Soviet and Post-Soviet Politics and Society (SI
ISSN 1614-3515

General Editor: Andreas Umland,
Stockholm Centre for Eastern European Studies, andreas.umland@ui.se

Commissioning
London, mjh@ibiden

EDITORIAL COMMITTEE*

DOMESTIC & COMPARATIVE POLITICS
Prof. **Ellen Bos**, *Andrássy University of Budapest*
Dr. **Gergana Dimova**, *Florida State University*
Prof. **Heiko Pleines**, *University of Bremen*
Dr. **Sarah Whitmore**, *Oxford Brookes University*
Dr. **Harald Wydra**, *University of Cambridge*

SOCIETY, CLASS & ETHNICITY
Col. **David Glantz**, *"Journal of Slavic Military Studies"*
Dr. **Marlène Laruelle**, *George Washington University*
Dr. **Stephen Shulman**, *Southern Illinois University*
Prof. **Stefan Troebst**, *University of Leipzig*

POLITICAL ECONOMY & PUBLIC POLICY
Prof. **Andreas Goldthau**, *University of Erfurt*
Dr. **Robert Kravchuk**, *University of North Carolina*
Dr. **David Lane**, *University of Cambridge*
Dr. **Carol Leonard**, *University of Oxford*
Dr. **Maria Popova**, *McGill University, Montreal*

FOREIGN POLICY & INTERNATIONAL AFFAIRS
Dr. **Peter Duncan**, *University College London*
Prof. **Andreas Heinemann-Grüder**, *University of Bonn*
Prof. **Gerhard Mangott**, *University of Innsbruck*
Dr. **Diana Schmidt-Pfister**, *University of Konstanz*
Dr. **Lisbeth Tarlow**, *Harvard University, Cambridge*
Dr. **Christian Wipperfürth**, *N-Ost Network, Berlin*
Dr. **William Zimmerman**, *University of Michigan*

HISTORY, CULTURE & THOUGHT
Dr. **Catherine Andreyev**, *University of Oxford*
Prof. **Mark Bassin**, *Södertörn University*
Prof. **Karsten Brüggemann**, *Tallinn University*
Prof. **Alexander Etkind**, *Central European University*
Prof. **Gasan Gusejnov**, *Free University of Berlin*
Prof. **Leonid Luks**, *Catholic University of Eichstaett*
Dr. **Olga Malinova**, *Russian Academy of Sciences*
Dr. **Richard Mole**, *University College London*
Prof. **Andrei Rogatchevski**, *University of Tromsø*
Dr. **Mark Tauger**, *West Virginia University*

ADVISORY BOARD*

Prof. **Dominique Arel**, *University of Ottawa*
Prof. **Jörg Baberowski**, *Humboldt University of Berlin*
Prof. **Margarita Balmaceda**, *Seton Hall University*
Dr. **John Barber**, *University of Cambridge*
Prof. **Timm Beichelt**, *European University Viadrina*
Dr. **Katrin Boeckh**, *University of Munich*
Prof. em. **Archie Brown**, *University of Oxford*
Dr. **Vyacheslav Bryukhovetsky**, *Kyiv-Mohyla Academy*
Prof. **Timothy Colton**, *Harvard University, Cambridge*
Prof. **Paul D'Anieri**, *University of California*
Dr. **Heike Dörrenbächer**, *Friedrich Naumann Foundation*
Dr. **John Dunlop**, *Hoover Institution, Stanford, California*
Dr. **Sabine Fischer**, *SWP, Berlin*
Dr. **Geir Flikke**, *NUPI, Oslo*
Prof. **David Galbreath**, *University of Aberdeen*
Prof. **Frank Golczewski**, *University of Hamburg*
Dr. **Nikolas Gvosdev**, *Naval War College, Newport, RI*
Prof. **Mark von Hagen**, *Arizona State University*
Prof. **Guido Hausmann**, *University of Regensburg*
Prof. **Dale Herspring**, *Kansas State University*
Dr. **Stefani Hoffman**, *Hebrew University of Jerusalem*
Prof. em. **Andrzej Korbonski**, *University of California*
Dr. **Iris Kempe**, *"Caucasus Analytical Digest"*
Prof. **Herbert Küpper**, *Institut für Ostrecht Regensburg*
Prof. **Rainer Lindner**, *University of Konstanz*

Dr. **Luke March**, *University of Edinburgh*
Prof. **Michael McFaul**, *Stanford University, Palo Alto*
Prof. **Birgit Menzel**, *University of Mainz-Germersheim*
Dr. **Alex Pravda**, *University of Oxford*
Dr. **Erik van Ree**, *University of Amsterdam*
Dr. **Joachim Rogall**, *Robert Bosch Foundation Stuttgart*
Prof. **Peter Rutland**, *Wesleyan University, Middletown*
Prof. **Gwendolyn Sasse**, *University of Oxford*
Prof. **Jutta Scherrer**, *EHESS, Paris*
Prof. **Robert Service**, *University of Oxford*
Mr. **James Sherr**, *RIIA Chatham House London*
Dr. **Oxana Shevel**, *Tufts University, Medford*
Prof. **Eberhard Schneider**, *University of Siegen*
Prof. **Olexander Shnyrkov**, *Shevchenko University, Kyiv*
Prof. **Hans-Henning Schröder**, *SWP, Berlin*
Prof. **Yuri Shapoval**, *Ukrainian Academy of Sciences*
Dr. **Lisa Sundstrom**, *University of British Columbia*
Dr. **Philip Walters**, *"Religion, State and Society", Oxford*
Prof. **Zenon Wasyliw**, *Ithaca College, New York State*
Dr. **Lucan Way**, *University of Toronto*
Dr. **Markus Wehner**, *"Frankfurter Allgemeine Zeitung"*
Dr. **Andrew Wilson**, *University College London*
Prof. **Jan Zielonka**, *University of Oxford*
Prof. **Andrei Zorin**, *University of Oxford*

While the Editorial Committee and Advisory Board support the General Editor in the choice and improvement of manuscripts for publication, responsibility for remaining errors and misinterpretations in the series' volumes lies with the books' authors.

Soviet and Post-Soviet Politics and Society (SPPS)

ISSN 1614-3515

Founded in 2004 and refereed since 2007, SPPS makes available affordable English-, German-, and Russian-language studies on the history of the countries of the former Soviet bloc from the late Tsarist period to today. It publishes between 5 and 20 volumes per year and focuses on issues in transitions to and from democracy such as economic crisis, identity formation, civil society development, and constitutional reform in CEE and the NIS. SPPS also aims to highlight so far understudied themes in East European studies such as right-wing radicalism, religious life, higher education, or human rights protection. The authors and titles of all previously published volumes are listed at the end of this book. For a full description of the series and reviews of its books, see www.ibidem-verlag.de/red/spps.

Editorial correspondence & manuscripts should be sent to: Dr. Andreas Umland, Department of Political Science, Kyiv-Mohyla Academy, vul. Voloska 8/5, UA-04070 Kyiv, UKRAINE; andreas.umland@cantab.net

Business correspondence & review copy requests should be sent to: *ibidem* Press, Leuschnerstr. 40, 30457 Hannover, Germany; tel.: +49 511 2622200; fax: +49 511 2622201; spps@ibidem.eu.

Authors, reviewers, referees, and editors for (as well as all other persons sympathetic to) SPPS are invited to join its networks at www.facebook.com/group.php?gid=52638198614
www.linkedin.com/groups?about=&gid=103012
www.xing.com/net/spps-ibidem-verlag/

Recent Volumes

268   *Nadiia Koval, Denys Tereshchenko (Eds.)*
Russian Cultural Diplomacy under Putin
Rossotrudnichestvo, the "Russkiy Mir" Foundation, and the Gorchakov Fund in 2007–2022
ISBN 978-3-8382-1801-4

269   *Izabela Kazejak*
Jews in Post-War Wrocław and L'viv
Official Policies and Local Responses in Comparative Perspective, 1945-1970s
ISBN 978-3-8382-1802-1

270   *Jakob Hauter*
Russia's Overlooked Invasion
The Causes of the 2014 Outbreak of War in Ukraine's Donbas
With a foreword by Hiroaki Kuromiya
ISBN 978-3-8382-1803-8

271   *Anton Shekhovtsov*
Russian Political Warfare
Essays on Kremlin Propaganda in Europe and the Neighbourhood, 2020-2023
With a foreword by Nathalie Loiseau
ISBN 978-3-8382-1821-2

272   *Андреа Пето*
Насилие и Молчание
Красная армия в Венгрии во Второй Мировой войне
ISBN 978-3-8382-1636-2

273   *Winfried Schneider-Deters*
Russia's War in Ukraine
Debates on Peace, Fascism, and War Crimes, 2022–2023
With a foreword by Klaus Gestwa
ISBN 978-3-8382-1876-2

274   *Rasmus Nilsson*
Uncanny Allies
Russia and Belarus on the Edge, 2012-2024
ISBN 978-3-8382-1288-3

275   *Anton Grushetskyi, Volodymyr Paniotto*
War and the Transformation of Ukrainian Society (2022–23)
Empirical Evidence
ISBN 978-3-8382-1944-8

276   *Christian Kaunert, Alex MacKenzie, Adrien Nonjon (Eds.)*
In the Eye of the Storm
Origins, Ideology, and Controversies of the Azov Brigade, 2014–23
ISBN 978-3-8382-1750-5

Gian Marco Moisé

THE HOUSE ALWAYS WINS
The Corrupt Strategies that Shaped Kazakh Oil Politics and Business in the Nazarbayev Era

With a foreword by Alena Ledeneva

Bibliographic information published by the Deutsche Nationalbibliothek
Die Deutsche Nationalbibliothek lists this publication in the Deutsche Nationalbibliografie; detailed bibliographic data are available on the Internet at http://dnb.d-nb.de.

Bibliografische Information der Deutschen Nationalbibliothek
Die Deutsche Nationalbibliothek verzeichnet diese Publikation in der Deutschen Nationalbibliografie; detaillierte bibliografische Daten sind im Internet über http://dnb.d-nb.de abrufbar.

ISBN (Print): 978-3-8382-1917-2
ISBN (E-Book [PDF]): 978-3-8382-7917-6
© *ibidem*-Verlag, Hannover • Stuttgart 2024
All rights reserved.

No part of this publication may be reproduced, stored in or introduced into a retrieval system, or transmitted, in any form, or by any means (electronic, mechanical, photocopying, recording or otherwise) without the prior written permission of the publisher. Any person who commits any unauthorized act in relation to this publication may be liable to criminal prosecution and civil claims for damages.

Alle Rechte vorbehalten. Das Werk einschließlich aller seiner Teile ist urheberrechtlich geschützt. Jede Verwertung außerhalb der engen Grenzen des Urheberrechtsgesetzes ist ohne Zustimmung des Verlages unzulässig und strafbar. Dies gilt insbesondere für Vervielfältigungen, Übersetzungen, Mikroverfilmungen und elektronische Speicherformen sowie die Einspeicherung und Verarbeitung in elektronischen Systemen.

Printed in the United States of America

Contents

List of Figures 9

List of Tables 9

Foreword by *Alena Ledeneva* 11

Note on the Transliteration 17

Introduction: A World of Oil 19

    1.   Research Objectives 21

    2.   Defining the Case(s) 25

    3.   Plan of the Book 29

I   Informality and the Kazakh Oil Sector 31

    1.   The Link between Corruption and Informal
       Governance 33

    2.   Corruption in Oil Economies 35

    3.   Informal Governance in Kazakhstan: The Network of
       Nursultan Nazarbayev 38

    4.   The Dawn of Informality in the Kazakh Oil Sector 43

    5.   Kazakhstan as Stable Kleptocracy 47

II Petroleum in Kazakhstan 49

    1.   The Kazakh National Oil and Gas Company and the
       Sovereign Wealth Fund 53

    2.   Upstream: Oilfields 55

        2.1 Suspicious Deals: Kashagan 56

        2.2 Suspicious Deals: Karachaganak 58

        2.3 Suspicious Deals: Kenkiyak and Zhanazhol 59

        2.4 Suspicious Deals: Uzen and Kumkol 59

        2.5 Suspicious Deals: Zhetybay and Kalamkas 62

        2.6 Suspicious Deals: North Buzachi; Alibekmola and
            Kozhasai; Karazhanbas 63

    3.   Downstream: Refineries 65

	3.1 Suspicious Deals: Atyrau	65
	3.2 Suspicious Deals: Pavlodar	66
	3.3 Suspicious Deals: Shymkent	67
4.	A Rich Poor Country	69

III Patrimonial Embezzlement ... 73

1. Patrimonial Embezzlement in Kazakhstan ... 75
   1.1 The Kazakhgate ... 75
   1.2 The Sale of Soviet-Era Companies ... 78
2. Patrimonial Embezzlement in Venezuela ... 82
3. Patrimonial Embezzlement in Oil Economies ... 85
4. Cementing Power Through Rent ... 88
5. Summary Sheet: Patrimonial Embezzlement ... 90

IV State Racketeering ... 93

1. State Racketeering in Kazakhstan ... 95
   1.1 Kumkol: 1997–2005 ... 99
   1.2 Karazhanbas: 2006 ... 104
2. State Racketeering in Russia ... 105
3. State Racketeering in Oil Economies ... 108
4. Racketeering as Business Strategy ... 110
5. Summary Sheet: State Racketeering ... 113

V Fine Threats ... 115

1. Fine Threats in Kazakhstan ... 116
   1.1 Tengiz: 2002 and 2007 ... 117
   1.2 Kashagan: 2004, 2008, and 2013 ... 119
   1.3 Karachaganak: 2010 and 2015 ... 123
2. Fine Threats in Chad ... 127
3. Fine Threats in Oil Economies ... 132
4. Forcing Renegotiations ... 135
5. Summary Sheet: Fine Threats ... 137

VI Specious Contract Cancellations ... 139

1. Specious Contract Cancellations in Kazakhstan ... 141

1.1	Biedermann International: 1996–1999	141
1.2	CCL Oil: 2001–2004	143
1.3	Liman Caspian Oil: 2007–2010	144
1.4	Caratube International Oil Company LLP: 2008–2014	147
1.5	Caratube International Oil Company LLP II: 2013–2017	148
1.6	Anatol Stati: 2010–2021	150
1.7	Türkiye Petrolleri Anonim Ortaklığı: 2011–2014	155
1.8	Aktau Petrol Ticaret and Som Petrol Ticaret: 2015–2017	156
1.9	Big Sky Energy Corporation: 2017–2021	158

2. Specious Contract Cancellations in Mexico 158
3. Specious Contract Cancellations in Oil Economies 162
4. Pettiness over Reputation 164
5. Summary Sheet: Specious Contract Cancellations 166

VII Bid Rigging 169

1. Bid Rigging in Kazakhstan 171

1.1	ENI: 2001–2007	172
1.2	Baker Hughes: 2007	173
1.3	Parker Drilling: 2010	175
1.4	Bateman et alia: 2012	176
1.5	International Tubular Services Limited: 2014	177
1.6	Unaoil: 2016	178

2. Bid Rigging in Brazil 180
3. Bid Rigging in Oil Economies 182
4. Sub-Contracting Bribing 185
5. Summary Sheet: Bid Rigging 188

VIII Corruption on Kazakhs' Skin 191

1. Working in a Kazakh Oil Region 193

1.1	Informal Recruitment: Nepotism, Ghost, and Conditional Employment	193

	1.2	Informal Work: Economisation on Security, Resource, and Wage Embezzlement	196

1.2 Informal Work: Economisation on Security, Resource, and Wage Embezzlement 196

1.3 Kazakhization and Social Justice 198

2. Living in a Kazakh Oil Region 200

2.1 Good Initiatives Turned Bad: The EITI 200

2.2 Good Initiatives Turned Bad: CSR 205

2.3 Good Initiatives Turned Bad: The Aarhus Convention 207

3. The Tick-the-Box Strategy 211

Conclusion: Understanding Strategies and Informal Rules 215

1. The Trickle-Down Effect of Corruption 220

2. Practices at Play in Kazakhstan 223

3. On Limitations and Use of These Findings 227

References 231

Appendix: The Methodological Challenge of Studying Corruption 255

1. On Choices of Research Design 257

2. The Literature Gap 258

3. Methods to Retrieve Literature 261

3.1 Systematic review: Corruption and oil 265

3.2 Systematic review: Oil and Kazakhstan 266

3.3 Systematic review: Corruption and Kazakhstan ... 268

3.4 Systematic review: Informality/informal and Kazakhstan 268

3.5 Systematic review: Oil and Venezuela 270

3.6 Systematic review: Oil and Chad 270

4. Methods to Retrieve Data 271

4.1 Document analysis 273

4.2 Interviews 275

4.3 An example of advanced unit of analysis: Elite 279

List of Figures

Figure 1   A Glimpse in Nazarbayev's Network 42
Figure 2   Oilfields by company in 2022 62
Figure 3   Gini index in Kazakhstan since 2001 69
Figure 4   Visualisation of patrimonial embezzlement 91
Figure 5   Visualisation of state racketeering 113
Figure 6   Visualisation of fine threats 138
Figure 7   Visualisation of the Liman Caspian Oil Case 145
Figure 8   Visualisation of specious contract cancellations 167
Figure 9   Visualisation of bid rigging 189
Figure 10   Conditional employment 195
Figure 11   Major Kazakh Oilfields and Cities 276

List of Tables

Table 1   Main macro-economic indicators of the oil sector in Kazakhstan 50

Table 2   Major Kazakh oilfields ranked according to proven resources 56

Table 3   The actors, roles, and goals of patrimonial embezzlement 87

Table 4   Patrimonial embezzlement transferability to the target population 90

Table 5   The actors, roles, and goals of state racketeering 110

Table 6   State racketeering transferability to the target population 112

Table 7   Actors, roles, and goals of fine threats 135

Table 8   Fine threats transferability to the target population .. 137

Table 9   Actors, roles, and goals of specious contract cancellations 164

Table 10   Specious contract cancellations transferability to the population 166

Table 11   Actors, roles, and goals of bid rigging 185

Table 12	Bid rigging transferability to the target population...	188
Table 13	Actors and goals of informal practices on the job......	198
Table 14	Objectives of informal practices	218
Table 15	Categorisation based on the corruption suggested ...	221
Table 16	Factors of attractiveness for kleptocratic decision-makers..	225
Table 17	Fifteen most influential persons in the oil sector of Kazakhstan in 2009 and 2019..	283
Table 18	Studies to be included in the updated systematic review of 'corruption' and 'oil'.....................................	287
Table 19	Studies included in the systematic review of 'oil' and 'Kazakhstan'	295
Table 20	Studies included in the systematic review of 'corruption' and 'Kazakhstan'	313
Table 21	Studies included in the systematic review of 'informality' / 'informal' and 'Kazakhstan'.................	326
Table 22	Studies included in the systematic review of 'oil', 'Venezuela', and 'Gomez'...	333
Table 23	Studies included in the systematic review of 'oil' and 'Chad'	335

Foreword

'Follow the oil' is the starting point of this forensic inquiry into Kazakhstan's informal practices. The reader is about to embark on an unusual journey, more nuanced than Daniel Yergin's *Quest for Oil*. Context–specific, but also comparative. By establishing five universal patterns of informal governance in rentier states, tested against the cases of Venezuela, Russia, Chad, Mexico, and Brazil–patrimonial embezzlement, state racketeering, fine threats, extra–legal contract cancellations and bid rigging — Moisé offers a taxonomy of political corruption in rentier states. The taxonomy fits within the wider typologies of post–communist corruption (Karklins 2005) while also linking the established patterns with the idea of informal governance.

There is a blurred line between corruption and informality (Ledeneva 2014). One can distinguish between these two categories by their relation to the legal and social norms: while corrupt practices are both illegal and unethical, informal practices are either legal but unethical, or illegal but socially acceptable. Informal practices become corrupt if/when qualified as such in law. Some complications emerge where legal norms are either not in place, as during post–communist transitions, regime change or constitutional crises, or cannot be enforced as the legal institutions are 'captured'. Further complications emerge from the ambivalence of social norms, or double standards, applied to us and them, insiders and outsiders, and the ambivalence of social networks — the relationships can be both social and instrumental, depending on the context and positionality: 'If I do it, it is friendship, if others do it, it is a favour'. Similar logic can differentiate between gift and bribe: 'If I give it, it is a gift, if I am forced to give it, it is a bribe'.

In corruption studies, the operationalisation of the concept tends to rely on bribes, which are material, instrumental, measurable, traceable, associated with a particular office.

Informality is less instrumental and more diffuse: informal practices rely on social ties (intimate relationships, family connections, friendships, and professional networks) to reach out, pull strings, or use connections to help children, relatives and friends, which are a default mode of human existence and cooperation, but also are instrumental for getting things done. Some informal transactions such as gifts (otherwise known as 'brifts'), hospitality, nepotism and patron–client relationships are included in the typologies of corruption (Listovaya 2021; Polese 2021), yet they are also forms of accepted human behaviour.

The crossover between sociability and instrumentality — the doublethink that allows for a relationship to be both sociable and instrumental — is only one of the four types of ambivalence, found to be characteristic of informal practices around the globe (Ledeneva et al. 2018; 2024). The ambivalence of the doublethink, double deed, double standards and double motives, which becomes resolved only in a particular context, makes the conceptualising of informality context bound: the context determines the *modus operandi* of a social tie.

Just like in the uncertainty principle in quantum physics, where particles exist in a state of superposition before observation, the informal transactions become categorised by observers, while the insiders might choose to remain oblivious to the instrumentality of a social tie until the latter is broken. As noted by Luc Boltanski, human transactions move between regimes of love, driven by common humanity, and regimes of justice, driven by ideas of the common good (2012). Norms of reciprocity — in the regimes of affection, equivalence or power — qualify informal transactions further, but often are not clearly articulated, which is the case with the overlap of family and power relationships in Nazarbayev's networks.

Informality is notoriously difficult to research. A scientific rigour of naming, describing, and classifying informal practices works at cross–purposes with the context–bound, bottom–up nature of informality, racing ahead of the top–down, regulatory efforts. For different reasons, capturing these elusive practices is a challenge for both native ethnographers and outsider researchers alike. The observers cannot help relying on their insider respondents, yet also maintain a critical perspective. This book does a good job at the balancing act of the insider–outsider perspectives, however difficult it may be. It strikes a rare equilibrium between data analysis and theorising informality. Gaining access to the closed–door data through in–depth interviews and open sources, as well as questioning the existing theoretical frameworks of categorisation of informal practices, do make this book stand out. There are three theoretical puzzles that it helps to solve.

First, this book is essential as it claims back some territory for the informality studies from the corruption field, and usefully discerns the concept of informality from that of corruption. Moreover, the informality angle serves to carve out the grey areas as distinct, even where practices of corruption and informality are intertwined in a seamless fashion. Such an approach is non–normative and fills the void in political sciences that lack discourses for capturing the 'grey zones' in non–democratic and non–market political regimes. Such approaches explore the ways in which patronal power works (Hale 2020).

Secondly, the book tackles the issue of the invisibility of informal practices, especially those with no colloquial names. Following the logic of Wittgenstein's linguistic turn, *The Global Informality Project* (www.in-formality.com) has adopted a so–called bottom–up approach that relies on linguistic filters as sufficient proof of the existence of practices. In other words, once the meanings of idiomatic names of informal practices are understood and shared, some spread of practices within a user community is a given. This heuristic cut–off point made it possible to identify new practices in unfamiliar contexts and reach out globally to researchers capable of capturing informal practices while navigating local contexts. Thus, the question of non–articulated practices remained open. In this book, the author ventures into the unarticulated and aims to capture informal practices without their linguistic signifiers.

Identifying practices without names has long been a puzzle, unresolvable without some top–down input of 'categorisation' by a researcher. The outcome in this case, however, is promising. Each chapter offers insights on a particular set, or cloud, of practices that account for non–articulated transactions and policies. There have been attempts to categorise informal practices as *strategies* of

14   THE HOUSE ALWAYS WINS

cooptation, control, and camouflage in the 3Cs model of informal governance (Baez Camargo & Ledeneva 2017; see also Magyar & Madlovic 2020).

In my own research of power networks, whereby the non–articulation is the *modus operandi*, I have qualified the unarticulated practices of informal governance indirectly, through the types or uses that those networks perform. For example, in a wider range of informal governance tools available for leaders, the power networks operate on the basis of *informal incentives, informal affiliations, informal agendas and informal signals* that drive and divert the workings of formal institutions (Ledeneva 2013: 236-9).

Informal governance, or network–based system of governance, serves to mobilise and coopt people; to access and control resources, to ensure that policy implementation is aligned with informal agendas and that informal signals entail compliance and stability. The goals of informal governance are not so different from that of formal governance institutions. But the means are network-based. Membership in such networks is meant to be beneficial for their members, but also comes with a cost: vulnerability to prosecution, limited property rights, lock–in effect etc, misreading the informal signals or losing the practical sense, effectively pointing to the ambivalence of networks. The double–edged functionality of networks, or their ambivalence, complicates the difficulties of the categorisation of invisible and non–articulated practices further. To pin down informality, one tends to rely on the concepts of institutions, networks and practices, and in the best examples is an interdisciplinary endeavour.

Thirdly, the ambivalence of oil is an important takeaway from this book. Petroleum is not an accidental object of this inquiry. The biggest industry in the world, oil has become not only a key axis of geopolitics but also a key target for the securitisation of the world order. Furthermore, the reliance on cheap oil underpins the 20th century environmental *modus operandi*, whereas the drive for economic growth intertwines with undermining planetary survival. Hence, oil is a basis of globalisation (food, energy, mobility, development), but also entails global divides, intricate interdependence between producers and consumers and corrupt alliances, which are ultimately detrimental to the environment — and this ambivalence of oil are in the focus of this book.

It is no accident that the so-called grand corruption related to political leadership takes root in oil fields. As Moisé puts it, "transnational corporations and national companies become oil predators, whereas resource-rich governments sell it to satisfy their rent addiction." The author's formulations, short yet profound, are worth particular note, as reading this accessible book is a pleasure, as well as a revelation. In the spirit of informality, such shortcuts embody the wisdom that allows the reader to grasp complex contexts and articulate both formal and informal constituents in the workings of institutions.

With a rare exception, the paradox of rational choice strategies that inevitably result in the collective corrupt behaviour of political and business elites, while being associated with the moral decay of individual kleptocrats, gets ignored. This is a blind spot for the majority of modernist discourses on democracy and markets that presume the best barrelling there is for the rotten apples. This book aims to shift the focus on the informal ways the barrels really work.

By reviewing the 30-year history of oil development in Kazakhstan, the book offers fascinating insights into the open secrets, unwritten rules, and hidden practices in the oil sector. The reader will enjoy the meticulous research drilling and the critical evaluation of policies adopted by the Kazakhstan government to improve the sector.

Alena Ledeneva

References

Baez Camargo, C. and Ledeneva, A., 2017. 'Where does informality stop and corruption begin? Informal governance and the public/private crossover in Mexico, Russia and Tanzania', *Slavonic & East European Review*, 95(1), pp.49–75.

Boltanski, L., 2012 (1990). *Love and Justice as Competences*. Cambridge: Polity Press.

Hale, H.E. 2020 'Freeing Post-Soviet Regimes from the Procrustean Bed of Democracy Theory,' in Magyar, B. (ed.) *Stubborn Structures: Reconceptualizing Post-Communist Regimes,* Budapest: CEE 2019.

Karklins, R., 2002. 'Typology of post–communist corruption', *Problems of Post–communism, 49*(4), pp.22–32.

Ledeneva, A.V., 2013. *Can Russia Modernise?: sistema, power networks and informal governance.* Cambridge: Cambridge University Press.

Ledeneva, A.V., 2014. 'The ambivalence of blurred boundaries: Where informality stops and corruption begins?' *RFIEA Perspectives, 12*(hiver), pp.19–22.

Ledeneva, A. ed., 2018. *The Global Encyclopaedia of Informality, Volume 1: Towards Understanding of Social and Cultural Complexity.* UCL Press.

Listrovaya, L., 2021. 'What Does a "Thank you" Cost? Informal Exchange and the Case of "Brift" in Contemporary Russia.' *Qualitative Sociology, 44*, pp.479–505.

Magyar, B. and Madlovic, B. 2020. *The Anatomy of the Post–communist Regimes.* Budapest: CEU Press.

Polese, A. 2021. "What Is Informality? (Mapping) 'the Art of Bypassing the State' in Eurasian Spaces — and Beyond." Eurasian Geography and Economics. https://doi.org/10.1080/15387216.2021.1992791.

Radaev, V. and Kotelnikova, Z., 2022. *The Ambivalence of Power in the Twenty–First Century Economy: Cases from Russia and beyond.* UCL Press.

Note on the Transliteration

In writing this book I wanted to ensure both a scientific transliteration of terms from Russian and an efficient retrievability of information. For this reason, most of the names of people or companies used in the text follow the international English standard. This means, for instance, that the former President of the Soviet Union is written 'Mikhail Gorbachev' and not 'Mihail Gorbačëv'. Similarly, the names of Kazakh companies such as KazMunayGas and MangistauMunaiGaz, are, among them, contradictory because I chose to transcribe them as they are commonly found on the web. In principle, the naming of Kazakh companies is simple, consisting of the composition of names of cities or regions with the terms oil and, at times, gas. Still, in KazMunayGas, 'gas' ends with 's' while in MangistauMunaiGaz with 'z'. Similarly, 'мунай', meaning oil in Kazakh, is alternatively transliterated as 'munay' or 'munai'. Instead, in footnotes reporting sources for the transliteration of books and articles from Russian I followed the GOST 16876–71 standard developed by UN experts because readers can follow the hyperlink leading to the source. Another remark should be made on the alternative use of the adjective 'Kazakh' and 'Kazakhstani'. The use is not accidental, I preferred Kazakh whenever I referred to the state, its institutions, or generally to the whole citizenry of the state. On the other hand, I chose Kazakhstani when I specifically referred to ethnic Kazakhstani people, mainly from the Western oil regions. Finally, there are several figures in the book. To avoid issues of copyright I chose to do portraits of the people mentioned as normally done by courtroom sketch artists. Any resemblance or lack thereof is my sole responsibility.

To the victims of the Zheltoksan uprising
(*Желтоқсан көтерілісі*, 1986),

the Zhanaozen massacre
(*Жаңаөзен оқиғасы*, 2011),

and those of the Bloody January
(*Қанды қаңтар*, 2022).

Introduction
A World of Oil

> What does the repetition reveal and conceal? It highlights similarities and points out common patterns of human interaction, regardless of geographical or historical specifics.
> Alena Ledeneva (Ledeneva et al. 2018b).

After gaining its primacy over the 1960s, with 53,181 terawatt-hours in 2019 oil is nowadays the most consumed energy source worldwide.[1] Petroleum is used as transportation fuel, the source for heating and electricity, and raw material for by–products such as asphalt, chemicals, plastic, and synthetic materials.[2] Oilfields are spread worldwide, but some countries have more reserves than others. The disparity is not simply caused by the location but by the combination of a series of factors, including the size of the population, industrialisation level, patterns of energy consumption and production. For example, while being one of the biggest energy producers worldwide, China remains a major oil importer. On the other hand, countries like Kazakhstan and Iraq export much more than what they consume.[3] This interplay creates frictions and patterns of dependency between different countries: transnational corporations and national companies become oil predators, whereas resource–rich governments are eager to satisfy their rent addiction.

As it often happens, the outset of the oil industry in the late 1850s was not accompanied by a systematic formalisation, legal or administrative. Rather, the *de facto* monopoly created by John D. Rockefeller was deemed a problem only after decades of activity (Maugeri 2006, 17–18). The sector was progressively formalised in the US, but with the increasing demand of new sources, oil majors

---

1   "How Much Energy Does the World Consume?," Our World in Data, https://ourworldindata.org/energy-production-consumption

2   "What are petroleum products, and what is petroleum used for?," EIA, https://www.eia.gov/tools/faqs/faq.php?id=41&t=6

3   S. Stebbins, "These 15 countries, as home to largest reserves, control the world's oil," USA Today, https://eu.usatoday.com/story/money/2019/05/22/largest-oil-reserves-in-world-15-countries-that-control-the-worlds-oil/39497945/

20   THE HOUSE ALWAYS WINS

ventured abroad hoping to profit off informal settings by taking advantage of dictators' thirst for bribes. Despite an increasing number of norms approved to curb them, informality and corruption never actually disappeared from the oil industry,[4] but changed form and adapted to the new circumstances. In fact, the unchanged role of oil in the worldwide energy consumption pattern only reiterated the actors' ends: corporations needed oil as resource-rich governments money.

While I always found corrupt behaviours logical outcomes of rational actors' strategies,[5] it struck me that research on the topic never fully embraced the idea. Focusing on fixers, middlemen, shell companies, and the dazzling spending patterns of corrupt dictators (Gillies 2020b; Silverstein 2014), authors often criticised the moral decay as it did not stem from objective socio–political and economic circumstances. On the opposite, this work starts from the 'cynical' assumption that: we can never get rid of informality or corruption; we must expect that individuals in power will act primarily for themselves and only incidentally for the state they are representing; we must expect hypocrisy from states and companies. This is not so much a pessimistic take on human nature as it is a realisation that organisations are composed of different departments in which diverse people with differing moral standards operate. Furthermore, said moral standards should be analysed in reference to the quality of life and the scarcity of resources that these people experience. Informality will not disappear insofar as freedom and inequality exist. Hence, readers will have to expect a theoretical discussion of strategies that are logical considering the goal that the actors here presented intend to achieve.

At the same time, this book is a tale about thirty years of oil in Kazakhstan. Despite being an enormous country, the 'field' revealed to be a modest environment to research, where the extended network of experts frequently re–conducted me to the same key

---

4   The initial prediction was that informality would have disappeared with development (Lewis 1954).
5   For an overview of rational choice theory in political science check Andrew Hindmoor's *Rational Choice* (2010).

informants. Having roamed off the network is what makes the research interesting. In fact, by the time I arrived, I figured that I was 'alone' to understand the topic, faced with the walls of corporative secrets and the rule of silence of the Kazakh administration. As I continued to research it felt clear also the disconnect between 'common people' and 'the elite', and the impossibility to speak of both with either of them. Everyone knows everything about the feats of gods, but no one can say to have met them. Hence, my search had to focus on finding the priests of the dictator's faith. So far, you know that this work will be about oil, rent, corruption, and Kazakhstan. You are now ready to follow me in my rabbit hole.

1. Research Objectives

In general, the research asks: what are the informal practices taking place in a rentier state?[6] As an exploratory study, this work aims to create a taxonomy of informal practices offering details and context for the effects of corruption and bribing on the larger socio–political landscape; the question remains unaddressed in literature. A second question, this time case–specific, is: how do the actors of the oil sector of Kazakhstan shape their relationships through informality? This research aims to develop further the analysis started by Wojciech Ostrowski (2010) on the effects of the Kazakh authoritarian regime on the development of its oil industry. His book is the exemplification of the overlay between politics and the driving sector of the economy of a country in a rentier state.

Answering the more general question means identifying different strategies used by a series of different actors in the oil sector of Kazakhstan. As discussed in *The EU and European Transnational Companies in Central Asia: Relocating Agency in the Energy Sector* (Moisé and Sorbello 2022), these actors are often transnational corporations of the oil sector and home governments of resource–rich countries. An important proposition of the study (Yin 2018, 5:62) is that the interplay between these actors is the precondition for the

---

6   The research question considers the historical evolution of the industry development. As such, there are informal practices that do not take place anymore.

occurrence of informal practices framed in a context of kleptocratic exploitation. Contrarily to many geopolitical analyses downplaying the agency of 'minor' countries (Menon 2003; Dietl 1997; Borisov 2016), this research argues that energy transnational corporations followed the rules of the game set by the Kazakh elite (Cooley 2012).

Quantitative measurements describe Kazakhstan as a country crippled by widespread corruption. The levels registered by the Corruption Perception Index of Transparency International have remained high from 1999, the first year of its measurement in the Central Asian Republic, with a score of 2.3 out of 10,[7] until nowadays in 2021, with a score of 37 out of 100.[8] Likewise, several anthropological studies have shown how the country was affected by informal behaviours long before its independence (Kim 2003; Ledeneva 1998). Such levels of informality throughout the period suggested a high variation in the ways informal behaviours are carried out, offering a broader range of phenomena to analyse.

A recurring answer of many non–Western interviewees is that the term 'corruption' is unhelpful in explaining the reality of some societies because the phenomenon is not an exception but a rule. In line with their argument, this study aims to categorise and distinguish this different set of rules. The objective of the taxonomy is hence to make sense of an unidentified mass of phenomena offering a vocabulary and theoretical considerations to shed light on the driving sector of a rentier economy. When talking about corruption, the focus is often on bribery. Yet, bribing is but a goal of the protagonists of the informal strategies discussed in this work: there are more political, economic, and social consequences to examine. Acknowledging these strategies in their unfolding leads to an improved comprehension of informal politics in rentier states.

From a theoretical standpoint, this research is to evaluate as a continuation of the work of the *Global Informality Project*,[9] an online

---

7   A low CPI score is a sign of high levels of corruption.
8   "Corruption Perception Index 2021," *Transparency International*, https://www.transparency.org/en/cpi/2021/index/kaz
9   Global Informality Project, https://www.in-formality.com/wiki/index.php?title=Global_Informality_Project

encyclopaedia developed by UCL's Alena Ledeneva intending to document the various informal practices existing worldwide. As Ledeneva already convincingly demonstrated on the pages of her monographs on Russia (2006; 2013), informality is often an underplayed aspect in the study of politics that deserves to be addressed to complement our understanding of political developments both in Western and non–Western societies.[10]

A major theoretical problem of the taxonomy was the process of naming the practices. As she clarified in her preface, the approach of Ledeneva consists of pairing the practice with a popular expression used to identify it. While a popular name does not automatically decrease the bias of the researcher in the process of taxonomisation, its existence is certainly evidence of a valid identification. Yet, most of the practices discussed in the book are not acknowledged to that extent: partly, because the elite does not mean to promote their informal deeds, and partly because researchers tend to identify these practices simply as corruption. To mitigate this problem, the name of each practice resulted in an association between its defining characteristics and common expressions used to refer to similar informal acts. The naming had to be brief for practical reasons but precise to convey its main characteristics. English was preferred over any 'local' expression to emphasise the potential for generalisation of the practice. For instance, while *State Racketeering* presents two valid Russian expressions, the practice was named in this way to stress that there is no logical reason for which the practice could not be employed in countries where Russian is not spoken.

Based on these initial considerations and the analysis of the literature, a crucial hypothesis that the thesis aims to challenge is that in kleptocratic rentier states there is a trickle–down effect of grand corruption that further reinforces petty corruption, informality, and predatory practices. While Western actors believe that they can cooperate with kleptocratic elites to decrease petty corruption,

---

10 On a similar note, in 2020 Alexandra Gillies used cases from African countries to identify some of the key actors of corruption, both on the pages of *Crude Intentions* (2020b) and *The Extractive Industries and Society* (2020a).

hence improving the lives of local populations, this work argues that these initiatives are fruitless at their best and generate negative consequences at their worst. These attempts are to be understood as medications that try to cure the symptoms instead of the causes.

This topic borders upon the stream of literature on the resource curse. As thoroughly explained in *Corruption in the Oil Sector* (2020), the research stream of the resource curse began in the early 1990s with the work of Richard Auty (1993) and was later confirmed by the analyses of Sachs and Warner (1995; 1999; 2001). The core observation of these studies was that resource–rich countries proved to grow at a slower pace than economies without such endowments. Part of the reason was the 'Dutch disease', a deindustrialization of the manufacturing sector provoked by the combination of the real exchange rate currency appreciation, generated by increasing exports of natural resources, and the volatility of the price of oil (Devlin and Lewin 2005; Eisgruber 2013; Gelb 1988; Corden 1984; Corden and Neary 1982).

As esteemed by Hasanov, Mikayilov, Bulut, Suleymanov, and Alyiev in 2017, in Kazakhstan the 1% rise in real oil price led to a 0.28% appreciation of the real exchange rate, half of what measured for the Russian Federation (Hasanov et al. 2017). Still, while in 2006 the then Kazakh Minister of Economy Kairat Kelimbetov stated that Kazakhstan was showing the first symptoms of the disease, the 2007 study of Balazs and Egert concluded that the latest oil price increases did not cause the appreciation of the Kazakh real exchange rate nor produced negative effects in the non–oil manufacturing sector (2007, 162). Kazakh authorities have often been attentive in avoiding the risks of the Dutch disease. For example, at the beginning of the 1990s KazMunayGas frequently sold fuel from the Atyrau refinery below the market price to local farmers. In 1998, the then–CEO of KazakhOil Baltabek Kuandykov[11] let the price of oil products rise just before sowing season, and President Nursultan Nazarbayev dismissed him (Shammas and Nagata 2000, 518).

---

11   Kuandykov remained a prominent figure in the Kazakh oil industry but nowadays works for private firms.

Since the resource curse is also associated with bad governance, corruption, and predatory rent–seeking behaviours, a sub–stream of this scholarship focused on whether natural resources could hinder democratisation. After years of debate, on the pages of *What Have We Learned About the Resource Curse*, Michael Ross (2015) argued that petroleum[12] makes authoritarian regimes more durable, leads to heightened corruption, and triggers violent conflicts in low and middle–income countries (Ross 2015, 240). The first two conclusions are valid also for Kazakhstan, where since the early 1990s former President Nursultan Nazarbayev established a kleptocratic authoritarian regime still in place more than thirty years later, despite his recent siding. Given that the resource curse topic has been extensively debated in the literature and that its study featured numerous analyses involving Kazakhstan (Franke, Gawrich, and Alakbarov 2009), this work will not indulge further. Quite on the contrary, the results of previous studies will be assumed as a starting point.

2. Defining the Case(s)

The research was guided by a case study process of inquiry. A case study is understood as an in–depth inquiry into a phenomenon and its real–world context, especially 'when the boundaries between phenomenon and context may not be clearly evident' (Yin 2018, 5:46; George and Bennett 2005, 24). Since the literature showed no records of attempts to create a taxonomy of informal practices in the oil industry, the case of Kazakhstan is exploratory. Future research focused on different countries shall highlight additional practices and strategies. The choice of the Central Asian state was determined by empirical reasons. In political science, there is a limited possibility to observe events. Similarly, the development of a sector from its start can be rare, as most countries worldwide had already a developed oil sector by the 1990s.

---

12 Although it remains valid for most forms of rent dependency, including foreign aid and remittances (Askarov and Doucouliagos 2015; Ahmed 2013).

26   THE HOUSE ALWAYS WINS

This was not the case in Kazakhstan. Before 1991,[13] during the negotiations for the development of the Tengiz oilfield, Kazakhstan was a country with an underdeveloped potential. Contrary to Azerbaijan, where exploitation of petroleum started under Tsarist Russia during the first decades of the global commercialisation of oil, the Kazakh natural resource sector flourished only after 1991. This subtle but relevant detail facilitated access to informants and increased the amount of retrievable information.

The case study is single but embedded with multiple units of analysis (Yin 2018, 5:84). The units, or set of phenomena identified, are:

- Patrimonial embezzlement.
- State racketeering.
- Fine threats.
- Specious contract cancellations.
- Bid rigging.

To show that informal practices are strategies rather than exceptions, each chapter presents one or more indicative episodes. For instance, *State Racketeering* shows the emblematic cases of Hurricane Kumkol Munay and Nations Energy, but both cases refer to the same strategy, consisting of taking possession of oil enterprises through racketeering.

With the purpose of suggesting generalisations to rentier states, specific attention was devoted to the transferability of the case phenomena. To achieve this objective, units were often accompanied by other cases from different countries. These additional cases are not to be understood through the sampling logic, but as the replication of the phenomenon in different contexts (Yin 2018, 5:91). For example, the analysis of patrimonial embezzlement in Kazakhstan is accompanied by the presentation of the exact same phenomenon in Venezuela based on a systematic literature review of historical research.

Similarly, the replication of cases does not serve the purpose of comparison. Classical strategies of comparison in political

---

13   Negotiations started already during the Soviet Union, as discussed in Chapter I.

science are directed at finding the causes of a phenomenon (Sartori 1991). In these phenomena, the causes are clear: the kleptocratic regime uses identified practices to achieve its goals of rule and enrichment. On the other hand, phenomena must be distinguished from their context to relieve them from the general label of corruption, which flattens the analytical capacity of understanding governance in kleptocratic societies.

Most of the activities explained throughout the book refer to the classic definition of rent given by David Ricardo as: 'that portion of the produce of earth which is paid to landlord for the use of original and indestructible powers of the soil' (Ricardo 1821), but others do not have a connection with land (i.e. bid rigging). Hence, in this work rent is understood as any: 'payment in excess of transfer earnings',[14] a surplus that can be generated by any factor of production. Rent seeking therefore: 'occurs when an entity seeks to gain wealth without any reciprocal contribution of productivity'.[15] Rent seekers, on their part, are actors actively manipulating rules to acquire a source of surplus (typically companies or contracts) without investing in their productivity.

Finally, a rentier state is generally understood as a country with an economy depending preponderantly on a single sector, so important that political decision–makers base their policies around them. In general terms, there is no univocal way to assess if a country is rentier because there is no official threshold of revenue contributed to the GDP beyond which the state would become objectively rentier.[16] At the same time, contextual evidence, such as a disproportionate level of devotion dedicated to the sector by decision-makers, allows to identify a rentier state. In this sense, even if Wojciech Ostrowski (2010) argued that until 2005 Kazakhstan could not be considered a rentier state because the oil sector did not

---

14 Seth, Tushar. No date. "Modern Theory of Rent (Explained With Diagram)," *Economics Discussion*, https://www.economicsdiscussion.net/theory-of-rent/modern-theory-of-rent-explained-with-diagram/1783

15 Majaski, Christina. 2021. "Rent Seeking," *Investopedia*, December 3, https://www.investopedia.com/terms/r/rentseeking.asp

16 Although different sources argue differently. For example, Groce claims that a petrostate is a country in which oil rents form no less than 10% of the GDP (Groce 2020, 480).

apport a relevant addition to the state budget, there is no doubt that since the 1990s the government focused preponderantly on its development. The very existence of the Ministry of Energy is an indication of the fact that Kazakhstan cared, above all, about its oil and gas.

Often these economies revolve around energy or other forms of extracted resources highly sought on the market. Yet, as noted by Sanghera and Satybaldieva (2020), 'rentierism' does not limit to the energy sector (Sanghera and Satybaldieva 2020, 507). Particularly in Central Asia, other forms of rent include finance, land, natural monopolies, audio–television broadcasting, intellectual property, outsourcing activities, and intellectual platforms (Sanghera and Satybaldieva 2020, 512–13). All five practices have been paralleled with examples of other oil economies. Still, as it will become clear throughout the book, these practices have a different generalisation potential. In fact, while the first four practices deal directly with rent from oil, bid rigging falls in what Sanghera and Satybaldieva (2020) acknowledged as outsource activities, the: 'awarding contracts to other companies for the services to be provided' (Sanghera and Satybaldieva 2020, 513).

Even if they might fall out of this category once they start diversifying their economy, rentier states worldwide are numerous and include Arab (Beblawi 1987), African (Yates 2015), Latin American (Mazzuca 2013), as well as Asian countries (Ostrowski 2012). Still, since corruption is often not visible, there is no way to determine the existence of episodes of corruption without journalistic or police investigation assessing them. To ensure the parallelism of the different practices analysed, the cases had to feature countries with either high levels of corruption or where a relevant scandal had erupted. In other words, it made no sense to choose Canada or Norway if they could not offer terms for parallelism. Hence, case selection was not random, but rather subordinated to the availability of information. For instance, the case of Chad was picked because there was available information on fine threats, but any other rentier country where the strategy was employed could have been used. The parallelism is used to enrich the variations and highlight elements that are a constant feature of the strategy under scrutiny.

3. Plan of the Book

The book extends throughout nine sections inclusive of the introduction and conclusion. The initial idea of a chronological display of the evolution of the oil sector of Kazakhstan was early dismissed because it did not promise to deliver sufficient clarity in explaining the dynamics of informality. Rather, this work mirrors Ledeneva's *How Russia Really Works* (2006) in proposing a chapter for each relevant practice. Still, their order reflects a chronological unfolding of events that facilitates the readers' comprehension. Besides the five main practices identified, the last one encloses a series of minor informal practices and three major policies conceived to improve the functioning of the sector. This last analytical chapter is different from the others because it does not focus on informal strategies of the oil sector as much as on the consequences of grand corruption for workers of the industry and inhabitants of oil regions.

The next chapter blends the literature review with theoretical considerations of the major concepts that are employed in the analytical phase of the research. There is also an extended section that reflects on the state of informality in the Kazakh oil sector, communicating to readers the general sense of how business deals in the industry played out, while not yet acknowledging informal strategies. Finally, there is a section focusing on the political system that explains how informality is an essential dimension of the inner workings of the Kazakh authoritarian regime.

Chapter II, *Petroleum in Kazakhstan*, discusses the oil sector of Kazakhstan from a general standpoint, using literature and data to evidence the main characteristics and specificities of the industry in the Central Asian Republic. This chapter is essential for the overall comprehension of what is discussed in the rest of the book. In fact, by learning about oilfields, pipelines, and refineries, readers are made aware of the general features and limits dictating the choices of the political elite in developing the key industry of this rentier state.

From chapters III to VII, the book focuses on the analysis of the five major informal strategies adopted in the oil sector of Kazakhstan throughout thirty–one years of independence.

Patrimonial embezzlement, state racketeering, fine threats, specious contract cancellations, and bid rigging are discussed paralleling the Central Asian Republic with Venezuela, Russia, Chad, Mexico, and Brazil. While not formally comparing them, the parallelism enables to show constants as well as variations, hence improving the theoretical understanding of the practice.

As anticipated, chapter VIII, *Corruption on Kazakhs' Skin*, is different from the previous analytical sections because it features both a short analysis of the remaining informal practices taking place at the lowest levels of the industry and a critical evaluation of policies adopted by the Kazakh government to improve the sector. This section is decisive in completing the taxonomy, as well as proving the hypothesis of the trickle–down effect of corruption. In the conclusion, I answer the research questions while analysing the interplay of the practices discussed throughout the thesis. Finally, the methodological issues and the complete lists of studies identified through the systematic literature reviews are included in the appendix.

I Informality and the Kazakh Oil Sector

> This guy would spend all his time trying to circumvent the rule. It doesn't matter what the rule was, he would feel like it was his duty to circumvent it. I was continuously trying to get in his head: 'It's just easier to follow the rule. We are not going to lose anything. We got everything to gain because we do not leave any string behind that has to be cut off later on'.
> Former oil investor, interview by author, April 22, 2020.

The study of informality is often as approximate as the attempt to draw the map of a territory relying only on the tales of people who visited it. Despite a growing body of literature, the concept has not an agreed definition. According to Mische and Misztal (2002), the reason lies in the difficulty of translating such mundane terms into sociological theories, while for Alice Sindzingre (2006) the complexity is due to the absence of recurring characteristics that would distinguish the phenomenon. Abel Polese (2021, 3) recently defined the concept as: 'an activity, performed by an individual or a group of individuals (organization, family, clan), that eventually bypasses the state or the overarching entity regulating the life of that group or society.' As such, informality is acknowledged as activities concealed from the state, a space between formal rules, and an attempt to legitimise informal social norms.

Historically, the concept emerged as a specific branch of research on developing and transitional economies (Cowan 1954; Hart 1973; A. Lewis 1954; Polese 2021). Yet, social scientists soon realised that its use could be extended to the study of sociology and politics (Helmke and Levitsky 2004; Polese, Morris, and Kovács 2016). Already in 1985, Granovetter argued that despite the tendency of the classical and neoclassical schools to consider human action as atomised, the economy has always been part of a social structure that affects its mechanisms (Granovetter 1985). Literature has discussed informality as a social construct present even in the most economically advanced communities (Granovetter 2007), archiving the idea that the phenomenon takes place solely at the outset of development (Ledeneva et al. 2018b; Polese 2021).

Informality hence involves a broad range of sociological phenomena spanning from informal economy to informal governance, from informal payments and corruption to 'infrapolitics' (Polese 2021). The informal economy refers to those aspects of the economy bypassing state controls such as informal employment or tax evasion. On the other hand, informal governance includes the mechanisms of national and international political institutions that are not envisaged by formal channels (Polese 2018, 10). Often in between governance and economy, informal payments and corruption involve a whole range of exchanges that differ in intent and scale (Polese 2018, 13). Finally, 'infrapolitics' identifies widespread behaviours that systematically deviate from officially established rules (Scott 2012), aiming to change or substitute them.

At first glance, Polese's definition, which creates the impression of an 'informality of the masses', does not seem to acknowledge the practices identified in this taxonomy. While informality normally 'bypasses' laws or 'conceals' from the state, in this research the actors are often the state themselves and therefore have no need to hide. Patrimonial embezzlement, state racketeering, fine threats, specious contract cancellations, and bid rigging are hypocritical actions of an elite that aims to maintain the *status quo* and thrives on ambiguity and double standards. Building on this idea, this research considers informality those borderline aspects of governance where informal groups 'become the state' abusing laws and 'eventually' bypassing them, as foreseen by Polese's definition (2021, 3). Identified practices are hence strategies of informal governance relying on corruption as a means and often end.

This research was conceived in dialogue with Ledeneva's *Global Encyclopaedia of Informality* (Ledeneva et al. 2018b; 2018a; 2024) and the *Global Informality Project*.[17] Both studies assume the researcher as a passive observer of the phenomena, suggesting that once the practice is sufficiently developed it comes with a name given by those who perform it. Yet, practices are not always diffused to the point of earning a name, neither cultural–specific nor

---

17 About the Global Informality Project, https://www.in-formality.com/wiki/index.php?title=About_the_Global_Informality_Project

global. Quite on the contrary, studies of corruption often lack the vocabulary to identify practices that affect politics, economies, and society. This taxonomy proposes a partial remedy offering names inferred from the features of the practices. While focusing specifically on the oil sector, these practices have different potential for generalisations based on their diffusion to other branches of the economy.

1. The Link between Corruption and Informal Governance

The term 'corruption' dates to the origin of monotheist religions, conceived as a moral attribute opposite to integrity (Rothstein and Varraich 2017). Unlike informality, the concept has a number of definitions adopting various perspectives, an economic one (Reschke 1992; Mauro 1995), a legal one (Kaufmann and Vicente 2011), or a socio–anthropological one (Strønen 2017). Given the growing number of definitions, in 1970 Arnold Heidenheimer grouped them into three categories: public–centred, market–centred, and public–interest–centred. The first type focuses on public office and its possible deviations, the second one draws a parallel between public offices and business, while the third indulges in behaviours affecting the public interest (1970). With the purpose of being as inclusive as possible, in this work I define corruption as the: 'abuse of public power for private gain'.[18] What informality does for corruption is to provide context, integrating it into the social, political, and economic stratum in which originated.

Research on the topic is often accused of employing Western lenses to study non–Western realities. Yet, corruption is not a Western invention, because its understanding is shared in various parts of the world (Kurer, 2005; Strønen, 2017). Still, the accuse denotes a difference in perception with informal payments, a connection on which literature has never completely agreed on. For Gaal and

---

18 A common definition involves 'the abuse of *entrusted* power', where 'entrusted' may limit the phenomenon of corruption to elected officials. Transparency International. "What is Corruption?," https://www.transparency.org/en/what-is-corruption

McKee (2004) informal payments differ from corruption, while for Maureen Lewis (2007) they are just one of its possible expressions. The sociological study of Stepurko, Pavlova, Gryga, and Groot (2013) resorted to the general perception that society has of informal cash payments to give an answer to this dilemma, but the results showed a discontinuous overlap between simple forms of informal payments and corruption. In fact, a growing number of studies insist on the impossibility of drawing sharp boundaries between bribes and gifts (Polese 2016). Finally, the network Polese, Stepurko, Oksamytna, Kerikmae, Chochia, and Levenets (2018) argued that: 'If I receive it, then it is a gift. If I demand it, then it is a bribe' (Polese et al. 2018).

Still, these debates focus on petty corruption, small bribes paid by regular citizens to navigate around their daily problems, whereas grand corruption is rarely questioned. By growing in scale, each corruption scheme becomes less morally ambivalent, but also more dependent on politics and governance for its success. At times, corruption is so connected to the political life of a country that researchers describe those states as kleptocracies (Gillies 2020b). But this connection between corruption and politics is the simple acknowledgement of the fact that also governance has an important informal dimension.[19]

Alena Ledeneva (2006; 2013) was among the first researchers to discuss recurring practices of informal governance. In *How Russia Really Works* (2006), Ledeneva argued that in certain states it is not possible to understand the functioning of socio–political institutions by simply looking at normative rules because a number of actors use informal mechanisms to achieve objectives different from those declared officially (2006, 4). As in the *Global Encyclopaedia of Informality* (Ledeneva et al. 2018b), in this study, Ledeneva used the names of informal practices given by the professionals of that particular sector as an indication of their strength and

---

19   As argued in Corruption in the Oil Sector (Moisé 2020), academic studies on the topic limited to acknowledge the presence of high corruption, neglecting its social embeddedness and the resulting baggage of informal practices, a gap in knowledge that this taxonomy intends to address.

diffusion. In studying Russian politics, the author identified: *black piar*, the surfacing of negative information on a political competitor (2006, 41); *kompromat*, the disparaging of 'documents on a person subject to investigation' as a form of blackmail (2006, 58); *krugovaia poruka*, the joint responsibility of a group for the actions and obligations of its individuals (2006, 91). While focusing on the Russian economy, the author discussed *tenevoi barter*, another name for shadow economy and informal payments, and *dvoinaia bukhgalteriia*, double accountancy and financial scheming (2006, 142). Most of these practices are purely political and, unlike those identified in this taxonomy, do not liaise with the classical definition of corruption.

Like its Russian counterpart, Kazakh top–politics cannot be understood without considering its informal dimension. Rico Isaacs (2011; 2013) discussed them in the context of party system formation and regime consolidation, focusing particularly on the importance of informal networks and family ties in shaping the political landscape. Both Russia and Kazakhstan are rentier states whose economies rely on energy resources, and as any other rentier economy, they keep these sectors in high regard. As such, the functioning of the oil sector is inevitably connected with the actions of governments of resource–rich countries. In such a specific context, this taxonomy will show how corruption can translate into informal governance and vice versa in consideration of the specific objectives of the actors at play.

2. Corruption in Oil Economies

The stream of literature on the resource curse emerged when economists noticed an inverse relationship between the quantity of natural resources owned by a country and economic growth (Auty 1993; Sachs and Warner 1995; 1999; 2001). Yet, after an initial focus on economic development (Sharma and Mishra 2022), associations increased to include negative socio–political consequences (Ross 2015) such as the emergence of violent conflicts and their contribution to the stability of autocracies (Le Billon 2014; Farzanegan, Lessmann, and Markwardt 2018; Neudorfer and Theuerkauf 2014). But

36   THE HOUSE ALWAYS WINS

as anticipated, Kazakhstan avoided the Dutch disease and maintained high levels of corruption with no evident consequences on its economic growth.

On their part, transparency initiatives started as civil society movements aimed to hold companies accountable for their misbehaviours in the extractive industries and beyond. After initially adhering to the initiative, the CEO of BP blamed the "Publish What You Pay" campaign for the Angolan government retaliation that followed the disclosure of a signature payment (Moisé 2020). Several heads of government then promoted the creation of the Extractive Industries Transparency Initiative (EITI) to both protect the investments of corporations and increase transparency in the industry. The EITI is hence a platform where governments, companies and civil society cooperate to make the sector more transparent in the eye of the public. While in their systematic review Rustad, Le Billon, and Lujala (2017) pointed out how the EITI was largely successful in achieving operational and institutional goals, academics are often critical of the project because it did not decrease corruption (Furstenberg 2018; Öge 2017a), and given that governments joined the initiative for reputational concerns (Pleines and Wöstheinrich 2016; Jiyad 2019), in Kazakhstan it failed to make the industry more transparent. In fact, reports are not easy to decode, and in absence of mechanisms to hold companies and governments accountable, the citizenry has remained powerless (Fenton Villar and Papyrakis 2017; Montinola and Jackman 2002; Kolstad and Wiig 2009; Sovacool and Andrews 2015; Sovacool et al. 2016; Idemudia 2013; López–Cazar, Papyrakis, and Pellegrini 2021; Kasekende, Abuka, and Sarr 2016; Mawejje 2019).

Initiatives to ascertain the accountability of entrepreneurs were discussed decades earlier (Bowen 1953), but the concept found renewed strength in the 1990s during the fight for transparency. Yet, despite NGOs expected transparency to translate into greater accountability, the passage was not automatic (Fox 2007; Hood 2010). Initiatives of Corporate Social Responsibility became a common practice for multinational corporations extracting natural resources, but projects, often scattered, never addressed the core problems of the regions they were destined for (Gulbrandsen and

Moe 2007; Wiig and Kolstad 2010; Reynolds 2021). This attitude is economically more convenient for companies (especially given the tax discounts associated) than effectively protecting and servicing citizens living in villages located near the extraction sites.

Finally, oil management strategies include a whole series of studies dealing with country–specific developments of legislation and policies. While many studies focus on Nigeria as the perfect incarnation of the resource curse (Wenar 2013; Sala–i–Martin and Subramanian 2013; Idemudia 2013; Gonzalez 2016), a good number of studies dealt directly with Kazakhstan (Öge 2017a; Mommen 2007; Furstenberg 2018; Ostrowski 2010; Hosman 2009), offering good contextual evidence for the informal practices discussed in the book.

Similarly, this study inevitably collides with the literature stream of 'resource nationalism', a scholarship meant to describe the trend of nationalisations of the energy sector in the Latin American countries in the 1930s as well as the policies of Middle Eastern ones before the creation of OPEC (Sarsenbayev 2011; Nurmakov 2009). Yet, as pointed out by Kuanesh Sarsenbayev (2011), each case of resource nationalism is to be evaluated based on its specific context (Sarsenbayev 2011, 371). For instance, the author describes Kazakhstan as an example of 'economic' resource nationalism, a situation where governments of resource rich countries attempt the renegotiation of contracts whose terms have obsolesced. Typically, resource–rich governments will take control of the resource when its price is high, while favour privatisation when is low. This trend in the Kazakh economy is described extensively in Chapter V, where the thesis focuses on the means employed by the Central Asian government to force renegotiations.

Historically, the literature on resource nationalism was not only linked to the oil price cycle but to colonialism (Fattouh and Darbouche 2010, 1121). Yet, this is not the case in Kazakhstan, where companies were warmly invited by the government rather than used as foreign policy tools by their home countries. Moreover, contracts were re–negotiated but foreign oil companies were not chased away, because to this day Kazakhstan still needs their expertise, technology, and liquidity. Hence, on the one hand, the concept applies to the case study, while on the other, forces its association with countries and political movements that fought foreign ownership of the resource. Since it does not represent the political reality of the sector in Kazakhstan, in the book the expression 'resource nationalism' is never employed.

3. Informal Governance in Kazakhstan: The Network of Nursultan Nazarbayev

Analysing the elite of a country is a complex endeavour because in many cases official positions do not correspond to the real power structure in place. This is the case in Kazakhstan, where to understand the power network of the oil sector is necessary to analyse contracts, deals, and critical decisions affecting the sector over the years. This network of power is in constant motion and changes over time as actors are side–lined or expelled, while others grow closer to the centre of power.[20] As argued by Muratbekova–Touron, Lee Park, and Fracarolli Nunes (2021), insiders of informal groups are more prone to corruption than outsiders, and for the purpose of this research, even a partial understanding of the composition of the network is fundamental because it has been the engine for forms of 'patronage, clientelism, corruption and bonds of personal loyalty' characterising the life of the country for decades (Isaacs 2013, 1055).

Until January 2022,[21] in the authoritarian personalised regime of Kazakhstan, at the top of the pyramid of power there was Nursultan Nazarbayev, not the person occupying the presidential post, but him (Isaacs 2013, 1061), even after his resignation in March 2019. The formal role of Qasym–Jomart Tokayev did not change the fact that the informal political network leading Kazakhstan revolved around the figure of the first president (Tipaldou 2021).[22]

---

20 Political risk analyst, interview by author, June 21, 2021.
21 L. Anceschi, "The week that changed Kazakhstan forever," Open Democracy, January 6, 2022, https://www.opendemocracy.net/en/odr/the-week-that-changed-kazakhstan-forever/
22 Political analyst, interview by author, Almaty, November 25, 2019. Economist, interview by author, Almaty, November 29, 2019. Journalist, interview by

The resignation was a reshuffle intended to dissipate the growing discontent spreading throughout the country and preserve its democratic façade, but also a way for Nazarbayev to remain in charge of the critical decisions while not having to deal with the day by day running of the government (Isaacs 2020).[23] His network was conceived with one centre. Yet, at times, members of the network looking for personal glory created their own influential circles distancing from him. While independence has been always tolerated, excessive autonomy has led to frictions and sanctions. This is the result of loose government regulations allowing: 'officials to steal resources in large proportions until the problem is big enough for the ruler to step in and solve it' (Tutumlu and Rustemov 2019, 8). In the worst cases, members were expelled by the network and had to flee Kazakhstan.

In the 1990s, the informal network of Nazarbayev was composed of a series of different actors tied to him on the basis of 'family, friendship, work, education, and patron–client relationships' even though their interests remained purely economic (Isaacs 2013, 1060). Among them, there were his daughter Dariga Nazarbayeva, married to Rakhat Aliyev, his second daughter Dinara, married to Timur Kulibayev, the future second president of Kazakhstan Qasym–Jomart Tokayev, the former oil minister and prime minister Nurlan Balgimbayev, the American middleman James Giffen, the prime minister Akezhan Kazhegeldin, the future competitor of Nazarbayev Mukhtar Ablyazov,[24] and the trio of the Eurasian National Resource Corporation, Aleksandr Mashkevich, Patokh Chodiev, and Alijan Ibragimov (Isaacs 2013, 1068; Mesquita 2016, 384).

Not all of them were active in the energy sector though. For example, Rakhat Aliyev and Dariga Nazarbayeva only featured in

---

author, Almaty, December 17, 2019. 'I think that the most obvious sign of where the power still lies is the decision to separate KazTransGas from KazMunayGas. It was a decision that was taken completely out of the realm of Tokayev. He did not seem to feature at all in that entire process.' Political risk analyst, interview by author, June 21, 2021.

23 Political risk analyst, June 21, 2021.

24 Reportedly, Ablyazov took part briefly in the oil sector through Caspi Neft, later sold to associates of Kulibayev. Former manager of an oil trading company, interview by author, April 16, 2020.

the sale of MangistauMunaiGaz. While the eldest daughter of Nazarbayev dedicated her life to politics,[25] Aliyev worked for a long time with the Kazakh secret services and as an ambassador. After opposing the president in different moments, Rakhat Aliyev, Akezhan Kazhegeldin, and Mukhtar Ablyazov[26] were publicly discredited and pushed away from relevant roles in the country. The regime was never openly violent with opposers,[27] but the spectre of the Kazakh government lingers over the suspicious suicide of Rakhat Aliyev in an Austrian prison in 2015.[28]

Married to Dinara Nazarbayeva, Timur Kulibayev has been the most important man in the Kazakh energy sector for nearly two decades.[29] While Nazarbayev never trusted him with political roles,[30] his importance in the sector has remained unabated. Most of the protagonists of the oil sector interfaced at some point with men from his circle or with Kulibayev himself.[31] Yet, since 2014[32] the importance in the sector of the new rumoured husband of

---

25 The ouster of Dariga Nazarbayeva from the post of president of the senate on the 2nd of May 2020 paved the way for speculations on her political future. B. Pannier, "What's Behind the Ouster of Nazarbaev's Powerful Daughter in Kazakhstan?," *Radio Free Europe*, May 4, 2020, https://www.rferl.org/a/whats-behind-the-ousting-of-nazarbaev-s-powerful-daughter-in-kazakhstan-/305925 71.html

26 Ablyazov was prosecuted both in Kazakhstan and abroad, and while he was a part of the system, his prosecution was also politically motivated as discussed by Scott Newton in the second volume of the *Global Encyclopedia of Informality* (Newton 2018, 476). His name appeared in connection with the revelations of the Paradise Papers. "Mukhtar Ablyazov," *Offshore Leaks Database*, https://off shoreleaks.icij.org/stories/mukhtar-ablyazov

27 Yet, arrests of militants and activists of Ablyazov's party continue yearly.

28 "Kazakh leader's ex-son-in-law Rakhat Aliyev found dead in Austrian jail", *The Guardian*, February 24, 2021, https://www.theguardian.com/world/2015/feb /24/kazakh-leaders-ex-son-in-law-rakhat-aliyev-found-dead-in-austrian-jail

29 Oil investor, July 1, 2021.

30 The dispatch from WikiLeaks seems to suggest that already in 2010 Nazarbayev preferred others to Kulibayev. "Money and Power," *WikiLeaks*, January 25, 2010, https://wikileaks.org/plusd/cables/10ASTANA72_a.html

31 Executive director of a contractor company, interview by author, Atyrau, December 3, 2019. Former manager of an oil trading company, interview by author, April 16, 2020.

32 P. Sorbello, "Open Secrets: Expose Reveals a Kazakh Top Manager's Business Network," *The Diplomat*, September 27, 2021, https://thediplomat.com/2021 /09/open-secrets-expose-reveals-a-kazakh-top-managers-business-network/

Dariga, Kairat Sharipbayev, former head of KazTransGas, had grown exponentially.[33] Recently, he left his post following the events of January 2022.[34] To this day, Kulibayev and his wife are among the richest persons in the country.

As of 2022, there was an effective shift in power in favour of Tokayev. More than a regime change, the bloodiest January in Kazakh history marked a process of 'de–Nazarbayevification',[35] while retaining major elements of continuity.[36] Still, given the strong presence of Nazarbayev's relatives in the economy of the country, it is not known to what extent this process will affect the energy sector in the years to come.

---

33 'You can't understand the policy decisions if you don't know the key men in the political economy.' Political risk analyst, interview by author, June 21, 2021.

34 P. Sorbello, "The Richest Get Richer in Kazakhstan," *The Diplomat*, May 13, 2022, https://thediplomat.com/2022/05/the-richest-get-richer-in-kazakhstan/

35 C. Putz, "Nur Otan No More? Kazakhstan's Ruling Party Rebrands as 'Amanat'," *The Diplomat*, March 2, 2022, https://thediplomat.com/2022/03/nu r-otan-no-more-kazakhstans-ruling-party-rebrands-as-amanat/

36 P. Sorbello, "Kazakhstan's New Cabinet Features Many of the same Ministers," *The Diplomat*, January 12, 2022, https://thediplomat.com/2022/01/kazakhstan s-new-cabinet-features-many-of-the-same-ministers/

Figure 1   A Glimpse in Nazarbayev's Network

Family

Timur Kulibayev · Dinara Nazarbayeva · Nursultan Nazarbayev · Aliya Nazarbayeva · Dimash Dossanov

2nd daughter   3rd daughter

Husband   Husband

1st daughter

Rakhat Aliyev · Dariga Nazarbayeva · Kairat Sharipbayev

Deceased husband   Rumoured partner

Oil

Timur Kulibayev

Former chairman of Samruk Kazyna ('11)
Former vice-president of KazMunayGas ('02-'05)
Board member of Gazprom ('11-)

Kairat Sharipbayev

Former chairman of KazTransGas ('14-'22)

Dimash Dossanov

Former general director of KazTransOil ('16-'22)

James Giffen

Middleman
Sidelined amid the Kazakhgate scandal

Politics

Kassym-Jomart Tokayev

2nd President of Kazakhstan ('19-)
Former Prime Minister ('99-'02)

Karim Massimov

Former chairman of the National Security Committee ('16-'22)
Former Prime Minister ('14-'16)

Nurlan Balgimbayev

Former Prime Minister ('97-'99)
Former Minister of Oil and Gas ('94-'97)

Akezhan Kazhegeldin

Former Prime Minister ('94-'97)
Fled abroad

4. The Dawn of Informality in the Kazakh Oil Sector

Oilmen have been often fighting the liberalist idea of competition. For poor countries rich in oil, tenders had been always rare. If interested companies wanted a chance to negotiate, they had to create channels of communication with leaders of resource–rich countries. These channels were managed by middlemen, negotiators with a secret service aura that had business and cultural connections with target countries. In fact, middlemen had been key to the biggest oil deals of the 20th century: William D'Arcy facilitated the Mesopotamian Concession for British Petroleum (BP), Calouste Gulbenkian did the same with the Turkish Petroleum Company in Iraq, Frank Holmes and Karl Twitchell obtained concessions from Bahrain and Saudi Arabia for Standard Oil California (Yessenova 2015, 301). In the 1990s, at the beginning of its oil exploitation, Kazakhstan had its own middleman: James Henry Giffen.

In the late 1960s, Jim Giffen took his first steps in Soviet–American Trading at the helm of Satra, a subsidiary of Ara Oztemel's[37] empire. But it was only as advisor of C. William Verity Jr., head of Armco, that in 1976 Giffen would take credit for negotiating $100 million in Armco's contracts in the Soviet Union (LeVine 2007, 109). A few years later, with the support of Verity, he even set up his own consultancy company specialized in the US–Soviet trade, Mercator (LeVine 2007, 110).

By the mid–1980s, Mikhail Gorbachev's policies of *glasnost'* and *perestrojka* (openness and reconstruction) should have paved the way for many more American investors, but investments did not arrive overnight. As the head of the US–USSR trade council, Giffen proposed to allow American oil companies to drill wells in the Soviet Union.[38] Part of the earnings from the exported oil would

---

37   D.C. Johnston, "Ara Oztemel, 71, Businessman; Cultivated U.S.-Soviet Trade," *The New York Times*, February 9, 1998, https://www.nytimes.com/1998/02/09/business/ara-oztemel-71-businessman-cultivated-us-soviet-trade.html

38   As much as Nazarbayev tried to portray himself as the initiator of the Kazakh oilfield privatisation in his latest autobiography, *My Life* (2023), he was still a few steps behind Gorbachev. P. Sorbello, "Nazarbayev's Own Version of Ka

44 THE HOUSE ALWAYS WINS

be split between Moscow and the oil majors, while the rest would be used to foster other companies intending to invest in the Soviet bloc (LeVine 2007, 118). In 1987, exchanging ideas with Nicholas Brady, chairman of the investment bank Dillon Read and Co., Giffen designated the Californian oil major Chevron as the forerunner. A few months later, Giffen received Gorbachev's blessing for the venture and the front page of *The Wall Street Journal* titled: *An American in Moscow: James Giffen helps U.S. firms get a foot in the door* (LeVine 2007, 123).

But the effort was not all American. Since 1984, Margaret Thatcher urged her cabinet and the head of BP to work on a deal with Moscow (LeVine 2007, 143). Yet, it was another American middleman who created the connection that BP needed. Jack Grynberg was a petroleum engineer of Belarusian origins. His opportunity arose fortuitously when the State Department asked him to organise a visit to the US for the leader of the Soviet Republic of Kazakhstan Nursultan Nazarbayev. The American middleman hosted the Kazakh delegation in his house near Denver for a cocktail party and dinner. It was there that Nazarbayev talked about the Tengiz oilfield for the first time. Discussions on the possibility of creating a consortium of companies to develop the field continued in Almaty, where Nazarbayev had invited Grynberg (LeVine 2007, 145–46).

The American middleman proceeded to present the opportunity to BP's Tom Hamilton in London. Still, the British had a connection with Almaty but not with Moscow. Their only chance to beat Chevron was to sign an exclusive protocol for the negotiation of oilfield exploitation in the pre–Caspian basin with the Kazakh government as soon as possible, hoping that Nazarbayev would win Gorbachev's approval. While BP's John Browne and the Kazakh Prime Minister Uzakbay Karamanov signed the agreement, the British executives realised something was off. Only three weeks later, Giffen escorted Nazarbayev during a visit to the US that was sponsored by Chevron. Gorbachev had preferred the Americans. BP agreed with the Soviet Oil Ministry to withdraw from further

zakhstan's Oil History," *Vlast*, December 5, 2023 https://vlast.kz/english/5 7850-nazarbayevs-own-version-of-kazakhstans-oil-history.html

negotiations for the exploration of Tengiz in exchange for facilitated access to the oilfields of Baku (LeVine 2007, 151).

Throughout their visits, Americans remained astonished by the massive Soviet natural reserves. Chevron's executives had put their eyes on the Tengiz oilfield, a supergiant onshore gas and oil condensate whose untamable fire had burnt throughout 1985 (Kokh et al. 2016). When John Silcox, head of Chevron's overseas operations, visited Tengiz in 1987, he grew convinced that the Soviets did not have the technology to develop the oilfield in safety. His intuition was confirmed in July 1990, when a Chevron team led by Sandy Cornelius confronted the Soviet management in then Guriev, nowadays Atyrau, and learnt of the victims that their broken logistical processes in the oilfield had provoked (LeVine 2007, 155). But Soviets were not concerned for the safety of their workers as much as for the profits that Tengiz could have generated. Instead, they decided to offer the Korolevskoye oilfield, a neighbouring giant discovered in 1984 (LeVine 2007, 129). American executives remained convinced that their engagement in the region was worth a supergiant. In the end, the persistence of Chevron paid off. On the 2nd of June 1990, Gorbachev and the new head of Chevron, Kenneth Derr, signed a protocol granting them the right to negotiate the development of Tengiz (LeVine 2007, 138). As a mediator, Giffen benefited personally from the deal, entitled to 7.5 cents for each barrel of oil extracted by Chevron from the oilfield (LeVine 2007, 167).

The deal seemed closed, but the unpredictable happened: the Soviet Union fell, and on the 16th of December 1991 the Republic of Kazakhstan became independent. This simple fact invalidated the agreement signed between Chevron and Gorbachev. Luckily for the American oil company, Kazakhstan was in desperate need of cash. Nazarbayev contacted Derr on the possibility of resuming talks on Tengiz and received a positive response. While Giffen believed his role would have been essential, the new head of Chevron's overseas operations, Richard Matzke, imagined himself as the head of the delegation for the negotiations. Only a month after independence, with the complicity of the Kazakhs Derr excluded Giffen from the deal (LeVine 2007, 167).

46   THE HOUSE ALWAYS WINS

Negotiations did not remain free from middlemen for long. Soon, the Dutch Johannes Christiaan Martinus Augustinus Maria (John) Deuss joined the table.[39] Oil trader since the 1970s, Deuss was close to the Omani royal family, and in fact, chairman and co-owner of the national Oman Oil Company (Boon 2019; Executive Intelligence Review 1988). Introduced by the Kazakh oil negotiator Halyk Abdullayev, Deuss met in Almaty with Prime Minister Sergey Tereshchenko. Upon learning of the poor harvest that left the country almost without livestock, Deuss agreed with Tereshchenko to a $100 million loan by the Omani government to be repaid in oil (LeVine 2007, 171–72). Gained the trust of the Kazakhs, the Dutchman was designed as a technical advisor of Kazakhstan in the negotiation with Chevron. Kazakhstan also hired the British lawyers' firm Slaughter and May and the investment bank J.P. Morgan. Official negotiations started in February 1992.[40]

Discussions went long, with none of the parties willing to make the deal fail. On the 18th of May 1992, Nazarbayev and Derr signed a foundation agreement to state the terms of the final contract: Chevron would be entitled to 20% of the profits. After ten months of negotiations and reaching a consensus over the shared management of the venture, on the 6th of April 1993, the parties signed the final contract. On his part, Deuss was awarded the right to develop the Tengiz pipeline project through the Oman Oil Company. He then invited Russia to participate in what became known as the Caspian Pipeline Consortium (CPC). Yet, the unfortunate death of the Omani finance minister in 1995 led to the progressive loss of influence of Deuss in the Middle Eastern country. In the end, the CPC was realised without Oman.

---

39   S. Mazur, "Caspian Tales: John Deuss, Oil, Spooks & Cohibas," *Scoop*, November 29, 2007, https://www.scoop.co.nz/stories/HL0711/S00443/caspian-tales-john-deuss-oil-spooks-cohibas.htm

40   T.W. Lippman, "Chevron, Kazakhstan sign $20 billion oil agreement," *The Washington Post*, May 19, 1992, https://www.washingtonpost.com/gdpr-consent/?next_url=https%3a%2f%2fwww.washingtonpost.com%2farchive%2fbusiness%2f1992%2f05%2f19%2fchevron-kazakhstan-sign-20-billion-oil-agreement%2f45021b9f-af82-4162-836f-6e8c461bbb5d%2f

5. Kazakhstan as Stable Kleptocracy

With Panama, Paradise, and Pandora papers, in recent years the cases of grand corruption multiplied, and they often involved the oil sector. In 2020, on this topic, Alexandra Gillies, advisor at the Natural Resource Governance Institute, published a book called *Crude Intentions: How Oil Sector Corruption Contaminates the World* (2020b). This book had the objective to review major scandals of corruption in several countries, including Nigeria, Brazil, the United States, Angola, Russia, Azerbaijan, and Malaysia showing the commonality of patterns of corruption in the oil sector regardless of the national specificities. The most relevant advantage of this choice is that the author was able to show effectively how several schemes have been reproduced in all these countries throughout the years. This is also a major goal of this research.

In fact, it can be argued that this research and the book of Gillies (2020b) reinforce each other. For example, the cases of expropriation described in Russia as a way for President Vladimir Putin to ensure his grasp on the sector resemble those of the Kazakh context discussed in Chapter IV, *State Racketeering* (Gillies 2020b, 112). Therefore, Russia was chosen as a parallel case to prove the common patterns. Similarly, among the episodes detailed by the author, there are some with such global resonance that they had repercussions also in Kazakhstan, such as the cases of bid rigging involving Unaoil and Baker Hughes, here described in Chapter VII, *Bid Rigging* (Gillies 2020b, 184).

Gillies argued that modern corruption involves complex schemes of international transactions that have often nothing to do with classic bribes, and there are also a number of relevant blurry areas to consider that she defined as 'wining and dining' (Gillies 2020b, 31). One of the statements where this research departs from her analysis is the continuous reference to the idea that corruption is more frequent during oil booms. The author is right in pointing out that most scandals described in her book happened during booming phases of the sector. Yet, the analysis of the oil sector of Kazakhstan from 1991 to the present day shows how corruption and informality took place long before those years (Groce 2020). In other words, informal payments and corruption are not the result of the large affluence of capital, but also of its promise. On the one hand, corruption is a recurring pattern in autocratic regimes (Groce 2020), on the other, a way of conducting business in the energy sector for decades.[41]

One of the most solid theoretical foundations of Gillies' book is the use of the concept of kleptocracy, literally 'rule by thieves', that she used to qualify cases as stable or low–capacity based on their political connotations (Gillies 2020b, 106–7). This allowed her to distinguish countries such as Nigeria and Brazil, where the electorate was able to hold corrupt politicians accountable by voting them out of office, from states such as Angola, Azerbaijan, and Russia, where the rule of autocrats is so rooted that citizens are 'powerless' against their thefts. The argument had been already explored by Mancur Olson in his *Power and Prosperity* (2000), in a comparison of what was defined as roving and stationary bandits. The difference is that a stationary bandit steals less than a roving one because he does not intend to spoil the wealth that in the future he may benefit from. Olson elaborated this argument with the objective of explaining taxation in authoritarian states, but in a similar way, rentier ones are known for having governments relying on natural resources. By strengthening their relationship with multinational corporations, governments led by stationary bandits create a dynamic that resembles the cases presented by Olson. This research suggests that rentier states are to be considered as variations of this theory.

By Gillies and Olson's standards, Kazakhstan is certainly a stable kleptocracy ruled by stationary bandits, and this allows to show a wide spectrum of informal behaviours common for the sector.

41　As well as to enter it in the first place.

II Petroleum in Kazakhstan

> The blood of our economy, at this stage oil became the 'black gold' of the Kazakh land. Oil and gas have grown into our main resource, and a type of start–up capital since the first days of independence.
> Nursultan Nazarbayev (2007).

According to British Petroleum, at the end of 2020, Kazakhstan's proven oil reserves were 3.9 million tonnes or thirty thousand million barrels, namely 1.7% of the world's. This impressive amount is largely due to the offshore supergiant Kashagan, considered the largest discovery after the Prudhoe Bay Field in Alaska in the 1970s (Howie 2018; Babali 2009). But figures are permanently floating due to the continuous explorations and re–estimations of the number of recoverable resources from each field. Reading the official website of the National Oil Company KazMunayGas,[42] the Kazakh reserves of oil amount to 3% of the world. The economic success of Kazakhstan in the past decades is partially explained by the favourable price of oil between 2006 and 2014. Table 1 lists relevant indicators displaying the impact of oil export on the Kazakh economy. The price of Brent is the most similar to the varieties extracted from the numerous Kazakh oilfields.

---

42   BP, "Statistical review of world energy 2022"; BP, "Statistical review of world energy 2008"; BP, "Statistical review of world energy 2002". "Oil and Gas Sector," *KazMunayGas*, http://kmgep.kz/eng/about_kazakhstan/oil_and_gas_sector/

50   THE HOUSE ALWAYS WINS

Table 1 Main macro-economic indicators of the oil sector in Kazakhstan

Year	Production in thousands of barrels per day[1]	$ of spot crude per barrel of Brent[1]	Crude as % of exports[2]	Oil rents as % of GDP[3]	GDP growth in %[3]
1991	569	20	–	6.7	–11
1992	549	19.32	16	5.3	–5.3
1993	490	16.97	7.7	5	–9.2
1994	430	15.82	6.3	4.9	–12.6
1995	434	17.02	3.31	5.8	–8.2
1996	474	20.67	18	8.6	0.5
1997	536	19.09	23.9	7.2	1.7
1998	537	12.72	30	2.3	–1.9
1999	631	17.97	31.2	10.7	2.7
2000	744	28.5	52.9	24.7	9.8
2001	836	24.44	46.2	16.9	13.5
2002	1,018	25.02	50.2	18.7	9.8
2003	1,111	28.83	48.9	19.1	9.3
2004	1,297	38.27	52.9	21.3	9.6
2005	1,356	54.52	59.2	24.6	9.7
2006	1,426	65.14	59.1	21.1	10.7
2007	1,490	72.39	56.6	18.7	8.9
2008	1,405	97.26	57.6	22.9	3.3
2009	1,609	61.67	58.7	15.5	1.2
2010	1,676	79.5	61.8	14.4	7.3
2011	1,684	111.26	58.9	18.4	7.4
2012	1,664	111.67	55.5	16.1	4.8
2013	1,737	108.66	64.6	13.6	6
2014	1,710	98.95	64.2	13.4	4.2
2015	1,695	52.39	56.7	6.8	1.2
2016	1,655	43.73	50.3	6.9	1.1
2017	1,838	54.19	53.7	9.7	4.1
2018	1,927	71.31	59.7	15.1	4.1
2019	1,919	64.21	57.8	13.3	4.5
2020	1,806	41.84	49.6	7.1	–2.5
2021	1,811	70.91	40.2	14.8	4.3

Sources of data are British Petroleum[1], the Observatory of Economic Complexity,[2] and the World Bank[3]

Such a profitable sector attracted several investors, both domestic and foreign, as early as 1991. With the fall of the Soviet Union, an economic catastrophe was unfolding, but the former Soviet Republic did not own the knowledge, the technology, or the liquidity required to develop its oil sector. Hence, Nazarbayev turned to multinational energy corporations.

The types of agreements that states sign with companies in the extractive industries are four: concessionary, production sharing agreements, joint ventures, and service contracts. The logic behind these contracts is that profits should increase with risk. Thus, the greater the risk, the bigger the profit. In concessionary contracts, the property of the oil extracted is transferred to private corporations that bear both risks and gains but repay states through royalties or taxes. In production–sharing agreements the ownership of resources remains with the state, while private corporations participate in costs and risks in exchange for a share of production. In joint ventures, the state has its maximum return because becomes a partner of the consortium through its National Oil Company, but also bears the costs and risks connected to production. Finally, service contracts refer to all agreements connected to the supply of technology and services that will be exploited in the phases of extraction, refinement, and transportation. While these contracts do not benefit much the state budget, they are valuable for employment in the regions where oilfields are located (Kaiser and Pulsipher 2007, 1306; Kalyuzhnova and Nygaard 2008, 1834).

In Kazakhstan, negotiations with multinational energy corporations can be distinguished into two different phases in consideration of who, between companies and government, had the upper hand. The first phase started in 1993 when the Kazakh government signed with Chevron the contract for the development of Tengiz and Korolevskoye (Munns, Aloquili, and Ramsay 2000, 411; Hosman 2009, 19). The second phase began in 2002, when the Kazakh government strengthened its position and forced renegotiations of contracts with foreign corporations (Orazgaliyev 2018). Ironically, both phases started with negotiations or renegotiations with the American company Chevron on the terms of the contract

52   THE HOUSE ALWAYS WINS

for the exploitation of the resources of the Tengiz and Korelovskoye fields.

Already in 1994, the government decided to capitalise on its oilfields signing production–sharing agreements and selling extraction enterprises, starting what was later renamed the 'Sale of the Century' (Hosman 2009, 18). In this phase, officials from the regions were so independent that in '1995 nobody knew how many contracts were signed nor which were the terms' (Ostrowski 2010, 39). Yet, in 2008 the government amended the legislation eliminating the production sharing agreement regime, limiting the choice for future projects to concessionary agreements and joint ventures (Sarsenbayev 2011). The last piece of the puzzle was set with the introduction of the Mineral Extraction Tax with rates from 5 to 18%, an Excess Profit Tax and a Rent Tax on Export that could reach 32% (Palazuelos and Fernández 2012). Since then, the renegotiation of contracts has become more frequent. Only in 2010, twenty–eight subsoil use contracts were cancelled due to alleged violations of the Kazakh content law (Sarsenbayev 2011, 378).

Also, to widen the benefits of the oil industry for the locals, in 2004 the governments introduced 'local content' in the subsoil legislation, but many producers did not implement the rule until 2009, with the approval of the Law on Amendments to Some Legislative Acts on Kazakh Content (Howie 2018, 222; Kalyuzhnova et al. 2016, 109). Any company with a Kazakh owner, producing goods for the Kazakh market, legally registered in Kazakhstan and with no less than 95% of Kazakh workers can annually apply for local content certification.

After December 2012, a subsoil user that wanted to buy equipment or hire a subcontractor had to: buy a minimum of 15% of local goods; hire a minimum of 90% and 70% of local technical workers and executives respectively; buy a minimum of 70% of local services. Finally, in 2010 Kazakhstan adopted a new Law on Subsoil and Subsoil Use that set 50% mandatory certified local procurement (Howie 2018, 222). As testified by Azhgaliyeva and Kalyuzhonova (2013), corporations do not always respect local content legislation. Fines for this type of violation totalled $1.3 million in 2011 and $2.3 million in 2012. Generally, Kazakh employment and services improved, but companies are not always satisfied and occasionally prefer to pay fines rather than buy unreliable Kazakh goods.

As of 2018, KazMunayGas had become a member in all major oil projects of the country, but Kazakhstan did not reach its oil empowerment (Palazuelos and Fernández 2012). Full control over the oil cycle means ensuring a development from upstream to downstream and a sustained effort to guarantee the continuity of the sector. At the domestic level, this is represented by continued exploration of new reserves, their drilling, and refining. At the international level, it means having control over transport routes, sales conditions, and distribution of revenues (Palazuelos and Fernández 2012, 28). To achieve these results, a resource–rich country needs sufficient political power to negotiate with companies, the technological capacity to handle the oil cycle, and sufficient revenues to reinvest in the sector guaranteeing its continuity (Palazuelos and Fernández 2012, 29). Kazakhstan does not possess any of these requirements. While rich in resources, the country relies on the technical capabilities of multinational corporations. Also, given the landlocked position of the country, export routes depend on Russia and China.

1. The Kazakh National Oil and Gas Company and the Sovereign Wealth Fund

The first National Oil and Gas Company (NOC) was the Kazakhstan Oil and Gas Corporation, founded in 1991, and renamed KazakhstanMunayGas in 1992. The company had been created for the direct management of the country's energy resources, but in those years the company was overshadowed by the formerly Soviet enterprises MangistauMunaiGas, Embanaft, KazakhstanCaspiShelf, and TengizMunayGas (Ostrowski 2010). In 1994, the attempt of the Ministry of Oil and Gas Ravil Cherdabayev to transform one of them into the main NOC of the country was opposed by President Nazarbayev, whose goal was to concentrate the key oilfields under the management of KazakhstanMunayGas. The conflict between Cherdabayev and Nazarbayev is told at length in *Politics and Oil*, where Ostrowski showed how the regime interrupted the corporatist strategies that favoured the ascent of Cherdabayev in order to privilege patron–client networks (2010). In 1997, when most regional companies had been privatised, the president dissolved the Ministry of Geology, the Ministry of Oil and Gas, the State Tax Committee, the State Pricing Committee, and the State Property Management Committee to create KazTransOil (Palazuelos and Fernández 2012, 32). In 2001, the companies dedicated to the transport of oil and gas were merged to create Transneft Oil and Gas. Finally, in 2002, KazTransOil and KazTransGas were merged to create the NOC KazMunayGas (KMG) (Palazuelos and Fernández 2012; Peck 2004; Ostrowski 2010).

According to Anne Peck (2004), behind the accelerated creation of a major NOC, there was the ambition of Timur Kulibayev, son–in–law of former President Nazarbayev, to become manager of the most important Kazakh company (Peck 2004, 182). Kulibayev, the protagonist of some of the sales of the companies operating in the oilfields in the 1990s, was in fact appointed first vice–president of the company already in 2002.[43] KMG is extremely politicised and often acted as an arm of the government in negotiations with multinational corporations (Kalyuzhnova and Nygaard 2008, 1837). Nowadays, the company has participation in all major oil projects, Kazakh refineries, and a number of subsidiaries that operate from upstream to downstream (Orazgaliyev 2018, 37). The KazMunayGas Exploration and Production Joint Stock Company, a subsidiary of KMG, has been listed on the London Stock Exchange since 2006.

Similar malicious observations followed the 2008 creation of the Sovereign Wealth Fund. But the choice to create Samruk-Kazyna rumoured since 2005, can be read as a measure to limit the excessive power accumulated by KazMunayGas over the years. Also, the creation of a fund abroad is a necessary move to counteract the harmful effects of the fluctuations in oil prices. The model for Samruk–Kazyna was the Singaporean Temasek[44] (Chervinsky 2017, 185). Nowadays, the Kazakh fund manages the National Oil

---

43   More on the professional history of Kulibayev is outlined in 4, *State Racketeering*.
44   "A Generational Investor," *Temasek*, https://www.temasek.com.sg/en/index

Fund as well as participations in several companies: from Kazakh-telecom to Air Astana, from KazAtomProm to KazMunayGas. Samruk–Kazyna also controls the financial position of KazMunayGas, with important effects on the inter–institutional power balance. In 2015, for example, KMG was forced by Samruk–Kazyna to reduce its outstanding $18 billion debt by selling to the holding half of its shares in the Kashagan consortium[45] (Chervinsky 2017, 303). As of 2020, the National Oil Fund of Kazakhstan was $61.9 billion, a remarkable figure, but far from the $1 trillion of the Norwegian one.[46]

2. Upstream: Oilfields

In Kazakhstan, there are 172 oilfields, and eighty of them are under development. Yet, 90% of reserves are concentrated in the fifteen major ones: Tengiz, Kashagan, Karachaganak, Uzen, Zhetybai, Zhanazhol, Kalamkas, Kenkiyak, Karazhanbas, Kumkol, North Buzachi, Alibekmola, Central and Eastern Prorva, Kenbai, Korolevskoye. The regions hosting them are Aktobe, Atyrau, West Kazakhstan, Karaganda, Kyzlorda and Mangystau.[47] The richest oilfields are listed in Table 2 below.

---

45 The shares are owned through a subsidiary, the Dutch KMG Kashagan B.V.
46 S. Bhutia, "Tracking Kazakhstan's sovereign wealth funds through the last oil slump," *Eurasianet*, January 22, 2020, https://eurasianet.org/tracking-kazakhstans-sovereign-wealth-funds-through-the-last-oil-slump
47 "Oil and Gas Sector," *KazMunayGas*, http://kmgep.kz/eng/about_kazakhstan/oil_and_gas_sector/

56   THE HOUSE ALWAYS WINS

Table 2   Major Kazakh oilfields ranked according to proven resources

Oilfield	In service since	Proven reserves (thousand million barrels)
Kashagan	2016	15
Tengiz and Korolevskoye	1991	9
Karachaganak	1984	2.4
Kenkiyak and Zhanazhol	1967 and 1984	1
Uzen	1965	1
Kumkol	1989	0.6
Others		1

Estimate, compiled through the US Energy Information Administration 2019

2.1 Suspicious Deals: Kashagan

The Offshore Kazakhstan International Operating Company N.V. (OKIOC) was created as a consortium of international oil companies in 1993 and started an exploration of the Caspian.[48] In 1997, the government of Kazakhstan and OKIOC signed the North Caspian Production Sharing Agreement. Companies initially part of the project were the Italian Agip (today ENI), British Gas (BG), ExxonMobil, the Franco–Belgian TotalFinaElf (today Total SA), Royal Dutch Shell, and KazakhOil, each of them with 16.67% of the shares. But the effect of the Russian crisis of 1998 had serious repercussions on Kazakhstan, forcing KazakhOil to sell its 16.67% shares to the American Phillips Petroleum (nowadays ConocoPhillips) and to the Japanese Inpex (Ostrowski 2010; Pomfret 2005; Babali 2009). KazakhOil soon regretted its choice, because in 2000 the consortium announced the discovery of the immense Kashagan field.[49] The following year, Agip became the main operator of the group and the functions of OKIOC were transferred to the Agip–Kazakhstan North Caspian Operating Company (Agip–KCO). Given the

---

48   "Project," *KMG Kashagan B.V.*, https://www.kbv.kz/en/project/
49   "Enormous Field Discovered in Caspian Sea," *Oil and Gas Online: Where Upstream Clicks*, May 17, 2000, https://www.oilandgasonline.com/doc/enormous-oilfield-discovered-in-caspian-sea-0002

difficulty of the project and the need for further investments before the field could become productive, BG decided to sell its shares to the Chinese companies China National Offshore Oil Corporation and Sinopec. Yet, Shell exerted its pre–emptive right of denying the transaction. KMG seized the opportunity asking to become a partner of Agip–KCO.

After long negotiations, KMG bought 8.33%[50] of the shares of BG while the remaining 8.33% remained at the disposal of other members (Palazuelos and Fernández 2012; Ostrowski 2010). Despite clear opposition from ConocoPhillips, Prime Minister Daniyal Akhmetov announced that the government would try to buy the second half of BG shares.[51] The opportunity presented itself in September 2007, when a delay due to the technical difficulty of the project caused the government of Kazakhstan to request $10 billion of compensation from the consortium (Babali 2009, 1299). The reaction of the government was not surprising considering that the capital expenditure of the project would have increased from $57 billion to $136 billion. After months of negotiations that included the meeting of the Italian Prime Minister Romano Prodi and his Kazakh counterpart Karim Massimov (Guliyev and Akhrarkhodjaeva 2009, 3179), KMG was allowed to buy 8.48% of shares for $1.78 billion[52] (Palazuelos and Fernández 2012, 32). Moreover, Agip–KCO was substituted by the North Caspian Operating Company led by Shell, and Kazakhstan was offered $5 billion as compensation (Sarsenbayev 2011, 376). In 2013, ConocoPhilips announced the sale of its shares, initially offered to the Indian ONGC, but then sold for $5 billion to the China National Petroleum Corporation (CNPC).[53] Nowadays, the ownership of the consortium sees KMG at the 16.88%, ENI, Shell, Total, and ExxonMobil at 16.81% each, CNPC at

---

50 More details on the strategy employed by KMG to acquire shares of Agip-KCO are offered in 5, *Fine Threats*, 1.2 *Kashagan: 2004, 2008, and 2013*.

51 "Good cop, bad cop on Kashagan?," *Wikileaks*, February 2, 2005, https://wikil eaks.org/plusd/cables/05ALMATY378_a.html

52 This percentage included the original 8.33% shares of BP and 0.15% sold by all remaining members.

53 M. Gordeyeva, "China buys into giant Kazakh oilfield for $5 billion," *Reuters*, September 7, 2013, https://www.reuters.com/article/us-oil-kashagan-china/ china-buys-into-giant-kazakh-oilfield-for-5-billion-idUSBRE98606620130907

58   THE HOUSE ALWAYS WINS

8.33%, and Inpex at 7.56% (Levine 2016, 157; Ostrowski 2010; Palazuelos and Fernández 2012). Production, which should have started in 2013, was further delayed to 2016 because of a gas leak two weeks after the beginning of operations (Parkhomchik 2016, 144).

2.2 Suspicious Deals: Karachaganak

The Karachaganak field is a giant condensate of oil and gas close to the Russian border.[54] The Soviet Union started its exploitation in 1984 through a subsidiary of Gazprom, but as Kazakhstan became independent, in 1992 KarachaganakGazprom returned the property to Kazakhstan. In that same year, the government of Kazakhstan started negotiating with Agip and BG for the exploitation of the field. In 1997, Texaco and Lukoil were included in the project by signing a production–sharing agreement that determined the creation of the Karachaganak Petroleum Operating B.V. (KPO). In 2009, KPO was the only big project without the participation of KMG, as the ownership included ENI and BG at 32.5%, Chevron-Texaco at 20%, and Lukoil at 15% (Pomfret 2005; Levine 2016). In 2010, the Kazakh government fined the KPO consortium for a total of $2.5 billion for 'tax and environmental accusations of illegal gains and cost overstatements, and violations of immigration law' (Sarsenbayev 2011, 376).[55] KPO reacted by launching an arbitration. The parties negotiated the entry of KMG in the consortium, but the lack of an agreement pushed the government to utterly fine KPO for a total of $1.3 billion.[56] Mutual claims were dropped as the final agreement was reached in 2011 when KMG bought 10% of the shares of KPO. One last shift in property occurred in 2015 when Royal Dutch Shell bought the BG group.[57] Nowadays, KPO is

---

54 "Karachaganak Oil and Gas Field", *A Barrell Full*, http://abarrelfull.wikidot.com/karachaganak-oil-and-gas-field
55 More details on the strategy employed by KMG to acquire shares of KPO are offered in 5, *Fine Threats*, 1.3 *Karachaganak: 2010 and 2015*.
56 "UPDATE 1-Kazakhstan says Karachaganak case in arbitration," *Reuters*, May 27, 2010, https://www.reuters.com/article/kazakhstan-karachaganak-idUSLDE64Q14B20100527
57 "Combining Shell and BG: A Simpler and More Profitable Company," *Shell Global*, https://www.shell.com/about-us/what-we-do/combining-shell-and-bg-a-simpler-and-more-profitable-company.html

property of ENI and Shell at 29.25%, ChevronTexaco at 18%, Lukoil at 13.5%, and KMG at 10%.

2.3 Suspicious Deals: Kenkiyak and Zhanazhol

These fields in the Aktobe region are operated by Aktobemunaygas, formerly Aktyubiskneftgas. The tender for the sale of the company was announced in 1996, but due to lack of investors, it was concluded only in 1997 when the government decreased the value of the sale to 60.3% of the company. CNPC won the tender and later renamed the company CNPC–Aktobemunaygas (Kalyuzhnova and Lee 2014; Peck 2004). The remaining 39.7% was divided between the Kazakh government at 30.2%, and the employees at 9.5% in preferred shares. In 2001, the government gave its entire share of 25.12% to American Access Industries–Eurasia in trust management.[58] Yet, the original share of Kazakhstan was 30.2%, suggesting that another 5% had been previously sold to unknown privates (Peck 2004, 170). In 2003, CNPC bought 25.12% of the shares from the government reaching 85.42% (Palazuelos and Fernández 2012). Nowadays, KazakhOil–Aktobe owns the remaining 14.58% of the shares. This consortium is owned equally by KMG and Sinopec. The Chinese company Sinopec bought half of KazakhOil–Aktobe from Caspian Investment Resources which previously bought it from Nelson Resources.

2.4 Suspicious Deals: Uzen and Kumkol

MangistauMunaiGaz was the company that operated Uzen until 1994 when the field was separated from those of Zhetybay and Kalamkas to create the enterprise Uzenmunaigas. Despite an attempt to sell to CNPC, the company remained unsold. In 2004, KMG merged Uzenmunaigas and Embamunaigas in KMG Exploration and Production.[59]

---

[58] "Kazakhstan gave 25.12% state block in Aktobemunaigas to Access," *KASE.Kz*, March 26, 2001, https://kase.kz/en/news/show/129344/

[59] "Latest News," *EasternBlocEnergy*, April 2, 2004, http://www.easternblocenergy.com/news/1489/

60   THE HOUSE ALWAYS WINS

The Kumkol oilfield is distinguished in the northern and southern portions. The national company Yuzhneftegas owned the entirety of the Southern portion and 50% of Turgay Petroleum, owner of the Northern portion, in a joint venture with Lukoil (Marten 2007). Yuzhneftegas was sold in 1996 by then Prime Minister Akezhan Kazhegeldin through a tender won by the Canadian firm Hurricane Hydrocarbons Ltd. at a price of $120 million. Earlier that year, Sarybay Kalmurzayev, chairman of the interdepartmental tender commission responsible for the oil industry and head of the Committee for the Management of State Property, announced that the American Samson International was the likely winner of the tender, but when Hurricane won, no further explanation was given. Many oilmen, including the future Prime Minister Nurlan Balgimbayev, did not see the sale as a good development, labelling it 'the sell-out of the motherland' (Ostrowski 2010, 47). Yuzhneftegas was then renamed Hurricane Kumkol Munay (HKM) (Peck 2004, 158). At the time of the sale, the company was on the edge of bankruptcy. Yuzhneftegas' properties did not simply include the field, but also: a road building company; a farm of 6,400 square kilometres; 25,000 sheep; 450 camels; a few horses, pigs, and goats which provided food for employees; a transportation company responsible for transporting employees from Kyzlorda to Kumkol; eleven gasoline stations, and a construction company that built facilities at the field and housing in Kyzlorda. Moreover, Yuzhneftegas had 5,000 employees, most of them working in affiliated companies (Peck 2004, 159).

Less than a year after the sale, HKM became profitable. Yet, due to the contractual agreements linked to the acquisition of the field, HKM had to deal with the elevated costs of the Shymkent refinery and was brought again to the edge of bankruptcy. Also, in 2002 the government disputed HKM $20 million in unpaid taxes and contested its acquisition of a share of the Caspian Pipeline Consortium. After seeking court protection, the company found an agreement with the creditors, and owners of the Shymkent refinery. A merger between HKM and Central Asia Industrial Holdings solved the long dispute.[60] In 2003, Hurricane Kumkol Munay was renamed PetroKazakhstan. New problems emerged in 2004 when the Canadian company started a dispute with Lukoil because of disagreements on the prices paid for crude oil by their joint venture in the Northern portion of the Kumkol field. In 2005, Lukoil answered by filing an arbitration to a Swedish court.[61] Before the dispute was solved, after years of problems in Kazakhstan, HKM decided to sell its shares of PetroKazakhstan to CNPC (Palazuelos and Fernández 2012). Under the Law on Subsoil and Subsoil Use, CNPC had to sell a third of its shares to KazMunayGas. In 2006, CNPC transferred its remaining 67% to China Petroleum Engineering & Construction Company, a joint venture between CNPC and its subsidiary PetroChina (Kalyuzhnova and Lee 2014, 209). The arbitration started by Lukoil in 2005 continued under the new Chinese owners, and the result led to the Russian acquisition of the entire northern portion of the field (Marten 2007, 27). Nowadays, the property of Kumkol in the Turgay basin is shared between China Petroleum Engineering & Construction Company, Lukoil, and KazMunayGas. Figure 2 shows graphically the shares of the oil companies in the major fields of Kazakhstan.

---

60   More details on the strategy of the shadow owner of Central Asia Industrial Holdings to pressure HKM are offered in Chapter IV, *State Racketeering*.

61   I. McKinnon, "PetroKaz fires back at Lukoil," *The Globe and Mail*, April 15, 2005, https://www.theglobeandmail.com/report-on-business/petrokaz-fires-back-at-lukoil/article18221371/

Figure 2   Oilfields by company in 2022

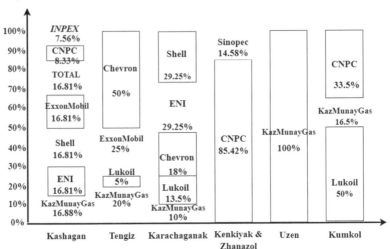

2.5 Suspicious Deals: Zhetybay and Kalamkas

In the 1970s, along with the Uzen oilfield, MangistauMunaiGaz (MMG) operated in the neighbouring fields of Zhetybay and Kalamkas. Like the other companies, MMG had a steady decline in production throughout the 1990s. The government announced its sale, but willing to participate in the decisional process, the workers staged protests. In 1997, the Indonesian Central Asian Petroleum Ltd. (CAPL) won the tender. The company had to face repeated protests throughout 1998 as workers asked to be paid for the eleven months since the tender was won. CAPL never invested in the enterprise, but the government never contested its role either. Central Asian Petroleum Ltd. was a joint venture of Setdco and the drilling company Medco whose owners were close friends of the son of the former Indonesian president Suharto. Funds for the acquisition of MMG were likely raised in the Netherlands from Central Asian Industrial Holdings, Central Asian Agriculture Holdings, and Central Asian Energy Holdings. These companies had the same financial management and Kazakh directors, including Askar Alshinbayev, managing director of Kazkommertsbank and CEO of Central Asian Industrial Holdings (Peck 2004, 168). In 1998, the owner of Medco, Arifin Panigoro was arrested for defrauding investors since bonds issued to finance investments in Kazakhstan remained unpaid. Panigoro later announced that he had sold his shares to Russian, American, and Kazakh companies. Another 30% share of MMG was sold to Ansdell Development, a group registered in the British Virgin Islands rumoured to be tied to Rakhat Aliyev and his wife Dariga Nazarbayeva (Peck 2004, 169). Finally, in November 2009, MMG was acquired, reportedly from CAPL,[62] in equal shares by CNPC and KMG (Kalyuzhnova and Lee 2014).

2.6 Suspicious Deals: North Buzachi; Alibekmola and Kozhasai; Karazhanbas

The field of North Buzachi, 250 kilometres North of Aktau, was put on sale in 1997.[63] Back then, the American Texaco bought 65% of the shares of the joint venture Buzachi Operating Ltd., later inherited by its successor ChevronTexaco, while the remaining 35% was taken by the British Nimir Petroleum Ltd. (Peck 2004). In 2003, the whole company was bought by CNPC (Mommen 2007). Still, in February 2004, CNPC bought half of Nelson Resources which in return obtained half of Buzachi Operating Ltd., renamed Nelson Buzachi Petroleum B.V. (Ostrowski 2010).[64] The ownership of Nelson Resources has been often unclear, but as testified by the leaked documents of the American ambassador in Almaty John Ordway, Americans believed that Nelson Resources was secretly owned by Nazarbayev's son–in–law Timur Kulibayev.[65] A few months later, also Nelson Resources decided to give up its shares. In 2005, Caspian Investments Resources Ltd. (CIR) was the owner of half of Nelson Buzachi Petroleum along with CNPC. That year, the equal

---

62 "UPDATE 2-CNPC, KazMunaiGas buy MangistauMunaiGas for \$2.6 bln," *Reuters*, November 25, 2009, https://www.reuters.com/article/kazmunaigas-cnpc -mangistaumunaigas-idAFGEE5AO12420091125

63 "North Buzachi Field," *nrgEDGE*, https://www.nrgedge.net/project/north- buzachi-field

64 "Nelson, CNPC to invest in North Buzachi field," *New Europe*, June 19, 2005, https://www.neweurope.eu/article/nelson-cnpc-invest-north-buzachi-field/

65 More details on Nelson Resources and Timur Kulibayev are offered in Chapter IV, *State Racketeering*. Kazakhstan: President's son-in-law resigns from state oil and gas company," *Wikileaks*, October 31, 2005, https://wikileaks.org/plusd/ cables/05ALMATY3912_a.html

participants of CIR were Lukoil and the Indian Mittal Investments (Palazuelos and Fernández 2012).[66] Eventually the Chinese Sinopec took over buying the shares from Mittal in 2010 and from Lukoil in 2015 (Kalyuzhnova and Lee 2014).[67]

The Alibekmola and Kozhasai fields were discovered in the 1980s, but their development started only in the early 2000s. The Alibekmola field is located 250 kilometres South of the city of Aktobe, while the Kozhasai field is 60 kilometres further South–West.[68] The first private company to benefit the exploitation of these fields was once again Nelson Resources, which had bought 50% of the shares of KazakhOil–Aktobe, the company responsible for the development of these fields.[69] As happened for the North Buzachi field, in 2005 CIR bought the shares of Nelson Resources. The ownership was hence shared between KMG, Mittal Investments, and Lukoil. In the same year, Sinopec bought the Indian share of CIR while Lukoil's share was purchased only in 2014 (Kalyuzhnova and Lee 2014). Nowadays, the owners of KazakhOil–Aktobe are therefore KMG and Sinopec in equal shares.[70]

Discovered in 1984, the Karazhanbas field is located on the seashore of the region of Mangistau. In 1996, the Canadian company Nations Energy bought Karazhanbasmunai, the company responsible for the field. Despite its success in making the field productive, after years of reported pressure[71] in 2006 the company sold

---

66   "Mittal acquires Kazakh firm for $980 mln," *The Economic Times*, April 25, 2007, https://economictimes.indiatimes.com/industry/energy/oil-gas/mittal-acqu ires-kazakh-firm-for-980-mn/articleshow/1954326.cms Lakshmi Mittal is a friend and business associate of Timur Kulibayev as detailed in Chapter IV.

67   "Russia's Lukoil completes Kazakh deal with China's Sinopec," *Kallanish Energy*, August 24, 2015, http://www.kallanishenergy.com/2015/08/24/russias-lukoil-completes-kazakh-deal-with-chinas-sinopec/

68   "Fact book 2011," *Lukoil*, http://lukoil.com/Handlers/DownloadPartialPdfHa ndler.ashx?fid=126252&fc=9&pages=24,48

69   "Latest News," *EasternBlocEnergy*, December 11, 2004, http://www.easternbloc energy.com/news/2552/

70   "Company Structure," *KazMunayGas*, http://www.kmg.kz/eng/kompaniya/ dochernie_organizacii/struktura_kompanii/

71   More details on the sale of Karazhanbasmunai are offered in Chapter IV, *State Racketeering*. E. Wilson, "Nations Energy sale marks the end of an era", *Euromoney*, April 30, 2007, https://www.euromoney.com/article/b13227814cx699 /nations-energy-sale-marks-the-end-of-an-era

its shares to the Chinese group CITIC Resources Holding Ltd.[72] Eventually, CITIC gave 50% of the shares to KMG (Kalyuzhnova and Lee 2014).[73]

3. Downstream: Refineries

Kazakhstan has also three refineries, in Atyrau, Pavlodar, and Shymkent. In 1994, a group of Japanese companies concluded a contract to build a new refinery in Mangistau, but work never started. (Peck 2004, 174). Largely unproductive and polluting, Kazakh refineries did not help the country to further improve its oil cycle, and that is why Kazakhstan still exports large quantities of crude rather than refined oil.

3.1 Suspicious Deals: Atyrau

Equipped with technology purchased through the American Lend–Lease program, the refinery of Atyrau was built in 1945. Yet, up to the Kazakh independence, the complex was not updated and revealed to be polluting and unequipped to process heavy sulphur crude oil from fields in Mangistau and Atyrau. As such, in 1997 the government opened a tender to find investors that could renew the refinery. Initially, the Essex Refinery Corporation, registered in the British Virgin Islands, was announced as the winner of the tender, but the government cancelled the contract, allegedly dissatisfied with the project proposal of the company.[74] Few months later, the Swiss company Telf bought 37.1% of the shares of the refinery from the management and employees. The government, who distributed the shares to employees in the first place, tried to buy them back, but it was unsuccessful. Telf had plans to update the refinery, but the government opposed them. While the refinery became idle

---

72 "Karazhanbas Oilfield, Kazakhstan," *CITIC Resources Holdings Limited*, http://resources.citic/eng/business/oil.htm

73 "Company Structure," *KazMunayGas*, http://www.kmg.kz/eng/kompaniya/dochernie_organizacii/struktura_kompanii/

74 While not supported by strong evidence, the unfolding of events suggests that the tender was rigged by Akezhan Kazhegeldin and the contract was cancelled when Nurlan Balgymbayev became prime minister. More details on this *modus operandi* are offered in Chapter III, *Patrimonial Embezzlement*.

66   THE HOUSE ALWAYS WINS

throughout 1997 and 1998, Telf increased its shares to 44.8%. Finally, in 1999 the government managed to buy back all shares from Telf (Peck 2004, 175), and nowadays KMG owns 99.4% of the refinery.[75]

In 2000, there was a first agreement between KazakhOil and the Japanese Marubeni to modernise it for an estimated price of $308 million, but the project of reconstruction was protracted until the present day (Chervinsky 2017, 152). Since 2015, the refinery has been modernised through an ongoing process worth $1.7 billion: the first phase has been carried out by Petromidia Navodari and Vega Ploiesti, a subsidiary of Rominserv Kazakhstan, with the financing of the Development Bank of Kazakhstan, Eximbank, and Kazakhstan National Bank; the second phase has been awarded to Sinopec Engineering and NC KazMunayGas; the third phase will be implemented by Marubeni, Sinopec Engineering, and KazStroy-Service, and financed by Nippon Export and Investment Insurance (NEXI), Bank of Tokyo–Mitsubishi UFJ (BTMU), and the Japan Bank for International Cooperation (JBIC).[76]

3.2 Suspicious Deals: Pavlodar

Opened in 1978, the complex of Pavlodar was conceived to refine crude oil from Siberia. Hence, its productivity was not affected by its technology, but rather by the shortages of oil in the dynamic between Russia and Kazakhstan. In 1997, the American CCL Oil won a five–year management contract for the Pavlodar refinery. Initially, the government was satisfied by the management because the company paid most of the debts. Yet, in 1998 the new Prime Minister Nurlan Balgimbayev announced the intention to annul the contract.[77] CCL Oil brought the government to court. During the

---

75 "Company Structure," *KazMunayGas*, http://www.kmg.kz/eng/kompaniya/ dochernie_organizacii/struktura_kompanii/

76 "Atyrau Refinery Modernisation Project, Atyrau oblast," *Hydrocarbons Technology*, https://www.hydrocarbons-technology.com/projects/atyrau-refinery-m odernisation-project/

77 Again, the tender was conducted under Prime Minister Kazhegeldin. More details on the sale of the Pavlodar refinery are offered in Chapter VI, *Specious Contract Cancellations*, 1.2 *CCL Oil: 2001-2004*.

hearings, it emerged that the agreement was unusual because two different contracts were signed with the same serial number and date but different terms. The court declared the act of the government illegal, and CCL Oil regained control of the refinery.

For a few months CCL Oil managed the refinery, but in 1999 MangistauMunaiGaz, which at that time was owned by CAPL and Ansdell development, claimed an unpaid debt from the refinery dating to 1996. After a failed negotiation, MMG brought CCL Oil to court. In May 1999, the Supreme Court awarded MMG 30% of the shares of the refinery as a repayment of the debt, but CCL Oil appealed the decision on the grounds that the company did not manage the refinery in 1996 and could not be held responsible. In 2000, the government revoked the concession from CCL Oil. The company appealed the decision, but this time the Supreme Court denied the claim. In 2000, the government divided the ownership of the refinery giving 51% of the shares to MMG and 49% to KazTransneftGas (Peck 2004, 177). Nowadays, KMG owns the refinery in its entirety.[78]

3.3 Suspicious Deals: Shymkent

Built in 1987, the refinery of Shymkent is the biggest and newest in the whole country, but like many other assets of the Kazakh economy by 1996 was full of debts. The government sold 85% of the shares of the complex for $60 million to Kazvit, a joint venture between Kazkommertsbank (KKB) and the Swiss trading company Vitol, operating through its subsidiary Vitol Munay (Pomfret 2005).[79] Still, already in 1997 Kazvit encountered its first problems: tax authorities reported that the company owed taxes for $4 million. Kazvit promptly paid $4.1 million, but soon the company was charged with tax evasion associated with the transfer–pricing scheme. This led authorities to arrest the president of the company and its financial manager. Unlike his collaborator, the president managed to flee the country, but during the trial of 1998, he was

---

78 "Company Structure," *KazMunayGas*, http://www.kmg.kz/eng/kompaniya/dochernie_organizacii/struktura_kompanii/

79 Once more, the sale took place under the government of Kazhegeldin.

68   THE HOUSE ALWAYS WINS

found guilty and banned from doing business in the country for five years. The share of the joint venture connected to Vitol was then sold to Central Asian Industrial Holdings (CAIH), a company connected to Timur Kulibayev.[80]

In that period, the Shymkent refinery was receiving crude oil from Hurricane Kumkol Oil (HKO), connected through the Pavlodar–Shymkent pipeline. Hurricane Hydrocarbons Ltd. made use of the services of the refinery as foreseen by the terms of its contract of acquisition of the rights of exploitation of the Kumkol field. Yet, the prohibitive costs of the Shymkent refinery brought the company to the edge of bankruptcy. In a struggle to diversify its options, the attempt of Hurricane to buy shares of the Caspian Pipeline Consortium was impeded by the government. HKO was accumulating debts while KKB and CAIH were pushing to obtain shares of the company (Peck 2004, 178). HKO sought court protection from creditors under the Companies Creditors' Arrangement Act.

In September 1999, the CEO of Hurricane wrote a letter to the Kazakh Prime Minister Balgimbayev where he threatened to bring the case to international arbitration. The situation was somehow overcome when Hurricane and KKB found an agreement that facilitated the relations with CAIH. In a mutual exchange of shares, CAIH obtained 30% of HKO while HKO obtained 88% of the shares of the refinery. Eventually, HKO, later renamed PetroKazakhstan, was entirely sold to the Chinese CNPC.[81] Nowadays the only owner of the Shymkent refinery is PetroChina, a subsidiary of CNPC.[82] In 2018, CNPC concluded the works of renovation and improvement of the refinery.[83]

---

80 The full story is detailed in Chapter IV, *State Racketeering*.
81 "Hurricane Hydrocarbons Ltd. History," *Funding Universe*, http://www.fundinguniverse.com/company-histories/hurricane-hydrocarbons-ltd-history/
82 "CNPC in Kazakhstan", *CNPC*, http://www.cnpc.com.cn/en/Kazakhstan/country_index.shtml
83 "CNPC completes upgrade at Kazakh Shymkent refinery," *ICIS*, http://www.mrcplast.com/news-news_open-342400.html

4. A Rich Poor Country

The picture drawn so far presents Kazakhstan as a country rich in resources but not fully in control of its oil cycle. The state strengthened its position in competitive cooperation with multinational corporations, but the macroeconomic indicators shown in the introduction do not disclose the full picture. The government is not simply asked to retrieve the maximum profit from natural resources, but also to distribute wealth homogenously among the population. As an indicator of the degree of distribution of wealth, Figure 3 shows the variation of the Gini index over the years in Kazakhstan.

Figure 3   Gini index in Kazakhstan since 2001

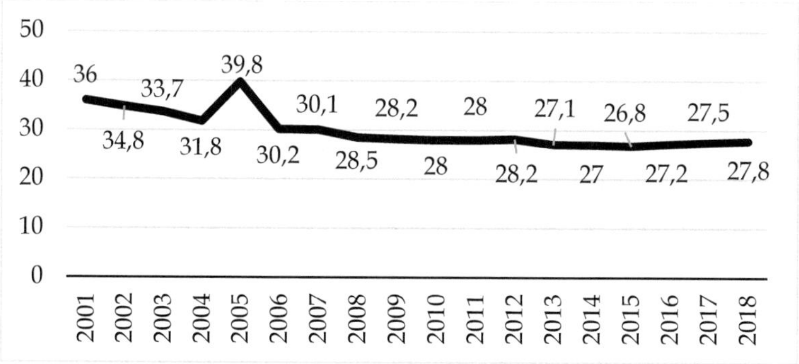

Source: The World Bank Data

As the index suggests, after 2005 there was a slow decrease in wealth inequality in Kazakhstan. The early 2000s were characterised by striking disparity between oil–producing and non–producing regions (Najman et al. 2007). In 2004, despite being a key region for oil production, Mangistau had 40% of its population living below the poverty line while in Astana and Almaty was only 2.2% and 4.1% respectively (Najman et al. 2007, 113). Similarly, while the poverty headcount tended to be generally higher in rural than in urban areas, in oil–producing regions the difference was twice or thrice higher. In 1996, a household settled in the north of the country had 30% higher living standards than one in Almaty (back then the capital city), while a household in the south had 45% lower standards (Najman et al. 2007, 117). Yet, in 2002 all other regions had significantly lower living standards than Almaty. The highly centralized taxation policy of Kazakhstan did not benefit oil–producing regions.

Even if the social expenditure per capita in oil regions was higher (Najman et al. 2007, 119), Almaty and Astana were benefiting more because development priorities were not in favour of poverty reduction. In 2006, 22% of the Kazakh GDP was spent on the construction of the new capital Astana (Franke, Gawrich, and Alakbarov 2009, 130). To increase regional budgets, regions started levying environmental fines on multinational corporations for greenhouse emissions, which led to the 2004 400% fines increase compared to the previous year. After that, macroeconomic indicators recovered, and in 2009 for the first time, the share of the population living below the minimum subsistence level decreased below 10% (Sakal 2015, 242). Yet, the result was not achieved through policies of wealth redistribution but through the general recovery of macroeconomic indicators caused by the sudden increase in oil prices (Sakal 2015). Poverty reduction was much slower; the Mangistau region had a poverty level that 'remained well above the Kazakhstan average until 2011' (Sakal 2015, 247). Central regions were luckier than the Western ones as they were indirectly exposed to the growth of Astana (Sakal 2015; Najman et al. 2007).

The government is not the only one responsible for the improvement of the living conditions of the population, especially in a country where multinational corporations are bound to develop so many oilfields. As the largest private investor in Kazakhstan, in those years the initiatives of corporate social responsibility of ChevronTexaco in the region of Atyrau included $50 million for development programs from 1993 to 1998. These programs financed the construction of a new heating plant, a medical clinic and a bakery in Atyrau, and a new medical clinic and a water treatment plant in Kulsary (Peck 2004, 156; Sakal 2015). The then consortium of Kashagan, the Agip–KCO, financed the building of schools, hospitals, and gas pipelines to villages, while in Karachaganak, KPO spent each year $5 million in the regions of Mangistau and Atyrau and $10 million in West Kazakhstan (Najman et al. 2007, 122).

These contributions were still relatively low compared to the earnings of the consortia. Inequality among regions remains a concern, and over the years oil workers have often protested wage inequalities between Kazakhs and foreigners (Sakal 2015, 248). Even if the country experienced an oil boom, common people did not reap its benefits. As a Kazakh living in Sarykamys, a settlement near the Tengiz oilfield, said: 'We have a lot of oil, but we're not the masters of this oil' (Najman et al. 2007, 125–26).

III Patrimonial Embezzlement

> The opening figure suggested by Giffen was $100 million. '[Nazarbayev] said, "Do you really think we can get $100 million just for negotiating rights?" 'I said, "You bet. In fact, I'm gonna ask for $150 million. How do you like that? I also think I can get $5 million to you by Friday — a couple of days to arrange the meeting, then a couple of more days for the money to get here." 'He said, "Go ahead." 'We finally settled on about $145 million.' Steve LeVine (2007).

> I have no doubt that you realise that the sort of concession that we are trying to get does not appeal to any government and that it is very difficult to obtain it in a country enjoying a real parliamentary system; it is to my mind only easy in countries of a one–man government like Mexico under President Diaz, Venezuela under Gomez or Colombia under Reyes.
> From a letter addressed to Weetman Pearson[84] (Philip 1982, 32).

Embezzlement is a crime defined as the misappropriation of funds or goods entrusted to an agent by its owner.[85] The principal–agent paradigm is very common in discussions about oil economies and corruption. Within this framework, citizens are owners of the resource and state authorities are agents entrusted to its management. Whenever the agent personally benefits from the sale of goods he is managing, it is possible to talk about embezzlement. The type of embezzlement discussed in this chapter procured a personal benefit to agents that awarded contracts of oil exploration or extraction but had also strong political connotations. In fact, in the cases presented, the practice has been adopted as a systematic strategy to cement political alliances and create new ones, which is what makes this form of embezzlement patrimonial.

To draw generalisations from the Kazakh case study, the chapter will make a parallelism with Venezuela. For the parallelism to work, countries should be analysed when the patrimonial embezzlement relies on oil contracts. Typically, this is at the outset of the oil industry, when numerous oilfields are discovered, and the

---

84 "Weetman Dickinson Pearson, 1st Viscount Cowdray. British engineer and politician," *Britannica*, https://www.britannica.com/biography/Weetman-Dickinson-Pearson-1st-Viscount-Cowdray

85 "Embezzlement", *Investopedia*, https://www.investopedia.com/terms/e/embezzlement.asp

74   THE HOUSE ALWAYS WINS

country has the possibility to issue contracts for extraction and exploration rights. If new oilfields are not discovered and the others are regulated with contracts valid for thirty years or more, such practice cannot take place. Said period reached its peak in the 1920s in Venezuela and the 1990s in Kazakhstan.

Another necessary precondition is high levels of corruption. Given that corruption may be present if not observed, a high level of perceived corruption indicates that the phenomenon has been detected. Looking at the Corruption Perception Index of Transparency International (CPI), Kazakhstan has been consistently at the bottom end of the rank since 1999, the first year that it was included in the measurements.[86] This shows, at least partially, that in the timeframe under analysis, the perceived corruption in Kazakhstan was high, as it was in 1920s Venezuela according to the accounts of historians (Yarrington 2003).

On the other hand, the international framework of anti–corruption norms is different because the two economies developed their oil sectors in different historical moments. In the early 1920s, colonialism was still a concrete reality and no international measure to counteract bribery abroad was in place. On the contrary, at the end of the 1990s the US Foreign Corrupt Practices Act was enforced,[87] which is also the reason that allowed the public to become aware of the embezzlement schemes of the Kazakhgate scandal. Corruption in Venezuela was reconstructed through the archival work of historians only decades after the facts took place.

The chapter aims to present the practice of patrimonial embezzlement in Kazakhstan. While the discussion mostly focuses on the embezzlement dimension, the patrimonial one has been deepened by Ostrowski (2010) in *Politics and Oil in Kazakhstan,* and acknowledged by Isaacs (2010; 2019). The analysis then moves to the case of Venezuela to show the numerous similarities with Kazakhstan and discuss the broader socio–political implications of the practice.

---

86   "Corruption Perception Index," *Transparency International,* 1999, https://www.transparency.org/en/cpi/1999

87   "Foreign Corrupt Practices Act," *The United States Department of Justice,* https://www.justice.gov/criminal-fraud/foreign-corrupt-practices-act

1. Patrimonial Embezzlement in Kazakhstan

Patrimonial embezzlement is a corrupt practice that autocratic leaders of rentier states use to cement political alliances when their grip on power is not yet strong. Still, the case of Kazakhstan shows how the same practice can present a chance for competitors of the autocrats to create their own circle of influence. With this purpose, this section discusses the dynamics of patrimonial embezzlement from the standpoint of the autocrat and his 1990s competitor.

1.1 The Kazakhgate

When talks over the CPC ran aground Giffen saw an opening and started to court the Kazakhs. In December 1994, the newly appointed oil minister Nurlan Balgymbayev nominated Giffen as main advisor (LeVine 2007, 309). The friendship with Balgymbayev was a determinant for the American middleman. It was in conjunction with the oil minister that in 1995 Giffen was able to negotiate the investments of another American major to Tengiz,[88] Mobil Oil. This deal earned Giffen $51 million and helped him to win the admiration of Nazarbayev (LeVine 2007, 351; Pomfret 2005, 866; Yeager 2012, 444). On the 1st of August 1995, the Kazakh president hired Giffen as his counsellor. He was given a diplomatic passport and authorised to represent the Central Asian Republic in oil transactions (Biegelman and Biegelman 2010, 183). From such a privileged position, the middleman managed to negotiate a number of deals throughout the 1990s: Mobil's agreement to finance the processing of gas from Karachaganak in 1995;

Amoco's purchase of shares in the CPC in 1997; Texaco's purchase of shares in Karachaganak in 1998; Mobil's purchase of exploration rights in the Caspian Sea in 1998; Phillips Petroleum's purchase of exploration rights in the Caspian Sea in 1998.[89] Yet, he did not realise that his moves had drawn the attention of international investigators.

---

88   The other one is Chevron.
89   R. Kupchinsky, "Alleged Bribery in Almaty and Elsewhere," *Radio Free Europe*, May 15, 2003, https://www.rferl.org/a/1342367.html

In 2003, Giffen was arrested at the JFK airport in New York accused of bribing foreign officials, racketeering, laundering money, and engaging in fraud.[90] The investigation started when Rakhat Aliyev, son-in-law of the president, warned Belgian authorities on the fact that Akezhan Kazhegeldin, former prime minister and opposer of Nazarbayev, intended to buy a house outside of Brussels with the money collected from the colossal privatisation of the 1990s. After the whistleblowing, Belgian authorities warned Swiss colleagues that shady individuals may have attempted to launder money in their banks. The prosecutor in Geneva Daniel Devaud asked Swiss banks to check accounts under the name Kazhegeldin or containing the word Kazakhstan. This control of routine unveiled an attempt to move $85 million in two Kazakh state accounts in Crédit Agricole Indosuez and Pictet & Cie (LeVine 2007, 465). Realising that the owner had been tipped, Devaud asked to freeze the accounts.[91]

While the direct involvement of suspects part of foreign governments would have not allowed the investigators to proceed, the discovery that the accounts were in fact manoeuvred by Giffen and that they channelled payments from American oil majors (Mobil, Texaco, Phillips Petroleum, and Amoco) towards Kazakh officials allowed the investigation to move forward. In April of 2000, Swiss investigators and US authorities started cooperating on the case. The investigators discovered that Giffen had been managing shell companies in the British Virgin Islands (Orel Capital Ltd, Altay, Tulerfield Investment Inc., Pio Ltd, Denlay Associated Ltd, Hovelon Trading SA, and NTC International Inc.), Bahamas (Condor Capital Management Ltd, Balicar Securities Ltd) and Panama (Berkut Holdings Ltd) (Peck 2004, 152–53). These companies were created in favour of President Nazarbayev himself, his daughter Dinara, Rakhat Aliyev, Akezhan Kazhegeldin, and the prime minister and former oil minister Nurlan Balgimbayev. The flux of money

---

90   R. Stodghill "Oil, Cash and Corruption," *The New York Times*, November 5, 2006, https://www.nytimes.com/2006/11/05/business/yourmoney/05giffen.html

91   S. Levine and J. Tagliabue, "Swiss Freeze Bank Account Linked to Kazakh President," *The New York Times*, October 16, 1999, https://www.nytimes.com/1999/10/16/world/swiss-freeze-bank-account-linked-to-kazakh-president.html

was consistent from 1994 to 2000, and among other things, the middleman used those funds to pay for: the maintenance of Balgimbayev's family home in Massachusetts, $30,000 worth of fur coats for Nazarbayev's wife and daughter, a speedboat for the president, as well as $45,000 in Swiss boarding school fees for his daughter (LaPorte 2017, 95). Giffen himself was said to have received $41 million as a commission for his work.

In September 2000, Nazarbayev travelled to the United States and in several meetings with the then Secretary of State Madeleine Albright asked to unfreeze the funds. Unsuccessful, in 2001 the Kazakh government lobbied the Bush administration expecting it would be well disposed towards them after the 9/11 and later pressured the construction company Halliburton with the objective to convince his former CEO, Vice President Dick Cheney, to shut down the investigation (Ostrowski 2010). While all the efforts in the US failed, Nazarbayev squashed critics at home: Emurat Bapi, director of *Soldat*, the newspaper that hosted publications on the Kazakhgate, was sentenced to one year of prison for 'insulting the dignity and honour of the president'; Lira Bayseitova,[92] the journalist reporting the news, lost an eye after being attacked by unidentified thugs; whereas the newspaper *Vremia Po* was forced to stop all publications (Ostrowski 2010). Finally, the president created a special crisis group, led by Bulat Utemuratov, to handle the long-term consequences of the corruption scandal.

The trial did not revolve on whether the facts had been committed, but rather on the motive. The defence argued that the middleman was often acting under the instruction of the CIA. During the hearings, Giffen's lawyers cited the former CIA official Robert Baer, who recalling an episode in which Toby Gati, US Special Assistant to the President and Senior Director for Russia, Ukraine, and the Eurasian States had contacted Giffen in reference to Kazakhstan selling weapons to North Korea and Iran. After the middleman's intervention, President Nazarbayev presumedly stopped the sales (Yeager 2012, 446). Prosecutors objected that this was not enough to

---

92 "Lira Bayseitova," *WikiLeaks*, https://wikileaks.org/wiki/Lira_Bayseitova

prove that Giffen's actions were to be considered lawful (Yeager 2012, 447).

The case of James Giffen and Mercator was concluded in 2010,[93] after 7 years of pre-trial litigation. The investigation produced 250 boxes of documents, but none of them were publicly available (Yeager 2012, 443). In 1990, at the XXVIII Congress of the Communist Party in Moscow Nazarbayev asserted: "We are for the market!" (Yessenova 2015, 291), but a few years later Jim Giffen would make him change his mind, and facilitating the access of oil companies to the biggest oilfields of the country *de facto* curtailed competition (Yeager 2012, 455). On the 19th of November, the American middleman was sentenced to serve one day and to pay a special assessment fine of $25. His company, Mercator, was sentenced to a criminal fine of $32,400. Until his death, Chevron paid Giffen 7.5 cents of commission per barrel of Tengiz crude (LeVine 2007, 167). The money frozen in the Swiss accounts was eventually donated to charity.[94] The sentence of the Kazakhgate is, for own admission of the US Judge William Pauley III, a recognition that the system built by Giffen was corrupt, but that his crimes had to be considered in light of the benefits procured to the American multinational corporations (Yeager 2012, 456). On October 29, 2022, James Giffen died at the age of 81.[95]

1.2 The Sale of Soviet–Era Companies

As illustrated in the previous chapter, Kazakh oilfields are numerous and diverse. Most of them are onshore small gushers developed by the Soviets already in the 1970s. In these cases, the government of independent Kazakhstan did not sell concessions for oil

---

93 S. Levine, "The Giffen strategy: Waiting out the CIA, hoping prosecutors lose heart or interest," *Foreign Policy*, June 4, 2010, https://foreignpolicy.com/2010/06/04/the-giffen-strategy-waiting-out-the-cia-hoping-prosecutors-lose-heart-or-interest/

94 R. Solash, "After Seven Years, 'Kazakhgate' Scandal Ends With Minor Indictment," *Radio Free Europe*, August 10, 2010, https://www.rferl.org/a/After_Seven_Years_Kazakhgate_Scandal_Ends_With_Minor_Indictment_/2123800.html

95 The New York Times. 2022. "James Giffen, Who Was Embroiled in 'Kazakhgate', Dies at 81," November 4, https://www.nytimes.com/2022/11/04/business/james-giffen-dead.html

extraction or exploration rights, but whole Soviet–era enterprises that owned the rights to smaller oilfields. These companies were often in bad shape, with outdated equipment and full of redundant personnel. In the early 1990s, Kazakhstan did not have the budget to save those companies and needed foreign investors who were not looking for a bargain, but rather for a chance to restructure an asset and turn it profitable. These deals were conducted by then Prime Minister Akezhan Kazhegeldin.[96]

A former KGB officer whose contacts had made him a rich dealer of chemical fertilizers and scrap metal,[97] Kazhegeldin was prime minister of Kazakhstan from 1994 to 1997 (LeVine 2007, 455). Born in Georgievka, in the region of Semipalatinks, in 1974 Kazhegeldin began his career as a schoolteacher. In 1976, he served in the army and was employed under the KGB in his region. In 1979 he started working for the party, and in 1987 he was enrolled at the KGB Superior School of the USSR. Doctor in economy, since 1990 he directed the productive complex Semey. By 1991, he became active politically, but most of his biography had been redacted. His case was not unique, because many former secret agents across the post–Soviet space were hired to liaise with Western companies (Ostrowski 2010).

He became known for being the promoter of the wave of privatisations that characterised the 1990s: 'I considered it my main task to attract foreign investment capital'.[98] This is one of the reasons for which American oil executives and US diplomats considered him closer to Western values than Nazarbayev. As recounted by Steve LeVine in *The Oil and the Glory*, he even replaced the oil

---

96 A. Grant, "The Naked King of the Kazakh Opposition", *New Eurasia*, https://www.neweurasia.info/archive/2001/tribuna/02_07_Grant.html "Ambassador's meeting with Otan party leader Yermegiyayev," *WikiLeaks*, January 4, 2005, https://wikileaks.org/plusd/cables/05ALMATY13_a.html

97 It is not clear how Kazhegeldin became rich. When asked by the press he always gave contradicting explanations. Still, he admitted taking part in illegal sales of weapons to Arab countries. A. Grant, "Golyj korol' kazahskoj oppozicii," [The Naked King of the Kazakh Opposition], *New Eurasia*, February 7, 2001, https://www.neweurasia.info/archive/2001/tribuna/02_07_Grant.html

98 "Speech by Akezhan Kazhegeldin in the City Club of Cleveland," 12 November 1999, quoted by Ostrowski (2010).

80   THE HOUSE ALWAYS WINS

minister of his government with Nurlan Balgimbayev after an exchange with Chevron's Espy Price (LeVine 2007, 317). Balgimbayev had in fact been trained by Chevron but endorsed by Nazarbayev he proved to be more than a simple puppet in the hands of American executives.

Similarly, reading Kazhegeldin as a pro–democratic and pro–Western stateman is an oversimplification. The business deals he concluded were opaque and 'made no business sense' (LeVine 2007, 455). Likely, during his mandate as head of the government he profited from rigging tenders,[99] selling most of the Soviet–era companies to unknown business groups for less than their market value. A first example was the 1995 sale of Kazchrom to the Japan Chrome Corporation, a company registered in the British Virgin Islands. To the questions of the reporters, the Japanese embassy answered that the company was in fact not Japanese. To journalists asking why all assets ended up being bought by unknown enterprises, Kazhegeldin replied that even if they were not famous at that time, the companies will be known in the future (Chervinsky 2017, 74).[100] Most of these unknown companies were tied to the British shell company Trans World Group, property of the brothers Chornoy and Ruben, and politically protected by the former Russian Deputy Prime Minister Oleg Soskovets, old business partner, promoter, and friend of Kazhegeldin.[101] A case involving the oil sector was the 1997 tender for the Atyrau refinery, initially won by the Essex Refinery Corporation, registered in the British Virgin Islands, but cancelled months later when Balgymbayev became prime

---

99 The bid rigging strategy is discussed further on, while here the focus is on the patrimonial embezzlement of Kazhegeldin in creating his informal political group.

100 "Evrazijskaâ istoriâ," [Eurasian History], *Blogbasta*, September 11, 2013, http://blogbasta.kz/?p=2513

101 Grant, "The Naked King of the Kazakh Opposition", New Eurasia. In 2005, Armangeldy Yermegiyayev, the then leader of the pro-government party Nur-Otan, complained of opposition leaders such as Akezhan Kazhegeldin who personally benefited from the sales of the 1990s creating "this problem with corruption". "Ambassador's meeting with Otan party leader Yermegiyayev," *WikiLeaks*, January 4, 2005, https://wikileaks.org/plusd/cables/05ALMATY13_a.html

PATRIMONIAL EMBEZZLEMENT   81

minister. Similar destinies awaited the Shymkent and the Pavlodar refineries.[102]

When he became a political opposer, the regime moved allegations of tax fraud and money laundering to discredit him (LaPorte 2017; Isaacs 2013, 1069), while Western media kept him in high regard turning a blind eye to his dubious tenders. He ruined the plans of regional oilmen who repeatedly expressed their discontent with the sales, but also those of members of Nazarbayev's informal political network aiming to buy those companies (Ostrowski 2010). Giffen disliked Kazhegeldin as well, as the Kazakh prime minister prevented him from negotiating those assets for Kazakhstan.[103] While Nazarbayev may have been influenced by Giffen, over time he grew discontent with Kazhegeldin's premiership. At the end of 1997, the Kazakh prime minister resigned claiming health reasons and fled to Switzerland.

By 1999, he decided to run against Nazarbayev for the presidency. It was only at this point that Rakhat Aliyev initiated the whistleblowing that provoked the Kazakhgate to be unveiled by an unforeseen domino effect. Reportedly, shots were fired at Kazhegeldin outside a restaurant, and a newspaper he funded was firebombed (LeVine 2007, 455). When asked about it, the president said that Kazhegeldin orchestrated those acts of violence himself to discredit him. The exiled politician tried to mend the relationship asking to be candidate vice–president at the elections. Nazarbayev refused and Kazhegeldin was disqualified from the race. The former prime minister had been part of Nazarbayev's circle of trust but betrayed it. He was not a champion of democracy, but a politician with unclear ties with shady Russian businessmen. During an interview with the Kazakh newspaper *Vremâ po Grinviču* (The Time in Greenwich) on the 19th of May 2000, he admitted to not being entirely clean because he had worked for a long time in a corrupt system.[104] Nowadays, he keeps supporting opposition movements

---

102 The case of the Shymkent refinery has been detailed in Chapter IV, *State Racketeering*.
103 V. Loginov, "Krestnyj otec 'Kazahgejta'," [The Godfather of the 'Kazakhgate'], Nomad, September 2, 2004, https://nomad.su/?a=3-200409030118
104 Grant, "The Naked King of the Kazakh Opposition", *New Eurasia*.

82 THE HOUSE ALWAYS WINS

in Kazakhstan and often comments political elections in the country for foreign media.

2. Patrimonial Embezzlement in Venezuela

Like Kazakhstan in the early 1990s, at the beginning of the 20th century, Venezuela was a state in the making. Also back then, private companies, and governments through their agency, were looking for new sources of oil. In 1911, as First Lord of the Admiralty Winston Churchill was lobbying for the fuel conversion of the Royal Navy from coal to oil. This allowed Britain to maintain temporary fleet supremacy over the rising German one, but neither the country nor its colonies had known oil reserves (Maugeri 2006, 22–23). At that time, oil production was dominated by only three countries: the United States, the Russian Empire, and Mexico (McBeth 2009, 431). Yet, private oil companies had already started geological investigations in Venezuela. While the government had been issuing oil concessions since 1866 (Rubio–Varas 2015, 169), the first one involving a British company was sold in 1909 by John Allen Tregelles to the British–owned Venezuela Development Co. (McBeth 1983, 10). In 1913, when Churchill obtained the approval for the navy fuel conversion, Royal Dutch Shell, the Anglo–Dutch enterprise directed by Henry Deterding, entered the Venezuelan market by buying the Valladares and Vigas concessions (McBeth 1983, 12).

Since 1908, Venezuela was ruled by General Juan Vicente Gómez, a dictator who laid the foundations of the state by imposing his authority over local leaders, building 'a stable system of national finances and administration' he managed to improve the infrastructures connecting Venezuela's regions (Yarrington 2003, 10). However, modernisation and material achievements hid social injustice and cultural obscurity (Almandoz 2001). Gómez's Venezuela was in fact a patrimonial state (Rothstein and Varraich 2017; Rodríguez and Gomolin 2009) where political power was used as a tool to enrich the dictator as well as a means to consolidate alliances with the local elite (Yarrington 2003, 12; Maugeri 2006, 31; Rodríguez and Gomolin 2009, 107). Officials often joined their capital with Gómez's to buy land and cattle (Yarrington 2003, 15), but most of the money that Gómez used for these acquisitions was effectively embezzled from the state treasury (Yarrington 2003, 16). As Yarrington (2003) noted, Gómez enriched at Venezuela's expense throughout his career, long before oil was first extracted in the country (McBeth 1983, 13; Rodríguez and Gomolin 2009, 109). Yet, under his rule, Venezuela reduced its internal and external debt and by 1931 achieved a budget surplus of 40.2 million bolívares (McBeth 1983, 112).

World War I showed the importance of oil and petroleum products not only for the well–functioning of fleets, but also for convoys and warplanes. In December 1922, when Venezuela's Los Barrosos no. 2 was discovered, British investors owned seven of the twelve oil companies operating in the country, particularly through Shell (Almandoz 2001, 87; Rubio–Varas 2015, 169). In fact, the United Kingdom needed Venezuela to emancipate itself from its dependence on North American oil. Yet, anxiety over the oil shortage pushed the US to invest to the point of becoming the strongest presence in Venezuela by the mid–1930s (McBeth 2009, 435; Almandoz 2001, 87). Gómez did not really mind who was investing in the country's oil development as long as more than one actor was present. By 1933 foreign corporations were responsible for 99.2% of the country's production (McBeth 2009, 429). This allowed him to play them against one another to increase his and Venezuela's revenue whilst avoiding economic and political dependency (McBeth 1983, 45). Even if limited in scale this was a veritable multi–vectoral energy policy.

While Juan Vicente Gómez used oil concessions as a means to improve his relationship with local *caudillos,* his family benefited as well (Kingsbury 2019, 78). Among them, there were: his son José Vicente Gómez Bello; his brother Juan Crisostomo Gómez; his sons-in-law Julio F. Mendez and Carlos Delfino, married to his daughters Graciela and Josefa (McBeth 1983, 17); his brothers in law General F. A. Colmenares Pacheco and General J. A. Martínez Méndez, married to his sisters Emilia and Indalacia; and his cousin Santos Matute Gómez (McBeth 1983, 92). In 1914, José Vicente was even appointed as a member of the Comisión Permanente de Fomento of the Chamber of Deputies in Congress, joined the following year by

84   THE HOUSE ALWAYS WINS

Carlos Delfino. In this way, the family was informed about the developments in the oil and mining sector, knowledge that they used for their personal advantage (McBeth 1983, 17). The family's involvement became more evident in 1916, when Juan Crisostomo Gómez acquired an oil concession in Zulia for Arístides Soto Bracho of Maracaibo, and offered guidance that helped Julio F. Mendez and Addison H. McKay to acquire lucrative contracts in 1919 (McBeth 1983, 18-19). In 1920, José Vicente and Carlos Delfino acted as intermediaries deciding the awarding of 116 contracts of 10,000 hectares each. In 1925, they also sold thirty-seven oil contracts they co-owned to the Central Venezuelan Oil Corp. (McBeth 1983, 47-48).

The government approved oil laws in 1918, 1920, 1921, and 1922. While each version corrected inconsistencies of the previous ones and increased the state's revenue, oil companies believed that the 1922 law was the most advantageous of all Latin America (McBeth 1983, 66; Bucheli and Aguilera 2010, 365; Maugeri 2006, 31). This allowed Venezuela to become the second-world producer and the largest exporter by 1928 (McBeth 1983, 70; 2009, 428; Rubio-Varas 2015, 169). During Gómez's lifetime, oil companies acquired 2,434 concessions, half of the total, from 829 individuals, and 1,354, or 22%, from the government (McBeth 1983, 70). Even if close associates of the dictator mediated concessions to oil companies earning a cut, the final price was still profitable. Not all companies developed their properties, some simply resold them.

Operators were careless and large quantities of oil wasted through spillage and fires went untaxed (McBeth 1983, 191). Furthermore, in 1929 the government discovered that Gulf Oil and Lago had overinflated their transportation costs, resulting in a loss of 61,452,899 bolívares in unpaid royalties (McBeth 1983, 196). In fact, Venezuelan oil was not traded on any market as it was moved between different subsidiaries of the same corporation, and its price was deducted by subtracting transportation costs from oil of the same sort sold by the same companies elsewhere. Yet, in 1932 the Great Depression and the introduction of a tariff on imported oil in the US ended up decreasing investments and Venezuelan drilling activity by 40% compared to the previous five years (McBeth 2009,

456). Fearing that insisting on tax evasion would have driven investors away, the government dropped any claim. At that point, Gómez needed oil revenues more than oil companies needed oil (McBeth 1983, 212).

3. Patrimonial Embezzlement in Oil Economies

Developed roughly seventy years apart, the oil sectors of Kazakhstan and Venezuela diverge considerably. Yet, when the analysis is focused on their initial phases of development, the countries show striking similarities, including systematic embezzlement relying on the sale of oil contracts for extraction and exploration. From an economic standpoint, in those historical moments, both Kazakhstan and Venezuela had a desperate financial situation. The perspective of oil discoveries was the promise of a way out of default. Both Nazarbayev and Gómez undersold their assets to foreign investors with contracts that would be later renegotiated, but their countries had neither the capital nor the technology to develop them. Both leaders carefully balanced the size and number of assets conceded to different investors, achieving what has been often identified as Nazarbeyev's multi–vector foreign policy (Ipek 2007). Against the resource curse hypothesis, despite high levels of corruption, both countries were financially better off at the end of Nazarbayev and Gómez's presidential mandates.

While embezzlement was systematic in both countries, elites adopted different strategies to make it work. In Kazakhstan, Giffen mediated sales that hid personal profits for Nazarbayev and other members of his informal network, while Kazhegeldin organised rigged tenders that benefited his business partners. In Venezuela, plots of land with potential for oilfield exploitation were bought at a discounted price by businessmen close to Gómez and later resold to international oil companies for a much higher price. In the 1920s, geological investigations that anticipated a contract for oil exploration were rather primitive if compared to the 1990s, because plots of lands were sold before oilfields were discovered. Similarly, finance did not allow the creation of offshore bank accounts where autocrats could hide their revenues. Still, the continuous development of the energy sectors was paralleled by the personal enrichment of the dictators.

Not only autocrats profited personally from these contracts, but they used the practice as a tool of state building. In the periods analysed, Kazakhstan and Venezuela risked being torn apart by regional strongmen, but Nazarbayev and Gómez gained the loyalty of local leaders by sharing revenues and properties (Ostrowski 2010; McBeth 1983). Political patronage is hence at the heart of the long years of rule of the Kazakh dictator (Tipaldou 2021, 257), but the outcome was not granted, as Kazhegeldin used the same informal means to gain autonomy and rival him. It is not a coincidence that all major opposers of Nazarbayev emerged from its own informal network. Yet again, the use of embezzlement for patronage is not peculiar to natural resources, since Gómez used oil as a means of patronage as he did with cattle before that (Yarrington 2003).

Managers of international oil companies often attempt to limit their competition, and in line with their desires, none of these deals were concluded through tenders. This stems from the fact that these statesmen managed oilfields as if they were their personal property, and international oil companies were picked based on the personal connections of the mediators. By bypassing competition energy corporations obtained favourable contracts, and the bribes they had to pay to autocrats were a much smaller price to pay than a competitive proposal. Quite the opposite, tenders are conceived to facilitate the victory of the investor proposing the best project for the best price. This ensemble of elements draws the picture of oil colonialism based on the alliance between a corrupt elite and international companies, at the expense of the citizens of resource-rich countries (Kingsbury 2019, 83). Foreigners were invited to modernise the country (Kingsbury 2019, 84), but a side-effect of their intervention was empowering autocrats to foster their policies of patronage. Table 3 summarises the actors, roles, and goals of patrimonial embezzlement.

Table 3   The actors, roles, and goals of patrimonial embezzlement

Actors involved	Role in the practice	Goal
Patron	Passive receiver of embezzlement responsible for its patrimonial implications	Personal profit Patronage
Middleman	Initiator	Personal and patron's profit
International oil company	Money dispenser	Avoiding competition

The conclusion of the political career of Kazhegeldin in Kazakhstan is also connected to 'character assassination' (Samoilenko et al. 2018), a practice of informal governance employed to get rid of political competitors through the use of *kompromat* and manufactured evidence (Ledeneva 2006). The motivation behind trials is often political and rarely has to do with how grounded allegations are. Other cases of character assassination in Kazakhstan included: former Prime Minister Serik Akhmetov, former Minister of Environmental Protection Nurlan Iskakov, former Health Minister Zhaksylyk Doskaliev, former Minister of Energy Mukhtar Ablyazov, former Minister of Energy as well as former mayor of Almaty Viktor Khrapunov, former Minister of Tourism and Sport Talgat Ermegiyayev, former Minister of Internal Affairs Serik Baymaganbetov, former Minister of the Economy Zhaksybek Kulekeyev, former Minister of Transport and Communication Serik Burkitbayev, former Defence Vice–Minister Kazhimurat Maermanov, former Agriculture Vice–Minister Muslim Umiryayev, former Defence Vice–Minister Bagdat Maykieiev, former Vice–Minister for Emergencies Altai Sabdalin, former Vice–Minister of Transport and Communication Dulat Kuterbekov, former Vice–Minister for Education Sayat Shayakhmetov, former Minister of the Economy Kuandyk Bishimbayev, former Energy Vice–Minister Gani

88 THE HOUSE ALWAYS WINS

Sadibekov.[105] Most of them were accused of corruption or abuse of power.

4. Cementing Power Through Rent

Like Kazakhstan, the Venezuelan economy has depended on oil consistently throughout its history. Yet, unlike the Latin American one, the Kazakh oil industry has been lucrative and did not negatively affect the rest of the economy. Venezuela is in fact often listed among the typical examples of resource curse (Hammond 2011). The country has suffered from the Dutch disease following a series of poor economic choices (Fardmanesh 1991). In the 1970s, its oil industry experienced a boom that in the 1980s was followed by a bust, solved with the bailing of the IMF. Under President Hugo Chávez oil production increased as well as the country's dependency on it, producing negative effects on the manufacturing sector.[106] Economic distress reached its peak under Nicolás Maduro with hyperinflation and a plunging GDP.[107] Unlike Kazakhstan, in Venezuela the busts were never counterbalanced with the liquidity of a sovereign fund. The only real attempt was in 1998 with the creation of the Macroeconomic Stabilization Fund, but Chávez used most of its capital in the early years of his presidency to implement social projects.[108] As a result of the protracted crisis, as of 2020 Venezuela was no more among the top oil exporters.[109] Yet, at the outset of their oil industry, both leaders adopted the same strategy:

---

105 "Pâtiminutnyj putevoditel' po ministram, pojmannym za ruku," [A five-minute tour through ministers caught red-handed] *Esquire*, March 6, 2018, https://esq uire.kz/pyatiminutny-putevoditely-po-ministram-poymannm-za-ruku/

106 E. Schwartz, "How Venezuela Caught an Incurable Case of Dutch Disease," *Econlife*, March 12, 2019, https://econlife.com/2019/03/venezuelas-oil-crea tes-dutch-disease/

107 "What caused hyperinflation in Venezuela: a rare blend of public ineptitude and private enterprise", *The Conversation*, February 5, 2019, https://theconvers ation.com/what-caused-hyperinflation-in-venezuela-a-rare-blend-of-public-in eptitude-and-private-enterprise-102483

108 M. Khayan, "We Need a Sovereign Wealth Fund," *Caracas Chronicles*, September 9, 2019, https://www.caracaschronicles.com/2019/09/09/we-need-a-sov ereign-wealth-fund/

109 D. Workman, "Crude Oil Exports by Country," *World's Top Exports*, 2020, https://www.worldstopexports.com/worlds-top-oil-exports-country/

systematic embezzlement relying on contracts that provided autocrats the liquidity necessary to consolidate their rule over the country. After all, internal legitimacy is a dictator's main concern.

The first suggested generalisation drawn from the cases is hence that countries whose leaders are looking for means to cement their rule and centralise power will use rent, from extractive resources or other forms of export, to create a patrimonial state where loyalty is bought. Still, a necessary precondition is that the country should not have a solid national company, the liquidity, or the technology to develop the sector on its own. Similar situations have taken place in the first decades of the 20th century, particularly in Saudi Arabia with King Ibn–Saud (Maugeri 2006, 57). The dysfunctional relationship between a country needing cash and a corporation looking for oil and gas resources is the precondition for the occurrence of this type of embezzlement. Still, as the case of Kazakhstan has shown, when patrimonial embezzlement is employed, the authoritarian regime is not yet stable, and competitors nominated to posts of power can apply the same strategy to rival the autocrat.

The second suggested generalisation is that in rentier states, foreign companies will favour this mechanism by undersigning the disputable conditions set by corrupt leaders to undercut competition. This statement remained valid despite measures adopted by states to limit corruption and bribery of their national companies abroad. Paradoxically, companies will often have the upper hand in contract negotiations, but since the political elite aims at personal profit, the disadvantageous conditions of the contract will not be perceived as a loss by local leaders. The situation will be hence characterised as a win–win for the negotiators but as a loss, in the long run, for citizens of the rentier state. The table below shows a schematic version of the preconditions of transferability of the cases based on the M–STOUT scheme of external validity employed in quantitative analysis (Findley, Kikuta, and Denly 2021).

90   THE HOUSE ALWAYS WINS

Table 4   **Patrimonial embezzlement transferability to the target population**

Dimension	Kazakhstan	Venezuela	Rentier states
Mechanisms	Embezzlement	Embezzlement	Embezzlement
Settings	Established authoritarian rule	Established authoritarian rule	Predatory political elite
Treatments	Intervention of foreign oil companies	Intervention of foreign oil companies	Foreign investments
Outcomes	Modernisation, centralisation, and patrimonial state	Modernisation, centralisation, and patrimonial state	Modernisation, centralisation of power, and patrimonial state
Units	Kazakh oil industry	Venezuelan oil industry	Resource–rich country without strong national actors in the sector
Time	1990s	1920s	Phase of initial development of the oil industry

Patrimonial embezzlement is the first piece of the puzzle and the first element of the taxonomy. On the other hand, with reference to the case–specific question, both the 'Kazakhgate' and the rigged tenders organised by Kazhegeldin have shown how middlemen and government officials colluded with companies to increase their personal profit. Said profit was also used to cement alliances and networks, creating the basis on which other practices have developed: without these initial contracts there could not have been fine threats, specious contract cancellations, and bid rigging.

5. Summary Sheet: Patrimonial Embezzlement

Definition: patrimonial use of misappropriated funds to cement political power.

Actors involved: political elite (autocrat and competing networks), foreign oil and gas corporations, and middlemen.

Observed in: Kazakhstan, Venezuela.

PATRIMONIAL EMBEZZLEMENT   91

Outcomes: country modernisation, centralisation of power and patrimonial ties.

Context: resource-rich country without strong national actors in the sector.

Timeline: phase of the initial development of the oil industry.

Figure 4   Visualisation of patrimonial embezzlement

* Transnational Oil Corporations

IV State Racketeering

> Soon, intermediaries arranged an Idenov–Kulibayev meeting. Idenov said they both pretended to ignore the core problem—Kulibayev's, he alleged, avarice for large bribes. Idenov averred he told Kulibayev, 'Please watch your image and reputation. You have a real opportunity to improve your own image and the image of the nation.'
> *WikiLeaks*, January 25, 2010.[110]

> Former Deputy Energy Minister Vladimir Milov highlighted personal corruption in discussing Sechin with us, noting something that many others with whom we spoke also alluded to—that Sechin's new direct authority over the lucrative energy sector would give him 'better access to cash flow.'
> *WikiLeaks*, September 12, 2008.[111]

In the online version of the Global Informality Project, Irina Jantayeva (2020) described *otzhat'*, a Russian word meaning squeeze, wring out, press, or extract, as a slang term used to identify the act of taking over someone's property or property rights under threat. In the 1990s, the practice was most diffused among those whom Vadim Volkov (2016) described as violent entrepreneurs, criminals employing physical intimidation, kidnapping and murders to take possession of assets. Violence was set aside once former members of the secret services or businesspeople politically connected appeared on the market. Their business strategy relied on formally legal means abused in an informal way. Rather than violence these entrepreneurs were using arrests, the freezing of bank accounts, or unexpected tax inspections to jeopardise the target company's future through *zakaznoe bankrotstvo* (ordered bankruptcy).

Otzhat' can be seen as a general take on what Ledeneva (2013) identified as *reiderstvo*, a Russian version of corporate raiding, consisting of stealing a company with the objective of reselling it for a profit. It is a business worth 120 million roubles (roughly $4 billion) a year in Russia alone, where $120,000 spent in bribing officials to bankrupt a company can help thugs acquire $3 million in assets

---

110 "Money and Power," *WikiLeaks*, January 25, 2010, https://wikileaks.org/plusd/cables/10ASTANA72_a.html

111 "Russia—Bringing Sechin into Focus," *WikiLeaks*, September 12, 2008, https://wikileaks.org/plusd/cables/08MOSCOW2759_a.html

(Ledeneva 2013, 189). This type of 'piranha capitalism' has been thoroughly described by Stanislav Markus in his *Property, Predation, and Protection* (2015) as a general inability or unwillingness of the Russian and Ukrainian states to make citizens respect the right to property. In this context, citizens and business owners cannot be sure their properties will be guaranteed: 'In the Constitution, we have the right to property. Such right is conceived in a way that your properties are secure. Yet, reality is different. If you are a successful businessman, the right does not apply to you, and the state will often take your properties away. This is even more true in the oil sector.'[112]

In Kazakhstan and Russia, similar developments allowed the practice to thrive despite a formal transition to liberal democracy. Both semi–presidential republics, the countries have been ranked as moderate autocracies in the 2020 index of the University of Würzburg.[113] While in the 2020 World Justice Project Rule of Law Index[114] Kazakhstan outperformed Russia, the cases displayed a very similar pattern, suggesting that the rule of law does not work in the oil sector of these countries. Following the process of privatisation that interested both countries in the transition to market economies, the state racketeers aimed at retaking possession of the assets that had ended in 'the wrong hands'.

Unlike fine threats, discussed in the next chapter, when governments have the goal of renegotiating contracts, with *otzhat'* members of the informal political elite use corporate raiding for personal profit. This chapter presents the Kazakh and Russian cases, showing how the validity of the theories exposed by Ledeneva (2013), Markus (2015), and Volkov (2016) extend to a post–Soviet state not originally envisioned by their research. Timur Kulibayev's *modus operandi* can be largely ascribed to *reiderstvo*, while the cases of Igor Sechin are a different form of *otzhat'*, serving both personal and systemic goals. To facilitate its applicability to rentier

---

112 Political analyst, interview by author, Almaty, November 25, 2019.
113 "Ranking of Countries by Quality of Democracy," *The University of Würzburg*, https://www.democracymatrix.com/ranking
114 "2020 World Justice Project Rule of Law Index," *World Justice Project*, https://worldjusticeproject.org/our-work/wjp-rule-law-index

states where Russian is not in use, the practice has been named 'state racketeering' in search of a synthesis between *otzhat'* and *reiderstvo*. While the literature seldom talks of 'state capture' (Isaacs 2019, 4), this expression focuses attention on the act of personal appropriation of state institutions. On the other hand, 'state racketeering' suggests that an already–captured state engages in racket.[115] In other words, the goal here is not to evaluate the political system, but to highlight what happens in the driving sector of a rentier state as a result.

1. State Racketeering in Kazakhstan

1997 was the year of succession to the throne of informal businessman of the oil sector. Kazhegeldin was forced to abandon his role as prime minister and Timur Kulibayev became increasingly involved in a series of deals with shell companies. When asked about Kulibayev during an interview for El Pais on the 2nd of April 2007, the first president commented that at the beginning of the 1990s his son–in–law bought a bank for nothing and managed to get involved in affairs worth millions, at the beginning of the privatisation there were many violations, but Kazakhstan is full of stories like this (Chervinsky 2017, 208-9). In contradiction with what was declared by the first president, the story of his son–in–law seems rather unique.

Timur Kulibayev was born in Alma–Ata in 1966. In 1988 he graduated in economics from the Lomonosov Moscow State University and in 1999 he earned his PhD in economics with a thesis titled 'Enhancing business management system of an enterprise in market conditions (the case of oil industry).' By 1997, he was already the Vice President for Finance and Economics of Kazakhoil National Oil and Gas Company, and in 2002 he was First Vice President of KazMunayGas. Allegedly, Kulibayev was temporarily pushed away from Kazakhstan and the Samruk-Kazyna Sovereign

---

115 Kulibayev has long been a member of the informal network of Nazarbayev, the ally of members of governments (including former Prime Minister Massimov), and managers of KazMunayGas. This explains in what sense the practice is promoted by the state.

Wealth Fund[116] following the 2011 shooting of Uzenmunaigas workers and Zhanaozen residents to show that Nazarbayev held those responsible for the oil sector accountable.[117] Away from Kazakhstan, he joined Gazprom.[118] Kulibayev is a billionaire[119] and one of the richest men of Kazakhstan. He made money through banking, but as soon as the late 1990s he started to operate in the energy sector.

One of Kulibayev's favourite tools of intervention in the oil industry was Nelson Resources, a company registered in the Bermuda Islands that the son–in–law of Nazarbayev used in cooperation with his friend and business partner Arvind Tiku.[120] In the mid–1990s, the company was called Nelson Gold because most of its deals were related to gold mines in Tajikistan (Chervinsky 2017, 156). In 2000, Central Asian Industrial Holdings and Korinth Trade & Investment Corp acquired 35% each of Nelson Gold. In the same year, Nelson Gold was renamed Nelson Resources and Baltabek Kuandykov, a man of Nazarbayev's circle operating in the industry, became its president (Ostrowski 2010; Chervinsky 2017). All investments of Nelson Resources in the oil sector were financed by Kazkommertsbank and the National Bank of Kazakhstan, today owned at 73.3% by Timur Kulibayev and his wife Dinara (Chervinsky 2017).[121]

In the early 2000s, Kulibayev used Nelson Resources as a tool to deal with Chinese investors. In 2003, CNPC bought Buzachi Operating Ltd., an operator in the field of North Buzachi. Still, in 2004 the Chinese major bought also half of the shares of Nelson

---

116 "Timur Kulibayev," *People Pill*, https://peoplepill.com/people/timur-kulibay ev/

117 R. Paxton, "Analysis: Kazakh leader reinforces power with oil sackings," *Reuters*, December 23, 2011, https://www.reuters.com/article/us-kazakhstan-suc cession-idUSTRE7BM0M820111223

118 "Timur Kulibayev," *Gazprom*, https://www.gazprom.com/about/managem ent/directors/kulibaev/

119 "Timur Kulibayev," *Forbes*, https://forbes.kz/ranking/object/40

120 "Arvind Tiku," *Forbes*, https://www.forbes.com/profile/arvind-tiku/#13623 a933681

121 "Kto vladeet 20 krupnejšimi bankami Kazahstana," [Who owns the 20 biggest banks of Kazakhstan], *Forbes*, September 19, 2014, https://forbes.kz/finances/ finance/kto_vladeet_20_krupneyshimi_bankami_kazahstana/

Resources, which on its part bought half of those of Buzachi Operating, hence becoming the main operator of the renamed Nelson Buzachi Petroleum B.V. (Ostrowski 2010). Already owner of Buzachi Operating, CNPC did not have any real interest to create a joint venture with Nelson Resources, but a connection existed since 2000, when Nelson Resources became shareholder of CNPC–Aktobemunaygas after its acquisition of half of the shares of KazakhOil–Aktobe.[122] As a result of these transactions, in 2004 the market capitalisation of Nelson Resources grew to $1 billion, making it the biggest Kazakh private company of the time. Over the years, Nelson Resources sold most of its shares in oilfields to Caspian Investments Resources Ltd. which by 2015 was entirely owned by the Chinese Sinopec.

In 2010, the long term opposer of President Nazarbayev Mukhtar Ablyazov accused Timur Kulibayev of corruption in a series of open letters published on the Kazakh *Respublika*.[123] According to the information disclosed by Ablyazov, in 2003 Kulibayev personally profited $166 million when CNPC bought 25% of Aktobemunaygas. For the transfer of money, CNPC used the shell company International Caspian Limited, founded in April 2003 in the British Virgin Islands with a start–up capital of $100. Soon, the company had sold 49% of its shares for $49 to Darley Investment Services, a company owned by Kulibayev's friend Arvind Tiku. CNPC transferred the $150 million necessary to buy 25% of Aktobemunaygas to International Caspian Limited, and over two years

---

122 "Hronologiâ sobytij," [Chronology of the Events], *KazakhOil Aktobe*, http://www.koa.kz/ru/hronologiya-sobytiy

123 D. Mavloniy, "Muhtar Ablâzov obvinâet Timura Kulibaeva v hišenii 20 milliardov dollarov," [Mukhtar Ablyazov accuses Timur Kulibayev of stealing $20 billion], *Radio Liberty*, March 3, 2010, https://rus.azattyq.org/a/mukhtar_ably azov_appeal_to_kazakhstan_society/1972361.html The American embassy presumed that the information leaked was provided either by Rakhat Aliyev, because at the time his relationship with the Nazarbayev family was already bad, or by another individual with contacts in the highest informal network of the country, as explained in "The President son-in-law tries, but fails to mute corruption allegations," *WikiLeaks*, February 12, 2010, https://wikileaks.org/plusd/cables/10ASTANA184_a.html

bought back from Darley Investment Services 49% of International Caspian Limited for $165.9 million (Cooley 2012, 141).[124]

In a different episode, CNPC bought MangistauMunaiGaz, which until 2009 was owned by Central Asian Petroleum Ltd. The company, reportedly Indonesian, was manoeuvred by Central Asian Industrial Holdings, Central Asian Agriculture Holdings, and Central Asian Energy Holdings. According to Ablyazov's reconstruction of the events, MangistauMunaiGaz was sold under a tender procedure even though it had been already agreed that CNPC would have bought it. The scheme was conceived to avoid paying the taxes connected to a normal sale.[125] The reaction of Kulibayev to these accusations was to file a lawsuit against the Kazakh newspaper that published Ablyazov's letters, resulting in Kazakh officials seizing the editions of five newspapers reprinting this information, and in a Kazakh court ordering journalists not to damage the honour of the son–in–law of president Nazarbayev (Cooley 2012, 141).[126]

Finally, in 2018 the investigative journalists of *Public Eye* drew the attention to Vitol, the biggest oil trader in the world, as a major source of Kulibayev's wealth.[127] As the article outlined, the Swiss company became the major trader of Kazakh oil by creating a system of shell companies (Ingma Holding B.V. in the Netherlands,

---

124 D. Mavloniy, "Ablâzov vovlek v svoû intrigu protiv Kulibaeva daže samogo Hu Czin'tao," [Ablyazov includes in his intrigue against Kulibayev also Xu Jintao], *Radio Liberty*, February 2, 2010, https://rus.azattyq.org/a/hu_jintao_mukhtar_ablyazov_timur_kulibaev_compromat/1945300.html

125 The letter of Mukhtar Ablyazov to the Parliament of the United Kingdom, "Letter to the Chair from Mukhtar Ablyazov," *www.parliament.uk*, https://publications.parliament.uk/pa/cm200910/cmselect/cmfaff/memo/human/m21702.htm Kulibayev was likely involved in the management of a $5 billion loan from the Chinese Export-Import Bank to the Development Bank of Kazakhstan owned by the National Fund Samruk-Kazyna as discussed in "China National Petroleum Corporation acquires 50% stake in MangistauMunaiGas," *WikiLeaks*, April 23, 2009, https://wikileaks.org/plusd/cables/09ASTANA678_a.html

126 In a public outcry, the court decision was reversed with the justification that also judges commit mistakes as in "The President's son-in-law tries, but fails to mute corruption allegations," *WikiLeaks*, February 12, 2010, https://wikileaks.org/plusd/cables/10ASTANA184_a.html

127 "Vitol, the king of oil in Kazakhstan," *Public Eye*, 2018, https://stories.publiceye.ch/vitolinkazakhstan/index.html

Oilex Sàrl in Luxembourg, and Oilex N.V. in Curaçao, the Dutch Antilles) that benefited Arvind Tiku and Timur Kulibayev. The son-in-law of the president made Vitol the biggest player in Kazakh oil trading in return for public investments and personal profit.

Timur Kulibayev is certainly one of the darkest figures of the Kazakh regime. His allegiance with former Prime Minister Karim Massimov allowed him to manipulate sentences and mobilise the police until the rightful owners of its targets had to capitulate by selling their assets to him or his associates. According to sources from the US embassy, he was the 'ultimate controller' of 90% of the Kazakh economy.[128] While estimations may be inflated, interviewees agreed he is the major actor in the energy sector: 'You can't really get any big project without Timur, and he's really the person behind all main decisions.'[129]

1.1 Kumkol: 1997–2005

The fact that Akezhan Kazhegeldin was organising tenders to sell Soviet-era companies to the 'wrong' buyers can be observed in the example of Yuzhneftegas, operator of the Kumkol oilfield. In 1996, when Kazhegeldin organised the tender, an inquiry by the Ministry of Oil and Gas showed that the oil extracted at Kumkol reached the refinery of Shymkent only after passing through 120 mediators (Chervinsky 2017, 76). Clearly, all transactions happened only on paper, and someone was profiting from a company on the verge of bankruptcy. In fact, the tender announcement found resistance from the local governors Erzhan Utembayev and Igor Rogov (Chervinsky 2017, 76). The procedure terminated with the victory of the Canadian Hurricane Hydrocarbons Ltd., but this conclusion is strange for two reasons: the price of $120 million seems very low for the potential of the oilfield, and before the announcement of Hurricane as winner, the head of the State Committee for the

---

128 "Money and Power," *WikiLeaks*.

129 'An advisor said that 95% of companies operating in the sector are somehow connected to T.', Employee of subcontracting company, interview by author, Aktau, 3 December 2019. Confirmed by: former manager of an oil trading company, former oil investor, oil investor, political risk analyst.

100 THE HOUSE ALWAYS WINS

Management of State Properties Sarybay Kalmurzayev announced that the likely winner was Samson International (Ostrowski 2010). Therefore, Kazhegeldin decided the winner unilaterally, probably for personal profit. The Nazarbayev circle was not pleased by the situation as proven by the objection of Nurlan Balgimbayev (Peck 2004; Ostrowski 2010).

In confirmation of the fact that the sale had not been good for the government, in 1997 Hurricane Kumkol Munay was already profitable (Peck 2004, 160). Yet, the Canadian owners were probably unaware that the company was already a target of Nazarbayev circle. The contract for the sale of Yuzhneftegas envisioned that the oil extracted at Kumkol had to be refined in the refinery of Shymkent but in 1997 the refinery was the property of Kazvit, a joint venture of Kazkommertsbank and the Swiss Vitol. In those months there were rumours suggesting that the real owner of the refinery was Akezhan Kazhegeldin. Whichever the truth, in early 1997 tax authorities conducted an audit and declared that Kazvit owed the government $4 million in taxes. Vitol paid $4.1 million, but this did not prevent authorities from charging Kazvit's president and financial manager with tax evasion. In 1998, after being banned from doing business in the country, the president of the company Gavin De Salis declared that the government tried to overturn the privatisation using him as an excuse (Shammas and Nagata 2000).[130] The shares of Vitol were then sold to Central Asian Industrial Holding, a daughter company of Kazkommertsbank (Chervinsky 2017). As anticipated, both Kazkommertsbank and Central Asian Industrial Holdings were connected, with some degrees of separation, to Timur Kulibayev and his business associates (Peck 2004, 168; Ostrowski 2010).

With full control of the refinery, the son–in–law of the president made the life of the Canadian company difficult. Obliged to refine its crude in Shymkent, Hurricane Kumkol Munay was on the

---

130 A. Macdonald, "British Oil Exec Vows to Fight After Kazakhstan 'Show Trial'," *The Moscow Times*, March 12, 1998, https://www.themoscowtimes.com/archiv e/british-oil-exec-vows-to-fight-after-kazakhstan-show-trial "KAZAKHSTAN —Chimkent Refinery," *The Free Library*, https://www.thefreelibrary.com/KA ZAKHSTAN+-+Chimkent+Refinery-a050193825

verge of collapse because the refinement costs remained high despite the sinking price of crude. When the company sought court protection and asked for the intervention of then Prime Minister Balgimbayev, the owners were not aware that they were interfacing with different members of the same informal political group. A first step towards the solution was reached once Hurricane understood that Central Asia Industrial Holdings aimed to its shares: Hurricane acquired 88% of the Shymkent refinery and Central Asia Industrial Holdings acquired 30% of Hurricane. According to Olga Elefteriadi, vice–president of Hurricane, the price paid for the shares of the refinery was overvalued. If she was correct, this may indicate that the inflated price was covering bribes. In the end, the fusion was realised, and Olga Elefteriadi lost her job as a result of the opposition to the deal (Chervinsky 2017, 117).

Still, while the Canadians had reached an armistice with the major informal group in the country, not all oilmen had been pleased. On the night of the 29th of November 2000, the former Kazakh director of the refinery Nurlan Bizakov, empowered by a regional court sentence advocating his reinstatement, occupied the complex of Shymkent escorted by special forces. Clearly, the action had not been supported by central authorities, because on the night of the 1st of December the new director, Marlo Thomas, regained control of the refinery escorted by forces of the Ministry of Interior (Chervinsky 2017, 145–46).[131] A few days later, the internal affairs department of South Kazakhstan filed a lawsuit against what was defined as Thomas's 'criminal expulsion' of Bizakov.[132]

Already in April 2001, the armistice had come to an end. Central Asian Industrial Holding made a bid to obtain a further 23% of

---

131 D. Parkinson, "Hurricane survives armed attack on Kazakhstan refinery," *The Globe and Mail*, December 4, 2000, https://www.theglobeandmail.com/report-on-business/hurricane-survives-armed-attack-on-kazakhstan-refinery/article25575266/

132 "Hurricane Hydrocarbons Ltd. History," *Funding Universe*, http://www.fundinguniverse.com/company-histories/hurricane-hydrocarbons-ltd-history/ The Kazakh press considered Nurlan Bizakov a member of the group of power of Kazkommertsbank which ultimately responded to President Nazarbayev. "Razdelennaâ èlita," [The Subdivision of the Elite], *New Eurasia*, 1999, https://www.neweurasia.info/archive/1999/analitica/06_11_Who0494.html

102   THE HOUSE ALWAYS WINS

the shares of Hurricane in an attempt to take control of the company. The bid was rejected, but in 2002 the government increased the pressure on the Canadians contesting them $20 million of unpaid taxes.[133] Finally, Hurricane got rejected its participation in the Caspian Pipeline Consortium and the Ministry of Energy established new export quotas that forced the company to reduce its production (Peck 2004, 165).[134] The troubled path of Hurricane in Kazakhstan terminated in 2005, with the sale of the company to the Chinese CNPC for $4.18 billion.[135] This was certainly a blessing for

---

133 The suspicious 'use of courts' has been noticed also by the American embassy in the sale of both PetroKazakhstan and Karazhanbasmunai as discussed in "Canadian oil company weathers legal assault," *WikiLeaks*, October 16, 2006, https://wikileaks.org/plusd/cables/06ASTANA90_a.html

134 In 2003, the company was also subject to price ceilings for some of its products. By its own admission, Hurricane violated the ceilings imposed, hence incurring a civil case for violation of antimonopoly legislation. In court, Hurricane declared to be the only company subject to those ceilings, and not to be the monopolist for the refined products contested. Therefore, its position was that the government had acted maliciously to distort market competition. "News Release," *PetroKazakhstan*, April 4, 2005, https://www.sec.gov/Archives/edgar /data/1013746/000127956905000220/ex991.htm   Furthermore, both Adil Nurmakov (2009) and Oleg Chervinsky (2017) recounted the numerous disagreements between the company and the government, from the refusal to sell oil products at a lower price to agricultural workers, to causes of presumed environmental and tax violations (Nurmakov 2009, 26–27). "PetroKazakhstan Inc.: Update on Antimonopoly Case," *KASE.kz*, July 7, 2005, https://kase.kz/ en/news/show/177022/ "KAZAKHSTAN−Chimkent Refinery," *The Free Library*, https://www.thefreelibrary.com/KAZAKHSTAN+-+Chimkent+Refin ery.-a0121086931

135 The sale did not actually terminate the troubles for PetroKazakhstan. In fact, the court cases against managers of PetroKazakhstan protracted until 2006. According to Tom Dvorak and Robert Goldsmith: 'PK's [PetroKazakhstan] legal problems were the result of a GOK [Government of Kazakhstan] plot (perhaps in collusion with Lukoil) to drive down PK's share price prior to a planned bid to buy the company' but when the case protracted after the sale they thought that the real reason for the court case was the fact that the government had been taken by surprise by the sale of PetroKazakhstan and wanted to have more leverage to bargain with the Chinese. This second hypothesis is confirmed by the embassy: 'Much evidence points to the fact that the GOK was caught unprepared by the sale, the most dramatic of which was a series of amendments which the GOK rushed into law before the deal was finalized (Ref B), which extended the GOK's "preemptive rights" and thus strengthened its negotiating position with CNPC. A KazMunaiGaz (KMG) contact told us at the time that the GOK had been unpleasantly surprised by the high price paid by CNPC−a price KMG would have to match, under the preemptive right legislation, to

the CEO Bernard Isautier, but the press judged the price excessive.[136] This detail becomes suspicious once learning that the competitor of CNPC was a joint venture of the Indian ONGC Videsh Ltd., an investment corporation owned by Lakshmi Mittal, a friend and business partner of Kulibayev in Zhaikmunay.[137] The unfolding of events seems to suggest that Kulibayev did not manage to artificially lower the price of the now renamed PetroKazakhstan[138] through court cases, because the sale of the company to CNPC was too fast. Most probably, the Chinese buyers accepted the first price proposed by Isautier just to anticipate other potential bidders. By own admission of Kulibayev, China is 'willing to pay a premium above the market price for Central Asian hydrocarbon resources'.[139] Still, the continuation of the court case against the staff of PetroKazakhstan must have convinced CNPC to cooperate with Kulibayev.[140] This is confirmed by the fact that CNPC ceded half of the shares of the Shymkent refinery after its acquisition.

---

acquire the PK assets." "PetroKazakhstan legal case winds down,' *WikiLeaks*, December 12, 2006, https://wikileaks.org/plusd/cables/06ASTANA817_a.ht ml The cable lists several indicators of the fact that the government used the court case to deal indirectly with CNPC.

136 M. Pottinger, "Chinese Oil Firm to Buy PetroKazakhstan," *The Washington Post*, August 23, 2005, https://www.washingtonpost.com/archive/business/2005/ 08/23/chinese-oil-firm-to-buy-petrokazakhstan/dc62219a-490c-4629-b1ed-3b 2ec0cb3154/ The 'premium price' is confirmed in two leaks from the American embassy in Kazakhstan. "PetroKazakhstan sold to Chinese CNPC subsidiary," *WikiLeaks*, August 23, 2005, https://search.wikileaks.org/plusd/cables/05AL MATY3075_a.html "Petrokazakhstan follow-up," *WikiLeaks*, August 26, 2005, https://search.wikileaks.org/plusd/cables/05ALMATY3143_a.html

137 A. Tikhonov, "Kulibayev's Belgian Connection," KazakhSTAN 2.0, July 25, 2018, https://kz.expert/en/news/analitika/956_kulibayevs_belgian_connect ion R. Orange, "Lakshmi Mittal to take \$300m stake in Kazakh oil services firm," *The Telegraph*, May 2, 2011, https://www.telegraph.co.uk/finance/new sbysector/energy/8488210/Lakshmi-Mittal-to-take-300m-stake-in-Kazakhoil-services-firm.html

138 The company was renamed in 2003, as discussed in Chapter II, *Petroleum in Kazakhstan*.

139 "Timur Kulibayev gives Das Feigenbaum oil and gas overview," *WikiLeaks*, August 28, 2006, https://search.wikileaks.org/plusd/cables/06ALMATY3027_a. html And confirmed later in "Special envoy Morningstar discusses energy, geopolitics with Timur Kulibayev," *WikiLeaks*, August 26, 2009, https://wikileaks .org/plusd/cables/09ASTANA1438_a.html

140 "PetroKazakhstan legal case winds down," *WikiLeaks*, December 12, 2006, https://wikileaks.org/plusd/cables/06ASTANA817_a.html

104 The House Always Wins

1.2 Karazhanbas: 2006

In 2006, Kulibayev's associates attempted to buy Karazhanbasmunai from the Canadian Nations Energy. The first reported attempt was in February through the Indian ONGC Videsh, close to Kulibayev's associate Lakshmi Mittal.[141] However, the CEO of Nations Energy Patrick O'Mara dismissed their bid very quickly defining them as 'clowns who did not have the cash'.[142] The second attempt is revealed in a very shady scheme originated in the US, where Zoran Savičić, owner of 17.9% of Karazhanbasmunai claimed more shares of the company from Nations Energy based on an agreement that he had made with its shareholders in 1994. Such agreement had been reportedly settled in 1998 but Savičić managed to make it void, claiming that he had been coerced into signing it. After obtaining a ruling in his favour in Nevada, where Nations Energy was registered, Savičić managed to continue the court procedure in Kazakhstan transferring the claim to Karazhanbasmunai. In August the court of Mangistau ruled in favour of Nations Energy's shareholders. On September 16, O'Mara told the economic officer of the American embassy that he had reason to believe that behind Savičić's assault in the Kazakh courts, there were Timur Kulibayev, the head of the Presidential Administration Adilbek Dzhaksybekov, and the managers of KMG Askar Balzhanov and Zhakyp Marabayev. O'Mara suspected that the scheme originated in 2004 when there were the first rumours that Nations Energy intended to sell Karazhanbasmunai. They wanted to acquire 50% of the company corrupting judges and driving down the price asked by Nations Energy.

O'Mara referred that in November of 2005, CNPC executives forwarded him texts they had received from Marabayev and Balzhanov where they were asking the Chinese company to stop the bid for Karazhanbasmunai to give Kulibayev the time to lower

---

141 As confirmed by the CEO of Nations Energy Patrick O'Mara in "Canadian oil company weathers legal assault," *WikiLeaks*, October 16, 2006, https://wikileak s.org/plusd/cables/06ASTANA90_a.html
142 "LUKoil, Chinese bidding for 'Nations Energy'," *WikiLeaks*, February 14, 2006, https://wikileaks.org/plusd/cables/06ALMATY603_a.html

the price of $700–800 million through fines and legal actions. In October of 2005, CNPC had just completed the acquisition of PetroKazakhstan[143] and hence the texts received from Marabayev and Balzhanov fit the timeline and explain why CNPC did not push through for the acquisition of Karazhanbasmunai from Nations Energy. O'Mara also declared that Savičić had a business history with Kulibayev, as they had partnered in illegal sales of oil during the embargo of Saddam Hussein's regime.[144] Ultimately, Kulibayev's efforts were halted by O' Mara's threat to reveal the plot to the public. In a meeting with the former Prime Minister Karim Massimov, long–term associate of Kulibayev,[145] the premier had confirmed the involvement of insiders in Savičić's attempt to gain control of Karazhanbasmunai, declaring also that he would have put an end to the scheme. O'Mara concluded by reporting that Kulibayev's revenge took place as a raid of the financial police in the offices of Nations Energy on September 11. He also confessed that the company kept receiving offers and threats, but in the end, Karazhanbasmunai was sold to the Chinese CITIC.[146]

2. State Racketeering in Russia

In 1999, when Vladimir Putin entered office, the Russian oil sector was already populated by several private actors who profited from the wave of privatisation of the early 1990s. Buying Soviet–era companies at relatively low prices allowed oligarchs to make a fortune and rival the power of the president (Gillies 2020b, 108). Yet, Putin's *systema* (Ledeneva 2013) pledged to retake control over the sector by orchestrating aggressions relying on the judiciary. According to

---

143 "CNPC completes acquisition of PetroKazakhstan," *CHINA Daily*, October 27, 2005, http://www.chinadaily.com.cn/english/doc/2005-10/27/content_4883 14.htm

144 "Canadian oil company weathers legal assault," *WikiLeaks*, October 16, 2006, https://wikileaks.org/plusd/cables/06ASTANA90_a.html

145 As confirmed by the then KMG director Maksat Idenov in "Canadian oil company weathers legal assault," *WikiLeaks*, October 16, 2010, https://wikileaks.or g/plusd/cables/10ASTANA72_a.html

146 "Sale of Nations Energy – To be or not to be?," *WikiLeaks*, December 26, 2006, https://wikileaks.org/plusd/cables/06ASTANA927_a.html

Ledeneva, *systema* is a system of governance relying on informal practices; in the narrow sense it describes power and state authorities, but in a wider one involves governance, leadership, and the bureaucratic order (Ledeneva 2013, 19–20). While *systema* has a rather hierarchical structure, like in Kazakhstan the members of this informal political group have agency. As for Kulibayev, the actions of Igor Sechin may have been ordered by Putin, agreed with him, or at times, only tolerated.

Igor Sechin was born in 1960 in nowadays Saint Petersburg. Graduated in 1984 from the Leningrad State University as a linguist, during the Soviet Union Sechin worked as an interpreter. In the early 1990s, he collaborated with Putin at the mayor's office in Saint Petersburg, served as his deputy head between 2000 and 2008, and deputy prime minister between 2008 and 2012. Since 2004, he has been chair of Rosneft, and the company's president since 2012 (Gillies 2020b, 109). According to Ledeneva, Sechin is fourth in the chain of command of *systema* and the head of Putin's circle of *piterskie chekists*, former secret service officers from Saint Petersburg (Ledeneva 2013, 56). Since his entrance on the board, Rosneft became Sechin's tool to operate in the oil sector. In fact, in 2004 the company was responsible only for 5% of Russian oil production, but by 2014, that share rose to 39% (Gillies 2020b, 109). As discussed by Alexandra Gillies in *Crude Intentions* (2020b), the spectacular ascension of Rosneft is due especially to three acquisitions orchestrated by Sechin (2020b, 113).

The first is the renowned case of Yukos. After a few successful years in the banking sector, in 1995 Mikhail Khodorkovsky bought the oil company Yukos for $350 million[147] through a rigged auction organised by his own bank, Menatep (Hoffman 2011; Gillies 2020b, 109). The company needed restructuring but had access to some of the biggest Siberian oilfields. By the early 2000s, Khodorkovsky managed to turn it profitable, but Sechin was plotting his demise

---

147 T. Macalister, "Mikhail Khodorkovsky: how the Yukos tycoon became Russia's richest man," *The Guardian*, December 20, 2013, https://www.theguardian.com/world/2013/dec/20/mikhail-khodorkovsky-russia-richest-man

leveraging on the oligarch's original sin.[148] The attacks started in 2000, when the tax agencies claimed Yukos unpaid contributions, and culminated in October 2003, when authorities raided the company's offices and arrested Khodorkovsky, accused of fraud and tax evasion (Gololobov 2007).[149] According to the government, Yukos owed over $24 million in back taxes, and the company's assets were frozen by court orders. In 2004, the government announced an auction for Yuganskneftgaz, owner of the most prolific oilfields of the Yukos group. Organised in one month, the tender was won by an unknown company whose registered address was the same as a grocery store in Tver.[150] Rosneft had lent $9 billion to the ghost company to buy Yuganskneftgaz to avoid its direct involvement. Two days after the sale, Rosneft bought out the new owner of Yuganskneftgaz (Gillies 2020b, 111). In the years that followed, Rosneft obtained all Yukos' assets until the company's final bankruptcy in 2007.

A second episode in which Sechin's informal participation was hinted at by internal sources of the US embassy in Moscow,[151] was Rosneft acquisition of the TNK–BP joint venture, co–owned by BP and some of the biggest Russian oligarchs. When in 2008 tensions arose between TNK–BP owners, the Kremlin started pressuring BP by raiding its offices and revoking work permissions for its foreign staff.[152] The TNK–BP CEO Robert Dudley was even named in a discrimination lawsuit by some of the company's Russian employees.[153] Finally, following a decision of the Russian shareholders, he was replaced temporarily by the oligarch Mikhail Fridman. To solve the impasse, in 2011 Sechin proposed to buy TNK–BP. He

---

148 "Sechin as Energy Czar: More Powerful, More Vulnerable," *WikiLeaks*, September 17, 2008, https://wikileaks.org/plusd/cables/08MOSCOW2802_a.html

149 S. Mydans and E. E. Arvedlund, "Police in Russia Seize Oil Tycoon," *The New York Times*, October 26, 2003, https://www.nytimes.com/2003/10/26/world/police-in-russia-seize-oil-tycoon.html

150 C. Belton, "State steps in for Yukos unit," *The Guardian*, December 23, 2004, https://www.theguardian.com/business/2004/dec/23/russia.oilandpetrol

151 "TNK-BP Update: BP Pulls Staff as AAR Ratchets up Pressure", *WikiLeaks*, July 24, 2008, https://wikileaks.org/plusd/cables/08MOSCOW2137_a.html

152 "TNK-BP Update," *WikiLeaks*.

153 "Mechel Bashing," *The Economist*, August 2, 2008, https://www.economist.com/business/2008/07/31/mechel-bashing

offered $16.7 billion and 12.8% of Rosneft shares to Dudley, who by then had become CEO of BP, and $28 billion to Fridman and his partners (Gillies 2020b, 114). While not fully satisfied, neither BP nor the Russian oligarchs felt they had a choice in negotiating with Sechin. As a result, Rosneft bought TNK–BP and Maxim Barsky was nominated new CEO.

The third great acquisition of Rosneft was Bashnet. In 2014, the Russian police arrested Vladimir Yevtushenkov, owner of the oil company operating in northern Kazakhstan.[154] As a result of the arrest, the company's value decreased, allowing Rosneft to buy 72% of its shares. In 2016, Sechin was granted the right to buy the remaining shares of Bashneft from the government for $5.3 billion. The then Minister of the Economy, Alexei Ulyukayev tried to oppose the deal but he was arrested and accused of corruption: he had presumedly attempted to extort $2 million from Rosneft to allow its acquisition of the government's shares in Bashneft.[155] In 2017, Yevtushenkov was released from house arrest, but he had to negotiate a $1.7 billion payment to Rosneft in a lawsuit for allegedly stripping Bashneft of its assets prior to its acquisition (Gillies 2020b, 115).

3. State Racketeering in Oil Economies

Over the years, both Timur Kulibayev and Igor Sechin have proven to be racketeers abusing state powers to acquire prolific oil companies. Their main tactic involved the use of the judiciary to drive down the prices of target companies and put the owners in a position where they would see selling as their only viable option. This served the racketeers, who benefited personally, and the patrons, who knew those assets would end in the secure hands of members of their inner circle instead of those of potential political rivals. In fact, both regimes proved to be unforgiving only with the oligarchs that tried to challenge their patrons. Yevtushenkov was released

---

154 "Russia Yevtushenkov arrest prompts Sistema share dive," *BBC*, September 17, 2014, https://www.bbc.com/news/world-europe-29234553

155 A. Winning, "Exclusive: Arrested Russian minister wanted state to cede control over Rosneft: sources," *Reuters*, November 29, 2016, https://www.reuters.com/article/russia-ulyujayev-rosneft-idINKBN13O1L5?edition-redirect=in

soon after the acquisition of Bashneft, and likely, Kazhegeldin's actions would have been tolerated if he had not tried to confront Nazarbayev at the presidential elections. On the other hand, Khodorkovsky spent years in prison for his political opposition to Putin and Sechin.

The fact that the elite used state racketeering in both countries is not a chance. This partly stems from Kulibayev's personal history as a Soviet man educated in Moscow, exposing him to a cultural way of doing business through racket. But it is also due to the friendship between Vladimir Putin and Nursultan Nazarbayev. Putin has always kept Nazarbayev in high regard, but he also mirrored his political choices and learnt from him directly.[156] It was this bond that allowed Kulibayev to become a board member of Gazprom, and to facilitate his schemes through the complacency of Russian businesspeople.[157] Still, there are a few differences between the Kazakh and Russian state racketeering in the oil sector.

The first difference is that Sechin worked from a more powerful position than Kulibayev's. In two of the three cases discussed, all he had to do was order the arrest of the company's owners and buy their assets. Kulibayev could not do it, because he was interfacing with foreigners, and their arrest would have provoked a reaction on the part of their governments. He had to wear them down, slowly undermining the conditions for the normal functioning of the company. This often took place by not renewing visas to foreign managers and workers,[158] as in the case of TNK–BP in Russia, but tax claims were even more frequent, as shown in the cases of Hurricane Kumkol Munay, Karazhanbasmunai, and Yukos.

The second difference is tied to the first one, and it is structural in the comparison between the Kazakh and Russian oil sectors. In

---

156 'Putin visited Nazarbayev many times at the beginning of his career as a president, so I'm sure he received his advice, and as a result, we've got very similar systems'. Oil investor, interview by author, July 1, 2021.

157 "No reaction from Kazakh elites as bombshell FT report says Nazarbayev's son-in-law siphoned millions from pipeline scheme," *bne Intellinews*, December 4, 2020, https://www.intellinews.com/no-reaction-from-kazakh-elites-as-bomb shell-ft-report-says-nazarbayev-s-son-in-law-siphoned-millions-from-pipeline -scheme-198235/

158 Political analyst, interview by author, Almaty, November 25, 2019.

both countries, the practice followed a widespread privatisation of the industry during the transition to the market economy. Yet, the better starting point of the Russian economy allowed local entrepreneurs to become oligarchs, while in Kazakhstan most of the assets had to be sold to foreigners.

The third difference is that unlike Sechin, who used the National Oil Company Rosneft to conduct his operations, Kulibayev was not allowed to rely on KazMunayGas. Yet, the son–in–law of the president had been an important member of Kazakhoil first and KazMunayGas then. Most likely, Nazarbayev did not want KazMunayGas to figure in opaque operations. In fact, Kulibayev never intended to own the target companies, but to acquire them at a low price and resell them for a profit. The intentions of the Kazakh racketeer were closer to what Ledeneva identified as *reiderstvo* (2013, 188) than a simple form of *otzhat'*. Also, the target companies of Sechin and Kulibayev were different in size and importance: Rosneft needed them to become the prime actor in the Russian oil market, but KazMunayGas would have not achieved the same result through Karazhanbasmunai or PetroKazakhstan/Hurricane Kumkol Munay. Table 5 summarises the actors, roles, and goals of state racketeering.

Table 5   The actors, roles, and goals of state racketeering

Actors involved	Role in the practice	Goal
Informal circle of a politically connected racketeer	Organising the aggression	Obtaining assets through informal means
Judiciary	Facilitating the aggression	Personal profit
Owner of the oil company	Target	Resisting the sale

4.   Racketeering as Business Strategy

Russia and Kazakhstan both figured in 2020 top ten of world oil exporters, occupying the second and ninth place respectively.[159] With $72.3 billion coming from crude oil alone and almost 40% of

---

159 D. Workman, "Crude Oil Exports by Country 2020," World's Top Exports, https://www.worldstopexports.com/worlds-top-oil-exports-country/

its budget depending on natural resources, Russia is a gigantic rentier state.[160] Kazakhstan, often referred to as the most Soviet of all Soviets republic, has a lot of commonalities with its neighbour, including its autocratic political system. Following the fall of the Soviet Union, the political elite of both countries decided to transition to the market economy. The process of privatisation that followed created the conditions for the market intervention of members of the informal political group of the patron. In the Russian Federation, Putin became president when the process had already occurred, while in Kazakhstan, Nazarbayev removed Kazhegeldin from the position of prime minister when most sales had already occurred. In both countries, patrons had to deal with the consequences by bringing back the assets under their indirect control. The adopted strategy was state racketeering, the informal use of legal means to steal the assets of other market actors.

The first suggested generalisation drawn from the cases is that in authoritarian rentier states, politically connected racketeers can leverage their informal affiliation to profit personally. There is no real limitation to their desires if the country's economy does not openly resent their performance and if the actions have the complacency of the patron. Their business success fulfils a double objective: they grow richer, and assets remain part of the patron's informal circle. The only way the patron can grow discontent is when state racketeers become arrogant and challenge them politically. In a way, this is what happened to Akezhan Kazhegeldin and Mukhtar Ablyazov. On the other hand, Kulibayev and Sechin kept a low profile, although not always in accordance with Nazarbayev and Putin respectively.

The second suggested generalisation that can be drawn from the parallelism is that in states where the rule of law is weak, criminal entrepreneurs can use legal means in an informal way to undermine the right to property, the quintessential symbol of

---

160 E. G. Abay, "Shift to clean energy may adversely affect Russian economy, its ties with EU," Anadolu Agency, October 8, 2021, https://www.aa.com.tr/en/economy/shift-to-clean-energy-may-adversely-affect-russian-economy-its-ties-with-eu/2386225

liberalism. This abuse of justice deriving from formal and informal uses of the law in post–Soviet societies is linguistically exemplified in the differentiation of legality (*zakonnost´*) and justice (*spravedlivost´*) (Ledeneva 2006, 41). As in the previous chapter, the table below shows a schematic version of the preconditions of transferability of the cases based on the M–STOUT scheme of external validity employed in quantitative analysis (Findley, Kikuta, and Denly 2021).

Table 6 **State racketeering transferability to the target population**

Dimension	Kazakhstan	Russia	Rentier states
Mechanisms	Racketeering	Racketeering	Racketeering
Settings	Established authoritarian rule	Established authoritarian rule	Corrupt judiciary
Treatments	All major assets of the oil sector had been privatised	All major assets of the oil sector had been privatised	Assets bought by actors external to the patron's informal circle
Outcomes	The assets change owners	The assets change owners	The patron's informal circle profits from the acquisitions
Units	Kazakh oil industry	Russian oil industry	Resource–rich country with an oil sector largely privatised
Time	End of the 1990s and the early 2000s	2000s	Phase following widespread privatisation of the oil industry

State racketeering is the second practice of the taxonomy and a further step towards answering the first research question. Similarly, explaining how Timur Kulibayev became the most important man in the energy sector of Kazakhstan partially explains how actors of the oil industry used state racketeering in shaping their relations. This practice is independent of patrimonial embezzlement but has a strong connection with fine threats and specious contract cancellations. The case of TNK–BP is evidence of the fact that when the national oil company is involved, the goal of the elite is what separates state racketeering from fine threats: personal profit and full ownership for the former, and renegotiation of contracts for the latter. On the other hand, specious contract cancellations can often be the latest resource conceived by racketeers to obtain the assets they are interested in. These differences will be clearer with the full presentation of the remaining practices.

5. Summary Sheet: State Racketeering

Definition: forced acquisition of assets with the complacent participation of corrupt judicial authorities.

Actors involved: politically connected racketeers, judicial authorities, target companies.

Observed in: Kazakhstan, Russia.

Outcomes: increased wealth and assets of the racketeers.

Context: resource–rich country with an oil sector largely privatised.

Timeline: phase following widespread privatisation of the oil industry.

Figure 5   Visualisation of state racketeering

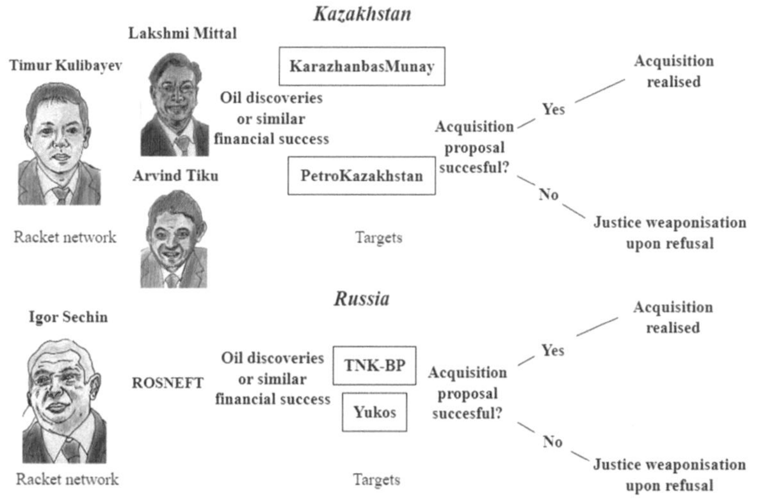

V Fine Threats

> Usually, they have a special target from their bosses to find something. If there is something behind this audit, usually they find significant amounts. But if there are no negotiations in place, audits are inconclusive. But audits, they can always find something honestly, because things cannot be perfect in companies, right?
> Financial department employee, interview by author, April 14, 2020.

> There is a clear difference between GOC [Government of Chad] officials' assertions that the tax dispute and renegotiation of the conventions are separate, and President Deby's public comments that appear to link the two initiatives. While Chevron and Petronas may resolve the short–term issue of their taxes, the GOC's clearly stated intention to pursue a majority share of the oil consortium will undoubtedly figure prominently in that negotiation.
> *WikiLeaks*, August 30, 2006.[161]

As a noun, the term 'fine' indicates a sum of money imposed as a punishment for an offence. Yet, in a state where justice is politically driven, the chances for the sanction to be based on actual violations are lower than in a liberal democracy. The practice of fining someone who committed an offence is formal, but when the presumed offender does not actually commit the fact, the law enforcer is likely acting maliciously for personal reasons, including but not limited to extortion. One of the classical examples of this use of sanctions in post–socialist countries is offered by traffic police (Nurgaliyev, Ualiyev, and Simonovich 2015).

In the oil sector, environmental fines are a consequence of alleged environmental violations, while accusations of tax evasion resulting from tax audits lead to requests for reimbursements accompanied by administrative amends. These actions are formal whenever the final goal of the judicial system is to punish a firm violating laws or regulations, but they become informal if the judiciary notified the penalty because instructed by political authorities. In these cases, law enforcement is not the protagonist but just a mediator of the action. Political authorities typically use the fine as a threat to force energy companies to renegotiate contracts. If companies play

---

161 "Chevron/Petronas Tax Dispute Update," *WikiLeaks*, August 30, 2006, https://wikileaks.org/plusd/cables/06NDJAMENA1095_a.html

116 THE HOUSE ALWAYS WINS

along, the fine remains a threat and eventually disappears, but if they do not, it is enforced regardless of the truthfulness of the accusations.

To draw generalisations from the Kazakh case study, the chapter will make a parallelism with Chad. As in *Patrimonial Embezzlement*, for the parallelism to work countries should be analysed when fine threats destined to renegotiate contracts are possible. As highlighted by Vernon in his *Sovereignty at Bay* (1971), countries lacking the technology to develop their energy sectors often rely on the work of international companies. Yet, over time the conditions underlying initial agreements are expected to 'obsolesce'.[162] In the cases analysed, fine threats are typically used by governments to signal the intention to renegotiate contracts, but it is their timing, when investments are sunk,[163] to force companies to the negotiation table. As a capital–intensive industry, the energy sector requires initial conspicuous investments on the part of companies, that usually spend years in development before starting to reap the benefits. Only in this phase, when companies cannot allow themselves to leave the country with empty hands, the governments of resource-rich countries start harassing them.[164] Curiously enough, this period roughly corresponded to the same years in Kazakhstan and Chad.

1. Fine Threats in Kazakhstan

While his study covered up to 2005, in his last chapter of *Politics and Oil in Kazakhstan*, also Ostrowski noted an initial effort of the executive to exert pressure on foreign oil companies (2010). Yet, while he defines the effort 'quasi–formal', scholarship tends to agree with the idea that if a formal mechanism is used not for its intended purposes, then the practice is simply informal (Ledeneva et al. 2018b).

---

162 Based on this expression, used to refer to the deterioration of the bargain, Vernon's theory is named 'obsolescing bargaining theory' (Gould and Winters 2007, 3).

163 Shown in Kazakhstan by Serik Orazgaliyev (2018).

164 Although, according to Collins, Jones, Krane, Medlock, and Monaldi (2021), the gas industry in the Vaca Muerta region, in Argentina, is not characterised by such predictable behaviours.

FINE THREATS 117

This analysis is completing the picture, initially hinted at by Ostrowski, offering a systematic overview of the strategy.

1.1 Tengiz: 2002 and 2007

In 2002, TengizChevrOil (TCO) was fined 11 billion tenge (around $45 million) for environmental violations by the regional court of Atyrau.[165] The contested violation regarded the storage of sulphur, a by–product of the oil extraction in Tengiz. While the court deemed the product polluting, the consortium argued that that the sulphur was perfectly safe and could be sold on the energy market. The fine was notified following the disagreement between KazMunayGas (KMG) and other partners of the consortium over the procedure to finance the project of expansion foreseen by the contract signed in 1993. The partners intended either to attract a new investor in the consortium or to pay the expansion with the dividends of the oil extraction. However, KMG did not want to decrease its shares in the consortium nor to renounce the dividends. The solution was found in 2003 when the parties decided to finance the expansion with foreign investments while acknowledging the government's $200 million a year of profits in addition to taxes (Chervinsky 2017, 160–61). As a result of the agreement the Kazakh Supreme Court reduced the fine for environmental violation originally inflicted on the consortium to one–tenth of its original size (Ostrowski 2010).[166]

In 2007, TCO was fined again for the storage of sulphur, but this time for $609 million.[167] The fine was unexpected. In fact, in a

---

165 P. Brown, "Byproduct that blights Caspian life," *The Guardian*, December 4, 2002, https://www.theguardian.com/business/2002/dec/04/oilandpetrol.news1

166 "Tengiz oilfield," Hydrocarbons Technology, https://www.hydrocarbons-technology.com/projects/tengiz/

167 E. Watkins, "Tengizchevroil fined for Tengiz field sulfur storage," *Oil&Gas Journal*, October 4, 2007, https://www.ogj.com/general-interest/article/17287174/tengizchevroil-fined-for-tengiz-field-sulfur-storage B. Schokay, "Neft' kačaetsâ, ušerb podsčityvaetsâ," [Oil oscillates, the damage is calculated], *Nomad*, February 22, 2008, https://nomad.su/?a=13-200802250006&__cf_chl_jschl_tk__=eb0282d13f728383faf191baa9de8a6c5f2557ca-1586064377-0-AQXkFrgU53h eDLJOHYe4P1PKVPnblZfqVyye1uDjsjnabznvlJrkkj09ailpK5CMVKGPOujn8r 2TwoTFNsng5_xYnc-4hj6LC2Uf89OGrtKU31ftmes2dAJZL4rxIX16ktQ7ycBjpz

118   THE HOUSE ALWAYS WINS

WikiLeaks cable of 2006, the TCO director Todd Levy had explained to the American ambassador John Ordway how the consortium had worked for the past months in cooperation with government representatives to reduce the amount of sulphur stored. In his words the joint efforts: 'seemed to have satisfied the GOK [Government of Kazakhstan] of TCO's intent to resolve the problem'.[168]

The need to get rid fast of the sulphur stored by TCO benefited the TTG group, a company that, according to the International Consortium of Investigative Journalists, is connected to Sauat Mynbayev through Meridian Capital, a shell company in the Bermuda Islands.[169] That year TTG bought more cars and leased them to TCO to ease the fast rail transport of the sulphur.[170] Sauat Mynbayev has been a recurring figure in the disputes over major consortia. In 2017, the name of the former minister and former head of KMG appeared in connection to the scandal of the Paradise Papers because from 2002 he was involved in the money transfers of Meridian Capital.[171] The then Minister of Energy and Mineral Resources had been also the main interlocutor with ENI since 2008 when the company had problems in Kashagan. According to the reconstruction of Italian prosecutors in Milan, the then CEO of ENI Paolo Scaroni contacted the Swiss middleman Giovanni Mahler to facilitate meetings with Mynbayev, who in the words of Mahler was: 'a friend, a brother'

ViyIovtjQldqqPe8lqkvhx62fM80q7EFa9LunuECqjgq674iXqVtggV6W1B4qmPt
6nrTuVOAKbh4c9WOuQQu16tLXdy28k9OJZTb5mZVsGSxBIzEP9BxZPNf9O
wvAYtIXxBVUcOMkUUtfNDM6wKfieSrBF4Zwv7cSE

168 "Tengiz Update: Riot Delays Production Increase," *WikiLeaks*, December 6, 2006, https://wikileaks.org/plusd/cables/06ASTANA737_a.html In another cable from 2009, the then director of KMG Maksat Idenov told the American ambassador that fining TCO for sulphur storage did not make sense as sulphur was not a 'waste product'. "KMG's Idenov entertains, reveals," *WikiLeaks*, February 27, 2009, https://wikileaks.org/plusd/cables/09ASTANA352_a.html

169 Sauat Mynbayev has been identified as a member of Timur Kulibayev's informal group. E. Merlink, "Vvedenie v kazahstanskuû oligarhologiû," [Introduction to Kazakh Oligarchology], *New Eurasia*, March 31, 2000, https://www.neweurasia.info/archive/2000/top5/03_31_anal.htm

170 As discussed in M. Patrucic and I. Lozovsky, "Top Kazakhstani Official Holds Stake in Secretive Transportation Empire," *OCCRP*, November 14, 2017, https://www.occrp.org/en/paradisepapers/top-kazakh-official-holds-stake-i n-secretive-transportation-empire

171 "Sauat Mukhametbayevich Mynbayev," *Offshore Leaks Database*, https://offsho releaks.icij.org/stories/sauat-mukhametbayevich-mynbayev

(Greco and Oddo 2018, 283).[172] The relationship between Scaroni, Mynbayev, and Mahler is documented at least until 2013.[173]

TCO never actually paid the 2007 penalty because the Supreme Court overturned the decision of the regional one. As revealed in a cable from WikiLeaks, the court's decision was the outcome of the gentlemen's agreement between the CEO of Chevron Dave O'Reilly and President Nursultan Nazarbayev.[174] As reminded by the Ambassador Richard Hoagland: 'He is the decider, on issues as strategically significant as the development of new oil export pipelines, or as mundane as administrative penalties for sulphur storage.'[175]

1.2 Kashagan: 2004, 2008, and 2013

When the project in Kashagan started in 2000, there was an internal competition among the participants of the consortium for who should have become the leading operator. One of the reasons that oriented Kazakhstan to pick ENI was certainly the guarantee of the beginning of the extraction in 2005, a promise that other participants deemed unrealistic. In fact, the oilfield has characteristics that make the extraction more difficult than in a standard oilfield, such as high pressure, extremely low temperatures of the water in winter, and high concentration of corrosive gas in the crude extracted (Totaro 2017). Yet, the government of Kazakhstan was so short-sighted and in need of cash that preferred an unrealistic promise over solid planning.

---

172 Investigators found an email from the 3rd of March 2008 where Mahler communicated to Scaroni the plan of Mynbayev's trip of and the modalities to organise a meeting with him. C. Gatti, "Spunta il mediatore svizzero," [The Swiss mediator appears], *Il Sole24 Ore*, February 5, 2015, https://st.ilsole24ore.com/art/commenti-e-idee/2015-02-05/spunta-mediatore-svizzero-i-kazaki-081208.shtml?uuid=AB99FnpC

173 Scaroni described the 3,700 Swiss francs dinner at the Dracula Club of Sankt Moritz with Mynbayev and Mahler in a recorded phone call. Replying to the questions of journalists Mahler denied being ENI's middleman in Kazakhstan.

174 'All relevant ministries [...] have consented to abide by the agreement', "Chevron CEO discusses meetings with Nazarbayev, Berdimuhamedov," *WikiLeaks*, November 12, 2009, https://wikileaks.org/plusd/cables/09ASTANA2005_a.html

175 Ibidem.

The first delay was announced in 2003, leading BG to withdraw from the consortium. The threat of a fine of $500 million arrived in 2004 when it became clear that the consortium could not guarantee the commencement of extraction in 2005. The official justification was tax evasion (Chervinsky 2017, 172). This was not an expense that the consortium was willing to pay, especially because the delay meant a $10 billion increase of costs in the first phase of the project. The government and the partners then negotiated a compensation of $150 million, $50 million for every year of delay (Chervinsky 2017, 173). Moreover, KMG managed to obtain 8.33% of the shares of BG. The fine for tax evasion was cancelled as soon as the acquisition was realised (Chervinsky 2017, 182).

In 2006, ENI declared that the consortium had spent $5 billion beyond the budget and that the esteemed costs for the end of the first phase would have increased further.[176] This disclosure was followed in 2007 by another delay in production with the first extraction expected for 2010 (Collier and Venables 2012, 162; Tekin and Williams 2011, 132).[177] ENI justified the delay with concerns connected to ecological risks. In August, the Minister of Environmental Protection Nurlan Iskakov accused the consortium of violation of the limits of gas emissions provoking increasing deaths of birds and seals on the shore of the sea. The statement was shortly followed by the opening of a criminal procedure for tax evasion against Agip–KCO in the Atyrau region (Chervinsky 2017, 206–7). The situation worsened in 2008 when ENI further postponed the first extraction to 2013. As reimbursement for the lost profits, Kazakhstan obtained a compensation of $300 million, to be paid before the end of 2011, and KMG acquired the remaining shares of BG for $1.78 billion through a payment delayed until the commencement of production (Sarsenbayev 2011, 376; Chervinsky 2017, 217–18). The official

---

176 N. J. Watson, "Problems for Kazakhstan at the country's biggest field," *Petroleum Economist*, December 11, 2014, https://www.petroleum-economist.com/articles/politics-economics/europe-eurasia/2014/problems-for-kazakhstan-at-the-countrys-biggest-field

177 "Kazakhstan: Kashagan Delay Official," *Petroleum Economist*, April 1, 2007, https://www.petroleum-economist.com/articles/upstream/exploration-production/2007/kazakhstan-kashagan-delay-official

FINE THREATS 121

punishment for not meeting the target was the conclusion of ENI's experience as a single operator; Agip–KCO was substituted by the North Caspian Operating Company (NCOC).

Yet, as discussed in *The EU and European Transnational Companies in Central Asia: Relocating Agency in the Energy Sector* (Moisé and Sorbello 2022), mainstream media did not report that the punishment was much more severe. In an episode of the Italian TV programme *Report*, a Kazakh banker explained to journalist Paolo Mondani how the further delay of ENI cost Italy the forced purchase of ATF, a bank property of Bulat Utemuratov, a close ally of President Nazarbayev.[178] In 2007, the then Prime Minister Romani Prodi flew to Kazakhstan along with the CEO of ENI Paolo Scaroni, the CEO of UniCredit Alessandro Profumo, and several other entrepreneurs. The participation of Profumo is especially significant when learning of UniCredit's acquisition of ATF a few weeks later. The Italian bank paid $2.275 billion for the acquisition, even if testimonies reported that ATF's value did not exceed $850 million.[179] In 2013, UniCredit resold the Kazakh bank for $464 million to Galimzan Yesenov, son–in–law of the mayor of Almaty Akhmetzhan Yesimov.[180] But UniCredit also guaranteed $630 million of ATF's debts until 2015, utterly discounting the purchase. The journalist investigation suggested that the transactions were inflated by

---

178 Introduced already in Chapter III, *Patrimonial Embezzlement*, Bulat Utemuratov is described in Ken Silverstein's *The Secret World of Oil* (2014) as the most trusted man of Nazarbayev. Contacting him was seen as an unavoidable passage for an interaction with the first president. The episode of Report is available at: "L'ostaggio," [The Hostage], *Report*, 104. November 25, 2013, https://www.ra iplay.it/video/2013/11/Report-del-25112013-3b2061ff-643d-4599-a1c6-65f6d0 1f8496.html and here, http://www.report.rai.it/webdoc/l-ostaggio/#Slide_1 _Cap1

179 "UniCredit buying ATF for $2.3bn," *Financial Times*, https://www.ft.com/con tent/30578378-201f-11dc-9eb1-000b5df10621

180 As discussed in M. Gordeyeva, "UniCredit may sell ATF Bank to Kazakh firm for $500 million," *Reuters*, January 31, 2013, https://www.reuters.com/article /us-unicredit-kazakhstan/unicredit-may-sell-atf-bank-to-kazakh-firm-for-500 -million-idUSBRE90U0O220130131 Akhmetzhan Yesimov has been identified as a close ally of President Nazarbayev by the political analyst Dosym Satpayev in "Political Analyst discusses 'Hawks and Doves' Around the President," WikiLeaks, October 2, 2009, https://wikileaks.org/plusd/cables/09ASTANA1761 _a.html

122   THE HOUSE ALWAYS WINS

bribes for Nazarbayev and his allies to avoid further sanctions for ENI. As a result of the deal, Utemuratov became a billionaire overnight, whereas Profumo, forced to leave his role as CEO of UniCredit in 2010, became a member of the board of ENI (Moisé and Sorbello 2022).[181]

Another relevant case involved the service company Parker Drilling, operating the Sunkar rig in the Caspian Sea for Agip–KCO. In 2006, the company reported to the economic officer of the American embassy that a court ruling on alleged tax duties of $53 million had been manipulated to facilitate KMG's acquisition of that rig. The vice president for operations Mike Drennon was particularly disturbed by the fact that during the hearings one of the three judges had been replaced. According to Drennon, shortly after the sentence the company was informed that the judgement had been indeed manipulated by KMG insiders, but if they had accepted to sell the rig, their tax problems would have disappeared.[182] As of today, the rig is still property of Parker Drilling.[183] In light of the 2010 sentence for corruption that Parker Drilling received in the US, this fact may be an indication that the company agreed with KMG on a way to maintain the property of the Sunkar rig while not having to pay the fine.[184]

In 2013, NCOC officially started the extraction, but after two weeks, leaks in the pipelines proved the necessity to change 200 kilometres of tubes. The beginning of the extraction had hence to be postponed to 2016 (Chervinsky 2017, 272–74). As expected, the

---

181 Through Verny Capital, Utemuratov was also the second shareholder of Kazzinc, immediately after the Swiss Glencore. The assets of Utemuratov are presented in "Bulat Utemuratov," *Forbes*, https://forbes.kz/ranking/object/41

182 Mike Drennon position is presented in "Parker Drilling's legal woes," *WikiLeaks*, June 28, 2006, https://search.wikileaks.org/plusd/cables/06ALMATY2 301_a.html The Energy News Bulletin presented the case as a symptom of power play by the Kazakh government in A. Hardy, "Kazakhstan impounds Parker Rig," *Energy News Bulletin*, July 6, 2004, https://www.energynewsbul letin.net/asia/news/1057667/kazakhstan-impounds-parker-rig

183 "Parker Drilling: Investor Presentation," *Parker Drilling*, 2018, https://d1io3yo g0oux5.cloudfront.net/_e51f4e3b51274965924d104c630ca8bd/parkerdrilling/ db/384/2903/pdf/Investor+Presentation+-+May+2018+v8+-+2018.03.31.pdf

184 The sentence of Parker Drilling for corruption is presented in Chapter VII, *Bid Rigging*.

delay was followed by the threat of a fine of 134 billion tenge (around $710 million). This time the justification was environmental violations, but also in this case the fine was cancelled when the parties reached an agreement on the 13th of December 2014. NCOC committed to financing a series of social projects in the Atyrau and Aktau regions and provided $50 million for the 2017 EXPO Astana (Chervinsky 2017, 294–95).[185]

1.3 Karachaganak: 2010 and 2015

In 2010, Kazakhstan indirectly manifested its intention to become a member of the Karachaganak Petroleum Operating (KPO), consortium led in joint operatorship by ENI and BG, by launching a series of controls by tax authorities followed by fines of 20 billion tenge (around $136 million) for tax evasion in 2004, one of $1.25 billion for overprice of the oil extracted between 2002 and 2007, and one of $700 million for illegal extraction of oil (Chervinsky 2017, 243).[186] The press revealed that in an attempt to solve the issue, in 2010 KPO sold 5% of its shares to KMG for $1 billion, but Kazakhstan deemed the shares insufficient. According to the American ambassador John Ordway, KMG was close to obtaining shares in KPO already in 2005, when BG tried to sell some of them in exchange for support for the single operatorship.[187] In lack of an agreement, in 2011 the state continued to exert pressure sanctioning the consortium with an environmental fine of $27 million (Sarsenbayev 2011, 377).[188] The litigation ended in the same year, when KMG obtained further 5% of shares for $2 billion, transaction on which KPO had to pay $1

---

185 L. Suleymenova, "Vsë spisali i ešë ostalis' vsem dolžny," [They kept on writing off debts and owe still], *Ak Zhayik*, February 17, 2015, https://m.azh.kz/ru/ne ws/view/26595

186 R. Orange, "Kazakh tax has Western oil firms over a barrel," *The Telegraph*, August 29, 2010, https://www.telegraph.co.uk/finance/newsbysector/energy /oilandgas/7970628/Kazakh-tax-has-Western-oil-firms-over-a-barrel.html

187 "KMG looking to buy Karachaganak," *WikiLeaks*, November 18, 2005, https://wikileaks.org/plusd/cables/05ALMATY4106_a.html

188 "Kazakhstan fines gas group on environment breaches," *Reuters*, January 25, 2011, https://www.reuters.com/article/kazakhstan-karachaganak/kazakhst an-fines-gas-group-on-environment-breaches-idINLDE70O0QP20110125

124　THE HOUSE ALWAYS WINS

billion of taxes. On its part, Kazakhstan gave access to a limited use of the transportation system of the Caspian Pipeline Consortium (Chervinsky 2017, 260).[189]

These were not the only sanctions that Kazakhstan notified in 2010. According to the official reconstruction, Chevron opposed the participation of KMG in the consortium of Karachaganak with the result of being fined 212.4 billion tenge for violation of the depth of extraction in the oilfield of Tengiz (Chervinsky 2017, 244–45).[190] As a response to the accusation, Chevron stated that on the contract there was no term on the depth of extraction. The situation was solved through a meeting between the US special envoy Richard Morningstar, Prime Minister Karim Massimov, and the Minister of Oil and Gas Sauat Mynbayev. The minister, who previously had argued the opposite, confirmed to the press that on the contract there was indeed no term on the depth of extraction (Chervinsky 2017, 245).[191]

On the 20th of April 2010, Flavio Sidagni, financial director of Agip–KCO was arrested in Atyrau for dealing drugs on the territory of the Republic of Kazakhstan. Arrested in possession of 112.73 grams of hashish and 57.53 of cannabis,[192] he was sentenced to ten

---

189　"Konsorcium vo glave s BG i Eni otdal Kazahstanu 10% Karačaganaka," [The consortium headed by BG and ENI gave Kazakhstan 10% of Karachaganak], *Vedomosti*, December 14, 2011, https://www.vedomosti.ru/business/news/2011/12/14/konsorcium_vo_glave_s_bg_i_en_otdal_kazahstanu_10

190　S. Tasbulatova, "Gluboko kopaût. Protiv dolžnostnyh lic TŠO vozbuždeno ugolovnoe delo," [Depth digging. Executives of TCO prosecuted with a criminal case], *Ak Zhayik*, July 22, 2010, https://azh.kz/ru/news/view/4921 "Finpol vozbudil delo protiv Tengizchevroil," [The financial police started a criminal case against Tengizchevroil], *Nur.kz*, July 15, 2010, https://www.nur.kz/15 7383-finpol-vozbudil-delo-protiv-tengizshevrojl.html

191　S. Isaeva, "'Kazahgejt' lopnul - pretenzii k 'Tengizševrojlu' peresmatrivaûtsâ," [The Kazakhgate erupted—claims towards Tengizchevroil are reconsidered], *Radio Liberty*, August 16, 2010, https://rus.azattyq.org/a/tengizchevroil_sayat_mynbayev/2128940.html V. Kazakova, "Za 'Tengizševrojl' vstupilis' SŠA" [The US stood up for Tengizchevroil], *Kursiv*, July 29, 2010, https://kursiv.kz/news/vlast-i-biznes/2010-07/za-tengizshevroyl-vstupilis-ssha

192　R. Tashkinbayev, A. Satubaldina and T. Kuzmina, "Italian ex-top manager released on parole to stay in Kazakhstan," *Tengrinews*, October 16, 2014, https://en.tengrinews.kz/people/italian-ex-top-manager-released-on-parole-to-stay-in-256906/

years, reduced to six for mitigating circumstances.[193] While Sidagni himself excluded that his case could be connected to the interest of KMG in the shares of KPO,[194] the timing seems to suggest it. In fact, according to Sidagni, the problem was: 'that I was not arrested by normal police officers. In my house broke the KNB, the former KGB. So, the issue became immediately difficult, because with the police you can pay €1,000 and they turn a blind eye. But they arrived with cameras, witnesses, like in a movie, as they were looking for Pablo Escobar.'[195] Sidagni believes that he was framed by one of the many frequenters of his house who talked about him to the police to save themselves from an unpleasant situation.

While Sidagni's reconstruction is believable, the intervention of the KNB makes things more suspicious. Either the KNB received the information from a whistleblower and did not verify it, or someone wanted the KNB to arrest Sidagni. The first hypothesis is diminishing for the Kazakh secret services, while the second one would indicate that someone did not want Sidagni to escape police custody to have leverage with ENI during the negotiations with KPO. In the words of Sidagni, it is not impossible that: 'They found a fish in their net by chance.'[196] Whichever the truth, ENI immediately distanced itself from Sidagni: 'I was immediately isolated because ENI suspended me after a month. They forced me to sever ties with my friends. I could only speak by phone with one person to whom I made orders to send me stuff. Later, the attitude changed... but at the beginning, ENI gave the order to my friends not to have contact with me or they would be sent home. It was like

---

193 The sentence is normal for this type of crime in Kazakhstan: "Zakon Respubliki Kazakhstana ot 10 iulia 1998 goda nomer 279-I," [Law of the Republic of Kazakhstan from July 10, 1998 number 279-I], *Online Zakon*, https://online.zakon .kz/document/?doc_id=1009806#pos=447;-24 "Ugolovnyj kodeks Respubliki Kazahstan ot 3 iûlâ 2014 goda № 226-V," [The Criminal Code of the Republic of Kazakhstan from July 3, 2014 number 226-V], *Online Zakon*, https://online. zakon.kz/Document/?doc_id=31575252#pos=4236;-69
194 Flavio Sidagni, interview by author.
195 Ibidem.
196 Ibid.

126 THE HOUSE ALWAYS WINS

this for a year.'[197] A year later, in 2011, KMG concluded the negotiations to acquire shares in KPO.

Another interesting fact is that Sidagni was accused and sentenced for drug dealing, but the witnesses swore that he was not selling them drugs. The most solid piece of evidence was a video retrieved from Sidagni's laptop where he was smoking a joint with friends: 'There was a video where we were passing the joint among a number of people, and they interpreted it (I am not a lawyer but I always worked with lawyers and to me it is absurd), as a matter of passage of property.'[198] Clearly, Sidagni was the only one among those in the video that faced a trial. While these are simple speculations, the unfolding of events suggests that the decisions of the Kazakh judiciary may have been piloted to pressure ENI at the negotiation table.

Yet, the armistice between KPO and Kazakhstan did not last long. In 2015, the government started another dispute threatening the consortium with a $1.6 billion fine. The figure was the result of what the state defined as a wrong method of revenue sharing for the oil sold in past years (Chervinsky 2017, 304).[199] The real reason behind the fine is unclear, but the fact that the government refused KPO's proposal to increase its shares in the consortium may indicate that Kazakhstan was in shortage of cash due to the fall of oil prices.[200] After rejecting the consortium's offer of $300 million, on the 22nd of June of 2017, President Nazarbayev himself invited the new CEO of ENI Claudio Descalzi, the one of Shell Ben Van

---

197 Ibid.

198 Ibid.

199 "UPDATE 2-Kazakhstan files $1.6 bln claim against BG-ENI venture — Lukoil," *Reuters*, April 5, 2016, https://www.reuters.com/article/kazakhstan-karacha ganak-idUSL5N1780U7 Including a fine for environmental violation "Field developer in Kazakhstan pays large fine for environmental damage," *Kazinform*, March 3, 2016, https://www.inform.kz/en/field-developer-in-kazakhstan-pa ys-large-fine-for-environmental-damage_a2877208

200 S. Bellomo, "Causa in Kazakhstan per ENI e Shell," [Trial in Kazakhstan for ENI and Shell], *Il Sole24* Ore, April 6, 2016, https://st.ilsole24ore.com/art/finanza-e-mercati/2016-04-05/causa-kazakhstan-eni-e-shell-213617.shtml?uuid=ACC GIj1C

Beurden,[201] and the one of Lukoil Vagit Alekperov to discuss the issue in person (Chervinsky 2017, 316–18). The dispute was concluded in 2018 when KPO accepted to pay $1.1 billion and agreed to modifications on the method of sharing revenues of the oil sold.[202]

2. Fine Threats in Chad

The biggest oilfields of Chad are Kome, Miandoum, and Bolobo, a complex of 315 wells near Doba, a town of about 25,000 people close to the borders with Cameroon and the Central African Republic (Guyer 2002, 109). Already in 1969, the American Conoco obtained the rights of exploration for 20 million acres of Chadian territory, joined by Royal Dutch Shell two years later (Behrends 2011; Guyer 2002, 110; Massey and May 2005). As of 1975, reserves sufficient for domestic needs were retrieved at Sedigui, north of Lake Chad (Guyer 2002, 111). In 1980, the extraction was 1,500 barrels per day, but the international oil companies did not invest in further projects due to the unstable political situation in the country (Massey and May 2005, 253). The first real commitment was in 1988 when the government signed an exploration agreement with Exxon (ExxonMobil after the 1999 merger), Elf Aquitaine (nowadays Total SA), and Royal Dutch Shell (Gould and Winters 2007).

The 1996 agreement with Cameroon to build a 1,070–kilometer pipeline from Doba to the port of Kribi was expected to solve the biggest infrastructural problem of oil export from the landlocked Chad. The countries asked for the financial backing of the World Bank Group, but while the international institution only loaned 4% of the projected $3.7 billion costs (Gould and Winters 2007, 13), it encouraged private investment and endorsed the 'ethical' validity

---

201 As explained in Chapter II, *Petroleum in Kazakhstan*, Shell had recently bought BG and hence acquired its shares in Karachaganak.

202 K. Konyrova, "Kazakhstan, KPO consortium settle Karachaganak dispute," *New Europe*, October 4, 2018, https://www.neweurope.eu/article/kazakhstan-kpo-consortium-settle-karachaganak-dispute/ P. Sorbello, "Some Win, Some Lose as Kazakhstan Gets a $1.1 Billion Check," *The Diplomat*, October 3, 2018, https://thediplomat.com/2018/10/some-win-some-lose-as-kazakhstan-gets-a-1-1-billion-check/

of the project in the wake of other mismanaged, corrupt, and environmentally disastrous oil projects in Africa' (Massey and May 2005, 254).

When on the 18th of October 2000, works started, the Esso Exploration and Production Chad Inc. (EEPCI) consortium was composed of ExxonMobil at 40%, the Malaysian Petronas at 35%, and Chevron at 25% (Gould and Winters 2007; Massey and May 2005). Both Elf and Shell abandoned the project in 1999 following the opposition of NGOs to the project. Convinced of the success of the venture, the World Bank proceeded nonetheless; it established an oversight committee, the *Collège de Contrôle et de Surveillance des Ressources Pétrolières*, and pressured the Chadian Parliament to approve the 1999 Petroleum Revenue Management Law 001 (Gould and Winters 2007), including a schedule detailing how the government could spend its revenues: 10% were destined to a Future Generations Fund, 85% should be spent on pro–development sectors, with a special quota for community development projects in Doba, while the rest was assigned to the general budget (Winters and Gould 2011, 234; Guyer 2002). The pipeline was completed in 2003 ahead of schedule (Pegg 2009, 311), and as soon as oil started flowing, most of the state budget started depending on its export[203] (Colom–Jaén and Campos–Serrano 2013, 591).

Reportedly, France and the US frequently interfered in Chad's political life since the independence of 1960. When leaving the country, the former coloniser reached an agreement that ensured that oil resources could not be developed without the participation of Elf. Yet, in 1969, when then President François Tombalbaye turned to Conoco, he did it to prevent any French intrusion. Similarly, in 1982 Hissène Habré reached power with the financial and logistic support of the United States (Colom–Jaén and Campos–Serrano 2013), a prelude to his choice of Exxon as the main operator of the exploration consortium of 1988. Again in 1990, General Idriss Déby, a Muslim from the Zaghawa group, led a group of rebels from Sudan in a *coup d'état* supported by Libya and facilitated by

---

203 In 2009 the oil sector accounted for 21.6% of the total GDP, and in 2010 oil was 89.2% of its exports (Colom-Jaén and Campos-Serrano 2013, 586).

France (Gould and Winters 2007, 13; Colom-Jaén and Campos-Serrano 2013; Winters and Gould 2011, 230). Elf was then included in the consortium to Chevron's detriment. Even though the French energy corporation eventually left the consortium, many other French firms were involved in the pipeline construction (Colom-Jaén and Campos-Serrano 2013).

Still, Déby was never a French puppet; rather, he established an illiberal regime that allowed him to prevail in questionable elections every five years until his death in April 2021 (Winters and Gould 2011, 231; Colom-Jaén and Campos-Serrano 2013, 586). Furthermore, in 2003, as soon as oil money started to flow he used patrimonial embezzlement to strengthen his control over state institutions (Colom-Jaén and Campos-Serrano 2013; C.-Y. Lee 2015; Pegg 2006; Winters and Gould 2011, 236). As for Kazakhstan and Venezuela, this did not harm the country's economy. Quite on the contrary, Chad's GDP per capita was 7% in 2003 and reached 9.3% in 2005 (Pegg 2006, 10). But patrimonial embezzlement did not stop the dictator's thirst for petrodollars. In their analyses, Winters and Gould (2007; 2011) effectively employed the obsolescing bargaining theory to argue that once initial investments sunk, he was in the position to renegotiate the agreements to increase his control over oil money. The World Bank suffered Déby's assault in 2005, as did Petronas and Chevron in 2006, CNPC between 2013 and 2014, and ExxonMobil from 2014 to 2016.

After nominating his relative Moussa Faki Mahamat to the post of prime minister, thus ending a twenty-five year old tradition of nominating Christians from the South, Déby tightened his control over the *Collège* by choosing one of his associates as parliament's representative, and his brother-in-law, Idriss Ahmed Idriss, as head of the Central Bank (Gould and Winters 2007, 17; Pegg 2006). With indirect control over the institution, in 2005 the dictator pushed for unilateral revisions of the Petroleum Law and transferred $36 million from the Future Generation Funds to the general budget, but the World Bank reacted by freezing $125 million in oil royalties from the London escrow account and suspending $124 million in undisbursed International Development Agency loans (Gould and Winters 2007, 12).

The negotiation stalled until 2006 when the country's political situation started to fall apart. In March, it was revealed a plot to shoot down the aeroplane of Déby returning from Equatorial Guinea. Reportedly, a hundred Chadian soldiers were involved as the dictator failed to pay the wages of the military (Pegg 2009; Gould and Winters 2007). Again, in April rebels from the Darfur region caused fighting in N'Djamena to end his rule. He reacted by blaming Sudan and threatening the expulsion of 200,000 refugees. To avoid a human rights catastrophe the World Bank resumed negotiations with the government and agreed on signing a Memorandum of Understanding. Chad formally agreed to increase oversight and commit 70% of oil funds to poverty reduction projects, but the dictator *de facto* increased his control over oil rents. This was followed by the full repayment of the World Bank loans ending the partnership and its oversight of the project by 2008 (Gould and Winters 2007; Winters and Gould 2011).

Emboldened by the victory over the World Bank, on the 26th of August 2006, Déby ordered Petronas and Chevron's representatives to leave the country within twenty-four hours for not paying an outstanding debt of $486.2 million[204] in taxes (Gould and Winters 2007, 23; Winters and Gould 2011, 239; Pegg 2009, 315). Already on the 27th of August, the American embassy in N'Djamena reported that the government appeared: 'to have an overall strategy to pressure the oil companies to reap greater benefits from the country's oil production',[205] while officially arguing that the original agreement between the companies and state institutions was 'illegal' because the Chadian Parliament had never approved it.[206] Reportedly, the government intended to take over 60% of EEPCI owned by Petronas and Chevron through its newly founded

---

204 The exact figure fluctuates according to different sources due to reporters' simplifications in converting CFA francs to dollars. B. Faucon, "Petronas Agrees to Pay Taxes to Chad," *Rigzone*, September 18, 2006, https://www.rigzone.com/news/oil_gas/a/36252/petronas_agrees_to_pay_taxes_to_chad/

205 "Chad Delivers Oil Ultimatum," *WikiLeaks*, August 27, 2006, https://wikileaks.org/plusd/cables/06NDJAMENA1089_a.html

206 "Chevron/Petronas Tax Dispute Update," *WikiLeaks*, August 30, 2006, https://wikileaks.org/plusd/cables/06NDJAMENA1095_a.html

Chadian Hydrocarbons Company.[207] The companies denied the Chadian claim of having willingly underpaid taxes and negotiated a solution, reached in October with the disbursement of $289 million.[208]

A second episode of fine threat occurred in 2013 with CNPC (C.-Y. Lee 2015). The company had been operating in Chad since 2003, but Chinese investments intensified after 2006 when Déby switched the country's diplomatic recognition from Taiwan to China (Gould and Winters 2007; Pegg 2009). In Chad, CNPC owns 60% of the shares of the N'Djamena JV refinery and Block H in the Bongor Basin. In 2013, the government suspended the company for violating environmental standards in drilling and waste management.[209] Yet, shortly after improving its standards and resuming the extraction, in March 2014 CNPC was fined $1.2 billion.[210] After months of negotiations, in October the parties settled the case when the company agreed to pay $400 million and to cede 10% shares in its active oilfields to the National Oil Company.[211]

Finally, in 2014 Chad contested EPPCI $837.90 million of unpaid taxes.[212] ExxonMobil argued that the claim was not grounded, but in 2016 a Chadian court issued a massive $74 billion fine in addition to the presumedly unpaid taxes.[213] As usual, the case was

---

207 X. Rice, "Chad orders oil firms to quit," *The Guardian*, August 28, 2006, https://www.theguardian.com/world/2006/aug/28/oil.business "Chad seeks 60% stake in oil output," *Reuters*, August 29, 2006, https://www.aljazeera.com/news/2006/8/29/chad-seeks-60-stake-in-oil-output

208 E. Watkins, "Chevron, Petronas resolve Chad tax dispute," *Oil & Gas Journal*, October 6, 2006, https://www.ogj.com/general-interest/article/17281279/chevron-petronas-resolve-chad-tax-dispute

209 "Chad suspends China firm CNPC over oil spill," *BBC*, August 14, 2013, https://www.bbc.com/news/world-africa-23697269

210 M. Nako, "Chad fines China's CNPC unit $1.2 billion for environmental damage," *Reuters*, March 21, 2014, https://www.reuters.com/article/us-chad-cnpc-fine-idUSBREA2K1NB20140321

211 "Settlement is reached with CNPC," *Economist Intelligence*, November 5, 2014, https://country.eiu.com/article.aspx?articleid=672467451&Country=Chad&topic=Economy&subtopic=Fore_7

212 M. Nako, "UPDATE 1-ExxonMobil seeks settlement in $800 mln Chad tax dispute -sources," *Reuters*, March 11, 2014, https://www.reuters.com/article/exxon-chad-tax-idUSL6N0M83R720140311

213 A. L. Dahir, "Chad Republic has just fined Exxon Mobil $74 billion—almost seven times its GDP," *Quartz Africa*, October 6, 2016, https://qz.com/africa/80

132   THE HOUSE ALWAYS WINS

settled out-of-court, but the terms have not been disclosed.[214] As of 2020 both ExxonMobil and Petronas announced the intention to sell their stakes in oil projects in the country,[215] but the sudden death of Déby in combat in April 2021 may have led the companies to reconsider.

3.   Fine Threats in Oil Economies

Two landlocked countries that depended on foreign investors to build the critical pipeline system that allowed them to first export their precious crude, Kazakhstan and Chad are rentier countries whose oil industries developed in similar ways. Both Nazarbayev and Déby relied on patrimonial embezzlement to strengthen their positions in power while reaping personal benefits. But soon the political elite grew greedier and used fine threats to force companies to renegotiate contracts whose terms they found 'deteriorated'. In such conditions, the peculiar institutional asset of illiberal countries allows governments to take advantage of the judiciary and law enforcement agencies with the aim of threatening companies. As anticipated in Chapter I, literature often referred to these cases as 'resource nationalism', albeit an economic version that does not resemble the revolutionary acts of nationalisation of Latin American countries (Domjan and Stone 2010; Sarsenbayev 2011).

As testified by the interviews conducted in Kazakhstan, authorities are aware of the details of contracts and visit companies regularly to receive updates on their expenditures. These audits allow officers to be aware of irregularities and use them to their advantage when necessary.[216] Reportedly, officials know contracts better than financial employees themselves. With environmental

---

2916/a-court-in-chad-fined-exxon-mobil-a-record-figure-of-75-billion-in-fin es/

214 "Out-of-court settlement between ExxonMobil and Chad," *Economist Intelligence*, June 14, 2017, http://country.eiu.com/article.aspx?articleid=1935548177 &Country=Chad&topic=Economy&subtopic=Fore_4

215 "Petronas joins Exxon in seeking exit from Chad project," *Energy Voice*, March 10, 2020, https://www.energyvoice.com/oilandgas/africa/227327/petronas-joins-exxon-in-seeking-exit-from-chad-project/

216 Financial department employee, interview by author, April 14, 2020.

fines the situation is no different: 'As we understood from our colleagues at the environmental department, the calculation of fines was done in a strange way: sometimes duplicated, exaggerated, or overstated.'[217] Companies build their cases in court, but when negotiations are taking place at the governmental level, judges always reason in favour of authorities.[218] Fine threats are led with the goal of obtaining a specific advantage for both the state budget and the political elite, being it shares in the project (extended) or cash (limited): 'Because we already had the experience that after significant findings, during these audits we were asked to give a certain percentage from the consortium shares to the Republic. Now we have also the Republic as a parent company.'[219] The satisfaction of conditions imposed by governments during negotiations causes sanctions to disappear, revealing the penalty to be just a threat.

Likewise, in Chad, political authorities used threats of fines to force companies to negotiate alternative solutions. But a major difference is that while the Kazakh government sought more property shares in consortia, hence obtaining a steady inflow of petrodollars, the Chadian one settled for cash. A reason for the preference may be the National Oil Company. On the one hand, KazMunayGas is a much more credible player than the Chadian Hydrocarbons Company, but it is also true that shares in consortia only subsume financial responsibilities. Hence, the rationale likely lies in the relative stability of Nazarbayev and Déby's respective regimes: the former had nothing to fear and preferred a steady income, but faced with continuous fighting, the latter opted for immediate flows of money.

---

217 Ibidem.
218 Confirmed by Ostrowski (2010).
219 Ibid. 'Those were not problems. The government wanted to do as they did in Kashagan, meaning that he had become a partner of the consortium [...]', financial department director, interview by author, April 6, 2020. This understanding of what fines actually represent is shared also by Lawrence Markowitz of Rowan University: 'Contestation between Kazakhstan's government and multinational corporations centres on contracts and this could be a case of a government using fines and penalties to be more predatory on the wealth these deposits generate' as referred in P. Sorbello, "Kazakh government to fine Karachaganak $2b, say sources," *Conway Bulletin*, Issue 254, October 30, 2015.

The outlier in this set of examples is the negotiation of the Chadian government with the World Bank. In this case, the power balance was reversed in favour of the international institution and the government had no obvious weapon to force a renegotiation. Hence, Déby decided for unilateral revisions to the agreement that caused the freezing of revenues. The dictator had gambled, and only after months of stalling he managed to weaponize refugees for the sake of his negotiation on oil revenues. Unlike companies, the World Bank could not be threatened with fines, and possible failures on the part of Chad in repaying the loan for the pipeline did not jeopardise its activities.

Even in the case of Russia, discussed in the previous chapter, there was an episode involving fines. During the acquisition of Yukos, Sechin used presumed unpaid taxes as a tool to justify the arrest of Khodorkovsky. Although tax claims were involved, the goal was not to renegotiate contracts to increase revenues but to take over (*otzhat'*) assets eliminating competitors. Moreover, fines were not threatened but sanctioned to justify criminal charges of tax evasion. The goal of state racketeering is to eliminate competitors, whereas fine threats aim to send a message. Both Kazakhstan and Chad wanted to increase revenues but did not plan to eliminate companies that were developing oilfields for them.

Three key characteristics emerge from the parallelism: fine threats do not require precision, sanctions are set at a value too high to be paid, and cases are always settled out-of-court. While Kazakh authorities are more subtle, fine threats are often based on loose evidence, and at times, the sanctions are evidently ungrounded. In fact, authorities do not need to build a case in court because judges are influenced by the executive. Also, sanctions are disproportionate and unreasonable. Most of the time, if companies had to pay threatened amends, they would bankrupt or would not be able to turn a profit. Undoubtedly, governments do not want companies to pay the fine but rather force them to the negotiation table. As in any negotiation, governments use fines to declare the first price, but through bargaining, they always settle for an inferior amount. Finally, all cases are solved out-of-court because governments wish to maintain the façade of a credible justice system. Table 7 summarises the actors, roles, and goals of fine threats.

Table 7   Actors, roles, and goals of fine threats

Actors involved	Role in the practice	Goal
Government	Ordering fines to trigger a contractual renegotiation	Personal profit Increased inflow of cash, limited (direct payment) or extended (shares acquisition)
Judiciary	Fine dispenser	Personal and governmental profit
International oil company	Money dispenser	Avoiding the failure of the venture

4.   Forcing Renegotiations

In 2020, Kazakhstan was the ninth world oil exporter and Chad only the thirty–second.[220] Up to the present day neither country suffered Dutch disease symptoms, even though Chad has no sovereign wealth fund (Egert and Leonard 2007; Kablan and Loening 2012). Still, both countries have resources they could not develop on their own. Upon their arrival, multinational corporations bargained profitable contracts that justified their involvement in the oil industry. Rent allowed both countries to decrease poverty, but the process was slow, and dictators used part of it to strengthen their grip on power. Only after years, when corporations had realised the infrastructures needed to operate oilfields, both the Kazakh and Chadian governments started threatening them with fines to increase revenues.

The first suggested generalisation is that in countries where multinational oil companies have invested to develop oilfields or operate refineries, illiberal leaders will use fine threats to revert the bargaining disadvantage they had when the contract was first signed. This conclusion has been already discussed as part of the obsolescing bargaining theory and proved valid beyond oil

---

220 D. Workman, "Crude Oil Exports by Country 2020," *World's Top Exports,* https://www.worldstopexports.com/worlds-top-oil-exports-country/

economies. Yet, the use of fine threats has never been singled out as an informal tool forcing multinational companies to renegotiations. This practice reveals more layers of complexity in geopolitical debates overstressing the role of foreign superpowers in the economic life of resource–rich countries. While their influence can be relevant, they are not always a major concern.[221] For example, reporters present Kazakhstan as crossed by widespread Sinophobia,[222] even though Chinese oil companies frequently undersign any condition imposed by local governments. Fine threats show the real negotiatory power of resource–rich countries, and in doing this they echo the title of Alexander Cooley's book (2012) *Great Games, Local Rules*.

The second suggested generalisation is a direct consequence of the first one: companies will eventually play the game set by the resource–rich government to minimise losses and turn a profit after initial conspicuous investments. At times, multinationals were backed by their home governments as in the case of Chevron in Karachaganak in 2010. Yet, only in rare exceptions, resource–rich governments did not obtain any form of compensation. The frequent interventions of the Italian government in Kazakhstan had the only goal of minimising losses (Moisé and Sorbello 2022). Once set foot in the country, multinationals become hostage of governmental needs and moods. The table below shows a schematic version of the preconditions of transferability of the cases based on the M–STOUT scheme of external validity employed in quantitative analysis (Findley, Kikuta, and Denly 2021).

---

221 Still, the direct or indirect intervention of foreign governments in the political life of resource-rich governments has often been crucial, particularly in former colonies. For example, the British government crowned its local ally in Iraq, Faisal I bin Al-Hussein and attempted to kill Mohammad Mossadegh in Iran in 1953 in a joint operation with the US (Maugeri 2006, 28; 66).

222 Not always genuine as argued by Y. Plakhina "How Sinophobia is instrumentalized in Kazakhstan as a form of oppositional politics," *Global Voices*, June 15, 2021, https://globalvoices.org/2021/06/15/how-sinophobia-is-instrumentalized-in-kazakhstan-as-a-form-of-oppositional-politics/

Table 8   Fine threats transferability to the target population

Dimension	Kazakhstan	Chad	Rentier states
Mechanisms	Threatening fines	Threatening fines	Threatening fines
Settings	Established authoritarian rule	Established authoritarian rule	Predatory political elite lacking the means to develop oilfields in autonomy
Treatments	Oil industry developed by foreign oil companies	Oil industry developed by foreign oil companies	Oil industry developed by foreign oil companies
Outcomes	Increased oil rent, temporary or extended	Increased oil rent, temporary or extended	Increased oil rent, temporary or extended
Units	Kazakh oil industry	Chadian oil industry	Resource–rich country without strong national actors in the sector
Time	2002–2017	2006–2016	Phase following the sinking of investments

Fine threats are the third practice of the taxonomy and a further step towards answering the first research question. The discussion on how contracts were renegotiated in the oil sector of Kazakhstan also explains how the government and multinational corporations framed their relationship after the initial agreements of the 1990s. Clearly, the strategy of fine threats cannot take place if initial contracts are not signed. Therefore, also if there is not a direct connection with patrimonial embezzlement, these strategies can easily take place in the same country at different stages of the evolution of the energy sector.

5.   Summary Sheet: Fine Threats

Definition: the threat of sanctions issued to renegotiate contracts with the goal of increasing rent.

Actors involved: government, judicial authorities, target companies.

Observed in: Kazakhstan, Chad.

Outcomes: increased oil rent, temporary or extended.

Context: resource-rich country without strong national actors in the sector.

Timeline: phase following the sinking of investments.

Figure 6 Visualisation of fine threats

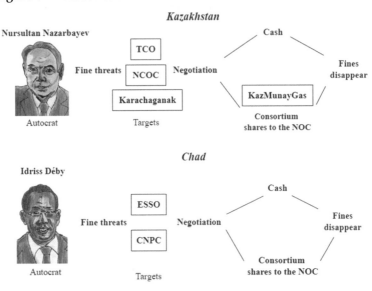

VI Specious Contract Cancellations

> I'm not interested in working with the government of Balgimbayev, that is engaged in state racketeering: first, he gives away the unproductive assets to investors, and when they drag them out of the crisis and put them to work, he takes the assets back.
> Aleksandr Krinichansky, former director of the Almaty international airport, 1999.[223]

> The president and the afore-mentioned treasury secretary used me to create a criminal conspiracy aimed at enriching themselves, not only by (taking) government funds, but also by extorting money from individuals and companies, fraud and deceit.
> Emilio Lozoya, former head of Petroleos Mexicanos, 2020.[224]

Contract cancellation, or termination, is a common practice in any industrial sector, but there are cases when contracts are cancelled for informal reasons. Rachel Wellhausen started her book *The Shield of Nationality: When Governments Break Contracts with Foreign Firms* by asking herself 'why do governments break contracts with foreign firms?' (2014, 9), and proposed four major explanations: 'enhancing revenue; responding to the particular circumstances of an asset or sector; achieving foreign policy goals; and catering to domestic interests' (Wellhausen 2014, 12). This chapter has a great deal of similarities with the conclusions of Wellhausen but expands upon them by focusing almost exclusively on Kazakhstan. In fact, contextual knowledge offers more articulate explanations, whose nuances are lost by simply grouping contract breaches.[225] For instance, the case of Anatol Stati, discussed at length by Wellhausen, is here put in perspective by showing several other cases that occurred in the Central Asian republic.

---

223 V. Hmelevskaya, "Biznes po-našemu: 'Ty menâ ne uvažaeš'!.'" [Business our way: 'You don't respect me!'], *New Eurasia*, March 31, 1999, https://www.new eurasia.info/archive/99/archives/march/ka_press/Sk0487.html

224 Associated Press, "Former Mexico President Enrique Peña Nieto directed corruption, says ex-official," *NBC News*, August 20, 2020, https://www.nbcnews .com/news/latino/former-mexico-president-enrique-pe-nieto-directed-corru ption-says-ex-n1237443

225 This 'sin' is common to Kuanysh Sarsenbayev (2011), who grouped contract cancellations without actually inquiring about the legitimacy of the action.

140   THE HOUSE ALWAYS WINS

Another example is Wellhausen's initial intuition that 'depending on the particular bilateral relations between the home and host country, a shield might be stronger or weaker' (Wellhausen 2014, 5). This statement is often correct, but it is also true that depending on the relationship between the company and the host government, the tie between home and host countries might also be affected. Between Italy and Kazakhstan, for instance, the only real driving interest was ENI's investment, and the Italian government even violated international treaties to protect its national oil company from sanctions (Moisé and Sorbello 2022).

As discussed in the previous chapter, to 'enhance revenue' it is more convenient to trigger fine threats. Also, in some cases understanding why governments respect contracts might be as important as why they violate them. Finally, Wellhausen possibly overstressed the 'foreign policy goal' in analysing the case of Stati versus Kazakhstan. While it is true that the contract cancellation harmed a competitor of the Moldovan President Voronin, the assets owned by the oligarch had also become the object of the interests of the Kazakh political elite following resource discoveries.[226] Having allies on the international stage is certainly important, but it is not realistic that Nazarbayev spent money on lawyers through eleven years of litigation just to please the Republic of Moldova's long dismissed autocrat. The presence of a kleptocratic elite 'catering to domestic interests' remains the most relevant informal objective of each of the informal practices proposed so far.[227]

The expression 'specious contract cancellation' is employed to distinguish the phenomenon under scrutiny from classic nationalisations that ultimately terminate contracts with foreign investors. Seldom called 'resource nationalism', the national reclaim of assets

---

226 An interviewee, when asked if the assets they were working on attracted the attention of Kulibayev and associates replied: 'Not at that point. Because you don't get their attention until it starts being recognised as having value and my development in [...] never got to that stage. They don't play their hand until there's something on the table worth winning.' International oil executive, interview by author, April 22, 2020.

227 As proven by Timur Kulibayev and Vitol's interests in the companies. Tikhonov, A. "On Guard for Vitol. Whose interest is in the Stati case?," *Kazakhstan 2.0*, October 31, 2019.

owned by foreign companies has often strong political connotations, and while specious contract cancellations may have political implications, they do not carry the same ideological weight. Rather, they are usually the outcome of elite infighting that might result in shifting equilibria in the political landscape. Also, specious contract cancellations can affect national investors as well. The only reason why contract cancellations involving only foreign investors are included in the chapter is the higher retrievability of information on the cases offered by international arbitrations databases.

The case used as parallel in this chapter is Mexico under the Peña Nieto administration. Given the wide applicability of specious contract cancellations, there is no specific time limit to analyse the practice. The only requirement is for the parties to have signed the contract. The choice of the Peña Nieto administration is justified by the presence of cases of international arbitration in a sector otherwise close to foreign investments. The arbitrations discussed in the chapter feature all the cases until 2022 in which Kazakhstan and Mexico were brought by foreign investors in front of international arbitrators accused of unmotivated unilateral contract cancellation. The cases were found using the United Nations Conference on Trade and Development and the International Energy Charter databases of treaty–based investor–state dispute settlement cases.

1. Specious Contract Cancellations in Kazakhstan

In its more than thirty years of independence, Kazakhstan was summoned nineteen different times in front of the International Centre for Settlement of Investment Disputes (ICSID), and in nine of them, the cases involved companies working in the oil sector.

1.1 Biedermann International: 1996–1999

In 1992,[228] the Californian banker Harold Biedermann entered the Kazakh oil market with his own Biedermann International by

---

228 Original name of the case: Biedermann International, Inc. v. Republic of Kazakhstan and Association for Social and Economic Development of Western Kazakhstan "Intercaspian", SCC Case No. 97/1996.

signing an agreement with Intercaspian to develop the oilfield of Kenbai, at the time owned by Embaneft (Chervinsky 2017, 27). Yet, the contract signing displeased Atyrau officials, including the regional governor Sagat Tugelbayev (Ostrowski 2010). To satisfy the regional elite, authorities terminated the contract arguing that the company had failed to live up to its contractual obligations. The Californian investor was given only six weeks of time before the decision of Kazakh authorities.[229] Shortly after the cancellation, the Atyrau Oil Joint Stock Company announced its intention to develop the field. The deputy director of Embaneft was appointed its president, while Sagat Tugelbayev and Mokhambet Khakimov obtained 25% of the shares. In 1996, Biedermann brought the case in front of the Stockholm Chamber of Commerce. Based on the treaty between the US and Kazakhstan on encouragement and reciprocal protection of investment, on the 1st of January 1999 the court decided in favour of the investor.[230] The $8.9 million compensation included sunk costs and interests, but less than 3% of the figure asked by the investor.[231] To this day the sentence is not public.

---

229 "Investment Law and Policy Weekly News Bulletin," *International Institute for Sustainable Development*, October 11, 2003, https://www.iisd.org/itn/wp-con tent/uploads/2010/10/investment_investsd_oct8_2003.pdf J. Hepburn, "Looking Back: In First Treaty Claim Under SCC Rules, Arbitrators in the Long-Opaque Bidermann Case Held Kazakhstan Liable for Breaching US-Kazak Bit, and Rejected Counterclaim for Merits," *Investment Arbitration Reporter*, November 1, 2017, https://www.iareporter.com/articles/looking-back-in-first-treaty-claim-under-scc-rules-arbitrators-in-the-long-opaque-biedermann-case-held-k azakhstan-liable-for-breaching-us-kazak-bit-and-rejected-counterclaim-on-me rits/

230 Treaty between the United States of America and the Republic of Kazakhstan Concerning the Encouragement and Reciprocal Protection of Investment, adopted on 19 May 1992.

231 "Biedermann v. Kazakhstan," *Jus Mundi*, https://jusmundi.com/en/docum ent/decision/en-biedermann-international-inc-v-the-republic-of-kazakhstan-and-the-association-for-social-and-economic-development-of-western-kazakh ntercaspian-award-friday-1st-january-1999 "Biedermann v. Kazakhstan," *UNCTAD Investment Policy Hub*, https://investmentpolicy.unctad.org/invest ment-dispute-settlement/cases/9/biedermann-v-kazakhstan "Biedermann International, Inc. v. Republic of Kazakhstan and Association for Social and Economic Development of Western Kazakhstan 'Intercaspian', SCC Case No. 97/1996," *italaw*, https://www.italaw.com/cases/149

1.2 CCL Oil: 2001–2004

In *Petroleum in Kazakhstan*, the issues encountered by CCL Oil in managing the Pavlodar refinery, target of Timur Kulibayev, were already discussed (Peck 2004, 176). In 1998, Prime Minister Nurlan Balgimbayev announced his intention to annul the contract hence regaining control of the refinery. Alarmed by the announcement, CCL Oil sought court protection in Kazakhstan and won the first case. Yet, in 2000 the wearing work of MangistauMunaiGaz concluded with the definitive revoke of the concession (Peck 2004, 177). In 2001, the company decided to bring the case in front of the Stockholm Chamber of Commerce and based on the treaty between the US and Kazakhstan on encouragement and reciprocal protection of investment, the court argued in favour of the state.[232]

Among the strongest arguments of the Kazakh lawyers was that by 2000 CCL Oil, represented by the ethnic Korean and Kazakh citizen Oleg Li, was an empty shell owned by Kazakh nationals (Chervinsky 2017, 84), and hence the court did not have the competence to conduct the arbitration. On their part, CCL Oil's lawyers claimed that the company had been owned by an American Mr X who shortly after the signature of the contract sold half of the shares to a group of investors led by the Russian Mr Y. In 1998, Mr X further decreased his shares to finance investments in New York, but after the loss of the concession in Kazakhstan, he regained 51% of the company. Mr Y and his allies decided not to seek compensation selling their remaining 49% to a company of the British Virgin Islands owned by Mr Z, a Geneva lawyer. Despite having failed to prove its ownership and activities, the court argued that the company registration in the US and the ownership of Mr X were enough evidence to ensure its competence (Shmatenko 2013, 28).[233]

---

232 "CCL Oil v. Kazakhstan," *UNCTAD Investment Policy Hub*, https://investment policy.unctad.org/investment-dispute-settlement/cases/69/ccl-oil-v-kazakhs tan "CCL v. Republic of Kazakhstan, SCC Case 122/2001," *italaw*, https://ww w.italaw.com/cases/227

233 While it is unclear who was behind CCL Oil over the years, there are several Kazakh sources confirming that the company was part of the group headed by Oleg Li. The businessmen had created an alliance with the group of Kazkommertsbank connected to President Nazarbayev. Following the court

144 THE HOUSE ALWAYS WINS

In a passage of the sentence, the judges commented on the ambiguous role played by the Kazakh General Prosecutor in revoking the concession of CCL Oil because: 'no explanation has been given why the Prosecutor General commenced his actions at this time.'[234] In its decision, the court did not award the €178,892,338 requested, arguing that the phrasing of the contracts[235] was too vague for compensation based on future profits of the refinery and that Kazakhstan had enacted an expropriation which was not 'creeping' nor 'covert'.

1.3 Liman Caspian Oil: 2007–2010

The case of Liman Caspian Oil[236] was brought in front of the ICSID in 2007.[237] Behind the claimants, court documents identify a Swiss citizen manoeuvring them through a third company, Z. In 2000, Kazakhstan granted company X the right to explore the Liman Block, but in 2002, X transferred the right to LCO. At the time of the assignment, X was owned at 99.9% by a British company Y and at 0.1% by two private individuals who filed a lawsuit to invalidate the agreement they had not been aware of. The Kazakh court invalidated the agreement *de facto* reverting back the rights of exploration to company X, which had then decided to transfer the rights to

---

reconstruction, Mr Y could have been Oleg Li. V. Kuklin, "Istinnaâ Vlast'," [True Power], *Perepliot*, http://www.pereplet.ru/text/kuklin09oct03.html "Razdelennaâ èlita," [The Subdivision of the Elite], *New Eurasia*, 1999, https://www.neweurasia.info/archive/1999/analitica/06_11_Who0494.html However, the resignation of Li occurred after the beginning of a criminal investigation against him related to unpaid debts. M. Popova, "Situaciâ vokrug Pavlodarskogo NPZ ostaetsâ poka nepredskazuemoj," [The Situation Around the Pavlodar Refinery Remains Unpredictable], *New Eurasia*, 1999, https://www.neweurasia.info/archive/archives/june/Oil255.htm

234 "Jurisdictional Award Rendered in 2003 in SCC Case 122/2001," *Stockholm Chamber of Commerce.* "Final Award Rendered in 2004 in SCC Case 122/2001," *Stockholm Chamber of Commerce.* "Supplemental Award and Interpretation Rendered in 2004 in SCC Case 122/2001," *Stockholm Chamber of Commerce.*

235 The contracts signed were in fact two as discussed in Chapter II, *Petroleum in Kazakhstan.*

236 Original name of the case: CCL v. Republic of Kazakhstan, SCC Case 122/2001.

237 "Liman Caspian Oil BV and NCL Dutch Investment BV v. Republic of Kazakhstan (ICSID Case No. ARB/07/14)," *International Centre for Settlement of Investment Disputes World Bank Group*, https://icsid.worldbank.org/en/Pages/cases/casedetail.aspx?CaseNo=ARB/07/14

SPECIOUS CONTRACT CANCELLATIONS   145

a third company dismissing LCO's claims. The argument of the claimants was that 10% of LCO was the property of Y, the majority shareholder of X. Z and Y had created the elaborate structure of companies with the objective of transferring the rights of exploration to LCO bypassing the will of the 0.1% owners of Y. The court did not award the compensation of $200 million requested by the claimants because they were not able to prove the alleged corruption of the Kazakh judges that annulled the agreement between LCO and X.[238]

Figure 7   Visualisation of the Liman Caspian Oil Case

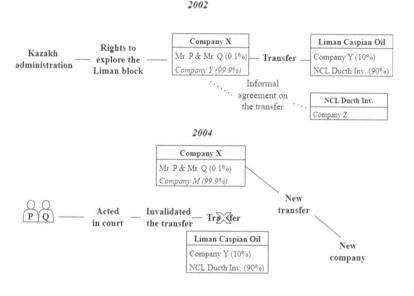

---

238 "Liman Caspian Oil v. Kazakhstan," *UNCTAD Investment Policy Hub*, https://investmentpolicy.unctad.org/investment-dispute-settlement/cases/248/liman-caspian-oil-v-kazakhstan "Liman Caspian Oil BV and NCL Dutch Investment BV v. Republic of Kazakhstan, ICSID Case No. ARB/07/14," *italaw*, https://www.italaw.com/cases/1977 N. Charalampidou, "Liman Caspian Oil BV and NCL Dutch Investment BV v Kazakhstan - ICSID Case No. ARB/07/14 - Excerpts of Award", *Transnational Dispute Management*, June 22, 2010, https://www.transnational-dispute-management.com/legal-and-regulatory-detail.asp?key=9444

146 THE HOUSE ALWAYS WINS

As reported on Glassdoor.com, Aurado Energy is Company Z and Aral Petroleum is Company X.[239] In 2004, at the time of the Kazakh sentence, X had become the property of company M. Aral Petroleum Capital, owned by Caspian Energy Inc.,[240] is Company M. Scrolling the list of the board members of Caspian Energy Inc. is possible to find the name of Baltabek Kuandykov,[241] president of Meridian Petroleum, a subsidiary of Meridian Capital, connected to Sauat Mynbayev.[242] Kuandykov was also the president of KazakhOil from 1997 to 2002 and a former president of Nelson Resources, connected to Timur Kulibayev. As a matter of fact, Caspian Energy Inc. reports on its website that its work in the North Block was conducted in cooperation with CNPC and Nelson Resources.[243] Likely, the company that received the rights of exploration of the Liman Block from Aral Petroleum in 2005 was KMG, because as soon as 2010 the Kazakh National Oil Company announced the discovery of oil in the Liman Block.[244] In other words, while there was an initial attempt to transfer the rights of exploration to another private company beyond Nazarbayev's informal circle, the decision of the Kazakh court led Aral Petroleum, meaning Kuandykov, Mynbayev and others, to sell to KMG. Timur Kulibayev was vice president of KMG until October 2005.

---

239 The description of Aurado Energy states that the company had the right to exploration of the Liman Block but such right was in contention with Aral Petroleum, "Aurado Energy," *Glassdoor*, https://www.glassdoor.com/Overview/Working-at-Aurado-Energy-EI_IE23894.11,24.htm

240 "Aral Petroleum LLP," *Russian Oil & Gas Technology*, https://rogtecmagazine.com/tag/aral-petroleum-capital-llp/

241 "Board Directors," *Caspian Energy Inc.*, http://caspianenergyinc.com/aboutus/board/

242 Among the protagonists of Chapter V, P. Sorbello, "Leaks Unveil Kazakhs Officials with Offshore Links," *The Diplomat*, November 17, 2017, https://thediplomat.com/2017/11/leaks-unveil-kazakh-officials-with-offshore-links/

243 "North Block," *Caspian Energy Inc.*, http://caspianenergyinc.com/operations/northblock/

244 "KazMunaiGas Discovers Oil in Liman Block," *Rigzone*, October 22, 2010, https://www.rigzone.com/news/oil_gas/a/100481/kazmunaigas_discovers_oil_in_liman_block/

SPECIOUS CONTRACT CANCELLATIONS 147

1.4 Caratube International Oil Company LLP: 2008–2014

In 2002, Caratube International Oil Company LLP,[245] a Kazakh company owned at 92% by US citizen Devincci Salah Hourani, acquired the rights to explore the oilfield of Caratube.[246] Over five years the relationship between the company and state authorities had been reportedly harmonious, but in 2008 the Ministry of Energy and Mineral Resources of Kazakhstan terminated the contract and froze the bank accounts of the company. On the 16th of June, Hourani brought the case in front of the ICSID,[247] claiming that the expropriation resulted from a fallout between President Nursultan Nazarbayev and his former son–in–law Rakhat Aliyev to whom Hourani was indirectly related.[248] In his request for arbitration, Hourani stated that he was repeatedly interrogated and harassed by the police but he was also reportedly told that a payment of $100,000 to an intermediary would have ended the molestation.[249]

---

245 Original name of the case: Caratube International Oil Company LLP v. Republic of Kazakhstan, ICSID Case No. ARB/08/12.

246 Kazakhstan gave the original concession to the Consolidated Contractors Company, which transferred it to Caratube International Oil Company shortly after.

247 "Caratube International Oil Company LLP v. Republic of Kazakhstan (ICSID Case No. ARB/08/12)," *International Centre for Settlement of Investment Disputes World Bank Group*, https://icsid.worldbank.org/en/Pages/cases/casedetail.as px?CaseNo=ARB/08/12 "Caratube v. Kazakhstan," *UNCTAD Investment Policy Hub*, https://investmentpolicy.unctad.org/investment-dispute-settlement /cases/297/caratube-v-kazakhstan "Caratube International Oil Company LLP v. The Republic of Kazakhstan, ICSID Case No. ARB/08/12," italaw, https://www.italaw.com/cases/211

248 The brother of Devincci, Issam, is married to Gulshat Aliyeva, "Issam Hourani," *LinkedIn*, https://www.linkedin.com/in/issam-hourani-6b2086137/?originalS ubdomain=lb

249 "Request for Arbitration between Caratube International Oil Company LLP and the Republic of Kazakhstan," *International Centre for Settlement of Investment Disputes World Bank Group*, June 2008. On page 20 of "Caratube International Oil Company LLP Memorial," International Centre for Settlement of Investment Disputes World Bank Group, May 2009, Hourani stated: 'It was quite clear to me that the questioning was aimed at finding out information about the connection between Mr. Aliyev and Issam, rather than any alleged wrongdoing by me or by any of my family's businesses. The interview with Colonel Kim took the form of an interrogation and the aggressive way in which it was conducted left me with the firm impression that there was extreme hostility towards me and my family.' On page 23: 'I felt under a lot of pressure and believed that the authorities were trying to scare me and my family, in order to force us to abandon our interests in Kazakhstan and leave the country for good.'

148   THE HOUSE ALWAYS WINS

In its counter–memorial Kazakhstan claimed that the company had violated terms of the contract.[250]

In 2009, the claimant asked the court to end the harassment by Kazakh authorities, but the tribunal did not comply as the criminal investigation by Kazakh authorities was not considered harassment.[251] The court also argued that Hourani's 92% shares of the company acquired with $6,500 was not enough to prove his ownership nor an economic investment (Verhoosel and Sheikh 2013, 305). Likely, the judges did not rule out the direct involvement of Aliyev and hence declared the court's lack of jurisdiction.[252] In 2012, the tribunal dismissed the case and asked the claimant to pay $3.2 million as a reimbursement for the respondent's expenses in the legal case.[253] Hourani found that the court had misinterpreted the requirements for its competence and in 2013 filed a request for the annulment of the award, instance dismissed in 2014.[254]

1.5   Caratube International Oil Company LLP II: 2013–2017

In 2013, the Hourani family presented again the claims of the first proceeding in front of the ICSID.[255] The substance of the case revolved around the cancellation of the contract over the rights of exploration in the Caratube oilfield, but while the former case was based on the Bilateral Investment Treaty between Kazakhstan and the US, the latter revolved around the contract between the parties

---

250 As clarified in "Counter-Memorial of the Republic of Kazakhstan," *International Centre for Settlement of Investment Disputes World Bank Group*, January 2009, during the discussion, the claimant argued that state authorities brought up these breaches only in 2008 when they decided to terminate the contract.

251 "Decision Regarding Claimant's Application for Provisional Measures," *International Centre for Settlement of Investment Disputes World Bank Group*, July 2009.

252 "Kazakhstan - United States of America BIT (1992)," *UNCTAD Investment Policy Hub*, https://investmentpolicy.unctad.org/international-investment-agreeme nts/treaties/bit/2218/kazakhstan---united-states-of-america-bit-1992-

253 "Award," International Centre for Settlement of Investment Disputes World Bank Group, June 2012.

254 "Decision on the Annulment Application of Caratube International Oil Company LLP," *International Centre for Settlement of Investment Disputes World Bank Group*, February 2014.

255 "Caratube Oil International LLP and Devincci Salah Hourani v. Republic of Kazakhstan, ICSID Case No. ARB/13/13," italaw, https://www.italaw.com/cas es/2131

and Kazakhstan's foreign investment laws. In 2017, the court awarded the Hourani brothers the victory of the case because the judges were convinced that: 'the real motivation behind the termination of the Contract was not [Caratube]'s allegedly deficient performance of the Contract, but rather lies in the family and political context underlying the case.'[256]

During the proceeding, the claimants requested the court to force Kazakhstan to reveal its role in the timely release of a website linked to the late Anastasiya Novikova, rumoured to be Rakhat Aliyev's lover. The woman died in 2004 falling from the top floor of a building owned by the Hourani brothers in Beirut, but her body was found only in 2007 in the town of Taraz, in Kazakhstan.[257] The court denied the request of the claimants,[258] but they pursued the cause suing Kazakhstan for defamation in the United States, where the case was dismissed in 2018.[259] By majority, the court awarded $39.9 million, $1.2 million in damages, and $10 million in interests, against the $991 million requested by the claimants.[260] In 2018, Kazakhstan appealed the decision asking the annulment of the award. The court established a stay of enforcement, a measure relieving the debtor from paying the debt until a decision on the annulment is

---

256 "Award," International Centre for Settlement of Investment Disputes World Bank Group, September 2017.

257 J. Lillis, "Kazakhstan: Rakhatgate Plot Thickens as Police Identify Body of Missing Television Host," *Eurasianet*, August 8, 2007, https://eurasianet.org/kaz akhstan-rakhatgate-plot-thickens-as-police-identify-body-of-missing-televisi on-host

258 "Decision on the Claimants' Request for Provisional Measures," *International Centre for Settlement of Investment Disputes World Bank Group*, December 2014.

259 M. Eckel, "U.S. Dismisses Defamation Lawsuit Linked To Kazakh Family Feud," *Radio Free Europe*, February 18, 2016, https://www.rferl.org/a/kazakh stan-nazarbaev-austria-killing/27560762.html

260 "Press Release on Behalf of Caratube International Oil Company LLP and Mr. Devincci Hourani," *Derains & Gharavi*, October 3, 2017, https://www.business wire.com/news/home/20171003005914/en/Derains-Gharavi-Press-Release-B ehalf-Caratube-International M. Abebe, "Kazakhstan held liable for expropriation of Hourani family's investment on second round of ICSID arbitration," *Investment Treaty News*, December 21, 2017, https://www.iisd.org/itn/2017/12 /21/kazakhstan-liable-expropriation-hourani-familys-investment-second-rou nd-icsid-arbitration-caratube-international-oil-company-llp-devincci-salah-ho urani-icsid-case-arb-13-13/

150 THE HOUSE ALWAYS WINS

achieved,[261] but in early 2022 the decision was still pending. In 2015, the Hourani brothers opened another case against Kazakhstan for expropriation of their pharmaceutical company.[262]

1.6 Anatol Stati: 2010–2021

The international arbitration involving the Moldovan investor Anatol and his son Gabriel Stati[263] is the longest and most complex in the entire history of the Republic of Kazakhstan. Stati had been investing in Kazakhstan since the Soviet era, but he entered the oil sector in 1999 with his Ascom S.A. acquiring shares in Tolkineftgas and Kazpolmunay LLP, companies working in the oilfields of Borankol and Tolkyn, in the Mangistau region, via Tristan Oil, a company registered in the British Virgin Islands. The Moldovans invested $990 million in ten years of activity in Kazakhstan, and by 2008 they had 100 active wells.

Problems began in July 2008, when investors announced a significant discovery in the Tabyl Block. In September, Ascom received several offers to buy the fields, including from KMG and Starleigh, a company owned by Timur Kulibayev.[264] However,

---

261 "Decision on Stay of Enforcement of the Award", International Centre for Settlement of Investment Disputes World Bank Group, December 2019.

262 "Hourani v. Kazakhstan," *Jus Mundi*, https://jusmundi.com/en/document/decision/en-devincci-salah-hourani-and-issam-salah-hourani-v-republic-of-kazakhstan-none-currently-available-thursday-16th-april-2015 "Hourani v. Kazakhstan," *UNCTAD Investment Policy Hub*, https://investmentpolicy.unctad.org/investment-dispute-settlement/cases/636/hourani-v-kazakhstan "Devincci Salah Hourani and Issam Salah Hourani v. Republic of Kazakhstan (ICSID Case No. ARB/15/13)," *International Centre for Settlement of Investment Disputes World Bank Group*, https://icsid.worldbank.org/en/Pages/cases/casedetail.aspx?CaseNo=ARB/15/13

263 Original name of the case: Anatolie Stati, Gabriel Stati, Ascom Group SA and Terra Raf Trans Traiding Ltd v. Republic of Kazakhstan, SCC Case No. V 116/2010.

264 "Witness Statement of Artur Lungu," Stockholm Chamber of Commerce, October 2013: 'We later learned that Starleigh was owned and controlled by the head of KazMunaiGas and son-in-law of the President of Kazakhstan, Timur Kulibayev, who essentially controlled Kazakhstan's energy sector.' Ascom, "Ascom Takes Government of Kazakhstan to Stockholm Court of Arbitration Under the International Energy Charter Treaty," *Cision PR Newswire*, September 8, 2010, https://www.prnewswire.com/news-releases/ascom-takes-government-of-kazakhstan-to-stockholm-court-of-arbitration-under-the-international-energy-charter-treaty-102416259.html

SPECIOUS CONTRACT CANCELLATIONS   151

upon refusal, the country's elite reacted; in 2009 the financial police contested Stati $220 million, accusing him of having postponed until 2007 the registration of Tolkineftgas to evade taxation (Chervinsky 2017, 229), and arrested Sergiu Cornegruță, director of Kazpolmunay (Sarsenbayev 2011, 377). Accused of illegally transporting 21.67 billion tenge ($147.8 million)[265] worth oil through the pipelines of KazTransOil, Cornegruță was sentenced to four years of prison (Chervinsky 2017, 230). He remained in jail until the 26th of August 2010 when the court conceded him probation. It was later revealed that he had paid $10 million to buy his freedom from the judge and to escape Kazakhstan without his passport. He flew from Atyrau to Almaty, and from there to Chişinău passing through Istanbul (Chervinsky 2017, 232–33).[266] As of 2010, the Moldovan assets were seized by Kazakh authorities and transferred to KMG.

Genuine elite interest for the assets mixed with international favours to fellow autocrats. At the end of 2008, the President of the Republic of Moldova Vladimir Voronin, accompanied by the Minister of Finance Oleg Reidman and the oligarch Vladimir Plahotniuc, met with President Nazarbayev in Kazakhstan. The visit followed a letter that the Moldovan president had forwarded to Nazarbayev on the 8th of October. In the letter, Voronin warned Nazarbayev to pay serious attention to Anatol Stati, accused of financing opposition parties in his home country (Wellhausen 2014, 176).[267] In April of 2009, after a controversial election in the Republic

---

265 As argued in the appeal to the Court, he was simply a salaried employee.

266 "Omul de afaceri moldovean, Sergiu Cornegruță, a evadat din închisoarea kazahă," [Moldovan businessman, Sergiu Cornegrutza has evaded from Kazakh prison], *News Point*, November 4, 2010, https://point.md/ru/novosti/proissh estviya/omul-de-afaceri-moldovean-sergiu-cornegrutza-a-evadat-din-inchiso area-kazaha A. Maytanov, "O pobege moldavskogo biznesmena iz kazahskoj tûr'my soobŝili spustâ polmesâca," [The escape of a Moldovan businessman from a Kazakh prison was reported after a month and a half], *Radio Liberty*, November 4, 2010, https://rus.azattyq.org/a/prison_break_moldavian_business man/2210397.html A. Maytanov, "Kto takoj Kornegruca, sbežavšij iz atyrauskoj kolonii?," [Who is that Cornegrutza that escaped from the Colony of Atyrau?], *Ak Zhaiyk*, November 4, 2010, https://azh.kz/ru/news/view/5502

267 R. Vladimirov, "Èto vse ne k Stati: Kazahskogo lidera Nazarbaeva lišâût 4 milliardov dollarov—kazalos' by, pri čem tut èks-prezident Moldovy Voronin?," [All of this is unfortunate: Kazakh leader Nazarbayev is being robbed of $ 4 billion - it would seem, what does the ex-president of Moldova Voronin have

152 THE HOUSE ALWAYS WINS

of Moldova, Chişinău was shaken by violent anti–communist rallies and Gabriel Stati was arrested with the accusation of being the organiser, but released two months later for lack of evidence (Moisé 2021).[268]

In 2010, Anatol and Gabriel Stati brought Kazakhstan in front of the Stockholm Chamber of Commerce (SCC) with a case based on the International Energy Charter.[269] In 2013, the Court found that the expropriation violated the treaty and decided to award the claimants a compensation of $497,685,101 plus interests matured since April 2009 and half of the claimants' legal expenses.[270] On their part, Kazakh lawyers advanced the argument that the award was not due because the $199 million SCC evaluation of the Liquefied Petroleum Gas plant operated by the claimants had been distorted by a fraudulent scheme including fake investments of the

---

to do with it?], *Komsomolskaya Pravda*, https://www.kp.kz/daily/26781/38154 39/ V. Gorbulin, "Komu meshayet ASCOM?," [Who is bothered by ASCOM?], *Moldavskie Vedomosti*, March 13, 2009, http://www.vedomosti.md/news/Ko mu_Meshaet_Ascom/2

268 A. Eftode, "Moldova's Richest Businessman Strikes Back," *Radio Free Europe*, July 16, 2010, https://www.rferl.org/a/Moldovas_Richest_Businessman_Strik es_Back/2101561.html "Moldova's rulers turn-up heat on business," *Financial Times*, https://www.ft.com/content/53e8b178-4baa-11de-b827-00144feabdc0 In 2010, Voronin was accused by a special committee of the Moldovan Parliament of having exceeded his constitutional powers by giving direct orders to the police, "Former Moldovan President Accused of Abuse of Power," *Radio Free Europe*, May 8, 2010, https://www.rferl.org/a/Former_Moldovan_Presid ent_Accused_Of_Abuse_Of_Power/2036157.html

269 "Stati and others v. Kazakhstan," *UNCTAD Investment Policy Hub*, https://investmentpolicy.unctad.org/investment-dispute-settlement/cases/379/stati-a nd-others-v-kazakhstan "Anatolie Stati, Gabriel Stati, Ascom Group SA and Terra Raf Trans Traiding Ltd. v. Kazakhstan, SCC Case No. V116/2010," *italaw*, https://www.italaw.com/cases/2358 "Anatolie Stati, Gabriel Stati, Ascom Group SA and Terra Raf Trans Traiding Ltd. v. Kazakhstan, SCC Case No. V116/2010," *International Energy Charter*, https://www.energycharter.org/wh at-we-do/dispute-settlement/investment-dispute-settlement-cases/28-anatoli e-and-gabriel-stati-ascom-group-sa-terra-raf-trans-traiding-ltd-v-kazakhstan/

270 N. Charalampidou, "Ascom and others v Kazakhstan - SCC Case No. V116/2010 - Award," *Transnational Dispute Management*, December 19, 2013, https://www.transnational-dispute-management.com/legal-and-regulatory-detail.asp?key=21912

shell company Perkwood.[271] This claim, dismissed in Sweden in 2016 and in the US in 2014, was upheld in Belgium in 2021.[272]

But until then, the lawyers' firms supporting Stati challenged Kazakhstan in jurisdictions where the state was believed to own assets through the Sovereign Wealth Fund Samruk–Kazyna. The case has been discussed in seven jurisdictions: the US, the UK, Belgium,[273] the Netherlands, Luxembourg, Sweden, and Italy. In 2017, the freezing of $22 billion of Kazakh assets in a dozen bank accounts of the Bank of New York Mellon's[274] branch in London by the Court in Belgium brought the case back to the attention of the public,[275] as the figure was about twice the 2018 GDP of the Republic of Moldova.[276]

The sum was then decreased to $530 million, which is what was due to Stati according to the Swedish award. Yet, these were not the only assets frozen: the Swedish Enforcement Agency suspended about $90 million in shares owned by Kazakhstan in 43 blue–chip companies (including Volvo, Scania, and Ericsson) and $85 million held in the Skandinaviska Enskilda Banken, sub–custodian of the National Bank of Kazakhstan and the Bank of New York Mellon.[277] In the Netherlands, the frozen assets amounted to $5.2

---

271 "Judgement SVEA Court of Appeal," *Stockholm Chamber of Commerce*, December 9, 2016.

272 S. Dolea, "ASCOM Case: Kazakhstan's request to set aside is rejected, the SCC award 'was not fraudulent'," *CIS Arbitration Forum*, January 10, 2017, http://www.cisarbitration.com/2017/01/10/ascom-case-the-kazakhstans-req uest-to-set-aside-is-rejected-the-scc-award-was-not-fraudulent/

273 "Belgian Court to Weigh Fraud in $506M Kazakh Award Fight," *Law 360*, https://www.law360.com/articles/1218498/belgian-court-to-weigh-fraud-in-506m-kazakh-award-fight

274 Incorporated in Belgium but with branches all over Europe.

275 "Amerikancy zamorozili $22 mlrd Nacfonda Kazahstana," [The Americans froze $22 billion of the National Fund of Kazakhstan], *Forbes*, December 21, 2017, https://forbes.kz/finances/finance/amerikantsyi_zamorozili_22_mlrd_natsfonda_kazahstana   P. Sorbello, "Lawsuits Threaten Kazakhstan's Oil Money," *The Diplomat*, January 12, 2018, https://thediplomat.com/2018/01/la wsuits-threaten-kazakhstans-oil-money/

276 "Data," *The World Bank*, https://data.worldbank.org/indicator/NY.GDP.MK TP.CD?locations=MD

277 According to Stati's lawyers, in 2019 the Swedish Enforcement Agency was about to sell the shares in partial enforcement of the award. Journalist, interview by author, March 10, 2020.

billion worth shares of KMG Kashagan B.V., hence blocking the inflow of dividends from the oilfield. In Luxembourg, frozen assets involved 40% of the Eurasia Resource Group,[278] whose estimated value is $1 billion, and dividends from Arcelor Mittal[279] and Cameco.

The court case in the UK was dismissed at the request of Stati's lawyers because they were not expecting to obtain a positive outcome.[280] The British Court believed that the accusation of fraud presented by Kazakhstan in the US trial had brought new evidence which could have been necessary in the redefinition of the award. Still, as anticipated, at the end of 2021 Stati lost the case in Belgium where the Court of Appeal endorsed the accusation of fraud proposed by Kazakh lawyers. Since the award was enforced based on misleading facts, the court relieved the frozen $530 million in the Bank of New York Mellon.[281]

Nevertheless, the case ended up endangering Kazakh assets abroad. As discussed in Chapter II, *Petroleum in Kazakhstan*, the negative effects of rent dependency can be mitigated by saving abroad funds to use them in case of low oil prices. The Kazakh Sovereign National Fund Samruk–Kazyna and the National Oil Fund were created with this purpose, but while the frozen accounts in London seem to reflect this idea, the Swedish shares in blue–chip companies raise the question of whom the money is destined for.

---

278 The remaining 60% of the shares are owned by Mashkevich, Chodiev, and Ibragimov.

279 As noted in Chapter IV, *State Racketeering*, Arcelor Mittal remains a strong operator in Kazakhstan due to the relationship between Timur Kulibayev and Lakshmi Mittal.

280 D. Lazic and D. L. Alonso Massa, "International Arbitration Case Law," *School of International Arbitration*, https://www.transnational-dispute-management.com/downloads/18887_case_report_stati_v_kazakhstan_june_2017.pdf

281 M. Bokanova, "Republic of Kazakhstan defeats Statis -- Belgium Court of Appeal conclusively determines Statis defrauded arbitral tribunal and 'deliberately misled' Swedish annulment courts -- reverses recognition and enforcement of USD 530 million arbitral award," *BusinessWire*, November 18, 2021, https://www.businesswire.com/news/home/20211118005635/en/Republic-of-Kazakhstan-defeats-Statis----Belgium-Court-of-Appeal-conclusively-determines-Statis-defrauded-arbitral-tribunal-and-%E2%80%9Cdeliberately-misled%E2%80%9D-Swedish-annulment-courts----reverses-recognition-and-enforcement-of-USD-530-million-arbitral-award

1.7 Türkiye Petrolleri Anonim Ortaklığı: 2011–2014

In 2011, Türkiye Petrolleri Anonim Ortaklığı (TPAO)[282] brought Kazakhstan in front of the ICSID[283] claiming a breach of the International Energy Charter.[284] Until 2010, TPAO was the sole owner of KazakhTurkMunay a subsidiary that conducted exploration and extraction in a few small oilfields in Western Kazakhstan. The subsidiary recovered its first commercial oil in 1996 and nowadays has exploration and extraction activities in six oilfields. In 2010, KMG acquired 51% of KazakhTurkMunay with $70 million while TPAO was left with a 49% stake.[285] The arbitration in front of the ICSID was likely started because of the aggressive takeover by KMG, but the documents of the trial are not public. According to the firm of lawyers Hughes Hubbard,[286] the arbitration was concluded in 2014 with an agreement between the parties. As of 2020, KazMunayGas is the only owner of KazakhTurkMunay after the acquisition of the remaining 49% of shares for $205 million.[287] Since the subsidiary did not announce major discoveries between 2010 and 2014, the figure agreed in court may include partial reimbursement for the 2010 acquisition.

---

282 Original name of the case: Türkiye Petrolleri Anonim Ortaklığı v. Republic of Kazakhstan, ICSID Case No. ARB/11/2.

283 "TPAO v. Kazakhstan," *UNCTAD Investment Policy Hub*, https://investment policy.unctad.org/investment-dispute-settlement/cases/439/tpao-v-kazakh stan "Türkiye Petrolleri Anonim Ortaklığı v. Republic of Kazakhstan (ICSID Case No. ARB/11/2)," *International Centre for Settlement of Investment Disputes World Bank Group*, https://icsid.worldbank.org/en/Pages/cases/casedetail.as px?CaseNo=ARB/11/2

284 "Türkiye Petrolleri Anonim Ortaklığı (Turkey) v. Kazakhstan," *International Energy Charter*, https://www.energycharter.org/what-we-do/dispute-settlemen t/investment-dispute-settlement-cases/30-tuerkiye-petrolleri-anonim-ortaklig i-turkey-v-kazakhstan/

285 "Istoriâ," [History], *Kazakhturkmunay*, http://www.kazakhturkmunay.kz/ist oriya/

286 "Hughes Hubbard Helps Turkish Company Settle Oil Dispute With Kazakhstan," *Hughes Hubbard*, https://www.hugheshubbard.com/news/hughes-hub bard-helps-turkish-company-settle-oil-dispute-with-kazakhstan

287 "Kazakhturkmunai contract areas," *Wood Mackenzie*, May 1, 2018, https://www.woodmac.com/reports/upstream-oil-and-gas-kazakhturkmun ai-contract-areas-551036

1.8 Aktau Petrol Ticaret and Som Petrol Ticaret: 2015–2017

The case of the two subsidiaries of the ASB Group[288] owned by the Turkish citizen Sitki Ayan was brought in front of the ICSID in 2015.[289] The claimants argued that Kazakhstan was in breach of the 1992 International Energy Charter and the Bilateral Investment Treaty between Turkey and Kazakhstan.[290] Between 2006 and 2014, the ASB Group had invested in: storage facilities, oil transhipment at the port of Aktau, a private railway that connected the state railway to the port, an oil terminal, and six hundred ninety–five railway tank cars. The dispute started in 2007 with a commercial agreement between Sitki Ayan and Askar Kulibayev,[291] the father of Timur Kulibayev. The Turkish had reportedly started the commercial relationship to facilitate his business in Kazakhstan, but the claimants argued that Kulibayev orchestrated court proceedings that led to the expropriation of the assets of the ASB Group. The counterargument of Kazakhstan was what the ASB Group did could not qualify as an investment because it only obtained shares from other companies.

The claimants accused Kazakhstan of judicial corruption based on the argument that the government had employed a

---

288 Original name of the case: Aktau Petrol Ticaret A.Ş. and Som Petrol Ticaret A.Ş. v. Republic of Kazakhstan, ICSID Case No. ARB/15/8.

289 "Aktau Petrol v. Kazakhstan," *UNCTAD Investment Policy Hub*, https://investmentpolicy.unctad.org/investment-dispute-settlement/cases/618/aktau-petrol-v-kazakhstan

290 "Aktau Petrol Ticaret A.Ş. and Som Petrol Ticaret A.Ş. v. Kazakhstan," *International Energy Charter*, https://www.energycharter.org/what-we-do/dispute-settlement/investment-dispute-settlement-cases/65-aktau-petrol-ticaret-as-and-som-petrol-ticaret-as-v-kazakhstan/ "Aktau Petrol Ticaret A.Ş. and Som Petrol Ticaret A.Ş. v. Republic of Kazakhstan (ICSID Case No. ARB/15/8)," *International Centre for Settlement of Investment Disputes World Bank Group*, https://icsid.worldbank.org/en/Pages/cases/casedetail.aspx?CaseNo=ARB/15/8

291 Defined by the lawyers of the claimants as a 'a manipulative, unprincipled and deceitful businessman'. "Hamid Gharavi and Melanie Van Leeuwen Secure a Third Consecutive Victory Against Kazakhstan for a US$30 Million Award," *Derains & Gharavi International*, http://www.derainsgharavi.com/2017/11/hamid-gharavi-and-melanie-van-leeuwen-secure-a-third-consecutive-victory-against-kazakhstan-for-a-us-30-million-award/

similar *modus operandi* in other cases.[292] The court responded that it could not accept propensity evidence as a sufficient indicator of Kazakhstan's responsibility in this particular proceeding.[293] According to the judges, the expropriation was not caused by Kazakh courts but rather by the authorities' implementations of those decisions, and while the claimants had done all they could to ask Kazakh courts to correct illegalities, the Kazakh judiciary remained uninterested. In one of the examples mentioned, the ICSID noted how the Kazakh tribunals took Aktau Petrol's shares in the railway in satisfaction of a $870,000 debt of another subsidiary of the ABS Group disposed in a different court judgement. Arbitrators qualified these behaviours as 'judicial apathy' rather than corruption. Also, the tribunal was not able to quantify the value of the assets because the last offer to buy them was made by Kulibayev's AKA Oil Trading. The court doubted his *bona fide* because the businessman had successfully chased other competitors, *de facto* eroding the conditions of a fair market competition. In 2017, Kazakhstan was sentenced to pay $22.7 million of damages plus the costs of the arbitration and interests, for a total of about $30 million. Yet, claimants were asked to pay their legal expenses because of the gravity of their unsupported allegation of judicial corruption.

---

292 Still, the Court recognised that the authorities initiated: 'a well-worn pattern of mistreatment of foreign investors who initiate and grow businesses in Kazakhstan, only to be deprived of their investments by unscrupulous Kazakh businessmen connected to the president, Nursultan Nazarbayev.' Ibidem, http://www.derainsgharavi.com/2017/11/hamid-gharavi-and-melanie-van-leeuwen-secure-a-third-consecutive-victory-against-kazakhstan-for-a-us-30-m illion-award/

293 The lawyers of the claimants justified by saying that some actions can only be proved by 'circumstantial evidence,' and that referring to the findings of other investment tribunals to show that the 'same players' are involved and that they 'use the judiciary as their puppets, tools' was their only option. Ibid., http://www.derainsgharavi.com/2017/11/hamid-gharavi-and-melanie-van-leeuwen-secure-a-third-consecutive-victory-against-kazakhstan-for-a-us-30-m illion-award/

1.9 Big Sky Energy Corporation: 2017–2021

In 2017, Big Sky Energy Corporation[294] brought Kazakhstan in front of the ICSID for a breach of the Bilateral Investment Treaty between the United States and Kazakhstan.[295] In an already well–known plot, the subsidiary Big Sky Energy Kazakhstan was expropriated of Kozhan LLP, operating in the fields of Morskoye, Dauletaly and Karatal, and Vector Energy West operating in the blocks Atyrau and Liman II, after a series of court proceedings that ended with the suspension of the contracts of the above–mentioned subsidiaries for not having respected the programs of investments since 2003. In 2015, the Eurasian Group of Mashkevich, Chodiev, and Ibragimov sold Kozhan JSC to the Chinese Geo–Jade Petroleum for $350 million.[296] The case was won by Kazakhstan on the 24th of November 2021, but no details have been disclosed.[297]

2. Specious Contract Cancellations in Mexico

The history of Mexican oil started when the engineer Weetman Pearson, famous for his work on the Panama Canal, was requested by the country's dictator Porfirio Díaz to study and carry out operations in his country. In 1901, he established his own company,

---

294 Original name of the case: Big Sky Energy Corporation v. Republic of Kazakhstan, ICSID Case No. ARB/17/22.

295 "Big Sky Energy Corporation v. Republic of Kazakhstan (ICSID Case No. ARB/17/22), *International Centre for Settlement of Investment Disputes World Bank Group*, https://icsid.worldbank.org/en/Pages/cases/casedetail.aspx?CaseNo =ARB/17/22 "Big Sky Energy Corporation v. Republic of Kazakhstan, ICSID Case No. ARB/17/22," *italaw*, https://www.italaw.com/cases/6162 "Big Sky Energy Corporation v. Kazakhstan," *UNCTAD Investment Policy Hub*, https://investmentpolicy.unctad.org/investment-dispute-settlement/cases/8 08/big-sky-energy-v-kazakhstan

296 "Sud'e arbitraža s učastiem Kazahstana ob"âvili otvod," [International arbitration involving Kazakhstan announced withdrawal], *inbusiness.kz*, May 10, 2018, https://inbusiness.kz/ru/last/sude-arbitrazha-s-uchastiem-kazahstana-obya vili-otvod

297 Ministry of Justice of the Republic of Kazakhstan, "The Republic of Kazakhstan won the arbitration process initiated by the American company Big Sky Energy Corporation," *JusMundi*, November 25, 2021, https://jusmundi.com/en/docu ment/other/en-big-sky-energy-corporation-v-republic-of-kazakhstan-the-rep ublic-of-kazakhstans-press-release-on-final-award-thursday-25th-november-2 021#other_document_21784

Mexican Eagle, and with the help of Everett DeGoyler, successfully managed to extract oil in exchange for royalties and a tax on surface occupation. In 1917, Pearson left the country by selling his company to Royal Dutch Shell, after having made Mexico the third world oil producer with up to 100,000 barrels per day (Maugeri 2006, 30).

After the fall of Porfirio Díaz, the relationship of foreign companies with the new revolutionary government worsened. During the 1920s, oilmen preferred the more liberal Venezuela over Mexico, and at the beginning of the 1930s the global oil market crashed. After previous unsuccessful attempts, in 1936 oil workers demanded an increase in salary. Foreign companies expected the government to take their side, but President Lázaro Cárdenas sent the matter to federal arbitration. The court decided for more than 30% raise, and while companies appealed the decision, the Supreme Court rejected their request (Joseph and Buchenau 2013, 132). Foreign investors, including Shell, then responsible for 65% of the Mexican oil production, decided to defy the court's decision. On the 18th of March 1938, the reaction of the Mexican president was tougher than what companies had envisioned, because in a radio broadcast, he announced a decree nationalising the oil sector (Maugeri 2006, 49; Joseph and Buchenau 2013, 133). From then, through its National Oil Company Petróleos Mexicanos (PEMEX), the country used oil to power its economic development.

The then Partido Nacional Revolucionario had ruled Mexico since its foundation by Plutarco Elías Calles in 1929. Renamed Institutional Revolutionary Party (PRI) in 1946, the party was not created to win elections, but rather to exercise the power it already had.[298] Established by the winners of the Mexican Revolution, the PRI ruled the country in a strict authoritarian fashion up to the 1990s. Until 1989, opposition parties never won a single state governorship, and unlike other Latin American unstable states, in Mexico, the rule of one party had 'a significant degree of consent among the governed' (Joseph and Buchenau 2013, 142). While intensified

---

298 F. Contreras, "PRI: A history of Mexico's ruling party," *CGTN America*, June 26, 2018, https://america.cgtn.com/2018/06/26/pri-a-history-of-mexicos-ruling-party

160 THE HOUSE ALWAYS WINS

under the 1976 presidency of José López Portillo, accusations of corruption towards the ruling elite had been circulating for decades. In the oil sector, British journalists estimated that during the oil boom almost every purchase by PEMEX involved a 10 to 15% kickback (Joseph and Buchenau 2013, 172).

The 1990s were characterised by rebellious movements and bloody repressions, but the country's opening to global capitalism led the PRI to approve a relatively fair and impartial electoral law. After seventy–one years, in the 2000 elections, Mexicans voted for a president who was not from the PRI. Nevertheless, the respite did not last long, because in 2012 the former governor of the state of Mexico Enrique Peña Nieto won the presidential race with almost 40% of the votes. His election was immediately met with popular protests warning against corrupt behaviours,[299] and the repeated scandals investing him are the likely reason behind the loss of the PRI in the 2018 elections.[300] As it turned out, in 2020 investigators opened a criminal case for corruption against former President Peña Nieto accused of taking bribes, amongst others, by the drug lord El Chapo.[301]

During Peña Nieto's mandate, the oil sector was not spared by accusations of corruption. Out of the thirty–five cases bringing Mexico in front of the ICSID, two comprised the forced suspension of service contracts with PEMEX. The number is still relatively low because the Mexican oil industry is nationalised, and the cases were initiated by foreign citizens who invested in the country indirectly through Mexican service companies. Commenced in 2018, both cases are still pending, but the arguments of the claimants display patterns of informal behaviour already observed in Kazakhstan.

---

299 "Mexicans protest against Peña Nieto's election win," *The Guardian*, July 8, 2012, https://www.theguardian.com/world/2012/jul/08/mexicans-protest-pena-nieto-election

300 D. Graham, "RIP PRI? Mexico's ruling party in 'intensive care' after drubbing," *Reuters*, July 4, 2018, https://www.reuters.com/article/us-mexico-election-pri-idUSKBN1JU1H1

301 "Mexico: Ex-President Enrique Peña Nieto accused of corruption and bribery," *BBC*, August 12, 2020, https://www.bbc.com/news/world-latin-america-537 46715

For instance, in the case of PACC Offshore Services Holding Ltd. (POSH) versus Mexico,[302] the government has been accused of targeting Oceanografía, S.A. de C.V. (OSA), with whom POSH had partnered, with a series of initiatives intending to bring it down.[303] The executive seemed to justify its choice of seizing OSA's assets backed by the claim of Citibank that $400 million of fraudulent invoices that the company had submitted questioned the validity of forty contracts with PEMEX. Yet, claimants insisted that the Peña Nieto Administration adopted public procurement sanctions, criminal investigations, insolvency proceedings and seizure of assets as revenge against the National Action Party, who 'spoiled OSA during Felipe Calderón's administration'.[304] POSH claimed that the actions of the government jeopardised the contracts and affected its investments. The case ended in January 2022 with the tribunal awarding the investor $6.70 million (out of $227.10 million requested) for breaches of fair and equitable treatment, denial of justice claims, most–favoured–nation treatment, and indirect expropriation.

In the case of Ampex Retirement Master Trust, Apple Oaks Partners, LLC, Brentwood Associates Private Equity Profit Sharing Plan and others versus Mexico,[305] US individuals owning 43% of Integradora de Servicios Petroleros Oro Negro S.A.P.I. de C.V. seek almost $1 billion of compensation claiming that the government's actions cost them their lease agreements. Between 2013 and 2015,

---

302 "PACC Offshore Services Holdings Ltd. v. United Mexican States (ICSID Case No. UNCT/18/5)," *International Centre for Settlement of Investment Disputes World Bank Group*, https://investmentpolicy.unctad.org/investment-dispute-settlement/cases/895/pacc-v-mexico

303 "Statement of Claim," *International Centre for Settlement of Investment Disputes World Bank Group*, March 20, 2019, https://www.italaw.com/sites/default/files/case-documents/italaw10469.pdf

304 "Claimant's reply," *International Centre for Settlement of Investment Disputes World Bank Group*, February 12, 2020, https://www.italaw.com/sites/default/files/case-documents/italaw10469.pdf

305 "Ampex Retirement Master Trust, Apple Oaks Partners, LLC, Brentwood Associates Private Equity Profit Sharing Plan and others v. United Mexican States (ICSID Case No. UNCT/18/4)," *International Centre for Settlement of Investment Disputes World Bank Group*, https://investmentpolicy.unctad.org/investment-dispute-settlement/cases/938/alicia-grace-and-others-v-mexico

162   THE HOUSE ALWAYS WINS

Oro Negro entered into five agreements to lease its offshore drilling platforms for three to five years with a daily rate of up to $160,000.[306] Yet, after the refusal to pay bribes to PEMEX employees and Mexican officials, the government singled out Oro Negro subjecting it to increasingly prejudicial and unfair treatment that ultimately resulted in the cancellation of the contracts. Clearly, so far Mexico has denied the accusations.[307]

3. Specious Contract Cancellations in Oil Economies

The fact that the Kazakh oil sector is largely privatised while the Mexican one relies on the strength of its own national oil company seems to put the cases at different ends of the rentier states' spectrum. Yet, both countries have been characterised by decades of authoritarian rule that reinforced patterns of corruption in the management of the oil industry. Those patterns were not entirely forgotten even after twelve years of absence of the Mexican PRI from power, because the executive seemed to maintain a strong influence over the judiciary.

If investors violate the terms of the contracts, rescinding them is a legitimate action, but the cases discussed show a coordinated action of the executive and the judiciary to eliminate market competitors. The arguments of claimants and defendants helped to illustrate the lingering political motives behind the cancellations, suggesting that the actions were informal. Surely, the cases of international arbitrations were not all won by investors, but the argument of judicial corruption is hard to prove in court, particularly if

---

306 "Notice of Arbitration," *International Centre for Settlement of Investment Disputes World Bank Group*, June 19, 2018, https://www.italaw.com/sites/default/files/case-documents/italaw10631.pdf

307 "Driller accuses government of collusion with Pemex over contract corruption," *Mexico News Daily*, July 25, 2018, https://mexiconewsdaily.com/news/driller-accuses-government-of-collusion-over-contract-corruption/ Oro Negro, the company accusing Pemex of bribery," *El Universal*, October 16, 2019," https://www.eluniversal.com.mx/english/oro-negro-company-accusing-pemex-bribery

the tribunal does not accept 'propensity evidence'.[308] From a legal standpoint this is right but does not help claimants to obtain satisfaction. On the other hand, the cases displayed show that investors were rarely honest businessmen without ties with the political elite of the country they had invested in. Rather, they often had political connections and even committed irregularities that backfired once they fell out of governmental grace. Hence, this conclusion is neither to be read as a critique of governments nor a defence of foreign investors, but as evidence of informal political patterns for which there is no possible trial.

The parallelism between Kazakhstan and Mexico highlights that the reasons guiding specious contract cancellations are political, and the assets involved are not to strategic interest for the country. Political is not intended as ideological, but as elite–centred and serving the goal of internal legitimacy, as one would expect from an autocratic government led by predatory leaders. While Mexico is closer to liberal democracy than Kazakhstan, the Peña Nieto administration was a step back towards 'incomplete democracy' and 'institutionalised impunity'.[309] In the cases considered, political implies elite infighting (Hourani versus Kazakhstan, CCL Oil versus Kazakhstan), favours to foreign allies (Stati versus Kazakhstan), revenge over other parties (POSH versus Mexico), but also elite self–enrichment (Liman Caspian Oil versus Kazakhstan, Aktau and Som Petrol Ticaret versus Kazakhstan, Oro Negro versus Mexico).

The 1938 Mexican nationalisation of the oil sector was 'resource nationalism', a political choice that led to the cancellation of several contracts with foreign corporations. The choice was then ideological, motivated by genuine concern over the exploitation of Mexican workers, and the action was intended as a governmental reappropriation of national wealth to move past the patrimonial embezzlement of the Díaz's dictatorship. Yet, given that the

---

308 "Hamid Gharavi and Melanie Van Leeuwen Secure a Third Consecutive Victory Against Kazakhstan for a US$30 Million Award," *Derains & Gharavi International.*

309 D. Dresser, "MEXICO: Why Mexico Fell Apart, and How to Fix It," *Berkeley Review of Latin American Studies,* Spring 2017, https://clas.berkeley.edu/mexico-why-mexico-fell-apart-and-how-fix-it

resulting contract cancellations have a 'political' dimension nonetheless, the adjective 'specious' helps distinguish the contract cancellations discussed in this chapter from those resulting from classic nationalisations.

While in most cases the figures discussed could not seriously worry governments, at times the reimbursements requested by claimants far exceeded the cash availability of these states ($500 million, but also $22 billion in frozen assets, in Stati versus Kazakhstan, and up to $1 billion in Oro Negro versus Mexico). This shows that the elites are short-sighted and arrogant in achieving their political objectives. Hiding behind the shield of sovereignty, kleptocratic elites successfully proved to be above national and international law on numerous occasions. Table 9 summarises the actors, roles, and goals of political contract cancellations.

Table 9   Actors, roles, and goals of specious contract cancellations

Actors involved	Role in the practice	Goal
Government	Requesting contractual cancellations	Political favours Personal profit
Judiciary	Cancelling contracts	Personal and governmental profit
Investor	Recurring in national courts and to international arbitrations	Avoiding losing money

4.   Pettiness over Reputation

The ninth and fifteenth world oil exporters of 2020 respectively,[310] Kazakhstan and Mexico have widely different oil histories. While the former has been in control of the sector only since its independence in 1991, the Central American country has extracted oil for well over a century and has fully governed the sector for more than eighty years. Yet, both the countries' governments have proved to recur to specious contract cancellations whenever they wanted to

---

310 D. Workman, "Crude Oil Exports by Country," *World's Top Exports*, 2020, https://www.worldstopexports.com/worlds-top-oil-exports-country/

take possession of assets or business deals avoiding the expensive process that the terms of contracts prescribed.

As anticipated in the introduction to this chapter, Rachel Wellhausen (2014) showed how contract cancellations are a widespread practice that is not limited to rentier states. This informal strategy has a much wider applicability and can occur in any country and economic sector. The first suggested generalisation is hence that for specious contract cancellations to occur the only real requirement is a predatory political elite aiming to take possession of business deals for either personal enrichment (Aktau and Som Petrol Ticaret versus Kazakhstan, Oro Negro versus Mexico), patrimonialism (Biedermann versus Kazakhstan, Big Sky Energy versus Kazakhstan), internal (Caratube I and II versus Kazakhstan) and external legitimacy (Stati versus Kazakhstan), political revenge (Caratube I and II versus Kazakhstan, POSH versus Mexico), or a mix of these reasons.

The second suggested generalisation is that specious contract cancellations often show the short sightedness of such predatory elites who risk governmental budgets and affect the country's reputation for unimportant business deals. Pettiness and elite infighting seem to be the prevailing reasons behind this informal practice, but also, specious contract cancellations seem to be the government's last resort when classic state racketeering does not work. As discussed in Chapter IV, *State Racketeering*, the case of CCL Oil falls into a process of reassignment of assets that, according to the Nazarbayev family's logic, should have not been sold to those players in the first place. On the other hand, the Caratube cases took place because of Aliyev's banishment from the informal political group leading the country (Lillis 2019).

Still, contract terminations, albeit specious, are common to all sectors and countries. As such, it is necessary to identify specificities for oil and rentier economies. The most evident peculiarity of these contract cancellations is that in the extractive industries, investments are so conspicuous that arbitrations can create serious problems for governmental budgets and jeopardise the original predatory purpose. The table below shows a schematic version of the preconditions of transferability of the cases based on the M–

166 THE HOUSE ALWAYS WINS

STOUT scheme of external validity employed in quantitative analysis (Findley, Kikuta, and Denly 2021).

Table 10 Specious contract cancellations transferability to the population

Dimension	Kazakhstan	Mexico	Rentier states
Mechanisms	Cancelling contracts	Cancelling contracts	Cancelling contracts
Settings	Established authoritarian rule	Predatory political elite	Predatory political elite intending to acquire assets or business deals
Treatments	Oil industry in development	Oil industry in development	Industry in development
Outcomes	Increased control over the oil sector and risk of international arbitration (in case of foreign investors)	Increased control over the oil sector and risk of international arbitration (in case of foreign investors)	Increased control over the sector and risk of international arbitration (in case of foreign investors)
Units	Kazakh oil industry	Mexican oil industry	Resource-rich country
Time	1992–2021	2012–2018	After the investor has spent capital as required by the contract

Specious contract cancellations are the fourth practice of the taxonomy and a further step towards answering the first research question. The court cases of the Kazakh oil sector offer a snapshot of how the local elite and foreign investors framed their relationship. The case of Mexico has shown how both specious contract cancellations and bid rigging can target service contracts. The difference consists in the fact that while bid rigging affects the tender phase, specious contract cancellations can take place only after the contract has been assigned.

5. Summary Sheet: Specious Contract Cancellations

Definition: unforeseen cancellation of contracts for informal reasons — personal acquisition, political revenge, or favours.

Actors involved: government, judicial authorities, target companies and investors.

Observed in: Kazakhstan, Mexico.

Outcomes: increased control of the racketeers on the sector.

Context: resource-rich country.

Timeline: after the investor has spent capital as required by the contract.

Figure 8   Visualisation of specious contract cancellations

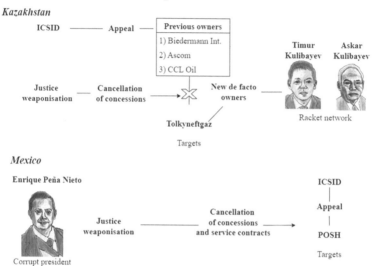

VII Bid Rigging

> tender 2007–0588 – Land Drilling Rig & Living Quarters: we can provide all the tender details, clarifications, evaluations, etc. The tender should be issued early Nov. 07
> tender 2007–0583 – Onshore Power
> Station–GlobalService Support Contract: we can provide only the Tender List, Tender Evaluation Plan, Estimated Cost and Schedule, Technical Evaluation (once approved), and final results (contract award recommendation). Practically all the EMCB Submissions.
> From an email of Stefano Borghi, former ENI executive, 2016.[311]

> Well, along the investigation we discovered that one money–laundering agent, Alberto Youssef, gave a luxury car in favour of one former Petrobras director, Mr. Paolo Costa … And when we talk about Petrobras, we are talking about the biggest Brazilian company at that point. It is one of the giants of the world in the matter of oil and gas, and its director led a field that had a budget bigger than the budget of many ministries in Brazil. He was not anymore a director when he received that car, but the fact that a money-laundering agent was giving a car to a former director of Petrobras was very suspicious.
> Deltan Dallagnol, former lead prosecutor in the Operation Car Wash investigation, 2018.[312]

Bid rigging is an informal practice consisting of competing parties colluding to determine the winner of a bidding process.[313] This form of anticompetitive collusion affects not only the outcome of the sale process but also contracts for jobs in which bids are submitted. Bid rigging can include bid suppression, cover bidding, or bidding at an artificially high price according to the number or value of contracts.[314] Finally, if the industry is sufficiently corrupt to allow it, bid rigging is also a form of collusion involving the very organiser of the tender. While it is not frequent, because a similar practice

---

311 "ciro," *The Age.com*, https://www.theage.com.au/interactive/2016/the-bribe-factory/common/emails/single-page-emails/2__ciro.pdf

312 Center on the Legal Profession, Harvard School, "Operation Car Wash," September/October 2018, https://clp.law.harvard.edu/knowledge-hub/magazin e/issues/brazilian-legal-profession/operation-car-wash/

313 "Bid Rigging," *Investopedia*, https://www.investopedia.com/terms/b/bid-rig ging.asp

314 "Bid Rigging," *Concurrences: Antitrust, Publications & Events*, https://www.con currences.com/en/dictionary/bid-rigging

harms the very organisation for which the colluded agents organising the tender are working, this is a tendency observed in the episodes described here. Even if the practice ultimately rigs whole tenders, the existence of an already viable expression was preferred over the simplistic 'rigged tenders'. There is already a dense quantitative literature on corruption in public procurement, and this facilitates the description of aspects of the practice that should be otherwise proven.[315]

To draw generalisations from this practice, the case of Kazakhstan is paralleled with that of Brazil. There is no specific time limit to identify bid rigging because. after the assignation of contracts to develop oilfields, there is a continuous process of sub–contracting in which companies choose service providers as well as companies to lease equipment from. In other words, when the sector is active there are always job contracts to win, particularly if the sum involved is conspicuous. Hence, the choice of the episodes discussed is related to the availability of information on the selected countries rather than their specificity. In the early 2000s, Ostrowski (2010) noted how winning tenders organised by KazMunayGas, and previously KazakhOil. did not mean being awarded contracts. Rather, to avoid the cancellation of the deal the winning company should have paid a bribe, at times equalling as much as 20% of the value.

Interestingly, the selected countries had almost the same overall score in the Corruption Perception Index of 2021, while separated by a few positions in the ranking.[316] Yet in 2014, the year in which Operation Car Wash was launched, Brazil held a spot in the ranking that was much higher than the Kazakh one.[317] Over the

---

315 Auriol, Straub, and Flochel (2016) discussed how rent-seeking favours corruption and deteriorates procedures for public procurement. Mara Faccio (2006) argued that politically connected firms are more likely to receive contracts, and Titl and Geys (2019) explained how donations lead to favouritism in lending contracts. Finally, Coviello and Gagliarducci (2017) associated longer terms in office with a higher probability of collusion between authorities and firms in public procurement. All these arguments effectively apply to Kazakhstan.

316 "2021 Corruption Perception Index," *Transparency International*, https://www.transparency.org/en/cpi/2021/index/kaz

317 Brazil was 69th and Kazakhstan the 126th in that ranking. "2014 Corruption Perception Index," *Transparency International*, https://www.transparency.org/en/cpi/2014

years, the Latin American country drew closer to the Kazakh position, whereas the Central Asian Republic improved slightly.

While the episodes of Kazakhstan may be slightly less known to readers, particularly because most of the sources on the topic are in Italian, Operation Car Wash has been discussed in all major media outlets worldwide (Mota Prado and De Assis Machado 2021; Lima–de–Oliveira 2020). This offers a glimpse into how media reporting of cases contributes to the distortion of perception based on the sensationalism of details. Just because in Kazakhstan corruption has been a key feature of the country for decades, it does not mean that this is in any way less relevant than in Brazil.

1. Bid Rigging in Kazakhstan

This section will not exhaust all cases of bid rigging in Kazakhstan,[318] but offers an overview of the major scandals that featured the practice of obtaining service contracts in the major oilfields of the country in the past two decades. While most of the cases described here feature the participation of governmental figures, it should be noted that minor service contracts are the most relevant illegal source of income for *akims*, regional governors. This is an important detail because the implicit acceptance that *akims* will participate in bid rigging is what ensured their loyalty to Nazarbayev. Through loyal governors, the autocrat exerted his control on the country at the regional level for decades (Ostrowski 2010). In this context, turning a blind eye has patrimonial implications, but it also provides the autocrat with evidence to blackmail governors in case they ever turn on him. As discussed in Chapter III, *Patrimonial Embezzlement*, this situation often leads to *character assassination* (Samoilenko et al. 2018). The cases discussed in this section were routed through empirical research and complemented with articles and books by investigative journalists.

---

318 In Kazakhstan, Alemgul Kuatova (2013) argued that one of the reasons for the widespread occurrence of corruption crimes in tenders is due to 'the lack of special provisions in the criminal code' (Kuatova 2013, 1422).

172 THE HOUSE ALWAYS WINS

1.1 ENI: 2001–2007

In 2001, when ENI became the main operator in Kashagan it came as a surprise to many, as the company did not have relevant experience in the management of such important projects. Malicious observers noted that one of the reasons behind the choice of the Kazakh government rested in the predisposition of the Italian company to offer the Kazakhs an increasing number of service contracts. For those with less than $100,000 of expected profit, there was no need to organise tenders, while for bigger contracts decisions could be taken behind closed doors. If a company close to Nazarbeyev's political circle manifested its interest in the contract, the executive director Pietro Cavanna managed to make that company the winner of the tender (Greco and Oddo 2018, 187).

The situation was no different in Karachaganak. After an internal investigation, the head of security Domenico Di Petrillo reported to the CEO Vittorio Mincato that ENI engineers were receiving wages of $2,500 a day, an alarming indicator of bribes. Mincato intervened by lowering their pay, but in 2001 the ENI executive in Moscow Mario Reali received information of more alarming practices. ENI and other members of the Karachaganak consortium were reportedly giving up millions of dollars in profits by selling the oil and gas extracted to unknown Russian and Kazakh companies chosen via bid rigging (Greco and Oddo 2018, 255). According to another member of security, Angelo Ruocco, in Kashagan and Karachaganak most of these decisions were taken by Cavanna and the executive Ernesto Ferlenghi (Greco and Oddo 2018, 188).

In 2007, during the broadcast of the investigative programme *Report,* Reali stated that Ferlenghi had Russian citizenship, implicating that he could be a collaborator of the Russian secret services.[319] Such a statement caused Ferlenghi to sue Reali and *Report* for defamation, but they were absolved because the investigations proved that Ferlenghi had, in fact, Russian citizenship since 1995. Ferlenghi's lawyer sent a letter to *Report* explaining that his client

---

319 "La Via del Gas" [The Gas Way], *Report,* https://www.raiplay.it/video/2009/01/La-via-del-gas-2b0c4299-25d3-48a3-bc27-d91edca454e3.html

received Russian citizenship because his mother was born in the Soviet Union (Greco and Oddo 2018, 268).

Unheard by the ENI headquarters, Reali forwarded his concerns on the tenders in Kashagan and Karachaganak to investigators in Rome. In his testimony, Reali referred to the words of Ferlenghi, explaining that the rigged tenders were organised by ENI executives in cooperation with Massimo Guidotti, an agent of Cifal, a company rumoured to be connected to the French secret services (Greco and Oddo 2018, 269). These tenders had been won by an Israeli company, Bateman, that had paid bribes of $100 million to ENI executives and Kazakh authorities. Reportedly, millions of dollars were deposited in offshore accounts and later moved to Luxembourg and Switzerland. The contact person for Kashagan was the engineer Luigi Diamante, who in cooperation with Guidotti, decided the size of bribes. Officially, bribes were reported as additional costs in contracts whose expenses had been inflated. According to Reali's testimony, Ferlenghi explained the situation because he needed his help to move $1.5 million from an account in Switzerland.

Investigators in Rome found partial correspondence to these declarations in testimonies of other ENI executives. Reali told the investigators that he had noted all names of the participants of the corruption scheme in a personal dossier that he kept in his office in Moscow, but since 2006 Ferlenghi had denied him access. Similarly, the documentation for service contracts was kept in the offices in Kazakhstan as required by the production–sharing agreement. On the 20th of October 2007, the judge archived the procedure considering there was not sufficient evidence to continue the investigation (Greco and Oddo 2018, 271).

1.2 Baker Hughes: 2007

In 2007, Baker Hughes, a Texan company that offers drilling services to major oil and gas companies in more than eighty countries worldwide, settled a federal probe connected to the violation of the Foreign Corrupt Practices Act (FCPA) paying $44 million, at that time the highest punishment ever inflicted for this type of crime.

174   THE HOUSE ALWAYS WINS

The investigation started with the complaint filed by Crude Accountability and the Berezovka Initiative Group to the Department of Institutional Integrity at the World Bank (Watters 2013, 179). These groups are respectively an American NGO and a group of activists that inquired about the environmental violations of the Karachaganak Petroleum Operating (KPO) consortium.[320]

In 1999, KPO announced the tender for a contract of approximately $200 million for oil drilling, logistics, and engineering, and KazakhOil was expected to approve the phase of contract bidding.[321] In early 2000, Baker Hughes' Roy Fearnley made contact with a key figure in KazakhOil (Holtzblatt and Tschakert 2014). In September, Fearnley heard from informal sources that Baker Hughes had been chosen as the winner of the tender, but also that KazakhOil requested him to hire an agent in connection with the tender. The headquarters of Baker Hughes in the US gave their consent to finalise the contract: Fearnley hired a company of the Isle of Man led by the UK banker Robert Kissin.[322] At the end of September, Fearnley agreed to pay a 2% commission on the earnings of Baker Hughes from the Karachaganak project, and in a different agreement, a 3% commission on revenues invoiced by the company in all future projects in Kazakhstan. In October, Baker Hughes was awarded the contract.[323] Between 2001 and 2003 the Texan company paid $4.1 million to the agent through a bank account in London

---

320 "Environmentalists charge oil majors with polluting Kazakhstan village," *Wikileaks*, April 12, 2005, https://search.wikileaks.org/plusd/cables/05ALMATY 1435_a.html

321 F. Norris, "Baker Hughes Admits to Overseas Bribery," *The New York Times*, April 27, 2007, https://www.nytimes.com/2007/04/27/business/worldbusin ess/27settle.html

322 D. Leigh, "WikiLeaks cables name UK banker as middleman in Kazakh corruption ring," *The Guardian*, December 12, 2010, https://www.theguardian.com/w orld/2010/dec/12/wikileaks-british-banker-kazakh-corruption

323 "SEC v. Baker Hughes Incorporated and Roy Fearnley, Civil Action No. H-07-1408, United States District Court for the Southern District of Texas (Houston Division)," U.S. Securities and Exchange Commission, April 26, 2007, https://www.sec.gov/litigation/litreleases/2007/lr20094.htm

under its name. Those expenses were registered as 'commissions', 'fees', or 'legal services'.[324]

In 2007, before the company was sentenced in the US, the senior vice president of Baker Hughes Alain R. Crain briefed the American ambassador and Prime Minister Karim Massimov. The vice-president warned that the name of Zhakyp Marabayev[325] was mentioned in the investigation. Marabayev left KMG shortly after Crain briefed Massimov.[326]

1.3 Parker Drilling: 2010

In 2010, the Texan company Parker Drilling was accused of international corruption by the Securities and Exchange Commission of the US Department of Justice because found in violation of the FCPA.[327] The company had paid bribes to government officials in Nigeria and Kazakhstan to secure commissions. Directors were said to have breached the fiduciary duty of their shareholders conducting business in countries where the risk of corruption was higher than normal.[328] The investigation started in 2007, and in May 2008 was followed by a parallel investigation on customs violations. In 2013, the sentence cost Parker Drilling $15.85 million (Chervinsky 2017, 246).[329] While the documents of the trial are not available,

---

324 "SEC Charges Baker Hughes with Foreign Bribery and with Violating 2001 Commission Cease-and-Desist Order," U.S. Securities and Exchange Commission, April 26, 2007, https://www.sec.gov/news/press/2007/2007-77.htm

325 Seen in Chapter IV, *State Racketeering*, 1.2 *Karazhanbas: 2006*.

326 "Baker Hughes seeks to limit fallout from FCPA case," *Wikileaks*, April 11, 2007, https://wikileaks.org/plusd/cables/07ASTANA919_a.html The Kazakh prime minister declared that the government was not interested in the guilty being named, revealing that Marabayev had effectively become expendable. "Information on Baker Hughes' FCPA case shared with government," *Wikileaks*, April 30, 2007, https://wikileaks.org/plusd/cables/07ASTANA1143_a.html

327 "Securities and Exchange Commission v. Parker Drilling Company, Civil Action No. 1:13CV461 (E.D. Va., April 16, 2013)," *U.S. Securities and Exchange Commission*, April 16, 2013, https://www.sec.gov/litigation/litreleases/2013/lr2 2672.htm

328 C. Langford, "Shareholders Say Oil Firm Paid Bribes," *Courthouse News Service*, June 7, 2010, https://www.courthousenews.com/shareholders-say-oil-firm-pa id-bribes/

329 "Parker Drilling uladila delo o vzâtkah v RK," [Parker Drilling Settles Bribery Case in Kazakhstan], *Forbes.kz*, February 16, 2013, https://forbes.kz//process/ probing/parker_drilling_uladila_delo_o_vzyatkah_v_rk/?

176 THE HOUSE ALWAYS WINS

the cases contested in Kazakhstan may have been connected to the Sunkar rig in the Caspian Sea.[330]

1.4 Bateman et alia: 2012

Having heard of Reali's testimony in Rome, in 2012 the Italian prosecutor in Milan Fabio De Pasquale opened an investigation for international corruption. The new investigation included ENI's manager in Kazakhstan Guido Michelotti, the director of Agip–KCO Umberto Carrara, once again Massimo Guidotti, and three executives of the Israeli Bateman. The company was the property of Beny Steinmetz, a businessman tied to former Prime Minister Ehud Olmert, convicted for corruption in 2015.[331] In a phone call recorded by his assistant, Olmert complained of Steinmetz's decision to stop paying him despite he had helped to deny the request of the Italian judges to search the offices of Bateman in Israel (Greco and Oddo 2018, 275). Despite the obstructions, the investigation continued for a few years. One of its possible outcomes could have been ENI's interdiction from organising further tenders connected to the Kashagan consortium, but the judge for preliminary investigations rejected the request of the prosecution.

The investigation was later extended to Iraq involving the Italian companies Saipem, Tecnimont, Ansaldo Energia, Elettra Progetti, Siirtec, Renco, and Prysmian that had supposedly over–inflated their commissions to allow payments to politicians through tens of companies in Bahamas, Cyprus, and the British Virgin Islands.[332] One of the companies paid by Bateman in connection with the Kashagan contracts was Enviro Pacific Investments, connected to Timur Kulibayev. During the investigation, De Pasquale searched the offices of the Enviro Pacific Investments despite the

---

330 Chapter V, *Fine Threats*, 1.2 Kashagan: 2004, 2008, and 2013.

331 "Former Israeli leader Ehud Olmert jailed for eight months for corruption," *The Guardian*, May 25, 2015, https://www.theguardian.com/world/2015/may/2 5/former-israeli-leader-ehud-olmert-jailed-for-eight-months-for-corruption

332 E. Randacio, "'Mazzette ai politici stranieri' sotto inchiesta i big del petrolio," [Bribes to Foreign Politicians, Under Investigation Oil Majors], *La Repubblica*, March 13, 2012, https://www.repubblica.it/economia/2012/03/13/news/ tangenti_petrolio-31432656/

opposition of the Kazakh police (Greco and Oddo 2018, 275). A few years later, it will be revealed that the funds that Kulibayev used to buy Prince Andrew's villa in Berkshire for £15 million came from that shell company.[333]

Italian prosecutors in Monza also opened a twin investigation that involved ENI's executive Paolo Dentali, Timur Kulibayev, KMG's executive Bolat Nazarov, and Maksat Idenov, former director of KMG but ENI's executive at the time of the investigation.[334] The scheme was the same foreseen by prosecutors in Milan: a contractor, the electrical society Dinamo, increased its commissions to ENI to facilitate the transfer of money to offshore companies tied to Kazakh influential figures. In 2016, both investigations were ultimately closed for lack of sufficient evidence.[335]

1.5 International Tubular Services Limited: 2014

After being purchased by Parker Drilling a few months before, in 2014 a company supplying drilling equipment to oil and gas majors, the Scottish International Tubular Services Limited, pleaded guilty in front of Scottish prosecutors for having paid bribes to secure a contract with a customer. The bribe was paid through a former employee based in Kazakhstan, and the deal helped the

---

333 R. Booth, "Prince Andrew tried to broker crown property deal for Kazakh oligarch," *The Guardian*, July 3, 2016, https://www.theguardian.com/uk-news/2 016/jul/03/prince-andrew-broker-crown-property-kazakh-oligarch The Swiss police investigated Kulibayev for money laundering between 2000 and 2005, in connection with this purchase: "Criminal investigations against Timur Kulibayev in Switzerland," *Open Dialogue*, November 9, 2010, https://en.odfoundati on.eu/a/29,criminal-investigations-against-timur-kulibayev-in-switzerland/ "Kazakh president accused of money laundering," Swissinfo.ch, February 13, 2012, https://www.swissinfo.ch/eng/kazakh-president-accused-of-money-l aundering/32117144 The case was abandoned in 2013, "How Vitol became king of oil in Kazakhstan," Public Eye, November 14, 2018, https://www.publiceye. ch/en/media-corner/press-releases/detail/how-vitol-became-king-of-oil-in-kazakhstan

334 The US ambassador Richard E. Hoagland reported that already in 2010 Idenov defined ENI and BG as corrupt, "Kazakhstan: Money and Power," *WikiLeaks*, January 25, 2010, https://wikileaks.org/plusd/cables/10ASTANA72_a.html

335 S. Vergine, "Kazakistan, niente petrolio molte mazzette," [Kazakhstan, no Oil but Many Bribes], L'Espresso, July 13, 2016, https://espresso.repubblica.it/plu s/articoli/2016/07/13/news/Kazakistan-niente-petrolio-molte-mazzette-1.27 6713

178   THE HOUSE ALWAYS WINS

company profit £172,000 (approximately $267,000).[336] The total amount was then reimbursed to the Scottish Consolidated Fund. As declared by Linda Hamilton, Head of the Civil Recovery Unit:

> 'Bribery and corruption undermines legitimate businesses and can harm economic development and we are committed to tackling it wherever it is found. In appropriate circumstances, the self–reporting initiative allows for companies to accept their involvement in corrupt practices, put in place effective systems to prevent it from recurring and repay the illegitimate profits.'[337]

Yet, the profiting of the company did not actively procure harm to the Scottish community, nor the sanction improve the Kazakh business environment as a result.

1.6   Unaoil: 2016

In 2016, the offices of the Monaco–based company Unaoil were raided by state authorities in cooperation with the UK Serious Fraud Office, the US Department of Justice, and the Australian anti–corruption police after that an investigation of Fairfax Media and the Huffington Post linked to the Panama Papers had revealed a worldwide corruption scheme.[338] In Kazakhstan, Unaoil operated as intermediary between companies that wanted to be granted

---

336   J. Jaeger, "Parker Drilling Unit Pays $267,000 for Bribery," *Compliance Week*, December 22, 2014, https://www.complianceweek.com/parker-drilling-unit-pa ys-267000-for-bribery/12829.article J. Kovensky, "Scottish Oil Services Firm Acquired by Parker Drilling Fined for Kazakh Bribes," Global Investigation Review, December 19, 2014, https://globalinvestigationsreview.com/article/jac /1023426/scottish-oil-services-firm-acquired-by-parker-drilling-fined-for-kaz akh-bribes

337   D. Herbert, "Scots Oil Firm Punished Over Bribery in Kazakhstan," *Express*, December 18, 2014, https://www.express.co.uk/news/uk/547543/Scottish-oil-firm-punished-over-bribery-in-Kazakhstan

338   S. Roque, "Unaoil Leaks: Investigation Spotlights Global Oil Industry 'Bribes-for-Contracts' Scandal," Organized Crime and Corruption Reporting Project, April 15, 2016, https://www.occrp.org/en/daily/5133-unaoil-leaks-investigat ion-spotlights-global-oil-industry-bribes-for-contracts-scandal "Monaco raids Unaoil offices over global oil corruption probe," Reuters, April 1, 2016, https://www.reuters.com/article/us-oil-companies-corruption-idUSKCN0W Y4S6 D. Pegg, "Serious Fraud Office opens criminal investigation into Unaoil," The Guardian, July 19, 2016, https://www.theguardian.com/business/2016/j ul/19/serious-office-opens-criminal-investigation-into-unaoil

contracts. Among these companies, there were Halliburton, Kellogg, Brown & Root, Petrofac, Rolls Royce, Aker Kvaerner, Gate, Keppel, and National Oilwell Varco. From 2004, these groups paid bribes to key influential figures in ENI or close to the government thanks to the intercession of Unaoil representatives. As an intermediary, the Monaco–based company retained a part of the bribe, normally no less than 3% of the value of a contract (Chervinsky 2017, 247). The emails of the executive of Unaoil Peter Willimont to the CEO Cyrus Ahsani show how being credible in the eyes of contractors consisted of guaranteeing access to contracts in light of personal relations with ENI and KMG representatives, referred to in the messages as 'spaghetti' and 'shashlik': 'We need to convince [Kellogg, Brown & Root] that we own the Spaghetti House and have a lease on the Shashlik takeaway'.[339]

In ENI, Unaoil had five contacts including Diego Braghi, Stefano Borghi, and Leonida Bortolazzo. Both Braghi and Borghi offered information, details, and clarifications on tenders in exchange for kickbacks.[340] Bortolazzo remained a key contact for Unaoil even after he left ENI for the Kazakh oil company KING, owned by Serik Burtikbayev, later jailed on corruption charges. In 2005, Bortolazzo was paid $80,000 a month to rig tenders for Unaoil's clients. The company also spent money on Kazakh government officials: paying for expensive hotel rooms in Monaco, submitting fraudulent visa requests, or setting up bank accounts in Bermuda and companies in the British Virgin Islands. However, most of the earnings were connected to service contracts with companies that these officials owned. From the emails, it is also possible to notice the efforts of Unaoil executives to win the favours of the billionaire Timur Kulibayev (Titl and Geys 2019).[341]

---

339 "RE: Confidential," The Age.com, https://www.theage.com.au/interactive/20 16/the-bribe-factory/common/emails/long-emails/17_spaghetti-house.pdf

340 "ciro," *The Age.com*, https://www.theage.com.au/interactive/2016/the-bribe-factory/common/emails/single-page-emails/2_ciro.pdf

341 N. McKenzie and R. Baker, "The Bribe Factory," The Age/Huffpost, https://www.theage.com.au/interactive/2016/the-bribe-factory/day-2/kaza khstan.html

2. Bid Rigging in Brazil

In Brazil, oil was first discovered in the state of Bahia following exploration activities in the 1930s. From the beginning, President Getúlio Vargas made clear that the Brazilian oil industry would have not been privatised. In 1938, with a move echoed years later by the slogan *o petróleo é nosso*, oil is ours, he established the National Petroleum Council (CNP). As discussed in the previous chapter, that same year Mexico nationalised its own oil industry in what seemed like a generalised attempt of Latin American oil producers to take control of their own destiny. In 1953, Getúlio Vargas approved law number 2.004 creating *Petróleo Brasileiro Sociedade Anonima* (Petrobras), the state-owned oil and gas company (Playfoot, Andrews, and Augustus 2015, 57). With the goal of maximising production, the CNP hired Walter K. Link, former Chief Exploration Geologist of Standard Oil New Jersey. The choice proved fruitful, and by 1957 Brazil extracted 40,000 barrels per day (Smith 1972, 187).

In those years, every move of Petrobras was under public scrutiny because the rhetoric of oil nationalism could not allow any form of collaboration with international oil companies, whose intervention was seen as imperialist interference (Smith 1972). Yet, in the 1960s Petrobras could not meet domestic demand and was forced to import oil from abroad. The global oil crisis of 1974 worsened the situation by decreasing the otherwise impressive Brazilian economic growth. While the 1967 Constitution formalised the state monopoly over the oil industry, in 1973 Petrobras' president Ernesto Geisel allowed the company to sign contracts with BP, Texaco, Exxon, ELF, Conoco, Marathon, and Total to improve domestic production (Playfoot, Andrews, and Augustus 2015, 57–58). The ambiguous situation was finally resolved in 1997 with partial liberalisation of the market. After a misstep in the 1970s in the creation of Braspetro, the Brazilian government started investing abroad to diversify its income. In 2003, Petrobras acquired the Argentinian Perez Companc Energia, and in 2005 entered the Japanese market by signing a contract with Nippon Alcohol Hanbai (Playfoot,

Andrews, and Augustus 2015, 60). Nowadays, Petrobras is regarded as one of the most important oil companies in the world.

Still, the proximity of such a powerful economic player to political circles did not end well. In 2014, the Federal Police of Brazil's Curitiba, in the state of Paraná, opened the criminal investigation known as '*Operação Lava Jato*', Operation Car Wash. Initially headed by the investigative judge Sergio Moro and then by Luiz Antônio Bonat, the case led to 295 arrests, 278 convictions, and 4.3 billion reais, approximately $803 million, returned to the Brazilian state throughout seven years of operation.[342] The investigation started as a small corruption case involving black market dealers who used petrol stations to launder money. Yet, investigators soon noted how dealers were answering directly to Paulo Roberto Costa, director of refining and supply at Petrobras. During his interrogation, Costa described how for years Petrobras had overpaid service contracts for construction, drilling, and exploration vessels guaranteeing contracts at lucrative terms in exchange for kickbacks from 1 to 5% into slush funds destined for politicians. The construction firm Odebrecht alone paid $3.3 billion (Guimaraes and Ribeiro 2019).

Diverted funds were funnelled to politicians and financed political parties.[343] Among the arrested politicians there were former Brazilian presidents Fernando Collor de Mello, Michel Temer, and Luiz Inácio Lula da Silva, but also businessmen and prominent politicians in Argentina, Colombia, Mexico, Panama, and Venezuela, including former Peruvian President Alan Garcia, who committed

---

342 R. Brito and G. Slattery, "After seven years, Brazil shuts down Car Wash anti-corruption squad," *Reuters*, February 4, 2021, https://www.reuters.com/articl e/us-brazil-corruption-idUSKBN2A4068 Sallaberry, Quaesner, Costa, and Flach (2020) did a complete evaluation of the damage caused by Car Wash on the pages of their Measurement of damage from corruption in Brazil. The authors concluded that the cost of corporate corruption reached '17.84% of the money amount of constructions' (Sallaberry et al. 2020, 1248).

343 J. Watts, "Operation Car Wash: Is this the biggest corruption scandal in history?," *The Guardian*, June 1, 2017, https://www.theguardian.com/world/201 7/jun/01/brazil-operation-car-wash-is-this-the-biggest-corruption-scandal-in -history

182 THE HOUSE ALWAYS WINS

suicide before facing imprisonment.[344] The investigation would not have achieved those results without the law on plea bargaining approved in 2013 after nationwide anti–corruption demonstrations[345] by the successor of Lula, Dilma Rousseff.[346] Yet, a 2019 investigative article of *Intercept Brazil* hinted that Sergio Moro was responsible of serious wrongdoing and abuse of power in the arrest of Lula, resulting in his exclusion as frontrunner of the Worker's Party at the 2018 presidential election.[347] While Sergio Moro has then become Minister of Justice and Public Security under Jair Bolsonaro, Lula, newly re–elected president, received satisfaction in 2021 when the Supreme Court ruled that the judge was biased in his corruption trial.[348] Operation Car Wash was officially closed in February 2021.[349]

3. Bid Rigging in Oil Economies

Brazil started developing its oil industry almost five decades before the Kazakh one. Unlike its neighbours, the Latin American country saw its natural resources as public wealth from the beginning, but while Petrobras grew stronger, the political elite progressively

---

344 D. Alarcón, "What Led Peru's Former President to Take His Own Life?," *The New Yorker*, July 1, 2019, https://www.newyorker.com/magazine/2019/07/0 8/what-led-perus-former-president-to-take-his-own-life

345 "Protests in Brazil Fuelled by Popular Discontent with Corruption and Bad Public Services," *European Research Centre for Anti-Corruption and State-Building*, June 24, 2013, https://www.againstcorruption.eu/articles/protests-in-brazil-fuelled-by-popular-discontent-with-corruption-and-bad-public-services/

346 "The Role of Plea Bargains in the Fight Against Corruption: A Presentation by Brazil's Attorney General, Rodrigo Janot," Wilson Center, July 17, 2017, https://www.wilsoncenter.org/event/the-role-plea-bargains-the-fight-agains t-corruption-presentation-brazils-attorney-general

347 A. Fishman, R. M. Martins, L. Demori, G. Greenwald, and A. Audi, "'Their Little Show'," The Intercept, June 17, 2019, https://theintercept.com/2019/06/17 /brazil-sergio-moro-lula-operation-car-wash/

348 "Brazil's Supreme Court rules judge Moro was biased in Lula corruption trial," France 24, March 24, 2021, https://www.france24.com/en/americas/20210324 -brazil-s-supreme-court-rules-judge-moro-was-biased-in-lula-corruption-trial

349 "MPF anuncia fim da força-tarefa da operação Lava Jato no Paraná," [MPF announces the end of the Car Wash Operation task force in Paraná] Poder360, February 3, 2021, https://www.poder360.com.br/lava-jato/mpf-anuncia-fim-da-forca-tarefa-da-operacao-lava-jato-no-parana/

increased its control over the company. As readers will have understood, KazMunayGas cannot be compared to Petrobras, neither in terms of experience nor capacity. Yet, both companies were active promoters of bid rigging. This suggests that the excessive politicization of national oil companies may be among the leading causes of systematic bid rigging.

The practice is better understood as the informal side of tenders. Winners may be selected pre–emptively based on recommendations or win them for merits. Still, if the political elite and the national company are corrupt, they will expect to be bribed as a reward for assigning the contract. This phase is so crucial that often decides the fate of the deal between the parties: if the agreement is not reached a new tender is arranged with the selection of a new potential sub–contractor. On the other hand, if the agreement is reached, the contract serves to hide a continuous flux of money to oil majors' executives and political officials.[350] With the justification of the pandemic and the fall of oil prices, at the end of March 2020, the Kazakh government allowed companies to find service providers without tender procedures, a choice that likely facilitated further bribing.

As clarified, the Kazakh elite is aware of the scheme because companies share bribes with them:

> 'They know everything, and they are also part of tender procedures, we have special group X,[351] which controls [...] In case of questions, they usually invite representatives of departments to understand the reason for the contract and why in some cases we choose a single source instead of having tender procedures. There is also a specific process of approval of contracts: there are major contracts, which should be reviewed by authorities, and there are minor contracts, which do not need to be reviewed by authorities. But anyway, authorities are quite strong with us, and sometimes it is difficult to prove something if we do not have a good basis. And since they are

---

350 Bid rigging is so diffused that companies do it in any aspect of service supply to oil companies, including catering, as happened in 2015 with Compass Group, owner of Eurest Support Services. C. Putz, "Catering to Bribes in Kazakhstan," *The Diplomat*, June 25, 2015, https://thediplomat.com/2015/06/catering-to-br ibes-in-kazakhstan/

351 Anonymised.

184   THE HOUSE ALWAYS WINS

aware of the situation, it is quite difficult to argue because they know the subject very well.'[352]

Both in Kazakhstan and Brazil, bid rigging was so organised that major companies colluded with the respective national oil companies to facilitate the flux of bribes towards staff and the political elite. The advantage of this level of organisation is that every participant in the scheme has a cut while not having to fear prosecution from the local judiciary. What seems clear through the examples discussed is that the cooperation between ENI and KMG's corrupt executives had created space for Unaoil to join the bid rigging business to the detriment of real economic activity. Unlike KMG, Petrobras was the company effectively looking for sub–contractors and the scheme was simpler. A second difference is that the Kazakh authoritarian landscape allowed the strategy to thrive, while the Brazilian independent judiciary shut off bid ridding through Operation Car Wash. This is a symptom of how widespread the practice is, showing that as specious contract cancellation, its potential for generalisation extends well beyond oil economies and authoritarian countries. In fact, bid rigging takes place in authoritarian and liberal democratic countries alike.[353]

Another relevant distinction displayed in the cases under scrutiny is that the practice's initiator varies. In the Kazakh case, the collusion between political actors and international oil companies created the framework for bid rigging to occur, while in Brazil the national oil company seemed the original promoter of the practice. This is likely what tells apart a kleptocracy from a flawed democracy affected by political corruption: in the former politicians ask for bribes, while in the latter businessmen try to bribe them. A final important remark is that bid rigging is not a prerogative of international companies, nor only occurs in public procurement. Even if in the case of Kazakhstan only international operators have been presented, in Brazil mostly Brazilian companies took part in the practice. Similarly, in Kazakhstan, all tenders were private and

---

352 Financial department employee, interview by author, April 14, 2020.
353 "Fighting Bid Rigging in Public Procurement," *OECD*, https://www.oecd
.org/competition/cartels/fightingbidrigginginpublicprocurement.htm

organised by the main operator of the consortium ENI, even when colluding with KMG. On the other hand, the Brazilian case showed only cases of bid rigging in public procurement.

While bid rigging shows similarities with patrimonial embezzlement, as both can involve tenders, there is reason to argue that the practices are indeed different. In Chapter III, *Patrimonial Embezzlement*, former Prime Minister Kazhegeldin was presented as the promoter of rigged tenders that were assigned to companies connected to his political allies. The major difference with the practice discussed here is that patrimonialism is not a factor in bid rigging. Rather, businessmen used bribes to guarantee contracts for their companies or business groups. In other words, the goal is economic and not political. Still, the practices easily blend when politicians aim to improve their position in the power game among the elite ranks and the national institutional landscape. In a way, bid rigging frequently leads to patrimonial embezzlement. Table 11 summarises the actors, roles, and goals of bid rigging.

Table 11 Actors, roles, and goals of bid rigging

Actors involved	Role in the practice	Goal
Political elite	Passive receiver of bribes, but responsible for its patrimonial implications	Personal profit
National oil company	Connected to the tender	Personal and political elite's profit
Service companies	Money dispenser	Avoiding competition

4. Sub–Contracting Bribing

When it comes to rentierism, Kazakhstan and Brazil are different for at least two reasons: one is an authoritarian country whereas the other a liberal, albeit flawed, democracy; the former has an oil industry with strong foreign participation and the latter has always defended its public ownership over natural resources. Yet again, in the past twenty years, both countries have been touched by relevant corruption scandals revolving around bid rigging in their respective oil sectors.

The first suggested generalisation emerging from the cases is that bid rigging can occur in several industries, and the only practice requirement is the presence of procurement, either public or private. Only in the presence of a tender, companies and the political elite can rely on this form of collusion. Yet, if the contract is assigned by the company promoting it, the case can only lead to simple bribing. At the same time, the tender façade helps promote the contract to a wider audience. In this way, the tender loses its original intent of increasing competition and improving services while retaining the function of offering the company seeking the service to browse different potential investors. Since ENI and KMG subcontracted the possibility of choosing service providers, for Unaoil was relatively easy to mediate the bid rigging business. Yet, overlooking the quality of offered services may be among the reasons that delayed for years the realisation, albeit challenging, of the Kashagan project. As in any corruption case, quality is sacrificed for greed.

The second suggested generalisation is that in some countries bid rigging seems the only way to undercut competition. In some instances, it becomes so systematised that requires international investors to adapt to the country's informal rule if they intend to make profitable business. As seen in Kazakhstan, bid rigging has been a basic requirement of any tender organised in key projects of the oil industry for years. Companies could not cluelessly participate in a tender whether they intended to win it, and this had the effect of reducing the penetration of the market by new investors. This is one of the reasons explaining the diffusion of consultancy firms that advise clients on the political risks of investing in specific sectors of a country's economy. This is for instance the purpose of consultancy firms specialized in political risk management.

> There are a lot of potential oilfields but there has not been a new major green field investment in an oilfield in Kazakhstan in years. As analysts, we see that the country desperately needs new investments because oil is running out and the country's economy is even more dependent on it. The government should be more open, but when you talk with IOCs [international oil companies] they say that the government is still very difficult to deal with.

> It does not make sense and it's an ongoing question we do not have an answer for.[354]

Possibly the answer is simpler than it looks. The kleptocratic ruling elite has been so focused on reaping the benefits of the oil industry through bribery that it lost sight of the sustainability of its actions in the long run. The country needs new investments, but the kleptocrats do not intend to give up the immediate benefits they receive.

Again, bid rigging is such a common crime, that it is useful to acknowledge the specificities of the oil and rentier cases. A peculiarity of the cases analysed is that the practice becomes so remunerative that it can become a professional route per se. This does not only involve Unaoil as a company but also employees who specialise in that specific career track. By reading the emails exchanged by managers at Unaoil it becomes evident that their work consisted mainly in matching potential investors with corrupt local executives and politicians. This suggests how the success and career of key figures revolved around political connections rather than the know–how of the oil industry. For instance, the once manager of KMG Maksat Idenov switched to ENI, but it was also mentioned the case of the Italian Leonida Bortolazzo who went to work for the Kazakh government–owned KING. The table below shows a schematic version of the preconditions of transferability of the cases based on the M–STOUT scheme of external validity employed in quantitative analysis (Findley, Kikuta, and Denly 2021).

---

354 Political risk analyst, interview by author, June 21, 2021.

188 THE HOUSE ALWAYS WINS

Table 12 Bid rigging transferability to the target population

Dimension	Kazakhstan	Brazil	Rentier states
Mechanisms	Bid rigging	Bid rigging	Bid rigging
Settings	Businessmen colluding with the political elite	Businessmen colluding with the political elite	Businessmen aiming to decrease competition
Treatments	Working oil industry	Working oil industry	Industry using public or private procurement
Outcomes	Continuous influx of money through bribes	Continuous influx of money through bribes	Continuous influx of money through bribes
Units	Kazakh oil industry	Brazilian oil industry	Resource-rich country
Time	2001–2016	?–2014	Phase following the sinking of investments

Bid rigging is the fifth practice of the taxonomy and the last one identified as a major corruption crime. While informal practices in employment and recruitment described in the following chapter are the final step to answer the first research question, they are to be identified as cases of petty corruption. Also, the Kazakh bid rigging scandals allow an understanding of the general patterns of public procurement in the country. Finally, bid rigging circles back to patrimonial embezzlement because service contracts are often offered to strengthen political connections and consolidate the status of the elite.

5. Summary Sheet: Bid Rigging

Definition: collusion over tender procedures leading to the piloted assignation of contracts via bribe dispensing.

Actors involved: political elite, national oil companies, service companies.

Observed in: Kazakhstan, Brazil.

Outcomes: continuous influx of money to racketeers through bribes.

BID RIGGING 189

Context: resource-rich country.
Timeline: phase following the sinking of investments.

Figure 9   Visualisation of bid rigging

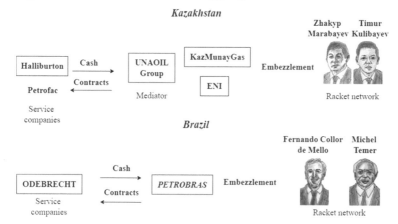

VIII Corruption on Kazakhs' Skin

> All key aspects of natural resources are handled by international companies and not Kazakh ones. This happens because the state can maneuver foreign companies using the arguments of ecology and visa.
> Political analyst, interview by author, Almaty, November 25, 2019.

> We sit on the top of a fortune, but we cannot seize it.
> Kazakh oil worker, interview by author, Aktau, December 7, 2019.

So far practices have been analysed with reference to decisions with a nationwide impact, but this chapter deals with local forms of informality. Whereas previous practices referred to the interaction between major oil companies and the government, here the local administration has a pivotal role. Throughout the 1990s, regional governors have been key pawns in Nazarbayev's strategy to control the oil sector. In fact, *akims* were appointed by the president himself, chosen on the basis of their loyalty to the patron (Ostrowski 2010). This allegiance rests on the possibility to reap the benefits of bid rigging as well as to exploit each interaction with companies to their advantage. Hence, in the long run, obedience to the regime is more remunerative.

Regional governors are still appointed by the central government, ensuring the capillary action of the elite. Nonetheless, since 2013 local *akims*, the equivalent of mayors of smaller cities and villages, are indirectly elected by *mäslihats*, local representative bodies voted by citizens. Still, in an untransparent electoral process with a dominant party, the presidential Nur–Otan (now Amanat), remained difficult to appoint representatives that felt accountable to the citizens of their areas. The reform of 2021 introducing the direct election of *akims* of small villages and rural districts improved the democratic governance of the Kazakh society,[355] but it had virtually no impact on the governance of the oil sector and its informality.

---

355 J. Musabayeva, "Vybory akimov: kak prohodit izbiratel'naâ kampaniâ v regionah," [Elections of the akims: how is the election campaign going in the regions], *Kazinform*, July 5, 2021, https://www.inform.kz/ru/vybory-akimov-kak-prohodit-izbiratel-naya-kampaniya-v-regionah_a3808909

The functions of *akims* include: creating plans for economic and social development of the territory; ensuring their implementation; managing the local budget; managing communal property; appointing and dismissing the heads of local executive bodies;[356] exercising other powers assigned to local executive bodies by law.[357] Therefore, *akimats* interact directly with companies on the fulfilment of local content requirements, in conjunction with the ministry of foreign affairs in deliberating visas for foreign employees; budgetary issues; designation of projects of corporate social responsibility; the respect of emission quotas and the correct disposal of waste materials from oilfields. The purpose of the *akimat* is simple: to ensure that companies abide by the law. Instead, *akims* have proven over and over to prefer to compromise on laws with corporations and face the discontent of citizens.

The chapter has been divided into two macro-sections: the first one focuses on the informal practices of the oil sector involving workers individually, whereas the second one discusses a series of good initiatives turned bad that directly affect the lives of citizens of the oil regions. The first section is directed at completing the taxonomy, whereas the second one has the objective of challenging the initial hypothesis on the trickle-down effect of corruption. Yet, the division is not clear-cut, because local content legislation, determining some of the practices discussed in the first macro-section, is also an example of positive initiatives that got corrupted, contributing to the overall discussion on the hypothesis.

Unlike in previous chapters, here there is no parallelism with other rentier countries. On the one hand, there is no need to prove the generalisation of practices widespread worldwide, while on the other there are several studies that have already asserted the strengths and weaknesses of most of the initiatives discussed (i.e. local content legislation, Extractive Industries Transparency Initiative, Corporate Social Responsibility, and ecological oversight in rentier countries).

---

356 Hence, potentially interfering with the work of directly elected officials.
357 "Akim," *Kazahstan. Nacional'naâ ènciklopediâ* [Kazakhstan. National encyclopaedia], Almaty, 2004. ISBN 9965-9389-9-7.

1. Working in a Kazakh Oil Region

Jobs in the oil sector are varied. In Kazakhstan as elsewhere, no job could be guaranteed without the continuous presence of an oil company, foreign or national, extracting crude oil and gas. Yet, the bulk of jobs is not in these companies as much as in the myriad of subcontractors offering them services: from enterprises realising infrastructures to those leasing boats and rigs for offshore operations, from transportation to catering services. As shown previously, these contracts are among the most eyed transactions by predatory managers. Monotowns were founded centring on the existence of oilfields where companies based their operations. Still, far from cities, *neftyaniki*, proud oil workers, settled with their families and contributed to the expansion of towns such as Aksai and Zhanaozen.

In his PhD thesis on *Industrial Relations in Kazakhstan's Oil Sector*, Paolo Sorbello (2021) argued that the implementation of neoliberal practices in Kazakhstan resulted in the precarisation of jobs (Totaro and Sorbello 2021). His study is a rare in-depth assessment of the transition of a vital sector for a rentier economy from a planned to a market economy. In his analysis of the industry, he divided the job into three phases: hiring, working, and outstaffing (Sorbello 2021), namely the demobilisation of workers at the end of the oilfield life cycle. Sharing the conclusions of the author, his division of the job phases is partially mirrored in this presentation of informal practices. While fieldwork for this research did not detect informal practices in the phase of outstaffing, their existence cannot be ruled out.

1.1 Informal Recruitment: Nepotism, Ghost, and Conditional Employment

In the recruitment phase, three major informal practices were observed:

- Nepotism.
- Ghost employment.
- Conditional employment.

194   THE HOUSE ALWAYS WINS

Nepotism is a form of favouritism based on relationships where someone in an official position exploits his or her power and authority to provide a job to a family member or friend, without regard to his or her qualifications.[358] This form of employment is more common in smaller, often Kazakh,[359] companies where a qualified employee uses his or her leverage within the company to facilitate the hiring process of relatives or acquaintances.[360] Still, also foreign companies succumb to the practice, particularly if the *akimat*, the local administration, pressures them to do it (Ostrowski 2010). This is often the result of negotiations to hire foreign specialists:

> The company needs a specialist and opens a general call. Based on the selection, said company decides to hire a qualified employee of nationality X. When the company requests the labour permit for this person, authorities often ask to hire a Kazakh instead. The company starts a negotiation to obtain the labour permit of the initially selected candidate by satisfying a condition: to hire the Kazakh one in a less relevant job position or part-time.[361]

These negotiations between companies and the *akimat* often result in ghost employment. As defined by an interviewee, ghost employees are people formally hired by foreign companies to meet the quotas required by the local content legislation, but that practically do not fulfil any function nor task in the organisation employing them, albeit receiving a small wage.[362] They can be well-connected individuals forced on the company registries by the *akimat*, or people with disabilities picked by companies just to meet the quotas (Sorbello 2021, 119). At times, these ghost employees do not even exist. Yet, as noted by Sorbello (2021), this negotiation over worker quotas is perceived as a nuisance by foreign companies that often delegate it to manpower agencies. In 2019, officers from the migration department were arrested with the accusation of taking bribes to speed up work permits of foreign workers (Sorbello 2021, 120). Clearly, this is but one of many cases of corruption where officials

---

358 "Nepotism," Transparency International, https://www.transparency.org/en/corruptionary/nepotism

359 Kazakh oil company employee, interview by author, Aktau, December 6, 2019. Financial department employee, interview by author, April 14, 2020.

360 Foreign oil company employee, interview by author, Aktau, December 3, 2019.

361 Executive director of a contractor company, interview by author, Aktau, December 3, 2019.

362 Kazakh oil company employee, interview by author, Aktau, December 6, 2019.

take advantage of their position for personal profit. Working permits are in fact one of the major tools that local authorities use to negotiate with companies.[363]

Finally, there is conditional employment,[364] a situation that requires the potential employee to satisfy specific conditions to get the job. The most requested ones are bribes[365] and sexual favours.[366] In Figure 10 below, there is an excerpt from a chat with an interviewee explaining the former.

Figure 10 Conditional employment

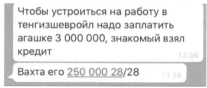

To get a job in TegizChevrOil[367] you need to pay to the agashka[368] 3 million tenge,[369] a friend took a loan. His shift is 250,000 tenge 28/28[370]

They say it depends on the wage, there are people with 100,000 tenge per shift
They have an extra 1.5 million tenge

Source: Catering contractor employee, interview by author, December 11, 2019.

---

363 Political analyst, interview by author, Almaty, November 25, 2019.
364 "What is a Conditional Employment Offer? (With Pros and Cons)," *Indeed*, November 15, 2021, https://uk.indeed.com/career-advice/starting-new-job/what-is-conditional-employment-offer
365 Refinery employee, interview by author, Nur-Sultan, February 27, 2020. Foreign oil company employee, interview by author, March 8, 2020. Atyrau activist, interview by author, March 21, 2020.
366 Catering contractor employee, interview by author, March 18, 2020. Catering contractor employee, interview by author, April 11, 2020.
367 Rather, the employment explained here is from a catering company working for TengizChevrOil. Hence, the American corporation is not the direct employer of these workers.
368 In Kazakhstan, this expression refers to an influential figure with strong personal connections allowing him to fulfil informal objectives (Oka 2018, 86).
369 Roughly $5,800, as of 2022.
370 The shift is based on 28 days; hence they are receiving 125,000 tenge per month ($242 in 2022).

196   THE HOUSE ALWAYS WINS

The unveiling of informal recruitment practices connected to local content legislation complements the study of Kalyuzhnova and Belitski (2019) on the interaction between local content legislation and corruption. In light of these practices, the authors' conclusion suggesting that corruption in local content implementation leads to more employment but not to more productivity is only logical (Kalyuzhnova and Belitski 2019, 73).

1.2   Informal Work: Economisation on Security, Resource, and Wage Embezzlement

In the work phase, there are three more informal practices taking place:

- Resource embezzlement.
- Wage embezzlement.
- Economizing on security.

Resource embezzlement takes place whenever workers steal equipment or resources they are responsible to produce or care for. While there were initial reports of oil disappeared in the early 1990s, interviewees confirmed it took place up until 2008.[371] The alleged reason is to resell the resource on the black market at a discounted price.[372]

Wage embezzlement is one of the major reasons behind the emergence of the first strikes in 2011 in the city of Zhanaozen.[373] Wage embezzlement does not consist of a direct embezzlement of the wage of workers. Rather, the practice consists of reporting higher wages paid to low–skilled workers to justify the appropriation of the company's earnings by managers. Wage embezzlement emerged in connection to KazMunayGas and its daughter companies in the region of Aktau:

> One of the workers wanted to get a certificate stating that he worked there and what his salary was in order to get a bank loan. He was not given a

---

371   Foreign oil company employee, interview by author, Aktau, December 3, 2019.
Kazakh oil company employee, interview by author, Aktau, December 6, 2019.
372   Ibidem.
373   Atyrau activist, interview by author, March 21, 2020.

certificate. He asked his sister, who worked at KazMunayGas in Astana to get this certificate, and it turned out that the salary reported was twice the amount he received. From there the conflict began.[374]

When strikes started in the region of Aktau in 2011, workers were indeed protesting the fact that their wages were too low to guarantee good living standards and that the management of the state-owned companies was profiting on their shoulders.[375] On the 16th of December 2011, the shooting of Zhanaozen workers and residents by the police and special forces in the monotown of the Aktau region has been a turning point for the industrial history of the Kazakh oil sector.[376] While the repression was authoritarian, resulting in sixty–four deaths and thousands of layoffs (Sorbello 2021, 97), afterwards working conditions in the region slowly improved.[377]

Finally, there is the economization of security measures and equipment. While interviewees working in Western oil companies reported of relatively high standards of security in their workplace,[378] those employed in Kazakh companies complained of theirs. Some of the examples include non–functioning fire alarms, cheap protective gloves and helmets that can lead to serious injuries and even death. The informal dimension here consists in the fact that companies frequently bypass rules by bribing security inspectors from the *akimat* to cancel inspections or directly paying the injured employee to avoid fines.[379]

---

374 Ibidem.
375 Proving a similar pattern in Russian national energy companies, Makarchev and Wieprzowski (2021) developed a model of state predation to understand the informal rules of these enterprises.
376 For an overview of the facts check the interviews at "The Zhanaozen Massacre: Kazakhstan on the 16th of December 2011," *Understanding Politics on YouTube*, December 16, 2020, https://www.youtube.com/watch?v=uQOkt8WTOCA and the testimony of E. Kostyuchenko, "What I didn't write about Zhanaozen," Open Democracy, January 17, 2018, https://www.opendemocracy.net/en/od r/what-i-didnt-write-about-zhanaozen/
377 Kazakh oil company employee, interview by author, Aktau, December 7, 2019. Foreign oil company employee, interview by author, Aktau, December 3, 2019.
378 Foreign oil company employee, interview by author, March 8, 2020. Refinery employee, interview by author, Nur-Sultan, February 27, 2020. Foreign oil company employee, interview by author, Aktau, December 3, 2019.
379 Kazakh oil company employee, interview by author, Aktau, December 6, 2019.

1.3 Kazakhization and Social Justice

While agreeing with Sorbello (2021) in assessing the harmful effect of the transition to the market economy, this research complements his picture by adding that the problem of exploitation is not only caused by neoliberal practices but also by 'deviated' or 'corrupted' ones. The trickle–down effect is here mirrored by the workplace culture of manpower agencies, that do exactly what Unaoil did for bid rigging. On the one hand, you have companies acquiring the monopoly of contract allocations, while on the other you have enterprises specialising in worker allocations to satisfy the formal requirements of local content legislation. Both actors take advantage of their dominant position requesting bribes from those they are supposed to serve. Table 13 summarises the actors and goals of each listed practice.

Table 13   Actors and goals of informal practices on the job

Practice	Actors involved	Goal
The Recruitment Phase		
Nepotism	Potential worker	Getting a job
	Recruiter	Personal profit
Ghost employment	Potential worker	Personal profit
	Recruiter	Satisfying local content requirements
Conditional employment	Potential worker	Getting a job
	Recruiter	Personal profit
The Work Phase		
Resource embezzlement	Worker	Personal profit
	Employer	Profit loss
Wage embezzlement	Worker	Wage loss
	Manager	Personal profit
Economizing on security	Worker	Increasing risk of injuries
	Employer	Increasing profit

All these practices have a strong potential for generalisation, not only to oil economies but to non–rentier countries and different sectors of the economy. It is, hence, more interesting to track down the reasons for the case–specific emergence of the practices. When Ostrowski published *Politics and Oil* (2010), he argued that

Nazarbayev managed to control the oil sector through patron–client networks and Kazakhization. To this, we shall add the precarisation of jobs in oil regions and the unequal socio–economic development of the country (Alzhanova and Nurzhaubayeva 2015).

By appointing trusted men of the regime as *akim,* the first president could control the sector, but since his control was based on clientelist relations, *akims* did not care to serve the people of their region as much as themselves and their patron. The *akimat* became the epicentre of petty corruption, where each administrative procedure was up for sale. Similarly, Kazakhization paved the way for more informality:

> I do not think that the Chinese are worse than the Canadians, they also have their own character. It's not about the Canadians or the Chinese, it's about our Kazakh side. The Kazakh side did not allow wages to be raised. They can dictate their terms to investors. The law of Kazakhstan applies here, you can do anything with these investors. In the worst case, you can take away money from the companies. They may demand, but I think that the fault is on the Kazakh side.[380]

Still, this is by no means a cultural–specific feature of Kazakhstani people. The reason why they violate rules is that they are left to fight with crumbles in a rigged game. Local content is, in principle, a good piece of legislation, but its implementation is distorted (Kalyuzhnova and Belitski 2019). In the early 2000s, Tokayev, Balgimbayev, and several other senior officials advocated for local content with the purpose of distracting protests in the Western regions from the regime[381] to foreign companies. What should have been a norm to allow Kazakhstani people to benefit from the wealth of their land became a measure to shift tensions from the Kazakh people–government axis towards the Kazakhstani–foreign investors axis. Many Kazakhstani employees became obsessed with how much more foreigners were paid, often without considering that they

---

380 Foreign oil company employee, interview by author, Aktau, December 7, 2019.
381 'You are living in poverty because all the money is going into the president's pockets' (Ostrowski 2010)

were compensated for working abroad and may have been more qualified for the job.[382]

Clearly, this should not exonerate oil multinationals complicit in the exploitation in the name of profit. Yet, the government dictate the rules, and instead of creating the conditions to facilitate the integration of foreign investors in the oil regions (i.e. courses to improve the preparation of the Kazakhstani workforce, issuing guidelines on minimal requirements to raise the quality of Kazakhstani products), they rooted a piece of legislation in a corrupt environment. Even though the quality of the fruit is excellent, eventually it gets corrupted in a basket full of rotten ones. This metaphor on the value of local content legislation in Kazakhstan is validated in the following section, where evidence shows how the intent of other functioning practices has been distorted.

2. Living in a Kazakh Oil Region

This section is dedicated to the initiatives promoted to improve transparency in the oil sector as well as the lives of citizens of the region. Yet, as it turned out, these initiatives ended up being corrupted by the decentralisation of corruption as well as, indirectly, by informal practices analysed so far: patrimonial embezzlement hinders the positive intents of the Extractive Industries Transparency Initiative (EITI), fine threats limit ecological oversight, and bid rigging at various levels affect them all. Sub–sections deal with the EITI, Corporate Social Responsibility (CSR) initiatives, and the Aarhus Convention respectively.

2.1 Good Initiatives Turned Bad: The EITI

The international community started to consider corruption a real problem at the end of the 1970s, when, as a reaction to the illegal political contributions made by foreign and domestic corporations

---

382 Foreign employees in Kazakhstan reported worrying episodes of violence perpetrated by Kazakhstani at the expense of Turkish, Indian, and Italian workers. Manager in a contractor company, interview by author, Aktau, December 5, 2019.

in the Watergate scandal,[383] the United States approved the Foreign Corrupt Practices Act[384] to criminalise the bribery of foreign officials by American firms. Still, a common effort started only in 1997 with the approval of the OECD's Anti-Bribery Convention,[385] that anticipated the creation of *ad hoc* national norms against bribery abroad in many Western countries (Olawuyi 2015). These norms were complemented by international treaties and mechanisms such as the Inter-American Convention against Corruption,[386] the Council of Europe's Group of States against Corruption,[387] or the United Nations Convention Against Corruption[388] (Pleines and Wöstheinrich 2016). A special tool designed for the extractive industry was the EITI, a mechanism conceived in the early 2000s to improve transparency while protecting oil companies from the repercussions arising from the unilateral disclosure of controversial payments (Moisé 2020).

Under the EITI scheme, a country can be either a candidate or compliant. To become a candidate, the government of the country is required to issue an official statement where it declares its intention to implement the EITI. During this phase, the government must declare its willingness to cooperate with civil society

---

383 A. Eberhardt, "How the Foreign Corrupt Practices Act Came to Be," *Corporate Compliance Insight,* July 3, 2018, https://www.corporatecomplianceinsights.com/foreign-corrupt-practices-act-came/

384 "Foreign Corrupt Practices Act (FCPA): Congressional Interest and Executive Enforcement," *Congressional Research Service* (1977), https://archive.org/stream/R41466ForeignCorruptPracticesActFCPACongressionalInterestandExecutiveEnforcement-crs/R41466%20Foreign%20Corrupt%20Practices%20Act%20%28FCPA%29_%20Congressional%20Interest%20and%20Executive%20Enforcement_djvu.txt

385 OECD, Convention on Combating Bribery of Foreign Public Officials in International Business Transactions and Related Documents (Paris November 21, 1997), https://www.oecd.org/daf/anti-bribery/ConvCombatBribery_ENG.pdf

386 OAS, Inter-American Convention Against Corruption (March 29, 1996), http://www.oas.org/en/sla/dil/inter_american_treaties_B-58_against_Corruption.asp

387 Council of Europe, Group of States Against Corruption, https://www.coe.int/en/web/greco

388 United Nations, United Nations Convention Against Corruption (December 9, 2003), https://www.unodc.org/documents/brussels/UN_Convention_Against_Corruption.pdf

representatives, appoint an independent personality to lead the implementation process, and then establish a multi-stakeholder group overseeing it. The candidacy period is characterised by the setup of procedures that all the companies operating in the extractive sector are requested to satisfy.[389] Reports should be produced following a process that is comprehensible, actively promoted, and publicly accessible. Information disclosed in the reports should include details of the call for proposals and bidding process for exploration; the terms of development contracts; payments by companies to governments, from royalties to taxes and signing bonuses; pricing decisions; the size of reserves; the location of resources; possible informed consent to communities affected by the agreements; government budgets on the distribution of resource rents (Haufler 2010). Once the country has fulfilled the sign-up, preparation, and disclosure requirements, it becomes compliant.

Since 2011, Kazakhstan has been an EITI-compliant country,[390] but on the pages of *State Responses to Reputational Concerns*, Saipira Furstenberg (2018) argued that the Kazakh elite had already learnt 'to bypass the international reforms that could threaten its informal practices' (Furstenberg 2018, 15). In a more nuanced way, NGO activists that participated in the initiative since its initial implementation argued that transparency in the extractive industry greatly improved since 2005, stating that the comparison with 2020: 'is like earth and sky'.[391] International consortia especially seemed more open towards transparency initiatives than Kazakh ones.[392] Yet, the effort is not fully clear to many of the civic participants,

---

389 EITI, How to become an implementing country, https://eiti.org/join-EITI

390 Although Öge (2017b; 2017a) argued that norms of transparency promotion, including the EITI, were only adopted because of strong incentives, such as 2014 Russia's annexation of Crimea.

391 Director of an NGO advocating for the environment, interview by author, Almaty, March 18, 2020. Confirmed also by the director of an NGO advocating for civic activism, interview by author, Almaty, March 18, 2020, and by the director of an NGO advocating for the environment, interview by author, Aktau, March 26, 2020.

392 Director of an NGO advocating for civic activism, interview by author, Almaty, March 18, 2020. Confirmed also by the director of an NGO advocating for the environment, interview by author, Atyrau, April 4, 2020.

because the roundtable strives to reconcile different figures supplied by government and companies.[393]

> One of the general purposes is that people should find no discrepancies between what is declared and what is paid. On the contrary, reports showed actual discrepancies. Not much, but they were there. Auditors asked if this was corruption and if something should be done. If we find discrepancies, do you give fines or jail someone? There was no answer. People have information but do not know what to do with it.[394]

As expected, though, financial department employees suggest that the reconciliation of figures is often done before reaching the multistakeholder platform of the EITI:

> They requested us to amend our budget, to move this portion to the next year, where their budget is higher than the previous one. That was a request from the *akimat*, and we could not say no. We tried our best to reduce this difference, but in the end, they pushed us, and we accepted it. We did as they said.[395]

As argued by Ofori and Lujala (2015), the EITI leads to information disclosure rather than transparency, because the latter implies the understanding of disclosed information. Yet, case studies from Ghana, Nigeria (Nwapi 2015), and the very own Kazakhstan (Öge 2017b), showed how the overly technical reports are understood only by experts in the sector (Kolstad and Wiig 2009). Interviewees for this research argued that Kazakhstan has a limited number of investigative journalists who can decipher reports and 'translate' them to the public. [396]

> To write about this, you need to immerse yourself in this topic, you need to understand it, and study the material. But there are very few journalists able to do this, especially in the peripheries. There are several people in Astana

---

393 Director of an NGO advocating for the environment, interview by author, Almaty, March 18, 2020. Confirmed also by the director of an NGO advocating for the environment, interview by author, Atyrau, April 4, 2020.

394 Director of an NGO advocating for the environment, interview by author, Pavlodar, March 21, 2020. Confirmed by the director of an NGO advocating for the environment, interview by author, Aktau, March 26, 2020.

395 Financial department employee, interview by author, April 14, 2020.

396 Director of an NGO advocating for civic activism, interview by author, Almaty, March 18, 2020. Director of an NGO advocating for the environment, interview by author, Pavlodar, March 21, 2020.

and Almaty, but all the rest mostly write *post–factum* reports, and only if there is a scandal. Nobody does investigative journalism. [397]

Also, neither the government nor companies have any real interest to draw the attention on the reports, which are put on a shelf and forgotten.[398]

> They started implementing hundreds of projects, many related to communication in administrations and schools. The effect is very weak. People are receiving the data, but as time passes there is no impact. [...] In the beginning, officials were very scared, expecting that normal citizens would start asking questions, but this did not happen.[399]

In their review of studies on the EITI, Rustad, Le Billon, and Lujala (2017) observed that the objective of increasing revenues through the reduction of corruption had been considered achieved only by 15% of the studies (Rustad, Le Billon, and Lujala 2017, 155). In line with this conclusion, most interviewees argued that the EITI did not improve corruption in Kazakhstan:[400]

> Corruption is hidden in the production sharing agreements that were made at the very beginning, and about which a lot of information is not available. They are undisclosed and both the government and companies want to keep it that way. If we talk about real corruption, then no, it has not decreased. Many contracts are still closed. What really happens, no one knows.[401]

Ineffective and underachieving, if judged by its results, the EITI is a waste of funds. In Kazakhstan, the initiative had been funded by

---

397 The director of an NGO advocating for the environment, interview by author, Aktau, March 26, 2020. Confirmed also by the director of an NGO advocating for free and independent media, interview by author, Nur-Sultan, March 21, 2020.

398 Director of an NGO advocating for civic activism, interview by author, Almaty, March 18, 2020.

399 Director of an NGO advocating for the environment, interview by author, Pavlodar, March 21, 2020. Confirmed also by the director of an NGO advocating for the environment, interview by author, Atyrau, April 4, 2020.

400 Director of an NGO advocating for the environment, interview by author, Atyrau, April 4, 2020. Confirmed by the director of an NGO advocating for the environment, interview by author, Aktau, March 26, 2020, and by the director of an NGO advocating for the environment, interview by author, Aktau, March 26, 2020.

401 Director of an NGO advocating for free and independent media, interview by author, Nur-Sultan, March 21, 2020.

the Soros Foundation with more than $1 million over twelve years.[402] Nevertheless, NGOs divided into factions and competed for funding, generating another undesired effect.[403] In 2016, the Soros Foundation decided to focus on other projects, leaving the burden of the EITI to the government. Yet, the executive did not accept the task, and NGOs part of the initiative had to look for new sources of funding, including the World Bank (Furstenberg 2018, 2). As for local content legislation, while the EITI is in principle a positive initiative with the potential to greatly improve the transparency of the extractive industry in Kazakhstan, the government promoted it with a different objective in mind. As argued by Furstenberg (2018), Kazakhstan joined the EITI to improve its reputation (Furstenberg 2018, 14).

2.2 Good Initiatives Turned Bad: CSR

CSR is an umbrella definition that includes a series of initiatives promoted by large corporations to produce a positive social impact and compensate for the negative externalities determined by their activity in the region. As testified by the behavioural change of companies such as Ford Motors, the awareness of corporations about the impact of their activity on the environment and societies increased enormously over the last century (Moura–Leite and Padgett 2011). Since Howard Bowen's *Social Responsibility of the Businessman* (1953), the understanding of what could be acknowledged as CSR grew to include any activity with the potential to enhance the sustainable development and welfare of societies (Kirat 2015). In the oil sector, the external costs of the action of national and international corporations have produced incalculable environmental damages, led to increasing unemployment, and impoverished the regions where oilfields are located (Onwuka 2005). In statistical terms, Will Hickey (2012) showed how production sharing agreements are associated with an inverse effect on human development capital investments.

---

402 Manager at the Soros Foundation, interview by author, Almaty, March 3, 2020.
403 Ibidem.

206   THE HOUSE ALWAYS WINS

As anticipated, consortia promoted initiatives of corporate social responsibility since their first involvement in Kazakhstan. Also in this case, projects are, in principle, a great opportunity for the social development of the regions where they are implemented, but as soon as greedy officials intervene, good intentions derail. A few good examples come from the region of Western Kazakhstan, where the money deployed by KPO was used to build the opulent 'Atakamen' culture building, realised with 9.5 billion tenge; a grand tennis court that cost 1.6 billion tenge in 2014; the bridal building 'Sultanat Sarayi', realised with $8.5 million in 2012; the 2015 reconstruction of the 'Youth Stadium', that cost 1.3 billion tenge; the embellishment of the right bank of the Chagan River.[404] None of these projects is a priority for the region, already suffering from insufficient infrastructures. Quite on the contrary, initiatives are often conceived for the wealthy individuals living in the area, particularly those connected with the *akimat*. But even so, the realisation is often short-sighted: the reconstruction of the 'Youth Stadium' revealed insufficient, as the building remained closed due to not functioning equipment; and the embellishment of the bank of the Chagan River caused environmental damage to the nearby forest.

This pattern is valid for each of the Kazakh oil regions. Globally, corporations adopt CSR initiatives as part of a public strategy to improve their reputation and leverage their position with local administrations and governments (Amujo et al. 2012; Wiig and Kolstad 2010; Uldam and Hansen 2017). In Kazakhstan, companies simply deploy money,[405] but it is the *akimat* to compile a list of priority projects to realise:[406] 'the *akim* of Mangistau prefers sport infrastructures, the *akim* of Eastern Kazakhstan spent 2 billion tenge

---

404 E. Lonkina, "Dvorec za 9,5 mlrd i drugie zdaniâ Ural'ska, postroennye na neftânye dividendy," [Palace for 9.5 billion and other buildings in Uralsk built on oil dividends], *Ak Zhalyk*, October 8, 2021, https://kz.kursiv.media/2021-10 -08/dvorec-za-95-mlrd-i-drugie-zdaniya-uralska-postroennye-na-neftyanye/

405 Director of an NGO advocating for free and independent media, interview by author, Nur-Sultan, March 21, 2020.

406 Financial department employee, interview by author, April 14, 2020. Confirmed also by the director of an NGO advocating for the environment, interview by author, Pavlodar, March 21, 2020.

on the hockey team, the *akim* of Atyrau spends more on hospitals and houses.'[407]

Chosen by the ruling elite, *akims* often pick projects based on their preference or needs because they feel unaccountable to the citizens of their region. At times, the infrastructure chosen can be useful, but the process through which the contractor has been selected is not regular, such as in the case of the central swimming pool in Atyrau.[408] After having won the tender either through a bid rigging or because of political connections, what firms build is often low quality products caused by savings on materials and equipment.[409] In Kazakhstan, as elsewhere, CSR initiatives have the potential to generate positive effects on the target regions, but in practice projects are scattered and ineffective (Gonzalez 2016; Andreas Engen, Mikkelsen, and Grønhaug 2010), useful only to fuel local corruption.

2.3 Good Initiatives Turned Bad: The Aarhus Convention

As obvious as it sounds, oil companies affect the lives of citizens also through their environmental impact. In general, each company receives yearly minor environmental fines from the administration and pays without contesting them.[410] Though, as seen with fine threats, when greater sanctions are inflicted the negotiations pave the way for informal agreements at the expense of the environment and citizens. In this aspect, international and Kazakh companies seem to be equally responsible when it comes to pollution, but big consortia have the highest share in terms of both emissions and waste. As reported by interviewees, international consortia have a

---

407 Director of an NGO advocating for the environment, interview by author, Almaty, March 18, 2020.

408 A. Vidianova, "Central'nyj plavatel'nyj bassejn v Atyrau okazalsâ nevostrebovannym," [The central swimming pool in Atyrau turned out to be unclaimed], Kapital, January 10, 2017, https://kapital.kz/business/56572/tsentral-nyy-plavatel-nyy-basseyn-v-atyrau-okazalsya-nevostrebovannym.html

409 At times initiatives are also good, as confirmed by a foreign oil company employee, interview by author, Aktau, December 7, 2019, and the director of an NGO advocating for the environment, interview by author, Aktau, March 26, 2020.

410 Refinery employee, interview by author, Nur-Sultan, February 27, 2020, but confirmed in most interviews with employees.

208 THE HOUSE ALWAYS WINS

greenhouse emission quota to respect, but these limits can be negotiated and bought by different operators.[411]

Since 2000 Kazakhstan has ratified the Convention on Access to Information, Public Participation in Decision Making and Access to Justice in Environmental Matters,[412] widely known as the Aarhus Convention. According to this international treaty, the affected population should be an active participant in decisions giving them the rights to: 'be informed of environmentally significant matters, to participate in environmentally significant decision making, and to legal redress in cases when their right to be informed or participate in decision making has been denied' (Watters 2013, 159).

Regardless of imposed restrictions, an operating extractive site is equally harmful to villages in proximity. The most famous case of air pollution that led to the poisoning of the local population was in the small village of Berezovka, located twenty-five kilometres from Aksai and only five from the oilfield of Karachaganak. Once a state-run collective farm, the village was the closest to the extraction site since the relocation of the citizens of Tungush to Uralsk in 2003 (Watters 2013, 157). Since 2002, members of the Berezovka Initiative Group started to associate: 'their worrisome health symptoms with the constant gas flaring, strong smell of sulfur, and increased industrial activity at Karachaganak' (Watters 2013, 160). Despite their continuous requests, KPO and the *akimat* agreed on a reduction of the sanitary protective zone to a three-kilometres radius, effectively avoiding the need to relocate the village (Watters 2013, 159).

From that moment, assisted by the American NGO Crude Accountability the activism of the Berezovka Initiative Group stepped up. Continuous activities included the intervention of the Office of the Compliance Advisor Ombudsman at the International Finance

---

411 Financial department employee, interview by author, April 14, 2020. Clearly, the market of greenhouse emissions has the potential to pave the way for new forms of informality.

412 "Convention on Access to Information, Public Participation in Decision Making and Access to Justice in Environmental Matters," *United Nations Economic Commission for Europe*, June 26, 1998, Denmark, chrome-extension://efaidnbmnnni bpcajpcglclefindmkaj/viewer.html?pdfurl=https%3A%2F%2Funece.org%2FD AM%2Fenv%2Fpp%2Fdocuments%2Fcep43e.pdf&clen=51257&chunk=true

Corporation, private investment arm of the World Bank (Watters 2013, 175; Weinthal and Watters 2010, 782); frequent health checks on villagers contradicting emissions reports issued by KPO; inquiries and articles on the local newspapers *Uralskaya Nedelya* and *Respublika*; repeated appeals to Nazarbayev (Weinthal and Watters 2010, 797). Finally, in solidarity with the Berezovka Initiative Group, Green Salvation,[413] an Almaty–based NGO, submitted two complaints against KPO for violation of the Aarhus Convention (Watters 2013, 158; Weinthal and Watters 2010, 794). In 2006, all this advocacy managed to force the government to reinstate the five-kilometre sanitary protection zone, arguing that previous changes had been done illegally (Weinthal and Watters 2010, 803). Still, the village was not relocated, likely because none of the actors involved intended to pay. Consistently ignored, the tragedy of Berezovka unfolded in November 2014, when twenty children and three teachers were rushed to the hospital for fainting, dizziness, and nose bleeds.[414] Citizens blamed intensified flaring from the oilfield, while in the aftermath the *akimat* continued supporting the thesis that the ecological situation was normal and KPO could not be blamed.[415]

Only in 2015, relocation was offered, with the excuse that KPO intended to expand the infrastructures of the oilfield and without admitting their responsibility for the 2014 accident. As for Tungush years before, the process of relocation was untransparent, not carried out by a third independent party but by the consortium itself. Also, rather than a cash compensation that could have allowed affected citizens to choose where to move, the consortium offered assigned houses.[416] Years later, in 2019, the artist and photographer Nata Li staged 'Afterwords' in Almaty, an exhibition of pictures of

---

413 Interview by author, Almaty, December 11, 2019.

414 J. Lillis, "Kazakhstan: Major Gas Field Suspected in Children's Poisoning," *Eurasianet*, December 4, 2014, https://eurasianet.org/kazakhstan-major-gas-field-suspected-in-childrens-poisoning

415 T. Kuzmina, "29 school students and teachers faint one after another in Western Kazakhstan," Tengrinews, December 1, 2014, https://en.tengrinews.kz/emergencies/29-school-students-and-teachers-faint-one-after-another-in-257706/

416 Crude Accountability, "Berezovka: Exodus," on YouTube, December 19, 2015, https://www.youtube.com/watch?v=srAdwG_U-Ds

210　THE HOUSE ALWAYS WINS

the abandoned buildings of Berezovka with tales from one of the children that survived the accident.[417]

A similar issue arose years earlier near the Tengiz oilfield. Located about twenty kilometres from the site, citizens of the village of Sarykamys spent months requesting the intervention of the *akimat* to force the American major to improve their living situation. While they presented medical evidence testifying the harmful effects of the emissions on their health, the company and local administration played again with rules, changing the limits of the sanitary zone: if in 1985, after the fire in Tengiz, the Soviet health ministry established a sanitary protection zone of thirty–two kilometres radius from the oilfield and forced the stop of operations until the full relocation of villages outside that area, since renewed activity in Tengiz the radius of the sanitary zone was decreased to ten. After months spent contesting medical evidence and citizens' concerns, finally, in November 2001 TengizChevrOil and the then Kazkhoil agreed to relocate the small village of Sarykamys at their expense (Peck 2004, 157). The stall was yet again for economic reasons.

In their 2020 documentary,[418] Lukpan Akhmedyarov and Raul Uporov, journalists of *Uralskaya Nedelya*, testified of worrying pollution levels for the citizens of the Aktyubinsk, Mangystau, and Atyrau regions. Yet, the documentary focused exclusively on oilfields managed by Chinese corporations, giving the false impression that only Chinese corporations are to blame. As discussed so far, all international companies are accountable for such irresponsible behaviour, including American (Chevron), Italian (ENI), and Anglo–Dutch (Shell) operators. In fact, it is the biggest consortium in the country with the participation of all major transnational corporations that caused water pollution in Kazakhstan's share of the Caspian Sea. Only in 1998, the drilling activity of the then OKIOK

---

417 E. Sorokina, "Images of the Abandoned Village of Berezovka, Kazakhstan, Showcased at George Washington University," Crude Accountability, February 24, 2020 https://crudeaccountability.org/images-of-the-abandoned-village-of-berezovka-kazakhstan-showcased-at-george-washington-university/

418 L. Akhmedyarov and R. Uporov, "The Other Side of Oil," *Crude Accountability* and on *YouTube*, March 26, 2020, https://crudeaccountability.org/the-other-side-of-oil-documentary/

consortium in Kashagan indirectly caused the death of 30,000 seals, as reported by the NGO *Caspyi Tabigaty* (i.e. Caspian Environment).[419]

Finally, waste management from extractive sites is a function often subcontracted to Kazakh operators that get rid of toxic substances dumping them not far from villages where people live. A good example is in the Mangistau region, near Zhetybay,[420] where for years people have been complaining about the work of the responsible society, Uralenergostroy, that was simply dumping toxic waste near the village. Again, even in this case, the *akim* has been defending the work of the company.[421] As discussed in Chapter V, *Fine Threats*, in Tengiz the sulphur storage and transportation was a way to enrich the owners of the TTG group, including Sauat Mynbayev, through lucrative contracts. These are just a few examples of the many environmental violations discussed with interviewees from Atyrau, Pavlodar, Zhetybay, Zhanaozen, and Aktau.

3. The Tick-the-Box Strategy

While explaining their approach, the interviewee from the Soros Foundation frankly outlined that in their organisation they distinguish files between initiatives where there is political will from those where there is not. If there is no political will, they do not dedicate much effort to the file because most of the care and money invested would be wasted.[422] On a similar note, another interviewee remarked how: 'Kazakhstan spends a lot of money on image events rather than on improvement of infrastructures.'[423] Both these positions reflect one simple truth: in an authoritarian regime

---

419 Director of an NGO advocating for the environment, interview by author, Atyrau, April 4, 2020.
420 Precisely at 43°37'15.5"N 52°07'05.07"E.
421 Olga Yurieva, "Žiteli posëlka v Mangistauskoj oblasti zadyhaûtsâ ot zapaha čërnogo zolota," [Residents of a village in the Mangistau region suffocate from the smell of black gold], *KTK*, March 11, 2013, https://www.ktk.kz/ru/news/video/2013/03/11/21662/
422 Manager at the Soros Foundation, interview by author, Almaty, March 3, 2020.
423 Director of an NGO advocating for the environment, interview by author, Almaty, March 18, 2020.

governments and administrations do not care about their citizens as long as their actions do not threaten their legitimacy.

The red thread connecting the informal practices in the work environment and the negative outcome of potentially positive initiatives is explained by a policy implementation lacking the political will to improve the lives of citizens. As a rule of thumb, the Kazakh elite repeatedly proved to be interested solely in its public image and reputation abroad but effectively changed the living situation of its citizens for the better only when forced, aware that each concession limited its ability to profit. This tick–the–box strategy is even more evident in the oil regions, where citizens had to fight for each social improvement, way before the Zhanaozen shooting. This last event was a turning point only for the average employees of state–owned enterprises, but major ecological problems remained unaddressed because citizens had virtually no negotiation power.

Inequal socio–economic development, precarisation of jobs, and corrupt practices favoured the diffusion of the six informal practices affecting work in the oil industry. For instance, nepotism is a hiring practice well–diffused worldwide, but the fact that is so widespread among Kazakhstani ranks suggests that the highly informal context contributes to its circulation. On the other hand, conditional employment becomes an informal hiring rule only if the justice system is utterly compromised. Also, ghost employment is the practice that connects more closely to the set of policies approved only for reputational concerns, because it allows companies to tick–the–box while not really employing Kazakhstani people. Both wage embezzlement and the economisation of security appliances show a widespread will of employers to abide by rules only on paper while trying to maximise their profit. On the contrary, resource embezzlement is an attempt by workers to make ends meet.

Yet, local content legislation was not the only policy whose intended objective was missed due to an insincere policy implementation. The EITI is widely ineffective, primarily because corruption is hidden among the pages of production sharing agreements. Initiatives of corporate social responsibility do not achieve their intended objective because projects are selected by an untransparent and unaccountable local administration. Finally, ecological oversight does not work, often relying only on the activity of NGOs and citizens' initiatives whose deeds remain unheard by the *akimat*. If transferred to the *Global Informality Project,* most of the examples shown in this chapter would fall in the cluster 'playing the letter of the rules against their spirit' and legislating for unfitting purpose, where: 'The latter deprives the formal/informal division of its sense: the formal law becomes an expression of informal interests'.[424]

---

424 "Category: Playing the letter of the rules against their spirit," *The Global Informality Project,* https://www.in-formality.com/wiki/index.php?title=Category :Playing_the_letter_of_the_rules_against_their_spirit

Conclusion
Understanding Strategies and Informal Rules

> You could knock at the door, but behind it there is a wall. And, of course, for foreigners… they enter five rooms, but there are ten more they cannot enter. To a certain extent it's like a labyrinth with a lot of corridors, but there are some doors which can help you to go from square one to the final.
> Former oil investor, interview by author, July 1, 2021

What are the informal practices taking place in a rentier state? As the research testified, the major informal practices identified in this taxonomy are five: patrimonial embezzlement, state racketeering, fine threats, specious contract cancellations, and bid rigging.

Patrimonial embezzlement is the practice taking place when money embezzled from the initial contracts of the rentier sector empowers the local elite to create a more stable authoritarian state resting on patron–client relations. It is not necessarily the money embezzled from these deals to develop the relationship; often the perspective of future enrichment is sufficient to guarantee the followers' loyalty. While in Venezuela, Gómez's embezzlement and patrimonialism were more evidently related, Nazarbayev's patrimonial embezzlement was limited to the elite circle. Still, he relied on the promise of bid rigging to ensure the regional grip of power through *akims*.

State racketeering consists of manipulation of rules and abuse of power to obtain assets otherwise unreachable. The criminal actions of the kleptocratic elite are backed by substantial impunity upheld by a partisan justice system. State racketeering is a versatile practice because can be used to strengthen the stability of the elite in power, or at the opposite, to challenge it. Hence, investigating cases of state racketeering allows us to assess the quality of the relationship between their promoters and the autocrat, predicting possible elite infighting.

Fine threats are used to re–negotiate contracts whose terms, according to the government, have obsolesced. While fines are a formal tool, in these cases their use becomes entirely informal because it entails convincing investors to join the negotiation table.

The use of fine threats by the local elite testifies to a shift in the power balance with investors. In fact, when the elite starts relying on these means the country has a relatively stable economy, whereas when contracts were first signed the government's desperate need for cash jeopardised its contractual power *vis–à–vis* foreign corporations. Discussed in *The EU and European Transnational Companies in Central Asia* (Moisé and Sorbello 2022) and expanded in Chapter V, *Fine Threats,* the ENI case study is a good example of this informal practice.

Specious contract cancellations consist of the irregular annulation of contracts on assets that the local elite would like to control. Like state racketeering, this is another form of hostile competition where private actors are leading the initiative. On the other hand, this practice makes more extensive use of local courts relying on the fact that foreign investors have a contextual disadvantage. In specious cancellations, targeted investors have a chance to defend their interests through international arbitrations, even though they rarely manage to recover their investments.

Finally, bid rigging is the practice consisting of the collusion of parties that determines the unfolding of an irregular tender outcome. This is the most diffused among the practices listed so far, particularly because the number of service contracts and companies involved is the highest of the whole sector: 'These contracts become prized assets for companies delivering the services, because they guarantee income for a fixed period of time' (Sanghera and Satybaldieva 2020, 513). This form of collusion is not sought after by top officials as much as minor governmental actors and regional governors willing to retain some of the earnings emerging from the exchange between their institution and the companies interested in those contracts.

As explained in Chapter III, *Patrimonial Embezzlement,* a final strategy connected to state racketeering and bid rigging is character assassination. Already an entry of the *Global Encyclopaedia of Informality* (Samoilenko et al. 2018), character assassination consists of the political killing of a public figure through the fabrication of evidence or *kompromat* (Ledeneva 2006, 58). While this is certainly a tool employed by the authoritarian regime of Nazarbayev throughout the years, this is a practice of informal governance with no impact on the economic management of the sector. Also, as demonstrated on the pages of *Populism in Moldova's Informal Political System* (Moisé 2021), this practice is not limited to authoritarian or rentier states.

While it is imprecise to talk about a hierarchy among these different practices, there is certainly a chronological implementation that derives from the workflow of the oil and gas industry. Clearly, without the original contracts on the development of the oilfields, neither of the practices listed could take place. Yet, once these contracts are signed, all practices can occur. The only real subordination exists between patrimonial embezzlement and fine threats because they refer to the original contract negotiation and to its subsequent renegotiation respectively. Still, both occur only in countries where the oil sector is not nationalised.

An element that allows to distinguish among the practices is the object of contention. More often the objective is contracts, but at times also whole companies. Yet, the difference is not significant because by taking control of companies, racketeers intend to gain control over the exploitation rights that these companies have over oilfields. In other words, what racketeers intend to acquire is not the oil itself but another source of rent.

While corruption is often discussed in connection to competitive market economies, the analysis of these practices suggests that the core problem is their anti–competitive nature. As remarked by Kartick Gupta (2017) on the pages of *Are Oil and Gas Firms More Likely to Engage in Unethical Practices than Other Firms*, competitiveness in the market and institutional settings are the main determinants of the levels of corruption (Gupta 2017). This means that although there is free competition, or the sector is nationalised, corruption is more likely to occur if there is excessive concentration of power both at the market and institutional level.

Finally, discussions on corruption make distinctions between the private and public nature of the goals difficult by design. It is assumed that all these practices procure, directly or indirectly, some form of enrichment for the actors promoting them. Yet, the main goal may be public in nature, such as consolidating the grip on power, strengthening the country's economy, or improving the relative stability of the national oil company. However, in the context of state capture, there is an indistinguishable mix between a state and a dictator's property. Hence, no generalisation is possible, and all considerations should be case or even episode–specific. At times, the elite will use national companies to justify their actions through the prism of policy, but on other occasions, some of its members will rely on private companies in their rise to power to own sufficient means to challenge the autocrat. Ultimately, to distinguish the practices it is necessary to understand the context as much as the *modus operandi* and the main objective. Table 14 below reflects the issues discussed so far.

Table 14   Objectives of informal practices

Practice	Object of contention	Main objective	Type of rentier economy
Patrimonial embezzlement	Contracts on oilfield exploitation	Embezzling money to create patron–client relationships	Open to foreign investment
State racketeering	Companies' property or contracts for oilfield exploitation	Taking over assets	Open or nationalised
Fine threats	Contracts on oilfield exploitation	Renegotiating contracts	Open to foreign investment
Specious contract cancellations	Contracts on oilfield exploitation	Taking over assets	Open to foreign investment
Bid rigging	Service contracts involving sub–contractors	Winning contracts	Open or nationalised

The reasoning focusing on the public or private property of assets echoes the debates on resource nationalism, but as anticipated in the introduction, the usefulness of this concept when discussing Kazakhstan is dubious. Already Koch and Perrault (2019) argued for a critical understanding of the concept. Their main argument focused on the idea that the traditional realist perspective tends to oversimplify the oil cycle expecting to predict specific behaviours from each involved actor (Koch and Perreault 2019, 3). Quite on the contrary, the critical approach proposed by the authors understands resource nationalism as a 'political discourse' (Koch and Perreault 2019, 1), where each term must be critically evaluated. When discussing Kazakhstan, the problem is double: the political discourse is in fact just a discourse, and neither term of the expression applies. It is true that Nazarbayev often presented oil as a means to empower the Kazakh nation to develop the country, but this was a rhetorical distortion to legitimise his actions. Particularly in the oil region, Kazakhstanis fought, protest after protest, to improve their living conditions. While the country's status improved overall, it never felt like a national achievement but rather as a scheme of elite enrichment in which citizens were not taken into consideration.

Therefore, it was never 'resource nationalism' as much as 'elite rentierism'. The Central Asian government never tried to take ownership of the 'resource' as much as the rent it produced. Also, when KazMunayGas came in possession of major shares in the biggest consortia, the 'nation' never enriched as a result, only members of Nazarbayev's circle did. The lack of distinction between the rhetoric of the Kazakh regime and its actions, and the equalization between 'statal' and 'national' property is what distinguished this analysis from both articles of Sarsenbayev (2011) and Domjan and Stone (2010). In fact, based on the assumption that a public company ultimately acquired the asset, the former presented the expropriation of Tristan Oil in Kazakhstan and the latter that of Yukos in Russia as examples of resource nationalism (Sarsenbayev 2011, 378; Domjan and Stone 2010, 41). Given that this work focused on both goals and ways in which the actors involved acquired the asset, Tristan Oil was discussed as a case of specious contract cancellation, and Yukos as an example of state racketeering. Neither of them was compared to the fine threats used in Tengiz, Kashagan, and Karachaganak because there was no effective re–negotiation of contracts whose terms had obsolesced. If resource nationalism stands for these authors' revised version of the concept, which limits to acknowledging that the state has acquired new assets linked to the exploitation of natural resources, then many other cases discussed here fall into this category. Yet, it can be argued that the theoretical utility of the expression becomes disputable.

1. The Trickle–Down Effect of Corruption

The second dimension of the taxonomy, and therefore answer to the research question, consists of six informal practices which are closer to everyday forms of informality than to grand corruption schemes. In the recruitment phase, there are nepotism, ghost, and conditional employment. In the work phase, there are economisation on security, wage, and resource embezzlement.

Nepotism is a form of favouritism in which a hiring manager exploits his or her authority to provide a job to a relative or friend, without regard for his or her qualifications. Ghost employment takes place when an employee is hired fictitiously to formally fulfil state requirements. Conditional employment is the act of offering a job position conditional to the satisfaction of requests from the hiring manager, such as bribes or sexual favours. All these practices have similar objectives: potential employees want the job, whereas the employer and the hiring manager seek personal benefit. Like previous practices, also these ones are characterised by an anti–competitive nature because decisions are not made through a regular selection but based on the satisfaction of informal requirements.

Economisation on security appliances is the act of saving on equipment and infrastructures to maximise profits. Yet, informality takes place only when bribes are paid to the *akimat* to skip controls or to avoid its involvement after accidents in the workplace. Wage embezzlement is the managerial practice of reporting higher remunerations for employees with the intent to embezzle excess retributions. Resource embezzlement consists of stealing appliances from the workplace with the purpose of reselling them on the black market. All these practices have similar but conflicting objectives: employees and employers try to defraud each other to maximise their profit. While none of them have noble reasons driving their actions, employees are partially justified by the fact that they must make ends meet.

These practices can be distinguished based on the type of corruption they are a symptom of. Nepotism and economisation on security are the most generalisable practices identified, easily spread worldwide. Their existence does not automatically mean that the country is extremely corrupt. On the other hand, conditional employment and resource embezzlement suggest widespread petty corruption because promoters are aware that they can compromise over police controls, convinced that the risk is worth the reward. This is supported by literature suggesting that reduced income increases corruption and vice versa (Cimpoeru and Cimpoeru 2015; Dzhumashev 2016; Borcan, Lindahl, and Mitrut 2014). Finally, ghost employment and wage embezzlement are symptoms of a trickle-down effect of corruption. Both practices are case-specific: local content legislation is employed by governments in contexts with a high concentration of foreign investments, whereas wage embezzlement was a result of excessive corruption decentralisation in the management of KazMunayGas. Table 15 below summarises this distinction.

Table 15   Categorisation based on the corruption suggested

Not a sufficient symptom of widespread corruption	Symptom of diffused petty corruption	Trick-down effect or decentralised corruption
Nepotism	Conditional employment	Ghost employment
Economisation on security	Resource embezzlement	Wage embezzlement

The trickle-down effect is an expression used in marketing to refer to the phenomenon describing the flowing of trends from upper to lower classes in society.[425] Here the general idea is that there is also a trickle-down of corruption. If the government appoints regional governors based on their loyalty and they do not have a direct share of the bribes, they will likely find their own way of earning from their position of power, leading to the decentralisation of

---

425 "Trickle-down effect," *Investopedia*, https://www.investopedia.com/terms/t/trickle-down-effect.asp

corruption. In *Economics of Trickle–Down Corruption*, Nuryyev and Hickson (2020) further argued that there is a positive correlation between state revenue and corruption decentralisation. This means that when state revenue decreases with the price of oil and gas, autocrats are more likely to centralise corruption to avoid elite infighting (Nuryyev and Hickson 2020). Yet, as noted by Tutumlu and Rustemov (2019), the central elite oversight does not always work because, with loose government regulations, Nazarbayev's circle frequently failed in preventing problems caused by: 'Bureaucrats who are empowered by information asymmetry and may resist implementing regulations from the ruler' (Tutumlu and Rustemov 2019, 3).

Both ghost employment and wage embezzlement are examples of decentralised corruption because they show how the local elite took advantage of a *laissez–faire* attitude on the part of the government. Knowing that is easier to compromise with the *akimat* than fighting over law implementation, companies found a way to formally fulfil the local content legislation through ghost employment. Similarly, knowing that decentralised corruption was tolerated, managers of KazMunayGas embezzled workers' wages, and the government was too late in intervening when the Zhanaozen shooting took place (Tutumlu and Rustemov 2019, 8).

In the previous chapter, there were further examples of good policies whose positive outcomes had been jeopardised by decentralised corruption. The EITI platform proved largely ineffective against corruption, although it improved transparency in the extractive industries. Initiatives of corporate social responsibility were often derailed by the arbitrary choices of corrupted *akims*. Finally, any form of ecological oversight did not work because of the strict relationship between companies and *akimat*. Also, previous practices indirectly affect all these policies: the EITI does not reflect the information enclosed in the original production sharing agreements that led to patrimonial embezzlement; fine threats and resulting compromises concluded at the governmental level limit the capability of the *akimat* to exert ecological oversight through environmental fines; and bid rigging foreshadows further forms of informal cooperation between companies and regional authorities.

After analysing the literature, I asked: 1) if corruption is so high, how could legislation on local content, the EITI, initiatives of Corporate Social Responsibility, or the Aarhus Convention lead to positive developments for the citizenry? 2) If the elite is draining most of the profits of the oil industry, how could poor people survive without relying upon informal practices? 3) If government and companies collude, will the former stand up to the latter to protect its citizens? Initial expectations were that: 1) these initiatives do not deliver the positive results they promise; 2) informal practices are often used to escape poverty; 3) at all levels, the government favours companies over citizens.

This led me to formulate a hypothesis about the existence of a trickle–down effect of grand corruption that further reinforces petty corruption, informality, and predatory practices because the decentralisation of corruption would distort the outcome of potentially good policies.[426] The systematic analysis of the Kazakh oil sector reinforced this conviction showing how the interplay of the different practices part of the taxonomy distorted them, and, generally, poverty, inequalities and widespread corruption strengthened informality. Yet, in conditions of low oil prices leading to decreased state revenue (Nuryyev and Hickson 2020), decentralised corruption takes place only when the autocrat opts for a pro–market approach resting on a loose governmental oversight (Tutumlu and Rustemov 2019, 4), hence resulting in a bureaucratic resistance to central orders. Clearly, only studies with bigger samples would be able to prove the validity of said hypothesis.

2. Practices at Play in Kazakhstan

How do the actors of the oil sector of Kazakhstan shape their relationships through informality? The taxonomisation of informal practices listed so far is a partial answer to this question. By setting the rules of the game, the Kazakh elite used patrimonial embezzlement, state racketeering, fine threats, specious contract

---

426 Similarly, Morena Groce (2020) argued that the informal network of the country would not allow functional reforms regardless of oil booms, busts, or the ownership of major assets in the oil sector (Groce 2020, 494).

cancellations, and bid rigging to satisfy internal economic and political demands.

At its independence, the elite of the country focused on developing its energy sector by opening the market to foreign investors. Nursultan Nazarbayev used a multi-vectorial foreign policy that allowed the government not to rely excessively on any country. Patrimonial embezzlement was used to increase its grip on power while companies obtained generous contracts for the exploitation of oilfields and the government temporarily solved its problems of liquidity. While other relevant figures close to the first president started concentrating assets and power through state racketeering and forcing specious contract cancellations, by the early 2000s some of the terms of the contracts had obsolesced and fine threats were used to renegotiate them.

As of early 2022, the Kazakh energy sector had seemingly stalled, at least at the macro level. Yet, in April 2023 the government hinted at starting an international arbitration to recover $16.5 billion from the consortia managing the Kashagan and Karachaganak oil fields in an effort to compensate for inflated costs.[427] This is an unprecedented behaviour on the part of the Kazakh government because the tool employed, the arbitration, is entirely formal. This suggests a few things: the government is relatively confident in winning the arbitration; the executive has not the same leverage it had when Nazarbayev and his informal circle were in power; and it is in shortage of cash. Besides cash, the main goal might be exposing these companies' past sins in the oilfields, which could serve the double purpose of winning the arbitration and weakening powerful elite members active in the energy sector.[428]

As outlined so far, there are different actors involved in the informal dimension of the oil sector, not only the elite and the

---

427 P. Sorbello. "Uncertain Rules of the Game Could Cost Oil Companies Billions in Kazakhstan," *Vlast*, April 26, 2023, https://vlast.kz/english/54930-uncertai n-rules-of-the-game-could-cost-oil-companies-billions-in-kazakhstan.html

428 Like during the 'bloody January', the real purpose might be elite infighting. Mazorenko, Dmitriy and Paolo Sorbello "Too little has changed in Kazakhstan in the year since 'Bloody January'," *Open Democracy*, January 5, 2023, https://www.opendemocracy.net/en/odr/kazakhstan-one-year-bloody-janu ary-no-change/

multinational energy companies, but also managers, employers, and oil workers. Still, there are visible differences among the involved actors. As discussed extensively in Chapter I, *Informality and the Kazakh Oil Sector*, the elite must be distinguished between a series of informal groups competing for power concentration. This became far more evident during January 2022 when a series of protests staged throughout the country were repressed in blood. While the autocrat and his inner circle used these practices to work towards regime consolidation, their competitors used the same practices to facilitate their rise to power.

Similarly, multinational corporations can be distinguished based on their overall performance in the informal game for resources. All of them had ultimately the same objective: maximising their revenue by gaining access to the most profitable oilfields. Yet, in a rigged informal competition, the factors at play to overpower competitors are different. If in regular tenders, reputation, the solidity of the project proposed, and technological innovation are some of the features that governments are looking for, in informal ones the most relevant aspects are: the availability of cash, governmental support, and predisposition to risk. In Table 16 below, three of the main foreign investors of the Kazakh oil sector, namely Chevron, ENI, and CNPC are distinguished based on these relevant characteristics.

Table 16   Factors of attractiveness for kleptocratic decision-makers

	Cash	Supporting government	Predisposition to risk
High/Strong	CNPC	Chevron and CNPC	ENI and CNPC
Low/Weak	Chevron and ENI	ENI	Chevron

These factors influence each other, adding or subtracting to the overall attractiveness that the company exerts on decision–makers. For instance, cash availability was a key element to win tenders in the Central Asian Republic for years, particularly if influential members of the elite such as Timur Kulibayev were directly involved. Among the listed companies, CNPC has the highest availability of cash, both to pay bribes and to offer liquidity to the Kazakh government, but even if ENI had a relatively scarce cash availability in comparison, its predisposition to risk allowed the company to outmanoeuvre competitors. On the one hand, the Italian energy company promised an unrealistic timeline for the oil extraction in Kashagan, and on the other, its managers contributed to creating a corrupt system of bid rigging that oiled the wheels of bureaucracy.

On paper, CNPC is the strongest candidate, because by having a high predisposition to risk and high availability of cash fits the expectations of the ruling elite, but the strong governmental support of the Chinese company decreased its overall attractiveness. In fact, for the Kazakh government was easier to 'bully' ENI than CNPC (Moisé and Sorbello 2022), because the only weapon of the Italian government during negotiations was diplomacy, posing no threat to Kazakh interests. On the contrary, as shown in Chapter V, *Fine Threats*, in 2010 Chevron was successfully backed by the American government when the Kazakh one 'crossed the line'. These factors are useful to estimate the capability of any other multinational corporation to win the rigged game but are less relevant for smaller foreign investors. In fact, the Kazakh elite seeks big investors to compensate for its shortage of technology and engineering expertise as well as shortness of cash but does not need help in developing oilfields less challenging from an engineering standpoint. As discussed in Chapter IV, *State Racketeering* and Chapter VI, *Specious Contract Cancellations*, this type of investors can easily become targets of the local elite. Finally, KazMunayGas cannot be evaluated based on the same standards because its high levels of politicization make it the *de facto* arm of the government.

Another set of actors discussed throughout the book is represented by managers and employed personnel. Their driving interests are far more obvious, and their informal interactions are well exemplified in the six informal practices involving employment: nepotism, ghost and conditional employment, economisation on security, wage and resource embezzlement. Lastly, for inhabitants of oil regions, informality is evident in the failed implementation of potentially good policies promoted by the government, including the EITI, the Aarhus Convention, and initiatives of corporate social responsibility. All these minor informal practices are the result of a trickle-down effect of corruption and unequal development in a rich but unequal country.

3. On Limitations and Use of These Findings

As anticipated, this research is limited by constraints of research design. As a case study, this work cannot claim generalisations common to all rentier states, but it can certainly suggest them based on parallelisms with similar cases. Also, the discussion of the informal practices has been conceived as an exploratory study, and future research should identify more strategies employed by the main actors of the oil sector. Finally, the hypothesis on the trickle-down effect of corruption suggested by the literature and confirmed by the case study should be tested on larger samples to verify or falsify it.

This research had the ambition of creating a vocabulary to explain corruption and to show continuity with informality. While the concept is increasingly studied by academics and activists, there is still a tendency to group different strategies as if they could not be identified as predictable behaviours of rational actors. If this book managed to do something is to shed light on some of the most common practices that could be expected by the ruling elite of a rentier state. Instead of talking generally about the need to curb corruption, analysts and researchers could focus on: how unchecked investments from multinational corporations could strengthen the position of autocrats through patrimonial embezzlement; how captured states can increase chances of state racketeering; how investing in a country with a rent-seeking elite can jeopardise investments in the long-run, either via fine threats or specious contract cancellation; or how bid rigging, in public and private procurement, affects the quality and costs of realised projects.[429] Academics and

---

[429] As explained, in most cases academics are already studying most of these phenomena (Ross 2015; Auriol, Straub, and Flochel 2016).

practitioners should devise methods to measure these phenomena to move beyond general country scores of corruption.

Politicization, centralisation, and internationalisation are the elements determining most of the informal practices identified. It is the competing interests of leading political actors and transnational energy corporations investing in Kazakhstan to shape the informal dimension of these economic strategies. This means, for instance, that a practice like fine threats is less likely to appear in countries with nationalised rentier sectors because the political authority can make decisions without pushing companies to renegotiate contracts. At the same time, while descending the hierarchical structure of the rentier sector, actors diversify and multiply, progressively decreasing the scale of informal practices from grand corruption, such as bid rigging, to everyday informal exchanges, such as conditional employment.

Having said that, each practice has its own degree of generalisation because each strategy is employed by different actors. Hence, practices such as specious contract cancellations and bid rigging are not tied to the extractive sectors or oil economies. Their use gives a glimpse of the activities to look for when a country is generically described as affected by systemic corruption. At the same time, it offers an understanding of how the legitimacy of the authoritarian regime of Kazakhstan was effectively determined by its ability to rule the oil sector of the country. Kazakhstan modernised with oil money as informality shaped the sector. The usefulness of the taxonomy is hence to create a proper vocabulary to talk about strategies with precise political and economic intents, rather than recurring to geopolitical oversimplifications. In conclusion, this book has proven beyond any reasonable doubt that resource-rich countries benefit enormously from their endowments. The house always wins; even when the house is not who we expect it to be.

Also, this study did not distinguish each case as either corruption or informal payments in an attempt to bring both concepts under the same umbrella (Polese 2021; 2016). If workers are asked to pay bribes to the private company, they will obtain the labour contract from it, the act does not qualify as corruption intended as 'abuse of public power for private gain' because there is no public authority involved. Yet, if widespread such informal payments can have serious socio–economic implications, and on their part, might be determined by corruption. Either way, the objective was to focus on the goals of the actors involved and on the consequences that these practices entail.

For policymakers and practitioners, the issue is more complex. If the EITI has taught us something, it is certainly that international mechanisms can force even autocracies to take steps to satisfy standards of transparency. Investing countries should hence act in the framework of international treaties that aim to address patrimonial embezzlement, state racketeering, fine threats, specious contract cancellations, and bid rigging individually. This would mean abandoning the double standards of morality that guided the way enterprises have been acting in the past century. On the other hand, only liberal democracy and fairer societies with functioning judicial systems could help resource–rich countries avoid informality in the workplace and address the negative externalities affecting the citizenry. Democracies and international organisations should invest in strengthening the civil societies of these countries to give citizens a chance to build better states. These objectives and risks remain valid considering the current transition from oil and gas to more green and sustainable sources of energy.[430]

Future research on informality should carefully examine contextual settings to evaluate to what extent informal practices are to be considered as grassroots spontaneous development and to what extent they are externalities of grand corruption and inequality. If it is true that informality is often a reaction to central government policies (Scott 1985), it can also be a form of homologation to the moral standards that the ruling elite set through its example. To conclude, this work has shown how informality scholarship can improve the understanding of the governance and economy of

---

430 This is a present-day debate as Kazakh authorities have already proposed themselves to the EU as a reliable supplier of raw materials necessary to build efficient batteries. Gotev, Georgi. 2022. "Kazakhstan tells EU: We can supply all 30 critical raw materials you need," *Euractiv*, November 18, https://www.euractiv.com/section/central-asia/news/kazakhstan-tells-eu-we-can-supply-all-30-critical-raw-materials-you-need/

corruption by assuming actors as rational operators with strategies and goals. At the same time, this work testifies to the need for broader analyses studying the interplay of different practices and their consequences on whole societies.

References

Ageev, Aleksandr, Anuar Bayschuakov, and Erlan Seytimov. 2008. *Элита Казахстана: Власть. Бизнес. Общество [The Elite of Kazakhstan: Power. Business. Society]*. Almaty: инес-ца.

Alexander, Catherine. 2018. "Homeless in the Homeland: Housing Protests in Kazakhstan." *Critique of Anthropology* 38 (2): 204–20. https://doi.or g/10.1177/0308275X1875887.

Aliyev, Huseyn. 2015. "Post-Soviet Informality: Towards Theory-Building." International Journal of Sociology and Social Policy 35 (3–4): 182–98. https://doi.org/10.1108/IJSSP-05-2014-0041.

Almandoz, A. 2001. "The Intelligentsia's Two Visions of Urban Modernity: Gómez's Caracas, 1908–35." Urban History 28 (1): 84–105. https://do i.org/10.1017/S0963926801000153.

Alzhanova, Nurzhan Sh., and Raissa D. Nurzhaubayeva. 2015. "Problems of Population Informal Employment in Monotowns of Kazakhstan in the Context of Globalization." Actual Problems of Economics 5 (167): 328–37.

Amujo, Olusanmi C., Beatrice Adeyinka Laninhun, Olutayo Otubanjo, and Victoria Olufunmilayo Ajala. 2012. "Impact of Corporate Social Irresponsibility on the Corporate Image and Reputation of Multinational Oil Corporations in Nigeria." Critical Studies on Corporate Responsibility, Governance and Sustainability 4 (January): 263–93. https://doi.org/10.1108/S2043-9059(2012)0000004020.

Andreas Engen, Ole, Aslaug Mikkelsen, and Kjell Grønhaug. 2010. "Critical Incidents and Social Construction of Corporate Social Responsibility." Social Responsibility Journal 6 (3): 345–61. https://doi.org/10.1108/17471111011064735.

Ashimbayev, Daniyar. 2010. Кто Есть Кто в Казахстане: Биографическая Энциклопедия 2010–2011 [Who Is Who in Kazakhstan: Encyclopaedic Biographies 2010–2011]. 11th ed. Almaty.

Auriol, Emmanuelle, Stéphane Straub, and Thomas Flochel. 2016. "Public Procurement and Rent-Seeking: The Case of Paraguay." World Development 77: 395–407. https://doi.org/10.1016/j.worlddev.2015.09 .001.

Auty, Richard. 1993. Sustaining Development in the Mineral Economies: The Resource Curse Thesis. 1st ed. London: Routledge. https://doi. org/10.4324/9780203422595.

Azhgaliyeva, Dina, and Yelena Kalyuzhnova. 2013. "The Evaluation of Local Content Implementation in Kazakhstan." *Vestnik Universiteta Kainar*, 51–59. https://centaur.reading.ac.uk/67517/3/Nadloc_paper_nobolashak2.pdf.

Babali, Tuncay. 2009. "Prospects of Export Routes for Kashagan Oil." *Energy Policy* 37 (4): 1298–1308. https://doi.org/10.1016/j.enpol.2008.11.013.

Beblawi, Hazem. 1987. "The Rentier State in the Arab World." *Pluto Journals* 9 (4): 383–98.

Behrends, Andrea. 2011. "Fighting for Oil When There Is No Oil Yet: The Darfur–Chad Border." In *Crude Domination: An Anthropology of Oil*, edited by Andrea Behrends, Stephen P. Reyna, and Günther Schlee, 81–106. New York and Oxford: Berghahn Books.

Biegelman, Martin T., and Daniel R. Biegelman. 2010. *Foreign Corrupt Practices Act Compliance Guidebook. Foreign Corrupt Practices Act Compliance Guidebook.* John Wiley & Sons. https://doi.org/10.1002/9781118268292.

Billon, Philippe Le. 2014. "Natural Resources and Corruption in Post-War Transitions: Matters of Trust." *Third World Quarterly* 35 (5): 770–86. https://doi.org/10.1080/01436597.2014.921429.

Boon, Marten. 2019. "Deuss' Demise: An Oil Trader's Struggle to Keep Up with the Market, 1970s-1990s." *Munich Personal RePEc Archive*, no. 95460: 1–39.

Borcan, Oana, Mikael Lindahl, and Andreea Mitrut. 2014. "The Impact of an Unexpected Wage Cut on Corruption: Evidence From a 'Xeroxed' Exam." *Journal of Public Economics* 120: 32–47.

Borisov, D. A. 2016. "The Great Game 2.0 in Central Asia (The Beginning: 1990-2000)." *Tomsk State University Journal* 407: 44–48.

Bowen, HR. 1953. *Social Responsibilities of the Businessman Harper & Row. New York.*

Bucheli, Marcelo, and Ruth V. Aguilera. 2010. "Political Survival, Energy Policies, and Multinational Corporations: A Historical Study for Standard Oil of New Jersey in Colombia, Mexico, and Venezuela in the Twentieth Century." *Management International Review* 50 (3): 347–78. https://doi.org/10.1007/s11575-010-0036-1.

Chervinsky, Oleg. 2017. *Чёрная Кровь Казахстана. Нефтяная История Независимости. [The Black Blood of Kazakhstan. The Oil History of Independence].* Almaty: Soz & DS.

Cimpoeru, Maria Violeta, and Valentin Cimpoeru. 2015. "Budgetary Transparency — an Improving Factor for Corruption Control and Economic Performance." *22nd International Economic Conference – IECS 2015 "Economic Prospects in the Context of Growing Global and Regional Interdependencies", IECS 2015* 27: 579–86.

Collier, Paul, and Anthony J. Venables. 2012. *Plundered Nations?: Successes and Failures in Natural Resource Extraction.* Edited by Paul Collier and Anthony J. Venables. *Choice Reviews Online.* Palgrave Macmillan UK. https://doi.org/10.5860/choice.49-3978.

Collins, Gabe, Mark P. Jones, Jim Krane, Ken Medlock, and Francisco Monaldi. 2021. "Shale Renders the 'Obsolescing Bargain' Obsolete: Political Risk and Foreign Investment in Argentina's Vaca Muerta." *Resources Policy* 74 (May): 102269. https://doi.org/10.1016/j.resourpol.2021.102269.

Colom–Jaén, Artur, and Alicia Campos–Serrano. 2013. "Oil in Chad and Equatorial Guinea: Widening the Focus of the Resource Curse." *European Journal of Development Research* 25: 584–599. https://doi.org/10.1057/ejdr.2013.25.

Cooley, Alexander. 2012. *Great Games, Local Rules: The New Great Power Contest in Central Asia. Great Games, Local Rules: The New Great Power Contest in Central Asia.* Oxford University Press (OUP). https://doi.org/10.1093/acprof:oso/9780199929825.001.0001.

Cooley, Alexander, and J. C. Sharman. 2015. "Blurring the Line between Licit and Illicit: Transnational Corruption Networks in Central Asia and Beyond." *Central Asian Survey* 34 (1): 11–28. https://doi.org/10.1080/02634937.2015.1010799.

Corden, W. M. 1984. "Booming Sector and Dutch Disease Economics: Survey and Consolidation." *Oxford Economic Papers* 36 (3): 359–80. https://doi.org/10.1093/oxfordjournals.oep.a041643.

Corden, W. M., and J. P. Neary. 1982. "Booming Sector and De–Industrialisation in a Small Open Economy." *Economic Journal* 92 (368): 825–48. https://doi.org/10.2307/2232670.

Coviello, Decio, and Stefano Gagliarducci. 2017. "Tenure in Office and Public Procurement." *American Economic Journal: Economic Policy* 9 (3): 59–105. https://www.jstor.org/stable/26598162.

Cowan, C. D. 1954. "Economics and Economic Policy of Dual Societies as Exemplified by Indonesia." *International Affairs* 30 (2): 259–60. https://doi.org/10.2307/2607628.

Cummings, Sally N. 2005. *Kazakhstan: Power and the Elite.* 1st ed. London, UK and New York, USA: I.B. Tauris.

Danilovich, Natalia, and Elmira Yessaliyeva. 2014. "Effects of Out-of-Pocket Payments on Access to Maternal Health Services in Almaty, Kazakhstan: A Qualitative Study." *Europe-Asia Studies* 66 (4). https://doi.org/10.1080/09668136.2014.897428.

Devlin, Julia, and Michael Lewin. 2005. "Managing Oil Booms and Busts in Developing Countries." In *Managing Economic Volatility and Crises: A Practitioner's Guide*, 186–212. Cambridge University Press. https://doi.org/10.1017/CBO9780511510755.008.

Dietl, Gulshan. 1997. "Quest for Influence in Central Asia: India and Pakistan." *International Studies* 34 (2): 111–43. https://doi.org/10.1177/0020881797034002001.

Dikkaya, Mehmet, and Bayram Veli Doyar. 2017. "Causality among Oil Prices, GDP and Exchange Rate: Evidence from Azerbaijan and Kazakhstan." *Bilig* 83: 79–98.

Domjan, Paul, and Matt Stone. 2010. "A Comparative Study of Resource Nationalism in Russia and Kazakhstan 2004–2008." *Europe-Asia Studies* 62 (1): 35–62. https://doi.org/10.1080/09668130903385374.

Dzhumashev, Ratbek. 2016. "The Role of Income Uncertainty in the Corruption Growth Nexus." *The B.E. Journal of Economic Analysis and Policy,* 16 (2): 1169–1201.

Egert, Balazs, and Carol S. Leonard. 2007. "Dutch Disease Scare in Kazakhstan: Is It Real?" *CESifo Working Paper Series.*

Eisgruber, Lasse. 2013. "The Resource Curse: Analysis of the Applicability to the Large-Scale Export of Electricity from Renewable Resources." *Energy Policy* 57 (June): 429–40. https://doi.org/10.1016/j.enpol.2013.02.013.

Executive Intelligence Review. 1988. "John Deuss, Shackley's Piggybank." 15 (26): 35–37.

Faccio, Mara. 2006. "Politically Connected Firms." *The American Economic Review* 96 (1): 369–86. https://www.jstor.org/stable/30034371.

Fardmanesh, Mohsen. 1991. "Dutch Disease Economics and the Oil Syndrome: An Empirical Study." *World Development* 19 (6): 711–17. https://doi.org/10.1016/0021-9169(78)90069-7.

Farzanegan, Mohammad Reza, Christian Lessmann, and Gunther Markwardt. 2018. "Natural Resource Rents and Internal Conflicts: Can Decentralization Lift the Curse?" *Economic Systems* 42 (2): 186–205. https://doi.org/10.1016/j.ecosys.2017.05.009.

Fattouh, Bassam, and Hakim Darbouche. 2010. "North African Oil and Foreign Investment in Changing Market Conditions." *Energy Policy* 38 (2): 1119–29. https://doi.org/10.1016/j.enpol.2009.10.064.

Fehlings, Susanne, and Hasan H. Karrar. 2020. "Negotiating State and Society: The Normative Informal Economies of Central Asia and the Caucasus." *Central Asian Survey* 39 (1): 1–10. https://doi.org/10.1080/02634937.2020.1738345.

Fenton Villar, Paul, and Elissaios Papyrakis. 2017. "Evaluating the Impact of the Extractive Industries Transparency Initiative (EITI) on Corruption in Zambia." *Extractive Industries and Society* 4 (4): 795–805. https://doi.org/10.1016/j.exis.2017.01.009.

Findley, Michael G., Kyosuke Kikuta, and Michael Denly. 2021. "External Validity." *Annual Review of Political Science* 24: 365–93. https://doi.org/https10.1146/annurev-polisci-041719-102556.

Fox, Jonathan. 2007. "The Uncertain Relationship Between Transparency and Accountability." *Development in Practice* 17 (4–5): 663–71. https://doi.org/10.1080/09614520701469955.

Franke, Anja, Andrea Gawrich, and Gurban Alakbarov. 2009. "Kazakhstan and Azerbaijan as Post–Soviet Rentier States: Resource Incomes and Autocracy as a Double 'Curse' in Post-Soviet Regimes." *Europe–Asia Studies* 61 (1): 109–40. https://doi.org/10.1080/09668130802532977.

Furstenberg, Saipira. 2018. "State Responses to Reputational Concerns: The Case of the Extractive Industries Transparency Initiative in Kazakhstan." *Central Asian Survey* 37 (2): 286–304. https://doi.org/10.1080/02634937.2018.1428789.

Gaal, Peter, and Martin McKee. 2004. "Informal Payment for Health Care and the Theory of 'INXIT.'" *International Journal of Health Planning and Management* 19 (2): 163–78. https://doi.org/10.1002/hpm.751.

Gelb, Alan. 1988. "Oil Windfalls: Blessing or Curse?" *Oil Windfalls: Blessing or Curse?* https://doi.org/10.1016/0304-3878(91)90059-5.

George, Alexander, and Andrew Bennett. 2005. *Case Studies and Theory Development in the Social Sciences. BCSIA Studies in International Security.* MIT Press. https://doi.org/10.1017/S0022381607080231.

Gillies, Alexandra. 2020a. "Corruption Trends during Africa's Oil Boom, 2005 to 2014." *Extractive Industries and Society* 7 (4): 1171–81. https://doi.org/10.1016/j.exis.2020.06.006.

—. 2020b. *Crude Intentions: How Oil Corruption Contaminates the World.* Oxford Scholarship. https://doi.org/10.1093/oso/9780190940706.001.0001.

Glasius, Marlies, Meta de Lange, Jos Bartman, Emanuela Dalmasso, Aofei Lv, Adele Del Sordi, Marcus Michaelsen, and Kris Ruijgrok. 2017. *Research, Ethics and Risk in the Authoritarian Field. Research, Ethics and Risk in the Authoritarian Field.* Amsterdam: Palgrave Macmillan UK. https://doi.org/10.1007/978-3-319-68966-1.

Gololobov, Dmitry. 2007. "The Yukos Money Laundering Case: A Never-Ending Story." *Michigan Journal of International Law* 28 (4): 711–64.

Gonzalez, Adrian. 2016. "Poverty, Oil and Corruption: The Need for a Quad-Sector Development Partnership (QSDP) in Nigeria's Niger Delta." *Development Policy Review* 34 (4): 509–38. https://doi.org/10.1111/dpr.12164.

Gould, John A., and Matthew S. Winters. 2007. "An Obsolescing Bargain in Chad: Shifts in Leverage between the Government and the World Bank." *Business and Politics* 9 (2). https://doi.org/10.2202/1469-3569.1199.

Granovetter, Mark. 1985. "Economic Action and Social Structure: The Problem of Embeddedness." *American Journal of Sociology* 91 (3): 22–45. https://doi.org/10.4324/9780429494338.

—. 2007. "The Social Construction of Corruption." In *On Capitalism*, 152–72. https://doi.org/10.1023/A:1010699110017.

Greco, Andrea, and Giuseppe Oddo. 2018. *Lo Stato Parallelo: La Prima Inchiesta Sull'ENI Tra Politics, Servizi Segreti, Scandali Finanziari e Nuove Guerre*. Chiarelettere.

Groce, Morena Skalamera. 2020. "Circling the Barrels: Kazakhstan's Regime Stability in the Wake of the 2014 Oil Bust." *Central Asian Survey* 39 (4): 480–99. https://doi.org/10.1080/02634937.2020.1812530.

Guimaraes, Denis, and Diaulas Ribeiro. 2019. "5 Years of Operation 'Car Wash': Revisiting Bid Rigging and Bribery Investigations." *Competition Policy International — Antitrust Chronicle*, 1–10. https://papers.ssrn.com/sol3/papers.cfm?abstract_id=3379136.

Gulbrandsen, Lars H, and Arild Moe. 2007. "BP in Azerbaijan: A Test Case of the Potential and Limits of the CSR Agenda?" *Third World Quarterly* 28 (4): 813–30. https://doi.org/10.1080/01436590701336689.

Guliyev, Farid, and Nozima Akhrarkhodjaeva. 2009. "The Trans-Caspian Energy Route: Cronyism, Competition and Cooperation in Kazakh Oil Export." *Energy Policy* 37 (8): 3171–82. https://doi.org/10.1016/j.enpol.2009.04.009.

Gupta, Kartick. 2017. "Are Oil and Gas Firms More Likely to Engage in Unethical Practices than Other Firms?" *Energy Policy* 100 (January): 101–12. https://doi.org/10.1016/j.enpol.2016.10.009.

Guyer, Jane I. 2002. "The Chad-Cameroon Petroleum and Pipeline Development Project." *African Affairs* 101 (402): 109–15.

Hammond, John L. 2011. "The Resource Curse and Oil Revenues in Angola and Venezuela." *Science and Society* 75 (3): 348–78. https://doi.org/10.1521/siso.2011.75.3.348.

Hanson, Margaret. 2017. "Legalized Rent–Seeking: Eminent Domain in Kazakhstan." *Cornell International Law Journal* 50 (1).

Hart, Keith. 1973. "Informal Income Opportunities and Urban Employment in Ghana." *The Journal of Modern African Studies* 11 (1): 61–89. https://doi.org/10.1017/S0022278X00008089.

Hasanov, Fakhri, Jeyhun Mikayilov, Cihan Bulut, Elchin Suleymanov, and Fuzuli Aliyev. 2017. "The Role of Oil Prices in Exchange Rate Movements: The CIS Oil Exporters." *Economies* 5 (2): 1–13. https://doi.org/10.3390/economies5020013.

Haufler, Virginia. 2010. "Disclosure as Governance: The Extractive Industries Transparency Initiative and Resource Management in the Developing World." *Global Environmental Politics* 10 (3): 53–73. https://doi.org/10.1162/GLEP_a_00014.

Heidenheimer, Arnold J. 1970. *Political Corruption : Readings in Comparative Analysis. New York.*

Helmke, Gretchen, and Steven Levitsky. 2004. "Informal Institutions and Comparative Politics: A Research Agenda." *Perspectives on Politics* 2 (4): 725–40. https://doi.org/10.1017/S1537592704040472.

Hickey, Will. 2012. "The Oil PSA and Its Inverse Effect on Human Resource Development (HRD)." *Procedia – Social and Behavioral Sciences* 65 (December): 1060–65. https://doi.org/10.1016/j.sbspro.2012.11.371.

Hindmoor, Andrew. 2010. "Rational Choice." In *Theory and Methods in Political Science*, edited by David Marsh and Gerry Stoker, Third, 42–59. Palgrave Macmillan.

Hoffman, David. 2011. *The Oligarchs: Wealth and Power in the New Russia.* New York, US: PublicAffairs.

Holtzblatt, Mark, and Norbert Tschakert. 2014. "Baker Hughes: Greasing the Wheels in Kazakhstan (FCPA Violations and Implementation of a Corporate Ethics and Anti–Corruption Compliance Program)." *Journal of Accounting Education* 32 (1): 36–60. https://doi.org/10.1016/j.jaccedu.2014.01.005.

Hood, Christopher. 2010. "Accountability and Transparency: Siamese Twins, Matching Parts, Awkward Couple?" *West European Politics* 33 (5): 989–1009. https://doi.org/10.1080/01402382.2010.486122.

Hosman, Laura. 2009. "Dynamic Bargaining and the Prospects for Learning in the Petroleum Industry: The Case of Kazakhstan." *Perspectives on Global Development and Technology* 8 (1): 1–25. https://doi.org/10.1163/156914909X403162.

Howie, Peter. 2018. "Kazakhstan's Diversification Strategy." In *Economic Diversification Policies in Natural Resource Rich Economies*, edited by Sami Mahroum and Yasser Al-Saleh, 203-35. Routledge. https://doi.org/10.4324/9781315660981-9.

Idemudia, Uwafiokun. 2013. "The Extractive Industry Transparency Initiative and Corruption in Nigeria: Rethinking the Links between Transparency and Accountability." *Afrika-Studiecentrum Series* 27 (January): 127-48. https://doi.org/10.1163/9789004251892_008.

Ipek, Pinar. 2007. "The Role of Oil and Gas in Kazakhstan's Foreign Policy: Looking East or West?" *Europe-Asia Studies* 59 (7): 1179-99. https://doi.org/10.1080/09668130701607144.

Isaacs, Rico. 2010. "Informal Politics and the Uncertain Context of Transition: Revisiting Early Stage Non-Democratic Development in Kazakhstan." *Democratization* 17 (1): 1-25.

—. 2011. *Party System Formation in Kazakhstan: Between Formal and Informal Politics. Central Asian Studies Series*. Routledge. https://doi.org/10.4324/9780203826003.

—. 2013. "Nur Otan, Informal Networks and the Countering of Elite Instability in Kazakhstan: Bringing the 'Formal' Back In." *Europe - Asia Studies* 65 (6): 1055-79. https://doi.org/10.1080/09668136.2013.802547.

—. 2014. "Neopatrimonialism and beyond: Reassessing the Formal and Informal in the Study of Central Asian Politics." *Contemporary Politics* 20 (2): 229-45. https://doi.org/10.1080/13569775.2014.907989.

—. 2019. "The Role of Party Interest Articulation in the Personalist-Authoritarian Regimes of the Central Asian Republics of Kazakhstan, Turkmenistan, and Tajikistan." *Problems of Post-Communism* 67 (4-5): 375-87. https://doi.org/10.1080/10758216.2019.1645606.

—. 2020. "Russia-Kazakhstan Relations and the Tokayev-Nazarbayev Tandem." *Russian Analytical Digest* 248: 2-5.

Janenova, Saltanat, and Colin Knox. 2020. "Combatting Corruption in Kazakhstan: A Role for Ethics Commissioners?" *Public Administration and Development* 40 (3): 186-95. https://doi.org/10.1002/pad.1873.

Jantayeva, Irina. 2020. "Otzhim (Russia)." Global Informality Project. 2020. https://www.in-formality.com/wiki/index.php?title=Otzhim_(Russia).

Jesson, Jill K., Lydia Matheson, and Fiona M. Lacey. 2011. *Doing Your Literature Review - Traditional and Systematic Techniques*. London: Sage Publications, Ltd. https://doi.org/10.7748/nr.19.4.45.s7.

Jiyad, Ahmed Mousa. 2019. "Transparency in Iraq Petroleum Sector: More Symbolic Formality than Impacting Effectiveness." *Journal of Contemporary Iraq and the Arab World* 13 (2–3): 145–65. https://doi.org/10.138 6/JCIAW_00004_1/CITE/REFWORKS.

Joseph, Gilbert M., and Jürgen Buchenau. 2013. *Mexico's Once and Future Revolution. Social Upheaval and the Challenge of Rule since the Late Nineteenth Century.* Durham and London: Duke University Press. https://doi.org/https://doi.org/10.1215/9780822377382.

Kablan, Sandrine A., and Josef L. Loening. 2012. "An Empirical Assessment of the Dutch Disease Channel of the Resource Curse: The Case of Chad." *Economics Bulletin* 32 (3): 2007–14.

Kaiser, Mark J., and Allan G. Pulsipher. 2007. "A Review of the Oil and Gas Sector in Kazakhstan." *Energy Policy* 35 (2): 1300–1314. https://doi.or g/10.1016/j.enpol.2006.03.020.

Kaliyeva, Gaukhar Keneskanovna. 2013. "Social–Legal Essence of Bribery of the Office Holders in the Territory of Kazakhstan in the End of the XIX Century." *World Applied Sciences Journal* 26 (11): 1526–29. https://doi.org/10.5829/idosi.wasj.2013.26.11.13587.

Kalyuzhnova, Yelena, and Maksim Belitski. 2019. "The Impact of Corruption and Local Content Policy in on Firm Performance: Evidence from Kazakhstan." *Resources Policy* 61 (January): 67–76. https://doi.org/1 0.1016/j.resourpol.2019.01.016.

Kalyuzhnova, Yelena, and Julian Lee. 2014. "China and Kazakhstan's Oil and Gas Partnership at the Start of the Twenty–First Century." *Emerging Markets Finance & Trade* 50 (5): 206–21. https://doi.org/10.2 753/REE1540–496X500515.

Kalyuzhnova, Yelena, and Christian Nygaard. 2008. "State Governance Evolution in Resource–Rich Transition Economies: An Application to Russia and Kazakhstan." *Energy Policy* 36 (6): 1829–42. https://doi.or g/10.1016/j.enpol.2008.01.035.

Kalyuzhnova, Yelena, Christian A. Nygaard, Yerengaip Omarov, and Abdizhapar Saparbayev. 2016. *Local Content Policies in Resource–Rich Countries.* Palgrave Macmillan. https://doi.org/10.1057/978-1-137-44786-9.

Kasekende, Elizabeth, Charles Abuka, and Mare Sarr. 2016. "Extractive Industries and Corruption: Investigating the Effectiveness of EITI as a Scrutiny Mechanism." *Resources Policy* 48 (June): 117–28. https://doi .org/10.1016/J.RESOURPOL.2016.03.002.

Kaufmann, Daniel, and Pedro C. Vicente. 2011. "Legal Corruption." *Economics and Politics* 23 (2): 195–219. https://doi.org/10.1111/j.1468–03 43.2010.00377.x.

Kesarchuk, Olga. 2018. "Deryban." In *The Global Encyclopaedia of Informality Volume 2*, edited by Alena Ledeneva, Anna Bailey, Sheelagh Barron, Costanza Curro, and Elizabeth Teague. UCL Press.

Kim, Byung-Yeon. 2003. "Informal Economy Activities of Soviet Households: Size and Dynamics." *PERSA Working Paper* 26: 1–23. chrome-extension://efaidnbmnnnibpcajpcglclefindmkaj/viewer.html?pdfu rl=https%3A%2F%2Fwarwick.ac.uk%2Ffac%2Fsoc%2Feconomics%2Fstaff%2Fmharrison%2Farchive%2Fpersa%2F026fulltext.pdf&clen=917739&chunk=true.

Kingsbury, Donald V. 2019. "Oil's Colonial Residues: Geopolitics, Identity, and Resistance in Venezuela." *Bulletin of Latin American Research* 38 (S1): 76–93. https://doi.org/10.1111/blar.12947.

Kirat, Mohamed. 2015. "Corporate Social Responsibility in the Oil and Gas Industry in Qatar Perceptions and Practices." *Public Relations Review* 41 (4): 438–46. https://doi.org/10.1016/j.pubrev.2015.07.001.

Knox, Colin, and Saltanat Janenova. 2019. "The E-Government Paradox in Post-Soviet Countries." *International Journal of Public Sector Management*. https://doi.org/10.1108/IJPSM-08-2018-0173.

Koch, Natalie, and Tom Perreault. 2019. "Resource Nationalism." *Progress in Human Geography* 43 (4): 611–31. https://doi.org/10.1177/0309132518781497.

Kokh, Svetlana, Artem Dekterev, Ella Sokol, and Sergey Potapov. 2016. "Numerical Simulation of an Oil–Gas Fire." *Energy Exploration & Exploitation* 34 (1): 77–98.

Kolstad, Ivar, and Arne Wiig. 2009. "Is Transparency the Key to Reducing Corruption in Resource-Rich Countries?" *World Development* 37 (3): 521–32. https://doi.org/10.1016/j.worlddev.2008.07.002.

Kuatova, Alemgul Sovetovna. 2013. "Corruption Crimes in Public Procurement in the Republic of Kazakhstan." *Middle East Journal of Scientific Research* 17 (10): 1419–24. https://doi.org/10.5829/idosi.mejsr.2013.17.10.12310.

Kutan, Ali M., and Michael L. Wyzan. 2005. "Explaining the Real Exchange Rate in Kazakhstan, 1996–2003: Is Kazakhstan Vulnerable to the Dutch Disease?" *Economic Systems* 29 (2): 242–55. https://doi.org/10.1016/j.ecosys.2005.03.009.

Kuzhabekova, Aliya, and Ainur Almukhambetova. 2019. "Women's Progression through the Leadership Pipeline in the Universities of Kazakhstan and Kyrgyzstan." *Compare*. https://doi.org/10.1080/03057925.2019.1599820.

LaPorte, Jody. 2017. "Foreign versus Domestic Bribery: Explaining Repression in Kleptocratic Regimes." *Comparative Politics* 50 (1): 83–102. https://doi.org/10.5129/001041517821864417.

Lasslett, Kristian. 2017. "Uncovering the Transnational Networks, Organisational Techniques and State–Corporate Ties Behind Grand Corruption: Building an Investigative Methodology." *International Journal for Crime, Justice and Social Democracy* 6 (4): 29–54. https://doi.org/10.5204/ijcjsd.v6i4.445.

Ledeneva, Alena, Anna Bailey, Sheelagh Barron, Costanza Curro, and Elizabeth Teague. 2018a. *The Global Encyclopaedia of Informality. Understanding Social and Cultural Complexity. Volume 1.* Edited by Alena Ledeneva, Anna Bailey, Sheelagh Barron, Costanza Curro, and Elizabeth Teague. London, UK: UCL Press.

—. 2018b. *The Global Encyclopaedia of Informality. Understanding Social and Cultural Complexity. Volume 2.* Edited by Alena Ledeneva, Anna Bailey, Sheelagh Barron, Costanza Curro, and Elizabeth Teague. *Global Encyclopaedia of Informality, Volume 2.* UCL Press. https://doi.org/10.2307/j.ctt20krxh9.

Ledeneva, Alena, Elizabeth Teague, Petra Matijevic, Gian Marco Moisé, Piotr Majda, and Malika Toqmadi. 2024. *The Global Encyclopaedia of Informality. A Hitchhiker's Guide to Informal Problem–Solving in Human Life. Volume 3.* Edited by Alena Ledeneva, Elizabeth Teague, Petra Matijevic, Gian Marco Moisé, Piotr Majda, and Malika Toqmadi. London, UK: UCL Press. https://doi.org/978-1-80008-616-6.

Ledeneva, Alena V. 1998. *Russia's Economy of Favours: Blat, Networking and Informal Exchange.* London: Cambridge University Press.

—. 2006. *How Russia Really Works: The Informal Practices That Shaped Post–Soviet Politics and Business.* New York, US: Cornell University Press. https://doi.org/10.7591/9780801461682.

—. 2013. *Can Russia Modernise?: Sistema, Power Networks and Informal Governance. Can Russia Modernise?: Sistema, Power Networks and Informal Governance.* Cambridge: Cambridge University Press. https://doi.org/10.1017/CBO9780511978494.

Lee, Chia–Yi. 2015. "Chinese Outward Investment in Oil and Its Economic and Political Impact in Developing Countries." *Issues and Studies* 51 (3): 131–63.

Lee, Pak K. 2005. "China's Quest for Oil Security: Oil (Wars) in the Pipeline?" *Pacific Review.* https://doi.org/10.1080/09512740500162949.

Levine, Ilya. 2016. *US Policies in Central Asia : Democracy, Energy and the War on Terror.* First. New York: Routledge.

LeVine, Steve. 2007. *The Oil and the Glory: The Pursuit of Empire and Fortune on the Caspian Sea.* Random House.

Lewis, Arthur. 1954. "Economic Development with Unlimited Supplies of Labour." *The Manchester School* 22 (2): 139–91. https://doi.org/10.1111/j.1467-9957.1954.tb00021.x.

Lewis, Maureen. 2007. "Informal Payments and the Financing of Health Care in Developing and Transition Countries." *Health Affairs* 26 (4): 984–97. https://doi.org/10.1377/hlthaff.26.4.984.

Lillis, Joanna. 2019. *Dark Shadows: Inside the Secret World of Kazakhstan.* London and New York: I.B. Tauris.

Lima–de–Oliveira, Renato. 2020. "Corruption and Local Content Development: Assessing the Impact of the Petrobras' Scandal on Recent Policy Changes in Brazil." *The Extractive Industries and Society* 7 (2): 274–82. https://doi.org/10.1016/J.EXIS.2019.08.004.

López–Cazar, Ibeth, Elissaios Papyrakis, and Lorenzo Pellegrini. 2021. "The Extractive Industries Transparency Initiative (EITI) and Corruption in Latin America: Evidence from Colombia, Guatemala, Honduras, Peru, and Trinidad and Tobago." *Resources Policy* 70 (March): 101907. https://doi.org/10.1016/J.RESOURPOL.2020.101907.

Mahood, Quenby, Dwayne Van Eerd, and Emma Irvin. 2014. "Searching for Grey Literature for Systematic Reviews: Challenges and Benefits." *Research Synthesis Methods* 5 (3): 221–34. https://doi.org/10.1002/jrsm.1106.

Makarchev, Nikita, and Piotr Wieprzowski. 2021. "Cuckoos in the Nest: The Co-Option of State–Owned Enterprises in Putin's Russia." *Post–Soviet Affairs* 37 (3): 199–221. https://doi.org/10.1080/1060586X.2020.1870372.

Markus, Stanislav. 2015. *Property, Predation, and Protection: Piranha Capitalism in Russia and Ukraine.* Cambridge University Press. https://doi.org/https://doi.org/10.1017/CBO9781316104743.

Marten, Kimberly. 2007. "Russian Efforts to Control Kazakhstan's Oil: The Kumkol Case." *Post–Soviet Affairs* 23 (1): 18–37. https://doi.org/10.2747/1060–586X.23.1.18.

Massey, Simon, and Roy May. 2005. "Dallas to Doba: Oil and Chad, External Controls and Internal Politics." *Journal of Contemporary African Studies* 23 (2): 253–76. https://doi.org/10.1080/02589000500176065.

Maugeri, Leonardo. 2006. *The Age of Oil: The Mythology, History, and Future of the World's Most Controversial Resource.* 1st ed. Westport, Connecticut, USA: Praeger Publishers.

Mauro, P. 1995. "Corruption and Growth." *The Quarterly Journal of Economics* 110 (3): 681–712. https://doi.org/10.2307/2946696.

Mawejje, Joseph. 2019. "Natural Resources Governance and Tax Revenue Mobilization in Sub Saharan Africa: The Role of EITI." *Resources Policy* 62 (August): 176–83. https://doi.org/10.1016/J.RESOURPOL.2019.04.001.

Mazzuca, Sebastián L. 2013. "The Rise of Rentier Populism." *Journal of Democracy* 24 (2): 108–22. https://doi.org/10.1353/jod.2013.0034.

McBeth, Brian S. 1983. *Juan Vicente Gómez and the Oil Companies in Venezuela, 1908–1935*. First. Cambridge: Cambridge University Press.

—. 2009. "Venezuela's Nascent Oil Industry and the 1932 US Tariff on Crude Oil Imports, 1927–1935." *Revista de Historia Economica – Journal of Iberian and Latin American Economic History* 27 (3): 427–62. https://doi.org/10.1017/S0212610900000835.

Menon, R. 2003. "The New Great Game in Central Asia." *Survival* 45 (2): 187–204. https://doi.org/10.1093/survival/45.2.187.

Mesquita, Michael. 2016. "Kazakhstan's Presidential Transition and the Evolution of Elite Networks." *Demokratizatsiya: The Journal of Post–Soviet Democratization* 24 (3): 371–97.

Mische, Ann, and Barbara A. Misztal. 2002. "Informality: Social Theory and Contemporary Practice." *Contemporary Sociology* 31 (5): 608. https://doi.org/10.2307/3090082.

Moisé, Gian Marco. 2020. "Corruption in the Oil Sector: A Systematic Review and Critique of the Literature." *Extractive Industries and Society* 7 (1): 217–36. https://doi.org/10.1016/j.exis.2020.01.002.

—. 2021. "Populism in Moldova's Informal Political System." *Journal of Extreme Anthropology* 5 (2): 1–26. https://doi.org/https://doi.org/10.5617/jea.8986.

Moisé, Gian Marco, and Abel Polese. 2021. "The Historical Conditioning of Languages and Ethnicities in Central Asia." In *European Handbook of Central Asian Studies: History, Politics, and Societies*, edited by Jeroen Van den Bosch, Adrien Fauve, and Bruno De Cordier, 1162. Ibidem.

Moisé, Gian Marco, and Paolo Sorbello. 2022. "The EU and European Transnational Companies in Central Asia: Relocating Agency in the Energy Sector." *Central Asian Survey* 41 (03). https://doi.org/10.1080/02634937.2022.2049590.

Mommen, André. 2007. "China's Hunger for Oil: The Russian Connection." *Journal of Developing Societies* 23 (4): 435–66. https://doi.org/10.1177/0169796X0702300403.

Montinola, Gabriella R., and Robert W. Jackman. 2002. "Sources of Corruption: A Cross–Country Study." *British Journal of Political Science* 32 (1). https://doi.org/10.1017/s0007123402000066.

Mota Prado, Mariana, and Marta R De Assis Machado. 2021. "Using Criminal Law to Fight Corruption: The Potential, Risks, and Limitations of Operation Car Wash (Lava Jato)." *The American Journal of Comparative Law* 69 (4): 834–79. https://doi.org/10.1093/AJCL/AVAC008.

Moura-Leite, Rosamaria C., and Robert C. Padgett. 2011. "Historical Background of Corporate Social Responsibility." *Social Responsibility Journal.* https://doi.org/10.1108/1747111111117511.

Munns, A. K., O. Aloquili, and B. Ramsay. 2000. "Joint Venture Negotiation and Managerial Practices in the New Countries of the Former Soviet Union." *International Journal of Project Management* 18 (6): 403–13. https://doi.org/10.1016/S0263-7863(99)00071-X.

Muratbekova-Touron, Maral, Camila Lee Park, and Mauro Fracarolli Nunes. 2021. "Insider's Corruption versus Outsider's Ethicality? Individual Responses to Conflicting Institutional Logics." *International Journal of Human Resource Management*, 1–29. https://doi.org/10.1080/09585192.2021.1945652.

Najman, Boris, Richard Pomfret, Gaël Raballand, and Patricia Sourdin. 2007. "Redistribution of Oil Revenue in Kazakhstan." In *The Economics and Politics of Oil in the Caspian Basin: The Redistribution of Oil Revenues in Azerbaijan and Central Asia*, 111–31. https://doi.org/10.4324/9780203940549.

Nazarbayev, Nursultan. 2007. *The Kazakhstan Way*. Astana: Stacey International Publisher.

—. 2023. *Моя Жизнь. От Зависимости к Свободе [My Life. From Dependence to Freedom]*. Fund Nazarbayev.

Neudorfer, Natascha S., and Ulrike G. Theuerkauf. 2014. "Buying War Not Peace: The Influence of Corruption on the Risk of Ethnic War." *Comparative Political Studies* 47 (13): 1856–86. https://doi.org/10.1177/0010414013516919.

Newton, Scott. 2018. "Conclusion: When Do Informal Practices Turn into Informal Institutions? Informal Constitutions and Informal 'Meta-Rules.'" In *The Global Encyclopaedia of Informality Volume 2*, edited by Alena Ledeneva, Anna Bailey, Sheelagh Barron, Costanza Curro, and Elizabeth Teague. UCL Press.

Noy, Chaim. 2008. "Sampling Knowledge: The Hermeneutics of Snowball Sampling in Qualitative Research." *International Journal of Social Research Methodology* 11 (4): 327–44. https://doi.org/10.1080/13645570701401305.

Nurgaliyev, Bakhyt, Kuatzhan Ualiyev, and Branislav Simonovich. 2015. "Police Corruption in Kazakhstan: The Preliminary Results of the Study." *Review of European Studies* 7 (3): 140–48. https://doi.org/10.5539/res.v7n3p140.

Nurmakov, Adil. 2009. "Resource Nationalism in Kazakhstan's Petroleum Sector: Curse or Blessing?" In *Caspian Energy Politics: Azerbaijan, Kazakhstan and Turkmenistan*, 20–36. https://doi.org/10.4324/9780203865231.

Nuryyev, Guych, and Charles Hickson. 2020. "Economics of Trickle-Down Corruption." *International Journal of Development Issues* 19 (1): 93–102. https://doi.org/10.1108/IJDI-09-2019-0164.

Nwapi, Chilenye. 2015. "Corruption Vulnerabilities in Local Content Policies in the Extractive Sector: An Examination of the Nigerian Oil and Gas Industry Content Development Act, 2010." *Resources Policy* 46 (December): 92–96. https://doi.org/10.1016/j.resourpol.2015.09.001.

O'Neill, Daniel C. 2014. "Risky Business: The Political Economy of Chinese Investment in Kazakhstan." *Journal of Eurasian Studies* 5 (2): 145–56. https://doi.org/10.1016/j.euras.2014.05.007.

Ofori, Jerome Jeffison Yaw, and Päivi Lujala. 2015. "Illusionary Transparency? Oil Revenues, Information Disclosure, and Transparency." *Society & Natural Resources* 28 (11): 1187–1202. https://doi.org/10.1080/08941920.2015.1024806.

Öge, Kerem. 2017a. "Transparent Autocracies: The Extractive Industries Transparency Initiative (EITI) and Civil Society in Authoritarian States." *Extractive Industries and Society* 4 (4): 816–24. https://doi.org/10.1016/j.exis.2016.12.010.

—. 2017b. "Elite Preferences and Transparency Promotion in Kazakhstan." *Communist and Post-Communist Studies* 50 (2): 135–43. https://doi.org/10.1016/j.postcomstud.2017.05.006.

Oka, Natsuko. 2013. "Everyday Corruption in Kazakhstan: An Ethnographic Analysis of Informal Practices."

—. 2018. "Agashka." In *The Global Encyclopaedia of Informality Volume 1*, edited by Alena Ledeneva, Anna Bailey, Sheelagh Barron, and Elizabeth Teague. UCL Press.

—. 2019. "Grades and Degrees for Sale: Understanding Informal Exchanges in Kazakhstan's Education Sector." *Problems of Post-Communism* 66 (5): 329–41. https://doi.org/10.1080/10758216.2018.1468269.

Olawuyi, Damilola S. 2015. "Legal Strategies and Tools for Mitigating Legal Risks Associated with Oil and Gas Investments in Africa." *OPEC Energy Review* 39 (3): 247–65. https://doi.org/10.1111/opec.12043.

Olson, Mancur. 2000. *Power and Prosperity: Outgrowing Communist and Capitalist Dictatorships*. New York, US: Basic Books. https://doi.org/10.2307/20049751.

Onwuka, E. C. 2005. "Oil Extraction, Environmental Degradation and Poverty in the Niger Delta Region of Nigeria: A Viewpoint." *International Journal of Environmental Studies*. https://doi.org/10.108/00207230500040823.

Orazgaliyev, Serik. 2018. "Reconstructing MNE–Host Country Bargaining Model in the International Oil Industry." *Transnational Corporations Review* 10 (1): 30–42. https://doi.org/10.1080/19186444.2018.1436646.

Osmonova, Kishimjan. 2016. "Experiencing Liminality: Housing, Renting and Informal Tenants in Astana." *Central Asian Survey* 35 (2): 237. https://doi.org/10.1080/02634937.2016.1146010.

Ostrowski, Wojciech. 2010. *Politics and Oil in Kazakhstan. Politics and Oil in Kazakhstan*. 1st ed. London: Routledge. https://doi.org/10.4324/9780203869161.

—. 2012. "Rentierism, Dependency and Sovereignty in Central Asia." In *Sovereignty After Empire: Comparing the Middle East and Central Asia*, edited by Sally N. Cummings and Raymond Hinnebusch, 282–303. Edinburgh University Press. https://doi.org/10.3366/edinburgh/9780748643042.003.0013.

Palazuelos, Enrique, and Rafael Fernández. 2012. "Kazakhstan: Oil Endowment and Oil Empowerment." *Communist and Post–Communist Studies* 45 (1–2): 27–37. https://doi.org/10.1016/j.postcomstud.2012.02.004.

Palinkas, Lawrence A., Sarah M. Horwitz, Carla A. Green, Jennifer P. Wisdom, Naihua Duan, and Kimberly Hoagwood. 2013. "Purposeful Sampling for Qualitative Data Collection and Analysis in Mixed Method Implementation Research." *Administration and Policy in Mental Health and Mental Health Services Research* 42: 533–44. https://doi.org/DOI 10.1007/s10488-013-0528-y.

Parkhomchik, Lidiya A. 2016. "Kazakhstan Pipeline Policy in the Caspian Region." *Handbook of Environmental Chemistry* 51: 139–51. https://doi.org/10.1007/698_2015_406.

Peck, Anne E. 2004. *Economic Development in Kazakhstan: The Role of Large Enterprises and Foreign Investment. Economic Development in Kazakhstan: The Role of Large Enterprises and Foreign Investment*. RoutledgeCurzon. https://doi.org/10.4324/9780203563427.

Pegg, Scott. 2006. "Can Policy Intervention Beat the Resource Curse? Evidence from the Chad–Cameroon Pipeline Project." *African Affairs* 105 (418): 1–25.

—. 2009. "Chronicle of a Death Foretold: The Collapse of the Chad–Cameroon Pipeline Project." *African Affairs* 108 (431): 311–20. https://doi.org/10.1093/afraf/adp003.

Pelizzo, Riccardo, Omer Baris, and Saltanat Janenova. 2017. "Objective or Perception-Based? A Debate on the Ideal Measure of Corruption." *Cornell International Law Journal*.

Pelizzo, Riccardo, and Colin Knox. 2021. "'Sobriety, Human Dignity and Public Morality': Ethical Standards in Kazakhstan." *Public Money and Management* 0 (0): 1–9. https://doi.org/10.1080/09540962.2021.19486 71.

Philip, George. 1982. *Oil and Politics in Latin America: Nationalist Movements and State Companies.* Cambridge: Cambridge University Press. https://doi.org/https://doi.org/10.1017/CBO9780511528149.

Playfoot, Jim, Phil Andrews, and Simon Augustus. 2015. *Education and Training for the Oil and Gas Industry: The Evolution of Four Energy Nations Mexico, Nigeria, Brazil and Iraq.* Volume 3. Amsterdam: Elsevier. https://www.sciencedirect.com/science/book/9780128009741.

Pleines, Heiko, and Ronja Wöstheinrich. 2016. "The International–Domestic Nexus in Anti–Corruption Policy Making: The Case of Caspian Oil and Gas States." *Europe–Asia Studies* 68 (2): 291–311. https://doi.org/10.1080/09668136.2015.1126232.

Polese, Abel. 2016. "Corruption State Trust and Informality in Ukraine." In *Addressing Security Risks at the Ukrainian Border Through Best Practices on Good Governance,* 129:31–41. IOS Press. https://doi.org/10.3233/9 78-1-61499-710-8-31.

———. 2018. "Informality and Policy in the Making: Four Flavours to Explain the Essence of Informality." *Interdisciplinary Political Studies* 4 (2): 7–20. https://doi.org/10.1285/I20398573V4N2P7.

—. 2021. "What Is Informality? (Mapping) 'the Art of Bypassing the State' in Eurasian Spaces – and Beyond." *Eurasian Geography and Economics.* https://doi.org/10.1080/15387216.2021.1992791.

Polese, Abel, Jeremy Morris, and Borbala Kovács. 2016. "'States' of Informality in Post–Socialist Europe (and Beyond)." *Journal of Contemporary Central and Eastern Europe* 24 (3): 181–90. https://doi.org/10.108 0/0965156X.2016.1261216.

Polese, Abel, Tetiana Stepurko, Svitlana Oksamytna, Tanel Kerikmae, Archil Chochia, and Olena Levenets. 2018. "Informality and Ukrainian Higher Educational Institutions: Happy Together?" *Policy Futures in Education* 16 (4): 482–500. https://doi.org/10.1177/147821031875881 2.

Pomfret, Richard. 2005. "Kazakhstan's Economy since Independence: Does the Oil Boom Offer a Second Chance for Sustainable Development?" *Europe – Asia Studies* 57 (6): 859–76. https://doi.org/10.1080/0966813 0500199467.

Reschke, Renate. 1992. "„Korruption"." *Nietzsche–Studien* 21: 137–62. https://doi.org/10.1515/9783110244403.137.

Reynolds, Douglas B. 2021. "Alaska's Corporate Social Responsibility: The Economics of the Corruption Case of VECO." *CSR, Sustainability, Ethics and Governance*, 567–78. https://doi.org/10.1007/978-3-030-56092-8_32/COVER.

Ricardo, David. 1821. *On the Principles of Political Economy and Taxation*. 3rd ed. London, UK: John Murray.

Rodríguez, Francisco, and Adam J. Gomolin. 2009. "Anarchy, State, and Dystopia: Venezuelan Economic Institutions before the Advent of Oil." *Bulletin of Latin American Research* 28 (1): 102–21. https://doi.org/10.1111/j.1470-9856.2008.00292.x.

Ross, Michael L. 2015. "What Have We Learned about the Resource Curse?" *Annual Review of Political Science* 18 (1): 239–59. https://doi.org/10.1146/annurev-polisci-052213-040359.

Rothstein, Bo, and Aiysha Varraich. 2017. *Making Sense of Corruption*. Cambridge University Press. https://doi.org/10.1017/9781316681596.

Rubio-Varas, María del Mar. 2015. "Oil Illusion and Delusion Mexico and Venezuela over the Twentieth Century." In *Natural Resources and Economic Growth: Learning from History*, edited by Marc Badia-Miró, Vicente Pinilla, and Henry Willebald, First, 160–83. London and New York: Routledge Taylor & Francis Group.

Rustad, Siri Aas, Philippe Le Billon, and Päivi Lujala. 2017. "Has the Extractive Industries Transparency Initiative Been a Success? Identifying and Evaluating EITI Goals." *Resources Policy* 51: 151–62. https://doi.org/10.1016/j.resourpol.2016.12.004.

Sachs, Jeffrey D., and Andrew M. Warner. 1995. "Natural Resource Abundance and Economic Growth." *NBER Working Paper 5398* 3 (December). https://doi.org/10.3386/w5398.

—. 1999. "The Big Push, Natural Resource Booms and Growth." *Journal of Development Economics* 59 (1): 43–76. https://doi.org/10.1016/S0304-3878(99)00005-X.

—. 2001. "The Curse of Natural Resources." *European Economic Review* 45 (4–6): 827–38. https://doi.org/10.1016/S0014-2921(01)00125-8.

Saivetz, Carol R. 2003. "Perspectives on the Caspian Sea Dilemma: Russian Policies since the Soviet Demise." *Eurasian Geography and Economics* 44 (8): 588–606. https://doi.org/10.2747/1538-7216.44.8.588.

Sakal, Halil Burak. 2015. "Natural Resource Policies and Standard of Living in Kazakhstan." *Central Asian Survey* 34 (2): 237–54. https://doi.org/10.1080/02634937.2014.987970.

Sala-i-Martin, Xavier, and Arvind Subramanian. 2013. "Addressing the Natural Resource Curse: An Illustration from Nigeria." *Journal of African Economies* 22 (4): 570–615. https://doi.org/10.1093/jae/ejs033.

Sallaberry, Jonatas Dutra, Liz Spinello Quaesner, Mayla Cristina Costa, and Leonardo Flach. 2020. "Measurement of Damage from Corruption in Brazil." *Journal of Financial Crime* 27 (4): 1239. https://doi.org/10.110 8/JFC-04-2020-0057.

Samoilenko, Sergei, Eric Shiraev, Jennifer Keohane, and Martijn Icks. 2018. "Character Assassination (Global)." In *The Global Encyclopaedia of Informality Volume 2*, edited by Alena Ledeneva, Anna Bailey, Sheelagh Barron, Costanza Curro, and Elizabeth Teague, 441–45. UCL Press.

Sanghera, Balihar. 2020. "Justice, Power and Informal Settlements: Understanding the Juridical View of Property Rights in Central Asia." *International Sociology* 35 (1): 22–44. https://doi.org/10.1177/02685809 19877596.

Sanghera, Balihar, and Elmira Satybaldieva. 2020. "The Other Road to Serfdom: The Rise of the Rentier Class in Post-Soviet Economies." *Social Science Information* 59 (3): 505–36. https://doi.org/10.1177/05390184 20943077.

Sari, N. 2001. "Consumer Out-of-Pocket Spending for Pharmaceuticals in Kazakhstan: Implications for Sectoral Reform." *Health Policy and Planning* 16 (4): 428–34. https://doi.org/10.1093/heapol/16.4.428.

Sarsenbayev, K. 2011. "Kazakhstan Petroleum Industry 2008–2010: Trends of Resource Nationalism Policy?" *The Journal of World Energy Law & Business* 4 (4): 369–79. https://doi.org/10.1093/jwelb/jwr017.

Sartori, Giovanni. 1991. "Comparing and Miscomparing." *Journal of Theoretical Politics* 3 (3): 243–57. https://doi.org/10.1177/09516928910030 03001.

Satpayev, Dossym. 2014. "Corruption in Kazakhstan and the Quality of Governance."

Schensul, Jean, and Margaret LeCompte. 2013. *Essential Ethnographic Methods: A Mixed Methods Approach. Ethnographer's Toolkit.* 2nd ed. Altamira Press.

Scott, James. 1985. *Weapons of the Weak: Everyday Forms of Peasant Resistance.* New Haven: Yale University Press.

—. 2012. *Two Cheers for Anarchism: Six Easy Pieces on Autonomy, Dignity, and Meaningful Work and Play.* Princeton University Press. https://doi.or g/10.1515/9781400844623.

Seriev, Bolat Abduldaevich, Amangeldi Gabdilkarimovich Tolamissov, Erbol Zhaksibekovich Beisov, and Ermek Talantuly Nurmaganbet. 2013. "Kazakhstan Model of Anti-Corruption Drive." *Middle East Journal of Scientific Research* 13 (Special Issue): 36–42. https://doi.org/ 10.5829/idosi.mejsr.2013.13.pl.14005.

Shammas, Pierre, and Koichiro Nagata. 2000. "Profiles of the Petroleum Sectors in Caspian Region Countries and the Potential for a New Caspian to Middle East Gulf Export Line Through Iran." *Energy Exploration & Exploitation*. Sage Publications, Ltd. https://doi.org/10.2307/43754164.

Sharipova, Dina. 2015. "State Retrenchment and Informal Institutions in Kazakhstan: People's Perceptions of Informal Reciprocity in the Healthcare Sector." *Central Asian Survey* 34 (3): 310-29. https://doi.org/10.1080/02634937.2015.1044199.

Sharma, Chandan, and Ritesh Kumar Mishra. 2022. "On the Good and Bad of Natural Resource, Corruption, and Economic Growth Nexus." *Environmental & Resource Economics* 82 (4): 889-922. https://doi.org/10.1007/S10640-022-00694-X.

Sheikhmohammady, Majid, D. Marc Kilgour, and Keith W. Hipel. 2010. "Modeling the Caspian Sea Negotiations." *Group Decision and Negotiation* 19 (2): 149-68. https://doi.org/10.1007/s10726-008-9121-2.

Shmatenko, Leonid. 2013. "An Overview of Kazakhstan's Investment Laws and Its Investor-State Arbitral Awards." *International Law Quarterly* 30 (4): 25-33.

Sholk, Dena. 2018. "Baraholka." In *The Global Encyclopaedia of Informality Volume 2*, edited by Alena Ledeneva, Anna Bailey, Sheelagh Barron, and Elizabeth Teague. UCL Press.

Silverstein, Ken. 2014. *The Secret World of Oil*. Verso.

Sindzingre, Alice. 2006. "The Relevance of the Concepts of Formality and Informality: A Theoretical Appraisal." In *Linking the Formal and Informal Economy: Concepts and Policies*. https://doi.org/10.1093/0199204764.003.0004.

Smith, Peter Seaborn. 1972. "Petrobras: The Politicizing of a State Company, 1953-1964." *Business History Review* 46 (2): 182-201.

Sorbello, Paolo. 2021. "Industrial Relations in Kazakhstan's Oil Sector (1991-2019)." Glasgow.

Sovacool, Benjamin K., and Nathan Andrews. 2015. "Does Transparency Matter? Evaluating the Governance Impacts of the Extractive Industries Transparency Initiative (EITI) in Azerbaijan and Liberia." *Resources Policy* 45 (September): 183-92. https://doi.org/10.1016/j.resourpol.2015.04.003.

Sovacool, Benjamin K., Götz Walter, Thijs Van de Graaf, and Nathan Andrews. 2016. "Energy Governance, Transnational Rules, and the Resource Curse: Exploring the Effectiveness of the Extractive Industries Transparency Initiative (EITI)." *World Development* 83 (July): 179-92. https://doi.org/10.1016/j.worlddev.2016.01.021.

Stepurko, Tetiana, Milena Pavlova, Irena Gryga, and Wim Groot. 2013. "Informal Payments for Health Care Services – Corruption or Gratitude? A Study on Public Attitudes, Perceptions and Opinions in Six Central and Eastern European Countries." *Communist and Post-Communist Studies* 46 (4): 419–31. https://doi.org/10.1016/j.postcomstud.2013.08.004.

Strønen, Iselin Åsedotter. 2017. *Grassroots Politics and Oil Culture in Venezuela: The Revolutionary Petro-State. Grassroots Politics and Oil Culture in Venezuela: The Revolutionary Petro-State.* Cham: Springer International Publishing. https://doi.org/10.1007/978-3-319-59507-8.

Tekin, Ali, and Paul Andrew Williams. 2011. *Geo-Politics of the Euro-Asia Energy Nexus: The European Union, Russia, and Turkey.* Edited by Ali Tekin and Paul Andrew Williams. *Choice Reviews Online.* Palgrave Macmillan UK. https://doi.org/10.5860/choice.49–0532.

Thompson, Theresa, and Anwar Shah. 2005. "Transparency International's Corruption Perceptions Index: Whose Perceptions Are They Anyway." In *Discussion Draft, March.*

Tipaldou, Sofia. 2021. "Kazakhstan 2.0: Change and Continuity?" In *Political Regimes and Neopatrimonialism in Central Asia: A Sociology of Power Perspective,* edited by Ferran Izquierdo-Brichs and Francesc Serra-Massansalvador, 249–93. Palgrave Macmillan.

Titl, Vitezslav, and Benny Geys. 2019. "Political Donations and the Allocation of Public Procurement Contracts." *European Economic Review* 111: 443–58. https://doi.org/10.1016/j.euroecorev.2018.11.004.

Totaro, Maurizio G. 2017. "Kashagan and the Shifting Landscapes of Capitalization in the North Caspian Oil Industry: Practical Lessons Beyong the Clichés." *Policy Paper: Around the Caspian.* http://caspianet.eu/2017/03/27/kashagan–shifting–landscapes–capitalizatio n–north–caspian–oil–industry–practical–lessons–beyond–cliches/.

Totaro, Maurizio G., and Paolo Sorbello. 2021. "Oil, Capital, and Labour Around the Caspian." In *The Routledge Handbook on Contemporary Central Asia,* edited by Rico Isaacs and Erica Marat, 496. Routledge.

Tutumlu, Assel, and Ilyas Rustemov. 2019. "The Paradox of Authoritarian Power: Bureaucratic Games and Information Asymmetry. The Case of Nazarbayev's Kazakhstan." *Problems of Post-Communism.* https://doi.org/10.1080/10758216.2019.1699432.

Uldam, Julie, and Hans Krause Hansen. 2017. "Corporate Responses to Stakeholder Activism: Partnerships and Surveillance." *Critical Perspectives on International Business* 13 (2): 151–65. https://doi.org/10.1108/cpoib–07–2015–0029.

Vasileva, Alexandra. 2018. "Otkat." In *The Global Encyclopaedia of Informality Volume 2*, edited by Alena Ledeneva, Anna Bailey, Sheelagh Barron, Costanza Curro, and Elizabeth Teague. UCL Press.

Verhoosel, Gaëtan, and Sabeen Sheikh. 2013. "Caratube International Oil Company LLP v Republic of Kazakhstan Revisiting Threshold Jurisdictional Questions – The Meaning of Foreign Control and Investment." *ICSID Review – Foreign Investment Law Journal* 28 (2): 301–6. https://doi.org/10.1093/icsidreview/sit023.

Vermeer, Eduard B. 2015. "The Global Expansion of Chinese Oil Companies: Political Demands, Profitability and Risks." *China Information* 29 (1): 3–32. https://doi.org/10.1177/0920203X14566177.

Vernon, Raymond. 1971. *Sovereignty at Bay: The Spread of U.S. Enterprises*. New York: Basic Books.

Volkov, Vadim. 2016. *Violent Entrepreneurs: The Use of Force in the Making of Russian Capitalism*. Cornell University Press.

Watters, Kate. 2013. "The Fight for Community Justice against Big Oil in the Caspian Region: The Case of Berezovka, Kazakhstan." In *Environmental Justice and Sustainability in the Former Soviet Union*, edited by Julian Agyeman and Yelena Ogneva–Himmelberger. MIT Press. https://doi.org/10.7551/mitpress/9780262012669.003.0008.

Weinthal, Erika, and Kate Watters. 2010. "Transnational Environmental Activism in Central Asia: The Coupling of Domestic Law and International Conventions." 19 (5): 782–807. https://doi.org/10.1080/096 44016.2010.508311.

Wellhausen, Rachel L. 2014. *The Shield of Nationality. The Shield of Nationality*. Cambridge University Press. https://doi.org/10.1017/cbo97813 16014547.

Wenar, Leif. 2013. "Fighting the Resource Curse." *Global Policy* 4 (3): 298–304. https://doi.org/10.1111/1758-5899.12069.

Werner, Cynthia. 2000. "Gifts, Bribes, and Development in Post–Soviet Kazakstan." *Human Organization* 59 (1): 11–22. https://doi.org/10.2307 /44126662.

Wiig, Arne, and Ivar Kolstad. 2010. "Multinational Corporations and Host Country Institutions: A Case Study of CSR Activities in Angola." *International Business Review* 19 (2): 178–90. https://doi.org/10.1016/j. ibusrev.2009.11.006.

Winters, Matthew S., and John A. Gould. 2011. "Betting on Oil: The World Bank's Attempt to Promote Accountability in Chad." *Global Governance* 17 (2): 229–45.

Yarrington, Doug. 2003. "Cattle, Corruption, and Venezuelan State Formation during the Regime of Juan Vicente Gómez, 1908–35." *Latin American Research Review* 38 (2): 9–33. https://doi.org/10.1353/lar.2003.0028.

Yates, Douglas A. 2015. "The Rise and Fall of Oil–Rentier States in Africa." In *New Approaches to the Governance of Natural Resources: Insights from Africa*, edited by Andrew J. Grant, Nadège W. R. Compaoré, and Matthew I. Mitchell, 45–64. London: Palgrave Macmillan UK.

Yeager, Matthew G. 2012. "The CIA Made Me Do It: Understanding the Political Economy of Corruption in Kazakhstan." *Crime, Law and Social Change* 57 (4): 441–57. https://doi.org/10.1007/s10611-011-9341-2.

Yessenova, Saulesh. 2010. "Borrowed Places: Eviction Wars and Property Rights Formalization in Kazakhstan." *Research in Economic Anthropology* 30: 11–45. https://doi.org/10.1108/S0190-1281(2010)0000030005.

—. 2012. "The Tengiz Oil Enclave: Labor, Business, and the State." *Political and Legal Anthropology Review* 35 (1): 94–113. https://doi.org/10.1111/j.1555-2934.2012.01181.x.

—. 2015. "The Political Economy Of Oil Privatization In Post–Soviet Kazakhstan." In *Subterranean Estates: Life Worlds of Oil and Gas*, edited by Hannah Appel, Arthur Mason, and Michael Watts, 1st ed., 291–306. Cornell University Press. https://doi.org/10.7591/9780801455407-017.

Yin, Robert K. 2018. *Case Study Research and Applications: Design and Methods. Paper Knowledge . Toward a Media History of Documents*. Sixth. Vol. 5. London, UK: SAGE Publications.

Appendix
The Methodological Challenge of Studying Corruption

Studying corruption is a complex endeavour for both qualitative and quantitative research. Among the most common indexes used in research to quantify corruption are the Transparency International Corruption Perception Index (CPI), the Control of Corruption of the World Governance Indicators, the measurement of corruption of the International Country Risk Guide of the PRS Group, and the Global Competitiveness Index's estimates of diversion of public funds. In a study destined to test the reliability of these indexes Pelizzo, Baris, and Janenova (2017) argued that these indexes cannot offer a solid estimate of the historical evolution of the phenomenon. The problem does not lie in the methodology used but rather in the source of data. In fact, an aggregation of subjective opinions cannot produce an objective measurement (Thompson and Shah 2005). Research uses the CPI not because there are no ways to produce an objective measurement, but because it is easy to retrieve. There are a number of researchers who tried to develop fact–based indexes, but as far as the research on the oil sector is concerned, as much as 93% of studies reviewed used perception–based indexes to evaluate the levels of corruption in a target country or even employed it in multivariate regressions through self–fulfilling prophecies (Moisé 2020, 223).

Furthermore, Cooley and Sharman (2015) argued how measuring corruption with a score for each country is senseless in a globalised world economy. It would be hard to imagine such advanced corruption schemes without banks in Switzerland and the advantageous corporate taxation of the Netherlands. As discussed in *Specious Contract Cancellations*, the Kazakh oil industry took advantage of the perks of globalisation several times: for example, by registering companies abroad using nominees. When discussing FDI in Kazakhstan in a working paper on corruption, Dossym Satpayev (2014) noted how in 2012, among the biggest investors in

Kazakhstan were the Netherlands in the first place, the UK in the second, the British Virgin Islands in the sixth, and Switzerland in the ninth. Unsurprisingly, almost every company operating in the oil sector of Kazakhstan is registered in one of these countries. Even the National Oil Company KazMunayGas used a branch from the Netherlands to acquire shares in the North Caspian Operating Consortium. In fact, in the Netherlands, there is a facilitated system of taxation for capital repatriation. In a similar fashion, the Italian oil company ENI has a branch registered in the Netherlands so that when repatriating to Italy, the capital has a lower taxation than if the company transferred it directly from Kazakhstan to Italy.[431] This is to say, that numerical data can be misleading, especially when they are not accompanied by a sound knowledge of the context.

Similarly, researching informality often translates into using a qualitative approach relying on ethnographic methods. This choice of research design tends to overemphasise the importance of national cultures, seldom leading authors to ungrounded theorisations. For example, Gaukhar Kaliyeva (2013) argued that the reasons for bribery should be found in the traditions of Kazakh society, and in a more prestigious publication, Huseyn Aliyev (2015) argued that post–Soviet informality is so peculiar that should be acknowledged as a whole different category. The problem with these arguments is that they do not emerge from a comparison of different cases but rather from case studies. This presumed exceptionalism is clearly not functional for theorisations whose objective is to generalise frameworks for processes, cases, and phenomena. Arguing that the oil sector of Kazakhstan is extremely corrupt because of the specific features of the Kazakh culture is inaccurate at best. While it is true that Kazakhstan was historically a country where informality was widespread, it is also necessary to acknowledge that the culture of the oil sector often involved cases of large–scale corruption in several countries (Moisé 2020, 219). In doing this, it is possible to argue that the business and local culture reinforced each other and acknowledge that every human experience is ultimately culture. The qualitative approach uses depth to

---

431 Financial department director, interview by author, April 6, 2020.

provide context for comparisons, not to produce unrelated pieces of knowledge.

Aware of the drawbacks of both approaches, this research aimed at proposing a taxonomy of informal practices with the final goal of improving the measurement of predatory practices as well as the understanding of evolutions in the political economic landscape of any rentier country. For instance, by monitoring specious contract terminations or by foreseeing the stages of negotiations between governments and foreign energy companies. The next section will focus on the choices of research design, the following one on the literature gap that the research aimed to address, the third on methods used to retrieve literature, and the final one on methods used to retrieve data for this research.

1. On Choices of Research Design

In classical political science, Giovanni Sartori (1991) argued that comparisons are used to control (verify or falsify) generalisations (1991, 244). Yet, the study envisioned cannot achieve that objective: firstly, there are no generalisations to prove yet; secondly, comparing two case studies that were purposefully selected cannot verify nor falsify generalisations. This is the reason for which the expression 'parallelism' was preferred over comparison. What this research aimed to achieve was to suggest generalisations that studies with broader samples can verify or falsify. At the same time, all the additional countries selected (Venezuela, Russia, Chad, Mexico, and Brazil) are comparable[432] because they are rentier states with high levels of corruption. The reasons for which they are paralleled are: 1) to show that the phenomena under analysis are not exclusive to Kazakhstan;[433] 2) and to put the phenomena in perspective, suggesting possible generalisations.

Another point that comparisons make is to ascertain the independent variable, which is the factor that explains why two countries are so similar in all aspects but the one which is under

---

432 Both to Kazakhstan and among themselves.
433 Hence avoiding what Sartori termed 'parochialism' (Sartori 1991, 247).

investigation (Sartori 1991, 250). The parallelisms fall within the category of most similar cases but the phenomenon under investigation is not different. On the opposite, the starting point of the whole reasoning is that the phenomenon is indeed similar. The resource curse literature has long dealt with why (and how) countries with similar resource endowments have managed to avoid the problems associated with the exploitation of their mineral wealth, but this is not the point that the book aimed to make. If there is a comparison, this is between the phenomena under scrutiny: patrimonial embezzlement in Kazakhstan and Venezuela; state racketeering in Kazakhstan and Russia; fine threats in Kazakhstan and Chad; specious contract cancellations in Kazakhstan and Mexico; and bid rigging in Kazakhstan and Brazil.

The generalisations suggested at the end of each of these chapters did not emerge from the comparisons of political systems or oil industries but between those of the practices. As an example, while state racketeering is similar in Kazakhstan and Russia, there are some key elements that differentiate how the strategy was employed in the two countries. These differences may be due to case-specific details, such as the institutional role of the perpetrator. Therefore, states are paralleled, whereas phenomena are compared. At the same time, phenomena are compared not to prove in what they differentiate, but to ascertain the conditions that set them in place or the objective they aim to achieve. In this way, these phenomena acquire an identity that sets them apart from others that are similar, but not quite the same. This is the reason why naming the practice is such a critical aspect of this analysis.

2. The Literature Gap

Many articles and books focused on the means devised to decrease corruption that, as authors noted, are often inefficient due to lack of political commitment. Starting from ethical codes and commissioners, whose role was expected to improve transparency in a number of sectors (Janenova and Knox 2020; Pelizzo and Knox 2021), to specific initiatives targeting the extractive industries, such as the EITI (Furstenberg 2018), policies to reduce corruption in Kazakhstan revealed to be nothing more than formal fulfilments. This has been well outlined by Pleines and Wöstheinrich (2016) in their analysis of the conditions to which Caspian states decided to participate in international anticorruption mechanisms. As the authors noted, the tension between transnational demands and national political elites does not often translate into serious conflicts, and there are different degrees to which governments commit to international treaties. Unlike Azerbaijan, that committed to the OECD ACN, GRECO, UNCAC, IFSWF, and the EITI, Kazakhstan only participates in the first, third, and last one. Yet, for both countries, these were tactical concessions rather than a genuine interest in fighting corruption. This is evident in the Kazakh oil sector, where oil swaps are done in secrecy, the Ministry of Finance publishes reports selectively, and PSAs and Joint Venture Agreements with international companies have undisclosed terms (Öge 2017b, 139).

Overall, the corruption scandals that received the attention of scholars were largely the same: the 'Kazakhgate' was mentioned seven times (Yeager 2012; Cooley and Sharman 2015; Öge 2017b; LaPorte 2017; Furstenberg 2018; Pleines and Wöstheinrich 2016; Knox and Janenova 2019), the bid rigging of Baker Hughes five times (Holtzblatt and Tschakert 2014; Cooley and Sharman 2015; LaPorte 2017; Furstenberg 2018; Knox and Janenova 2019), while the investigation of ENI in 2012 (Furstenberg 2018) and the suspect cases of Chinese buying of Kazakh assets (O'Neill 2014) were discussed only once.

Hotzblatt and Tschakert (2014) aimed to show red flags in international business deals that could indicate corruption, whereas Matthew Yeager (2012) discussed the Foreign Corrupt Practices Act court case as a failure of the US judicial system in delivering justice. In her study on repression in kleptocracies, also Jody LaPorte (2017) used them in justification of her choice of Kazakhstan as a case study. Likewise, Cooley and Sharman (2015) referred to those cases to show that while transnational corruption schemes often involve foreign 'legitimate' actors, such as unscrupulous lawyers and banks, international anticorruption norms focus solely on minor national players while ignoring the elephant in the room: the kleptocratic elite. Instead, Daniel O'Neill (2014) discussed the complex

260   THE HOUSE ALWAYS WINS

interplay between the Nazarbayev family and companies keen to pay any price to acquire more energy resources with the objective of problematise Chinese investments in Kazakhstan. While all these papers have been guiding the research, they had different analytical objectives.

The above-mentioned criteria have considerably narrowed down the search, hence reducing the inner variation of systematic literature reviews. The methods chosen by the authors of the studies were largely limited to descriptive statistics of the main economic indicators of the energy sector with seldom use of more advanced statistical tools to individuate possible symptoms of the Dutch disease (Egert and Leonard 2007; Dikkaya and Doyar 2017; Kutan and Wyzan 2005). In terms of topics, most of the literature focused either on the oil industry or more broadly on the energy sector. Within the studies on the oil industry it is possible to identify sub-topics discussing the international implications of the sector in terms of energy security (Parkhomchik 2016; Vermeer 2015; P. K. Lee 2005) or the relative strength of the state in controlling its resources (Nurmakov 2009; Domjan and Stone 2010; Sarsenbayev 2011). The only topics distinct from the energy sector, and therefore outliers of this sample, were those dealing with the negotiations on the status of the Caspian Sea (Sheikhmohammady, Kilgour, and Hipel 2010; Saivetz 2003) and those on the bargaining strategies of multinational corporations and rentier states in their dependent relationship (Hosman 2009; Sarsenbayev 2011).

The Global Encyclopaedia of Informality and the *Global Informality Project* were both surveyed to find possible overlaps with the practices discussed in this research, but apart from *otzhim* and *reiderstvo* discussed in Chapter IV, *State Racketeering*, nothing else was found.[434] On the one hand, Kazakh practices discussed by these studies are small in scale and even cultural-specific,[435] and on the other, global practices have a more general breadth that does not

---

434 Although the Ukrainian expression *deryban* (Kesarchuk 2018, 195), used to identify the distribution of public or state-owned resources to the elite circle, and the Russian *otkat* (Vasileva 2018, 274) come close to patrimonial embezzlement, this is in fact because both the expressions refer to some form of embezzlement.
435 Such as *agashka* (Oka 2018) or *baraholka* (Sholk 2018, 125).

necessarily involve rentierism nor kleptocratic strategies. Finally, while different in framing and scale, both Cynthia Werner (Werner 2000) and Natsuko Oka (2013) attempted to classify acts of informality and petty corruption in Kazakhstan: the former dealt with informal payments and relied on their cultural-specific names, whereas the latter addressed petty corruption in different public spheres.

Informal governance in Kazakhstan was addressed by Rico Isaacs (2011; 2013) in his research on the party system of the Central Asian Republic. While his analyses do not overlap with this study, Isaacs, and before him, Ostrowski (2010), remarked on the quintessential neo-patrimonial dimension of the Nazarbayev regime: 'where informal patrimonial politics such as personalism of office, patron-client networks and factional elite conflict are interwoven with formal legal-rational institutions' (Isaacs 2011, 8; 2010). As Isaacs warned (2014), neopatrimonialism does not define the regime, as much as its sources of authority and legitimation. At the same time, the concept describes the use of 'political power as a form of private property', blurring the division between formal and informal (Isaacs 2014, 231).

The clear precursor of this research is *Politics and Oil in Kazakhstan*, by Wojciech Ostrowski (2010). The book is an in-depth analysis of how, in the early years since independence, Nazarbayev gained control over the oil sector, relying at first on corporatist techniques and then on patron-client networks. This is the starting point of this research. In fact, the description of patrimonial embezzlement assumes that the embezzlement of funds by the circle of Nazarbayev translated into patron-client relationships. This study expands on the results of *Politics and Oil*, identifying the pressure exerted by the regime on foreign oil companies as a relevant strategy that the executive exploited throughout the years.

3. Methods to Retrieve Literature

Systematic reviews emerged in the early 1990s in clinical biomedical research in the UK, but since then have moved to other fields (Jesson, Matheson, and Lacey 2011, 105). Producing the review means offering all researchers interested in studying the topic the means to understand what has been already done and in which direction should future research be oriented. This is the traditional understanding of what a classic literature review does, except it does not, it only promises to do it because it lacks the certainty of having reviewed all relevant studies on a given topic. This last statement is reinforced by the fact that a number of studies published in relevant journals and included in the systematic reviews conducted for this research are very similar, adding very little to the discussion. This is not only the outcome of flawed literature reviews but also the effect of over–publishing under pressure generated by the increasing requirements of the academic industry.[436]

The best way to understand the efficiency of the different approaches to literature is offered by a comparison with the sampling of a population. A traditional literature review is not dissimilar from the snowball method used to create a sample: it can be a very useful tool, but is time–consuming and it does not guarantee the result. Besides its inherent flaws, in general, sampling methods do not tell anything about the population. This literature review is therefore problematic at its start because the process is potentially neverending, leaving the researcher with the uncertainty of not having completed a fundamental task for which will be blamed at a later stage. Conversely, a systematic review starts with the operationalisation of the topic in a few relevant keywords. If the topic is 'corruption', introducing the keyword in one of the relevant databases of social sciences (such as Scopus or the Web of Science of the Institute of Scientific Information) shows the size of the population under scrutiny, in this case, all the academic literature ever

---

436 Critiques of traditional reviews are becoming increasingly common as highlighted in Doing a Literature Review — Traditional and Systematic Techniques (Jesson, Matheson, and Lacey 2011, 24). Another major limit lies in the fact that less than only half of published studies are open-access, as shown in "Trends for Open Access to Publication," *European Commission*, https://ec.europa.eu/info/research-and-innovation/strategy/goals-research-and-innovation-policy/open-science/open-science-monitor/trends-open-access-publications_en, and this condition affects the quality of literature reviews of researchers from different contexts. In other words, a researcher from a good university will have access to more literature than a colleague from a worse one.

produced on the topic 'corruption'. In a systematic review, this phase is called identification.

The phase of identification is the one that requires more reflection because the researcher has not yet put any real effort into the search and has the opportunity to change his/her idea, project or population. In this phase, it becomes clear whether the research is feasible or not in consideration of the resources at disposal, namely time to read and access to the literature. This is when the researcher can decide to narrow down the topic reducing the size of the population indirectly. If the topic is corruption in Uganda, the operationalisation of the topic will produce two keywords, 'corruption' and 'Uganda', and the database will show an inferior number of entries. At this point, the researcher should proceed in creating a few criteria that will be necessary to identify the sample of the study, namely the literature to read. While these criteria are conceived to create the sample, they may have the positive side-effect of giving a more precise picture of the population. An example is the criterion 'all studies should be in the realm of social sciences'. On the one hand, this choice reduces your sample of studies, on the other hand, enforcing it allows the researcher to get rid of studies originally included in the population due to the inherent ambiguity of the keyword used. For example, by simply introducing 'corruption' in Scopus a researcher will obtain studies not relevant to the purpose of the search, such as 'corruption of digital images'. The creation of these pre-determined criteria is what makes the sampling of the literature potentially unbiased. In practice, the population and sample are never perfect, but the process is verifiable and falsifiable, and hence scientific in Popperian terms.

When the criteria are established, the process moves from identification to screening. This is when the researcher judges critically the titles and abstracts of the pool of results informed by the pre-determined criteria. The next phase is eligibility, the moment for the researcher to read the full text of the remaining studies. In a systematic review, the researcher starts reading an article aware that it will be useful, while in a traditional review, the reading may be unproductive. In fact, even if a study is not what the title and abstract promised it to be, the initial criteria may determine its exclusion from the final sample of studies. The literature review terminates with a full list of studies included in the sample.[437] This list, along with the description of the most important studies, is what will help future researchers to have a full account of the literature on a particular topic, at a given time, reading a few pages. As discussed by Mahood, Van Eerd, and Irvin (2014), for the completeness of a systematic review, grey literature, namely non-academic or unpublished studies,[438] can further complete the scope of the search to relevant documents neglected by academic databases.[439]

The objective of this research is to create a taxonomy of informal behaviours in the petroleum industry of Kazakhstan. As such, the keywords identified are four: corruption, informality, oil and Kazakhstan. The systematic reviews conducted for this research originate from an overlap of these concepts: 1) corruption and oil; 2) corruption and Kazakhstan; 3) informality/informal and Kazakhstan; 4) oil and Kazakhstan.[440] It is important to acknowledge that while these systematic reviews included all works respecting the pre-determined criteria, there were a number of published articles whose contribution was at the limit of the ideological, as in the case of *Kazakhstan Model of Anti-Corruption Drive* (Seriev et al. 2013), or simply flawed in terms of research design and methods chosen. As a rule of thumb, the samples reviewed corresponded to the population of studies. The following sub-sections address the rules adopted to conduct each systematic review. At the end of the chapter, there are tables listing studies included and excluded.

The choice of languages in the systematic reviews varied in consideration of the keywords employed: in corruption and oil, to limit the results only English was employed; in the others, both English and Russian were employed. The absence of Kazakh is

---

437 To complete the analogy, if the author of the review decides to read all the studies shortlisted, the sample and population will correspond while introducing a criterion like 'reviewing only studies with more than 50 citations' will inevitably shrink the sample when compared to the population.

438 Such as reports of international organisations and PhD theses.

439 Still, both Scopus and WoS have become extremely inclusive, listing conference papers as well as articles from specialised journals.

440 There are a few studies repeating in more than one search as it is possible to notice by reading the tables at the end of the appendix.

because academic literature from the region is only in English and Russian. As a post–Soviet country, Kazakhstan has a history of bi-lingualism that translated into the official recognition of both Ka-zakh and Russian as official languages of the state (Moisé and Polese 2021, 307). The former is widely spoken in the oil region, whereas the latter, acknowledged as the 'superior language' throughout the Soviet era, is not only spoken by the elite and intel-lectuals but also in Almaty and in the northern regions bordering the Russian Federation.

3.1 Systematic review: Corruption and oil

The systematic review of 'corruption' and 'oil' has been thoroughly described in *Corruption in the Oil Sector* (2020). The number of stud-ies included in the original review was 184.[441] The result has been updated to October 2022 including sixty–seven new studies (thirty-nine new from 'corruption' and twenty–eight from stemming the keyword 'corruption', corrupt*, and by adding the keywords 'bribe', 'graft', and 'kickback')[442] while respecting the criteria of the previous review, namely:

---

441 For more information check pages 227 to 232 of *Corruption in the Oil Sector* (Moisé 2020).

442 The stemming corrupt* created 643 results on Scopus (Social Sciences; Econom-ics, Econometrics and Finance; Business, Management and Accounting; Energy; Arts and Humanities; Environmental Science; Multidisciplinary) and 510 on the WoS (Economics; Environmental Studies; Political Science; Energy Fuels; Area Studies; International Relations; Business; Development Studies; Engineering Petroleum; Environmental Studies; Social Sciences Interdisciplinary; Law; Busi-ness Finance; Criminology Penology; Management; Public Administration; So-ciology; Anthropology; Ethics; Humanities Multidisciplinary; Geography; His-tory; History of Social Sciences; Social Work; Asian Studies; Ecology; Social Is-sues; and Social Sciences Mathematical Methods). Additional searches in-cluded: 'bribe' and 'oil': twenty-nine and eighteen results on Scopus and WoS respectively (listed in Table 19 at the end of the appendix), with seven results included. 'graft' and 'oil': sixty-eight on Scopus (Environmental Science; En-ergy; Multidisciplinary; Social Sciences; Arts and Humanities; Business, Man-agement and Accounting; Economics, Econometrics and Finance) and 124 on WoS (Multidisciplinary Sciences; Environmental Sciences; Energy Fuels; Busi-ness Finance; Environmental Studies; Geography; and Law), all the studies se-lected were doubles found in searches with different keywords. 'kickback' and 'oil': thirteen and four results on Scopus and WoS respectively, with no limits applied, all the studies selected were doubles of searches with different key-words.

a) The literature should remain in the realm of social sciences.[443]
b) Both the topics represented by their keywords should be included in the study, and at least one of them should be the primary focus of the research.
c) Studies should be in English.[444]

With the exception of the literature excluded by criterion c), the population of studies on corruption in the oil sector corresponds to the sample reviewed. Articles and books have been divided according to the major streams of literature identified, namely: the resource curse; transparency; accountability; oil management and energy strategies. Seventy–four new studies have been classified based on these categories. The full list of studies is displayed in Table 18 at the end of the appendix.

3.2 Systematic review: Oil and Kazakhstan

Conducted in August 2019 and complemented in January 2022 on the WoS and Scopus, the search of literature relied on the keywords 'oil' and 'Kazakhstan'. On the other hand, a Google search of the aforementioned terms was futile because the first twenty pages were crowded with results from several websites showing relevant statistics on petroleum, descriptions of oil companies working in the country, and newspaper articles that did not fit the review of

---

443 The subjects included in the WoS were: anthropology; area study; business; business finance; criminology penology; demography; economics; education educational research; energy fuels; engineering petroleum; environmental sciences; environmental studies; ethics; ethnic studies; geography; green sustainable science technology; health policy services; history; history philosophy of science; history of social sciences; hospitality leisure sport tourism; humanities multidisciplinary; industrial relations labour; international relations; law; management; multidisciplinary sciences; planning development; political science; psychology applied; psychology clinical; public administration; public environmental occupation; social issues; social sciences interdisciplinary; social sciences mathematical methods; social work; sociology; urban studies. The subjects included in Scopus were: business, management and accounting; economics, econometrics and finance; energy; environmental science; multidisciplinary; psychology; and social sciences.

444 A total of sixty-six (not checking duplicates) new studies were excluded based on their language.

the search. The total number of studies included is 143[445] and they have been identified respecting the following criteria:

a) The literature should remain in the realm of social sciences.[446]
b) Both keywords should be the primary focus of the research.
c) Studies should be in English or Russian.[447]
d) The literature should include only academic studies.

Criterion a) helped to narrow down the initial screening from 979 to five 503 results. Similarly, criterion d) was introduced to exclude news articles from specialised magazines such as the *Oil & Gas Journal*, narrowing down the number of studies from 480 to 183. While it is true that news can give good insights into the evolution of the oil sector of Kazakhstan, their search was targeted and limited to fill the gaps of academic sources in drawing the timeline of ownership in the sector. The search of January 2022 followed the same parameters[448] with the result of adding thirty more studies to the list.[449]

---

445 Table 19, at the end of the appendix, shows the full list of studies included in this systematic review.

446 The subjects included in the WoS were: anthropology; area studies; business; business finance; criminal penology; development studies; ecology; economics; energy fuels; environmental sciences; environmental studies; geography; geography physical; history; international relations; law; management; multidisciplinary sciences; planning development; political science; psychology applied; public administration; public environmental occupational health; social sciences interdisciplinary; and statistical probability. The subjects included in Scopus were: business, management and accounting; economics, econometrics and finance; energy; environmental science; multidisciplinary; psychology; and social sciences.

447 A total of ninety-four studies were excluded based on the language requirement. Out of them, twelve were retrieved in the WoS, eighty-two on Scopus. The overall number of studies excluded may have been inferior due to the likely presence of duplicates.

448 In the meantime, WoS changed the taxonomy of topics, this search hence included: area studies; business; business finance; ecology; economics; energy fuels; environmental science; environmental studies; geography; geography physical; history; humanities multidisciplinary; international relations; law; management; multidisciplinary science; and political science.

449 The search of the keywords limited to the timeframe 2019-2022 gave 362 results on Scopus and 707 on WoS but reduced to 213 and 228 applying parameters a) and c).

3.3 Systematic review: Corruption and Kazakhstan

The review of 'corruption' and 'Kazakhstan' was conducted in May 2020 and complemented in February 2022 using Scopus and the Web of Science. The number of studies included was sixty–nine, sixty–seven from the above–mentioned databases and two working papers of scholars working on the region found through a general search on Google. The full list of studies is displayed in Table 20 at the end of this appendix. The criteria respected were the following:

a) Both the topics represented by their keywords should be included in the study, and at least one of them should be the primary focus of the research.
b) Studies should be in English or Russian.

As indicated in the table, the studies have been distinguished in consideration of their approach, methods and sector of interest. Forty–nine of the sixty–nine studies adopted a qualitative approach, nineteen quantitative and only one study mixed them (Öge 2017a).[450] Only thirteen papers dealt with the oil sector or the extractive industries, whereas almost half of them, namely thirty out of sixty–nine, did not focus on sectors but undertook theoretical discussions on informal behaviours in the country, either trying to distinguish corruption from other forms of social interaction or discussing the Kazakh anti–corruption legislation and its needs for improvement.[451]

3.4 Systematic review: Informality/informal and Kazakhstan

The systematic review of 'informality' and 'Kazakhstan' was conducted in May 2020 and updated in February 2022 on the WoS and Scopus without any limiting criteria. The total number of studies included is eight and the only studies excluded were the five doubles between the databases. Given the scarce results of this search, a second one employing the keywords 'informal' and 'Kazakhstan' was conducted. This second search was more productive, showing

---

450 In percentages: qualitative 71.02%, quantitative 27.53% and mixed 1.45%.
451 In percentages: theoretical 43.47%, oil sector or extractive industries 18.84%.

that despite its broader conceptual implications, the term 'informality' remains associated with the subfield of the informal economy. Beyond those found through the WoS and Scopus, four more studies were identified through external sources as entries in *The Encyclopaedia of Informality* (Ledeneva et al. 2018b) and the *Global Informality Project*. The limiting criteria used for this search were the following:

a) The literature should remain in the realm of social sciences.[452]
b) Both the topics represented by the keywords should be the primary focus of the research.
c) The phenomena under scrutiny should fit the 'flavours of informality' as identified by Abel Polese (2018), or theoretical discussions of the concept, namely: theoretical discussion; informal governance; informal economy; informal payments and corruption; infrapolitics.[453]

The total number of studies included in the systematic review is fifty-three including both searches. They are shown in the same Table 21 at the end of the appendix. Breaking down the studies of this search based on the type of informality they fit in, it is possible to find out that 9.4% focused on informal governance, 15% on informal payments and corruption, 15% on infrapolitics, 45.4% on informal economy, and 13.3% on more than one category. This is a more

---

452 The subjects included in the WoS were: anthropology; area studies; business; business finance; demography; economics; education educational research; environmental studies; ethnic studies; geography; healthcare sciences services; health policy services; international relations; law; management; multidisciplinary sciences; political science; public administration; social sciences interdisciplinary; sociology. The subjects included in Scopus were: arts and humanities; business, management and accounting; economics, econometrics and finance; environmental science; psychology; and social sciences.

453 Some of the excluded forms of informality are informal vows of marriage, informal discussions, and informal information channels. The fourth type of informality is potentially so wide that could easily accommodate most informal phenomena that raise the attention of researchers, but not all analysed phenomena could be considered systematic deviations from the norms. Moreover, the second criterion excluded by default all studies in which informal phenomena under scrutiny were not the main objective of the analysis or central for the framing of the argument.

precise indication that, at least in the case of Kazakhstan, informality remains largely associated with the informal economy. The sectors analysed by the studies were education in two cases (Oka 2019; Kuzhabekova and Almukhambetova 2019), healthcare in three (Sharipova 2015; Sari 2001; Danilovich and Yessaliyeva 2014), informal settlements and housing in five (Yessenova 2010; Hanson 2017; Osmonova 2016; Sanghera 2020; Alexander 2018), trade and bazaars in five, mostly due to the special issue of *Central Asian Survey* edited by Fehlings and Karrar (2020). The remaining studies did not concentrate on specific economic sectors but more generally on politics, informal payments, and employment.

3.5 Systematic review: Oil and Venezuela

Literature on the early development of the oil sector under Juan Vicente Gómez was retrieved via a systematic literature review conducted on Scopus and Google in September 2021. The first search employed the keywords 'oil' and 'Venezuela' producing 3,538 results, but limiting the inquiry to 'social sciences', 'economics, econometrics and finance', and 'business, management and accounting', the results dropped to 313 studies. The second search relied on the keywords 'Venezuela' and 'Gomez' and gave forty-five results. The search on Google was limited to the first five pages of results. The only limitation employed throughout the screening was that studies should include a section on Gómez's policies in the oil sector. The final number of studies included is fourteen, and the full list is in Table 22 at the end of the appendix.

3.6 Systematic review: Oil and Chad

Literature on the development of the Chadian oil sector under Idriss Déby was retrieved via a systematic review conducted on Scopus in December 2021. The search employed the keywords 'oil' and 'Chad' producing 304 results, but limiting the inquiry to 'energy', 'social sciences', 'economics, econometrics and finance', 'business, management and accounting' and 'environmental science', the results dropped to eighty-four studies. The limitations employed throughout the screening were that studies should not include less than a dedicated section on the oil sector of Chad and that only published academic papers would be accepted.[454] The final number of studies included is twenty–nine and the full list is in Table 23 at the end of the appendix. As for Kazakhstan, the cases of fine threats in Chad were hinted by the literature. Yet, they were often overlooked in academic analyses, and the recollection of events had to be completed relying on journal articles and cables from WikiLeaks.

4. Methods to Retrieve Data

Given the sensitivity of the topic, conducting research on informal payments and corruption does not produce problems in theoretical discussions as much as in the phase of data retrieval. In this sense, there are two distinct qualitative approaches employed to respond to different scales of the phenomenon. The first one is ethnographic methods which have been frequently used to study everyday petty corruption and lower–scale informal payments. The second one is the corruption investigative framework which has been used to study grand corruption.

Ethnographic methods include participant observation, informal interviews in the field, as well as in–depth, open–ended interviews, focus groups, and surveys. Additional ways to gather data while conducting fieldwork consist in forms of mapping, elicitation of information through objects, drawings, photographs and materials, creation of personal and community timelines, and interactions with organisational charts (Schensul and LeCompte 2013, 112). While ethnographic methods are naturally associated with anthropology, they can be effectively used to analyse several everyday socio–political and economic contexts. The study of informality started with the acknowledgement of the embeddedness of economic transactions within the social context (Granovetter 1985) and owes much to the work of anthropologists, such as Alena Ledeneva (2018b).

---

454 Hence excluding news of specialised journals such as *The Oil & Gas Journal*, and conference papers.

The corruption investigative framework is a system of methods conceived by Kristian Lasslett (2017) to analyse grand corruption. It relies on systematic fieldwork to document 'in rich detail the national and transnational networks, schemes, mechanisms and infrastructure' necessary for its functioning (Lasslett 2017, 30). In practical terms, systematic fieldwork consists of digitally investigative methods devised to extract data used in combination with interviews and documentary records, such as company information, corporate registries, certificates of incorporation, and websites. Data are then analysed through the investigative social network and transaction mapping to create consolidation and triangulation (Lasslett 2017, 32). The corruption investigative framework creates an investigative vantage point starting from a set of elementary units of analysis such as nodes (actors), ties (relations), and transactions. The more advanced units of analysis are an enhanced version of these elementary units (Lasslett 2017, 31). Among them, there are node biographies, an advanced historical analysis of specific actors (individuals, companies, or public bodies) playing a relevant role in the functioning of the scheme; the transaction sequence, that follows the exchanges between the identified actors; and the network architecture, an analysis of the 'structured interrelativeness' of the relationships created with the objective of achieving said transactions (Lasslett 2017, 32).

These strategies may appear extremely dissimilar from the other one but rely on a similar set of methods. The most striking difference consists in the definition of the field of inquiry. While in classic ethnographic research the field of inquiry is concrete and well defined, climbing the pyramid of power of the oil industry means losing grasp of this field, which becomes more and more intangible. For example, while it is clear that the area of inquiry of Saulesh Yessenova in *The Tengiz Oil Enclave* (2012) was the Tengiz oilfield and the workcamp nearby, for Cooley and Sharman in *Blurring the Line between Licit and Illicit* (2015) the space of inquiry spanned from the office of the president of Kazakhstan to the headquarters of Mercator and Chevron. Only the work of journalists such as Steve LeVine (2007) can describe investigations of grand

APPENDIX 273

corruption as some sort of imagined observation.[455] Yet, both strategies have their validity, and this research oscillated between them while climbing the hierarchical structure of the Kazakh oil sector. The following subsections explain the concrete steps made to retrieve data and offer a relevant example of an advanced unit of analysis derived from the conceptual framework of the corruption investigative framework applied to the social context of Kazakhstan.

4.1 Document analysis

The analysis of documents relevant to this study started with the book of Oleg Chervinsky *Black Blood of Kazakhstan: An Oil History of Independence* (2017).[456] This work has been realised as a sort of crowning achievement of the years of work of the author as journalist and director of the Kazakh specialised journal *Petroleum*. The book was used as a historical atlas of the major facts that occurred in the Kazakh oil industry throughout the years. The writing style chosen resembles that of a report, far from the blatant criticism and sharpness of LeVine's investigative work. In fact, *Black Blood of Kazakhstan* is written in Russian, destined and sold to the Kazakh audience[457] by an author with a recognised position in the oil sector of the country[458] and that does not pose a threat to the regime. Still, by mapping the major transactions operated throughout the years it is possible to recreate the network of influential personalities that decided the fate of the sector in the past three decades. This analysis of web resources led to the recreation of often opaque transactions

---

455 *The Oil and the Glory: The Pursuit of Empire and Fortune on the Caspian Sea* (2007) is one of the richest descriptions of the transition of Azerbaijan and Kazakhstan from communism to capitalism. Through the narration of its investigative work, LeVine brings the reader into the rooms where decisions on such a key industry were made, in a way that only Wikileaks could do a few years later.

456 The title in its original language is Černaâ krov' Kazahstana: Neftânaâ istoriâ nezavisimosti.

457 An excellent review of the book is offered by Tarp Hansen M., "Black blood: a history of Kazakhstan's oil sector," *Open Democracy*, April 24, 2018, https://www.opendemocracy.net/en/odr/black-blood/

458 KazService listed Chervinskyi as the 50th most influential person in the oil sector of the country in 2019.

274　THE HOUSE ALWAYS WINS

that took place in the oil industry, which constitute an advanced unit of analysis in the corruption investigative framework.

Another set of documents analysed with a similar intent were several newspaper articles published both by international and local press. On a few occasions, these articles qualified as evidence of cases of corruption rather than simple points of reference for historical deals. Also, the work of Greco and Oddo *The Parallel State* (2018)[459] has been used as a starting point to discuss many general issues in the interviews on the basis of Chapter V, *Fine Threats,* and Chapter VII, *Bid Rigging.* Wikileaks has been surveyed in all its 1,394 cables from Astana[460] and 477 from Almaty, narrowing down the search to the cases that resonated with the companies operating in the oil sector of the country. While less relevant for this research, the Panama Papers and the Paradise Papers were also included, mediated by the work of the Offshore Leaks Database of the International Consortium of Investigative Journalists.

Chapter VI, *Specious Contract Cancellations,* hosts instead a thorough analysis of all available documents on the database of the treaty–based investor–dispute settlement cases of the United Nations Conference on Trade and Development. Of the nineteen cases listed on the Investment Hub of UNCTAD,[461] eight of them concerned foreign investors that had operated in the oil sector of the country. One of the cases, Caratube International Oil Company LLP v. Republic of Kazakhstan, was discussed in two different trials even if only one of them is shown in the list of UNCTAD. Not all court documents are available to the public, but some of the information was triangulated through interviews. Similarly, despite the anonymisation of the companies in one trial, a simple search through the websites of companies operating in Kazakhstan led to their identification allowing me to find more interviewees.

---

459 The title in its original language is Lo stato parallelo. La prima inchiesta sull'ENI tra politica, servizi segreti, scandali finanziari e nuove guerre.
460 Renamed Nur-Sultan between 2019 and 2022.
461 "Kazakhstan", *Investment Dispute Settlement Navigator,* UNCTAD, https://investmentpolicy.unctad.org/investment-dispute-settlement/country/107/kazakhstan

In Kazakhstan, newspapers outlets are often written in Russian, and while many are bilingual, those from the oil region can be published exclusively in Kazakh. While I do not know Kazakh, I used some of these articles to discuss the phenomena presented in Chapter VIII, *Corruption on Kazakh's Skin*. The translation was achieved by combining the use of a common translation software with suggestions by native Kazakh speakers befriended on the field.

4.2 Interviews

The fieldwork was conducted remotely in 2021 but in Kazakhstan in 2019 and 2020, with visits to the cities of Almaty, Nur–Sultan/Astana,[462] Aktau, and Zhanaozen. Almaty and Astana, respectively the former and the current capital of the country, are the cities where the major international oil companies have their headquarters and where it is most likely to meet with experts and international journalists. Atyrau is the renowned 'oil capital' of the country, where it is possible to find TengizChevrOil and North Caspian Operating Consortium headquarters as well as smaller companies such as Embamunaigas,[463] and it is the closest city to the biggest onshore oilfield of the country, Tengiz. Aktau is the biggest Kazakh city on the Caspian Sea and hosts the headquarters of Mangistau-MunaiGaz. Zhanaozen is a Kazakh monotown revolving around the work of the state–owned Uzenmunaigas and is known to the international audience for the infamous shootings of workers and inhabitants striking in December 2011. Uralsk is one the closest cities to the North–Western border with the Russian Federation and the biggest one in the proximity of the monotown of Aksai, hosting the headquarters of Karachaganak Petroleum Operating, the international consortium developing the gigantic oil and gas complex of Karachaganak.

---

462 Reverted to Astana after a short period as Nur-Sultan. The Guardian. 2022. "Kazakhstan to change name of capital from Nur-sultan back to Astana," 14 September, https://www.theguardian.com/world/2022/sep/14/kazakhstan-to-change-name-of-capital-from-nur-sultan-back-to-astana

463 Considering revenues but not in terms of staff.

Figure 11 Major Kazakh Oilfields and Cities

Map: Author • Source: Global Energy Monitor Wiki • Map data: © OSM • Created with Datawrapper

Interviews were realised with stakeholders believed to be more likely to share information on the ways in which informality takes place in the oil sector of the country. These included experts in the fields of political science and economy, journalists, representatives of NGOs and workers of the oil sector operating in various segments of the industry. Given the sensitivity of the topic, all interviews were anonymised with few exceptions. The interviews were not always conducted with the same degree of freedom in consideration of the understanding that the interviewee had towards the topic. Thus, common workers were given a structured interview while for journalists the process was often unstructured. Common workers asked about 'corruption' ventured into political statements digressing from the object of the discussion, while the word 'informality' did not produce any form of elicitation. Therefore, to retrieve valuable information it was necessary to discuss questions revolving around security in the workplace, the formality of their contracts, regulations on vacations, wages, overworking hours, as well as hiring processes. Quite on the contrary, asking journalists about cases of corruption in the sector would achieve the objective more directly.

The total number of interviews conducted was thirty–seven. Workers and managers interviewed were from TengizChevrOil, Karachaganak Petroleum Operating, North Caspian Operating Consortium, Karazhanbasmunai, Uzenmunaigas, Saipem, KIOS, and several smaller contractors. The research aimed at retrieving interviewees from different workplaces and with different career lengths in the sector. The NGO representatives interviewed included almost the entirety of the directors that participated as board members of the Extractive Industry Transparency Initiative and directly advocated in favour of environmental protection of their respective regions. Journalists interviewed were mostly Kazakh citizens with the rare exception of known international contributors. The sampling of interviewees did not aim to represent the workers of the sector but to identify different forms of informal practices. As such, the population of strategies taking place in the sector is unknown in size and its inductive search was meant to identify if not all, at least the most recurrent ones. Hence, the number of interviews alone is not indicative of the information retrieved. A few of them did not deliver any relevant information, while others were extremely insightful. Interviews were suspended once the forms of informality described by interviewees started repeating and all the major cities relevant to the functioning of the oil industry in the country were surveyed.

Not all the interviews were conducted in person, a large part of them took place through voice–over–internet protocol with a few managers that are not working in Kazakhstan anymore. The selection of interviewees was done with a combination of 'snowball' (or 'chain') and purposeful sampling, contacting potential interviewees through social media and email addresses retrieved online (Palinkas et al. 2013). The snowball method is a sampling method that relies on informants giving contact information to other informants (Noy 2008, 330). As such, the procedure of retrieving informants can be slow but it can also offer insights into social knowledge and power relations inherent to the group under analysis (Noy 2008, 329). For example, journalists part of this research often shared the contact information of three key figures acknowledged as experts on the topic under investigation. Interviews conducted with informants retrieved through the snowball method provided new information that had to be verified through other sources to achieve triangulation. Quite on the contrary, interviews conducted with informants selected through purposeful sampling confirmed or confuted information drawn from other sources. For instance, since the analysis of documents indicated that environmental fines may have hidden different intentions from those officially declared by public authorities, during an interview with a worker of the financial department of a big consortium the issue was addressed, and the suspicion was confirmed.

In Kazakhstan, English is becoming increasingly popular, both among younger generations and businessmen. In fact, Nazarbeyev's multi-vector foreign policy translated into a multi-vector political economy, *de facto* opening the energy sector to a variety of investors from all over the globe. As such, interviews were conducted in either English or Russian in consideration of the language that the interviewee felt more comfortable speaking. During my fieldwork, I did not meet a person who could speak only Kazakh,[464] and since the research did not feature a prolonged participant observation,[465] my personal limitations did not affect the quality of the work.

Doing research in an authoritarian state is an uneasy task, effectively described in *Research, Ethics and Risk in the Authoritarian Field* (Glasius et al. 2017). In Kazakhstan, conducting research on corruption is not a problem *per se* because officially the country wants to get rid of the problem to improve its reputation, but researchers will encounter a hard red line whenever discussing the wealth of the elite of the country (Glasius et al. 2017, 39). The sensitivity of the topic required the anonymisation of most interviews to protect the identity of the source, while specific information that could lead back to identifying interviewees was avoided altogether. In fact, the study aimed at understanding several *modi operandi* of

---

464 Yet, some inhabitants of oil regions do, as showcased in the documentary "The Other Side of Oil," by Lukhpan Akhmedyarov and Raul Uporov https://crud eaccountability.org/the-other-side-of-oil-documentary/

465 Albeit important informal phenomena might be grasped only by extended ethnographies (such as Maurizio Totaro's).

the sector rather than describing specific episodes. Informed consent on the reason and the outcome of the interview was always given upfront, but never in a written form, because interviewees worried that the existence of a physical document could be later used to blackmail them. Similarly, recordings of the interviews were done only in accordance with the interviewee. Standard encryption of data and devices was believed a sufficient precaution, while more electronic security may have raised the suspicion of authorities.

Due to origin and status, the researcher was often perceived positively by interviewees. Being from a liberal–democratic country, many Kazakh interviewees felt 'understood' in their fight for a freer society and being relatively young many others felt compelled to help. On the other hand, on a few occasions, these advantages turned into disadvantages because the research was belittled, considered not as incisive as the press, or because interviewees felt implicitly criticised: 'Why Kazakhstan? Is there not corruption in Italy?' Overall, the advantages outweighed the disadvantages, and the common Italian background of many interviewees helped reach a high number of reliable sources. As described in *Research, Ethics and Risk in the Authoritarian Field* (Glasius et al. 2017), refusals were never given in a straightforward way. On the contrary, interviews were often agreed in principle, but when it became necessary to agree on the details respondents invented 'a series of excuses to make it practically impossible' (2017, 59). This form of ghosting is so common that in this research it is possible to count at least one indirect refusal for any given interview. Whenever realised, interviews were conducted in a friendly and condescending way, the wording of questions was devoted the maximum care, and whenever possible topics were de–politicised.

4.3 An example of advanced unit of analysis: Elite

Elites are defined as small groups of people holding a disproportionate power and influence if compared to the rest of the population under analysis.[466] The concept is a recognised category both in sociology and politics and while the term is of common use in popular discourse, identifying the elite of a country is not an easy task. In trying to identify the political elite of Kazakhstan, Sally Cummings (2005) searched for individuals able to 'exercise "preponderant political influence"' (2005, 10). Among the techniques used to identify elites in political science there are positional, reputational, and decisional analyses as well as the 'snowball' method. For positional analyses, individuals derive power from their institutional role, reputational analyses rely on 'informal reputations of power' as a better representation of the dynamic, while decisional analyses focus on how decisions are reached (Cummings 2005, 11). In *Kazakhstan: Power and the Elite* (2005), Cummings opted for the 'snowball' method starting with interviewees holding relevant positions and asking them to identify other members of the elite. This list of names was then submitted and verified by a panel of experts that helped the author to achieve a tentative identification of the members of the Kazakh political elite.

Cummings herself acknowledged that none of the methods of identification is flawless and they could not be effectively used alone to identify the Kazakh elite. Given the relevance of informality in shaping the political dynamics in Kazakhstan, by looking only at the individuals in institutional positions there is the risk to overlook relevant players that are related to the former president of Kazakhstan through family ties. Moreover, reputation can result in the creation of real dynamics of power regardless of the actual situation. An example is the case of Unaoil described in Chaper 7, *Bid Rigging*: while the managers of the company never interfaced with the son–in–law of the first president of Kazakhstan Timur Kulibayev, they proved to be obsessed with the idea of creating a bond with him, because believed to be the most relevant decision–maker of the energy sector. Kazakhstan appears to have a taste for the concept of elite and for the cult of personalities. An implicit admission is the book of Daniyar Ashimbayev (2010), an encyclopaedia of

---

466 As explained in the Encyclopaedia Britannica. "Elites. Sociology", *Britannica*, https://www.britannica.com/topic/elite-sociology

biographies of relevant individuals in Kazakhstan titled *Who is Who in Kazakhstan: Encyclopaedic Biographies*.[467] In a more straightforward way, the multi-authored book realised by Ageev, Bayschuakov, and Seytimov (2008),[468] *The Elite of Kazakhstan: Power. Business. Society* starts with the cynical assumption that in any country the power does not belong to the people but to the elite, which constitutes about 10% of the total population (Ageev, Bayschuakov, and Seytimov 2008, 5). Still, looking at the people interviewed in this book, it is possible to understand how the authors identified the elite through positional method, and therefore, with the exception of the second president of Kazakhstan Kassym–Jomart Tokayev and the opposer of the regime Mukhtar Ablyazov, they often missed the target.[469]

While the analysis of Cummings (2005) focused on the political elite, Ageev, Bayschuakov, and Seytimov (2008) acknowledged that an elite can be identified in different aspects of the life of a society. In this sense, also in the oil sector, it is possible to identify an elite, and this is even more true considering its hierarchical nature. International oil companies depend on governments for concessions, contractors depend on the former for service contracts, and workers depend on all of them to be employed. At the top of the industry, there is the elite of the sector that has the power to decide over contracts. Given its strategic significance in the economy of the country, to some extent, it is the political elite to leads the oil sector, but also relevant international managers are part of this elite. The American James Giffen, for example, was one of the most influential figures in the Kazakh oil industry for years. Oil entrepreneurs of the Central Asian Republic are vain, and in an attempt at self-celebration, in 2017 the specialised journal *KazService* started to make a yearly list of the fifty most influential persons in the Kazakh oil and gas sector. Table 17 below has been created crossing the data of the fifteen most influential persons of the sector as reported in

---

467 This edition is from 2010, the original title is: Kto est' Kto v Kazahstane: Bio-grafičeskaâ Ènciklopediâ 2010-2011.

468 The original title is: Èlita Kazahstana: Vlast'. Biznes. Obŝestvo.

469 Still, this is not to be considered a scientific work and the authors probably ended up interviewing those who agreed to be interviewed.

the issues of *KazService* of 2017, 2018, and 2019[470] with an article by *Ak Zhalyk* from 2009.[471]

---

470 "50 Samyh vliâtel'nyh lûdej neftegazovoj otrasli Kazahstana", [The 50 Most Influential People of the Oil and Gas Sector of Kazakhstan: 50], Issue 3(21), *KazService*, July-September 2017. "Samyh vliâtel'nyh lûdej neftegazovoj otrasli Kazahstana: 50", [The Most Influential People of the Oil and Gas Sector of Kazakhstan: 50], Issue 3(25), *KazService*, July-September 2018. "Samyh vliâtel'nyh lûdej neftegazovoj otrasli Kazahstana: Top 50", [The Most Influential People of the Oil and Gas Sector of Kazakhstan: Top 50], Issue 3(29), *KazService*, July-September 2019.

471 "Samye vliâtel'nye lûdi neftegazovogo sektora Kazahstana", [The Most Influential People of the Oil and Gas Sector of Kazakhstan], *Ak Zhalyk*, November 18, 2009, https://azh.kz/ru/news/view/3567

Table 17 Fifteen most influential persons in the oil sector of Kazakhstan in 2009 and 2019

Position	2009	Role	Reason for absence in 2019	Corruption scandal (Chapter)
1	*Timur Kulibayev*	Vice–president of Samruk–Kazyna	Present	All major scandals (III, IV, VI, VII)
2	Nurlan Balgimbayev	Advisor of the President of Kazakhstan	Died on the 14th of October 2015	Kazakhgate (III)
3	Sauat Minbayev	Minister of Energy and Mineral Resources	3rd until 2018, reassigned to Temir Zholy (railway transport)	ENI service contracts (VII)
4	*Kairgeldi Kabildin*	President of KazMunayGas	47th in 2019	
5	*Zhakyp Marabayev*	Vice–executive director NCOC	Present	Nations Energy (IV) and Baker Hughes (VII)
6	*Kanatbek Safinov*	Executive secretary of the MEMR	5th in 2018, absent from the 2019 ranking	
7	Nurlan Kapparov	CEO of Lancaster Group	Died on the 26th of March 2015	
8	Kenes Rakishev	CEO of SAT Operating		
9	Askar Balzhanov	Executive director of KazMunayGas	Fired after the Zhanaozen massacre of 2011[472]	Nations Energy (IV)
10	*Kenzhebek Ibrashev*	General Director of KazMunayGas	28th in 2019	
11	Kairat Krimov	CEO of Mercury		

472 P. Legina, "Sud posle rasstrela," [Judgment after the execution], *Belorusy i Rynok*, December 26, 2011, https://belmarket.by/news/2011/12/26/news-11362.html

12	*Uzakbay Karabalin*	General Director of Mangistau-MunayGas	Present	
13	Maksat Idenov	Executive director of KazMunayGas	Fired by KazMunayGas, re-employed at ENI	ENI service contracts (VII)
14	Bolat Akchulakov	Executive director of Samruk–Kazyna	Present	
15	*Nurtas Schmanov*	Executive director of KazMunayGas	36th in 2019	
2019		**Role**	**2018**	**2017**
1	Kanat Bozumbayev	Minister of Energy	2nd	Not ranked
2	*Timur Kulibayev*	Independent director of the board of Gazprom	1st	1st
3	Makhambet Dosmu-khambetov	Vice–minister of Energy	4th	3rd
4	Alik Aidarbayev	CEO of KazMunayGas	Absent	Absent
5	Magzum Mirzagalyev	Minister of Geology, Ecology and Natural Resources	7th	Absent
6	Murat Zhurebekov	Vice–minister of Energy	10th	9th
7	Asset Magauov	Vice–minister of Energy	9th	6th
8	Daniyar Tiyesov	Deputy CEO of KazMunayGas	19th	Absent
9	Daniyar Abulgazin	CEO committee Oil&Gas Ataka-men	8th	14th
10	*Zhakyp Marabayev*	Deputy CEO of KazMunayGas	21st	19th

11	Kurmangazy Is-kaziyev	Deputy CEO of KazMunayGas	11th	10th
12	*Uzakbay Karabalin*	Samruk–Kazyna representative in the board of KazMunayGas	12th	5th
13	Bolat Akchulakov	General director of Kazenergy	6th	8th
14	Talgat Momyshev	Executive secretary of the Minister of Energy	Absent	Absent
15	Beket Izbastin	General director of PSA authority	Absent	Absent

286 THE HOUSE ALWAYS WINS

Table 17 was not created with the purpose of comparing two rankings realised with different rationales, but to show some of the names that recur the most. In fact, while the first ranking by the journalists of *Ak Zhalyk* seems more oriented towards a reputational analysis, the one of *KazService* seems more informed by a positional analysis. In italics, the table shows the names of those who remained among the fifteen most influential persons in the sector throughout the years. Moreover, the column indicating the reason for the absence in 2019 of some of those present in 2009 shows that in three cases they remained in the ranking but at a lower level. Therefore, the often-praised stability of the Kazakh state, fundamental to attracting foreign direct investments, is mirrored in the stability of the elite of its oil industry. Still, as suggested by Wojciech Ostrowski (2010), there is a difference between professional oilmen, members of families who worked in the oil industry for generations, and businessmen who used the oil industry as a vehicle to accumulate more capital.

One of these men is Kenes Rakishev, son-in-law of the former Prime Minister Imangali Tasmagambetov, a person whose own website indicates an 'international businessman'.[473] He was indicated as the negotiator of the sale of the Sunninghill Park residence of UK's Prince Andrew to President Nazarbayev or his son-in-law Timur Kulibayev (Mesquita 2016, 392). In a state as corrupt as Kazakhstan, the purposes of the corruption investigative framework and the process of elite identification overlap so much that the concept of elite can be acknowledged as an advanced unit of analysis of the former. In confirmation of this, the column on corruption scandals in Table 17 shows that as much as six out of the fifteen most influential men of the Kazakh oil sector were involved in relevant scandals of corruption. The number may be bigger considering that not all corruption cases end up being unveiled.

---

473 The website clearly identifies the diversified investments of Rakishev, as seen at Kenes Rakishev, https://www.kenesrakishev.com/

Table 18   Studies to be included in the updated systematic review of 'corruption' and 'oil'

Title	Author(s)	Year	Source	Field
A perfect storm: how high levels of risk and weak internal controls resulted in violations of the foreign corrupt practices act	Franz, D.	2021	CASE Journal	Oil management and energy strategies
Actors, networks and assemblages: Local content, corruption and the politics of SME's participation in Ghana's oil and gas industry	Ablo, A.D.	2019	International Development Planning Review	Oil management and energy strategies
Asymmetric oil price shocks, tax revenues, and the resource curse	Zakharov, N.	2020	Economic Letters	Resource Curse
Between altruism and self–aggrandisement: Transparency, accountability and politics in Ghana's oil and gas sector	Ackah, I. et al.	2020	Energy Research and Social Science	Oil management and energy strategies
Corruption trends during Africa's oil boom, 2005 to 2014	Gillies, A.	2020	Extractive Industries and Society	Oil management and energy strategies
Critical government and national oil company role in their petroleum resource development: lessons for Guyana petroleum sector	Azubike, V.C.	2020	Commonwealth Law Bulletin	Oil management and energy strategies
Crude oil price and government effectiveness: The determinants of corruption in oil abundant states	Madathil, J.C. et al.	2021	Journal of Public Affairs	Resource Curse
Cuckoos in the nest: the co–option of state–owned enterprises in Putin's Russia	Makarchev, N. & Wieprzowski, P.	2021	Post–Soviet Affairs	Oil management and energy strategies
Culture of abuse of power due to conflict of interest to corruption for too long on the management form resources of oil and gas in Indonesia	Riyadi, B.S.	2020	International Journal of Criminology and Sociology	Oil management and energy strategies

Deep Determinants of Corruption? A Subnational Analysis of Resource Curse Dynamics in American States	Tyburski, M., Egan, P. & Schneider, A.	2020	Political Research Quarterly	Resource Curse
De–escalation strategies for kleptocracy in Nigeria's oil sector	Das, V.	2020	Journal of Financial Crime	Oil management and energy strategies
Distortions in oil contract allocation and environmental damage in the presence of corruption	Akaeze, H.O.	2020	Review of Development Economics	Transparency/ Theoretical
Economics of trickle–down corruption	Nuryyev, G. & Hickson, C.	2020	International Journal of Development Issues	Resource Curse
Examining corruption prominence in SIDS – the curse and the cure for construction tender practices	Martin, H. et al.	2022	Journal of Facilities Management	Resource Curse
Extractive Sector Stakeholders' Perspectives of the Extractive Sector Transparency Measures Act (ESTMA)	Brown, K. et al.	2021	Accounting Perspectives	Transparency
Foreign aid, oil revenues, and political accountability: Evidence from six experiments in Ghana and Uganda	de la Cuesta, B. et al.	2020	Review of International Organizations	Accountability
Globalisation, governance, accountability and the natural resource 'curse': Implications for socio–economic growth of oil–rich developing countries	Adams, D. et al.	2019	Resources Policy	Resource Curse
How transparency improves public accountability: The extractive industries transparency initiative in Mexico	Lopez, L. & Fontaine, G.	2019	Extractive Industries and Society	Transparency
Institutions and the "Resource Curse": Evidence from Cases of Oil–Related Bribery	Mahdavi, P.	2020	Comparative Political Studies	Resource Curse

Kleptocracy and tax evasion under resource abundance	Mohtadi, H. et al.	2019	Economics and Politics	Transparency
Measurement of damage from corruption in Brazil	Sallaberry, J.D. et al.	2020	Journal of Financial Crime	Oil management and energy strategies
Natural resources, fuel exports and corruption policy in Africa	Onodugo, V.A. & Isijola, D.O.	2020	Corvinus Journal of Sociology and Social Policy	Oil management and energy strategies
Nigeria's upstream petroleum industry anti–corruption legal framework: the necessity for overhauling and enrichment	Olujobi, O.J.	2021	Journal of Money Laundering Control	Oil management and energy strategies
Oil, politics, and "Corrupt Bastards"	James, A. & Rivera, N.M.	2022	Journal of Environmental Economics and Management	Resource Curse
Opportunity entrepreneurship, oil rents and control of corruption	Torres, P. & Godinho, P.	2019	Journal of Enterprising Communities	Resource Curse
Optimal concession contracts for oil exploitation	Cerqueti, R. & Ventura, M.	2020	Energy Policy	Transparency
Production sharing contracts and rentierism: Reforming transparency gaps in Kurdistan's oil and gas contracts	Hasan, Q.M. & Perot, K.A.	2021	Extractive Industries and Society	Transparency
Rampant corruption: The dilemma facing economic diversification in oil–abundant MENA countries	Matallah, S.	2022	Resources Policy	Resource Curse
Re–examining corruption and economic growth nexus in oil dependent economy: Nigeria's case	Rotimi, M.E. et al.	2021	Journal of Money Laundering Control	Resource Curse
Rent–seeking practices, local resource curse, and social conflict in Uganda's emerging oil economy	Ogwang, T. et al.	2019	Land	Resource Curse

Spoils of Oil? Assessing and Mitigating the Risks of Corruption in Lebanon's Emerging Offshore Petroleum Sector	Leenders, R.	2019	Book chapter in *Future of Petroleum in Lebanon: Energy, Politics and Economic Growth*	Oil management and energy strategies
Sustainability of energy assets and corruption in the developing countries	Gani, A.	2021	Sustainable Production and Consumption	Resource Curse
The Drivers and Barriers of Corporate Social Responsibility: A Comparison of the MENA Region and Western Countries	Alizadeh, A.	2022	Sustainability	Accountability
The Extractive Industries Transparency Initiative (EITI) and corruption in Latin America: Evidence from Colombia, Guatemala, Honduras, Peru, and Trinidad and Tobago	Lopez–Cazar, I., Papyrakis, E. & Pellegrini, L.	2021	Resources Policy	Transparency
The impact of corruption and local content policy in on firm performance: Evidence from Kazakhstan	Kalyuzhnova, Y. & Belitski, M.	2019	Resources Policy	Oil management and energy strategies
The political economy of oil in the Democratic Republic of Congo (DRC): Corruption and regime control	Titeca, K. & Edmond, P.	2019	Extractive Industries and Society	Resource Curse
The Role of Accounting and Accountants in the Oil Subsidy Corruption Scandal in Nigeria	Abdul–Baki, Z., Uthman, A.B. & Kasum, A.S.	2021	Critical Perspectives on Accounting	Oil management and energy strategies
The Troubled Path Toward Greater Transparency as a Means to Foster Good Corporate Governance and Fight Against Corruption in the Energy Sector	Grasso, C.	2020	Book chapter in *Handbook of Energy Finance: Theories, Practices and Simulations*	Transparency

Title	Author	Year	Source	Theme
Voluntary, Self–Regulatory, and Mandatory Disclosure of Oil and Gas Company Payments to Foreign Governments	Healy, P.M. & Serafeim, G.	2020	Accounting Horizons	Transparency

Alaska's Corporate Social Responsibility: The Economics of the Corruption Case of VECO	Reynolds, D.B.	2021	CSR, Sustainability, Ethics and Governance	Accountability
Big, Bigger, Biggest Grand Corruption Scandals in the Oil Sector in Nigeria	Williams–Elegbe, S.	2018	Corruption Scandals and their Global Impact	Oil management and energy strategies
Corruption and Local Content Development: Assessing the Impact of the Petrobras' Scandal on Recent Policy Changes in Brazil	Lima–de–Oliveira, R.	2020	Extractive Industries and Society	Oil management and energy strategies
Corruption and the Energy Sector: Inevitable Bedfellows?	Low, L.A. & Battaglia, R.J.	2014	Book chapter in *Research Handbook on International Energy Law*	Resource Curse
Corruption and the Role of Natural Resources in Post–Conflict Transitions	Cheng, C. & Zaum, D.	2016	Governance, Natural Resources, and Post–Conflict Peacebuilding	Resource Curse
Corruption, Natural Resources and Development: From Resource Curse to Political Ecology	Williams, A. & Le Billon, P.	2017	Book	Resource Curse
Crude Oil Price and Government Effectiveness: The Determinants of Corruption in Oil Abundant States	Madathil, J.C., Palaniyappa Shanmugam, V. & Thippillikat, A.	2021	Journal of Public Affairs	Resource Curse
'How much do we get?' An Update on Transparency of Revenues from the Sales of Natural Resources	Poretti, P.	2018	Journal of World Energy Law and Business	Transparency

Title	Author	Year	Source	Category
Is Sunshine the Best Disinfectant? Evaluating the Global Effectiveness of the Extractive Industries Transparency Initiative (EITI)	Sovacool, B.K.	2020	Extractive Industries and Society	Transparency
Natural Resource Dependence, Corruption, and Tax Revenue Mobilization	Zalle, O.	2022	Journal of Economic Integration	Resource Curse
Oil and Property Rights	De Soysa, I., Krieger, T., & Meierrieks, D.	2022	Resources Policy	Oil management and energy strategies
Oil, Corruption, and Vote–Buying: A Review of the Case of São Tomé and Príncipe	Vicente, P.C.	2011	Book chapter in *International Handbook on the Economics of Corruption*	Resource Curse
Oil Corrupts Elections: The Political Economy of Vote–Buying in Nigeria	Onapajo, H., Francis, S. & Okeke-Uzodike, U.	2015	African Studies Quarterly	Resource Curse
Oil Price Shocks, Protest, and the Shadow Economy: Is There a Mitigation Effect?	Ishak, P.W. & Farzanegan, M.R.	2022	Economics and Politics	Resource Curse
Oil Wealth, Corruption, and the Multiple F(PH)Aces of Internal Colonialism in Ahmed Yerima's Hard Ground	Lawal, N.A.	2020	Anafora	Oil management and energy strategies
On the Good and Bad of Natural Resource, Corruption, and Economic Growth Nexus	Sharma, C. & Mishra, R.K.	2022	Environmental and Resource Economics	Resource Curse
Organized Criminals, Human Rights Defenders, and Oil Companies Weaponization of the RICO Act Across Jurisdictional Borders	Ofrias, L. & Roecker, G.	2019	Focaal–Journal Global and Historical Anthropology	Oil management and energy strategies
Russia, Transition and Poland's Energy Security: A Retrospective View	Ostrowski, W.	2021	Journal of Contemporary Central and Eastern Europe	Oil management and energy strategies

Title	Author	Year	Journal	Category
Scientific Ghostwriting in the Amazon? The Role of Experts in the Lawsuit against Chevron in Ecuador	Kirsch, S.	2022	Comparative Studies in Society and History	Oil management and energy strategies
Suspicion and Expertise: Following the Money in an Offshore Investigation	Fedirko, T.	2021	Journal of the Royal Anthropological Institute	Oil management and energy strategies
The Effect of Mandatory Extraction Payment Disclosures on Corporate Payment and Investment Policies Abroad	Rauter, T.	2020	Journal of Accounting Research	Transparency
The Extractive Industries Transparency Initiative and Corruption in Nigeria: Rethinking the Links Between Transparency and Accountability	Idemudia, U.	2013	Access to Information in Africa: Law, Culture and Practice	Transparency
The Impact of Oil Revenue on the Economic Corruption in Iran	Dadgar, Y. & Nazari, R.	2012	Actual Problems of Economics	Oil management and energy strategies
The Upsurge of Oil Theft and Illegal Bunkering in the Niger Delta Region of Nigeria: Is there a Way Out?	Boris, O.H.	2015	Mediterranean Journal of Social Sciences	Oil management and energy strategies
Transparency in Iraq Petroleum Sector: More Symbolic Formality than Impacting Effectiveness	Jiyad, A.M.	2019	Journal of Contemporary Iraq and the Arab World	Transparency
Using Criminal Law to Fight Corruption: The Potential, Risks, and Limitations of Operation Car Wash (Lava Jato)	Prado, M.M. & Machado, M.R.D.	2022	American Journal of Comparative Law	Oil management and energy strategies
Victims of their own Success Abroad? Why the Withdrawal of US Transparency Rules is Hindered by Diffusion to the EU and Canada	Kleizen, B.	2019	Journal of European Public Policy	Transparency

Who Profits from Windfalls in Oil Tax Revenue? Inequality, Protests, and the Role of Corruption	Alexeev, M. & Zakharov, N.	2022	Journal of Economic Behavior and Organization	Resource Curse
Search of 'bribe' and 'oil'				
Oil Hikes, Drugs and Bribes: Do Oil Prices Matter for Crime Rate in Russia?	Burakov, D.	2019	International Journal of Energy Economics and Policy	Oil management and energy strategies
Collusive Bidding in Brazilian Infrastructure Projects	Signor, R. et alia	2017	Proceedings of the Institution of Civil Engineers: Forensic Engineering	Oil management and energy strategies
Shell embroiled in Nigeria bribery scandal	No author	2017	TCE The Chemical Engineer	Grey literature
Brazil corruption probe compounds growing economic slump	Van Hampton, T.	2015	Engineering News–Record	Grey literature
Don't stand still for bribery requests	Wrage, A.	2006	Hart's E and P	Grey literature
Bribery: Time to share the limelight	Wrage, A.	2006	Hart's E and P	Grey literature
Bribes…Holzer hints at surrendering	No author	2000	European Chemical News	Grey literature

Table 19   Studies included in the systematic review of 'oil' and 'Kazakhstan'

Title	Author(s)	Year	Source
A Comparative Study of Resource Nationalism in Russia and Kazakhstan 2004–2008	Domjan, P. & Stone, M.	2010	Europe – Asia Studies
A Negotiation Support System for Resolving an International Trans–Boundary Natural Resource Conflict	Madani, K. et al.	2014	Environmental Modelling & Software
A Practical Approach to Oil Wealth Management: Application to the Case of Kazakhstan	Aktoty A. et al.	2015	Energy Economics
A Review of the Oil and Gas Sector in Kazakhstan	Kaiser, M. J. & Pulsipher, A. G.	2007	Energy Policy
Addressing the Growth and Employment Effects of the Extractive Industries: White and Black Box Illustrations from Kazakhstan	Sadik–Zada, E. R.	2021	Post–Communist Economies
Analysis on the Impact of International Oil Price Changes on Kazakhstan's Economy	Elmira, B., Feng, J. & Wang, X.	2017	International Conference on Economics, Management Engineering and Marketing
Back Yard Politics: Russia's Foreign Policy Toward the Caspian Basin	Griffith, B.	1998	Demokratizatsiya
Caspian Energy Phase II: Beyond 2005	Shaffer, B.	2010	Energy Policy
Caspian Oil and Gas: Production and Prospects	Gelb, B.A.	2011	Economic, Political and Social Issues of the Caucasus Region
Caspian Oil in a Global Context	Ahrend, R. & Tompson, W.	2007	Transition Studies Review
Causality Among Oil Prices, GDP and Exchange Rate: Evidence from Azerbaijan and Kazakhstan	Dikkaya, M. & Doyar, B. V.	2017	Bilig
Central Asia: A Major Emerging Energy Player in the 21st century	Dorian, J. P.	2006	Energy Policy

Title	Author	Year	Source
Central Asia: Mapping Future Prospects to 2015	Dowling, M. & Wignaraja, G.	2006	ERD Working Paper Series
Central Asia: Regional Developments and Implications for United States Interests	Nichol, J.	2012	Central Asia: Regional Affairs and U.S. Interests and Policies
Central Asia's Oil and Gas Pipeline Network: Current and Future Flows	Dorian, J. P., Rosi, I. S. & Indriyanto, S. T.	1994	Post–Soviet Geography
Central Asia's Security: Issues and Implications for U.S. Interests	Nichol, J.	2011	Economic, Political and Social Issues of Asia
Challenges for Kazakhstan's Energy Sector to 2050	Pomfret, R.	2017	Book chapter in: Sustainable Energy in Kazakhstan: Moving to Cleaner Energy in a Resource–Rich Country
China and Kazakhstan's Oil and Gas Partnership at the Start of the Twenty–First Century	Yelena K. & Lee, J.	2014	Emerging Markets Finance and Trade
China Gazes West: Xinjiang's Growing Rendezvous with Central Asia	Pannell, C. W.	2011	Eurasian Geography and Economics
China's Hunger for Oil	Mommen, A.	2007	Journal of Developing Societies
China–Kazakhstan Energy Relations	Kuteleva, A.	2022	Book chapter in China's Energy Security and Relations with Petro-states
China's Quest for Oil Security: Oil (wars) in the Pipeline?	Lee, P. K.	2005	Pacific Review
Chinese Energy Company Relations with Russia and Kazakhstan	Cutler, R. M.	2014	Perspective on Global Development and Technology
Circling the Barrels: Kazakhstan's Regime Stability in the Wake of the 2014 Oil Bust	Groce, M. S.	2020	Central Asian Survey
Coping with energy insecurity: China's response in global perspective	Calder, K. E.	2006	East Asia

Corporate Social Responsibility in Kazakhstan: Content Analysis of Annual Reports of the Listed Oil and Gas Companies	Markhayeva, B.	2016	Proceedings of the 4th International Conference on Management, Leadership and Governance
Country risk Volatility Spillovers of Emerging Oil Economies: An Application to Russia and Kazakhstan	Sun, X., He, W. & Li, J.	2009	Communications in Computer and Information Science
Creation of an Oil Shale Industry in Kazakhstan May Become a Reality	Yefimov, V.	1996	Oil Shale
Crouching Dragon, Hungry Tigers: China and Central Asia	Spechler, M. C.	2003	Contemporary Economic Policy
Crude "Oil Mercantilism"? Chinese Oil Engagement in Kazakhstan	McCarthy, J.	2013	Pacific Affairs
Dutch Disease Scare in Kazakhstan: Is it Real?	Egert, B. & Carol, L. S.	2008	Open Economies Review
Dynamic Bargaining and the Prospects for Learning in the Petroleum Industry: The Case of Kazakhstan	Hosman, L.	2009	Perspectives on Global Development and Technology
Economic Advance, Living Standards and Inequality in Oil–Producing Former Soviet Union Countries	Aliev, U. T.	2013	Экономика Региона
Economic Aspect of Personnel Management in Oil and Gas Companies of Kazakhstan	Duzelbaeva, G. B.	2012	Actual Problems of Economics
Economic Development in Kazakhstan: The Role of Large Enterprises and Foreign Investment	Peck, A. E.	2004	Economic Development in Kazakhstan: The Role of Large Enterprises and Foreign Investment
Effects of Oil Production on Economic Growth in Eurasian Countries: Panel ARDL Approach	Bildirici, M. E. & Kayikçi, F.	2013	Energy
Efficiency of the Investment Project Solution for Diversification in the Oil and Gas Industry	Razakova, A.A., Shalbolova, U.Z. & Yelpanova, M.A.	2019	Academy of Strategic Management Journal
Energy and the Environment in Kazakhstan	Dahl, C. & Kuralbayeva, K.	2001	Energy Policy
Energy Policy in Kazakhstan: Tendencies and Risks	Kozhabayeva, A.	2012	13th International Scientific Conference on International

			Relations 2012: Contemporary Issues of World Economics and Politics
Energy security and Sustainability in Eurasian Economic Union in the Terms of Economic Growth: The Case of Kazakhstan's Energy Sector up to 2040 Perspectives	Movkebayeva, G. et al.	2020	International Journal of Energy Economics and Policy
Energy Security in Kazakhstan: The Consumers' Perspective	Mouraviev, N.	2021	Energy Policy
Energy Service Centres: An Innovative Approach to Achieving Energy Efficiency in Kazakhstan	Zbrodko, Y. A., Novoseltsev, A.V. & Sankovski, A.G.	2017	Book chapter in: Sustainable Energy in Kazakhstan: Moving to Cleaner Energy in a Resource–Rich Country
Energy Wealth and Tax Reform in Russia and Kazakhstan	Weinthal, E. & Jones Luong, P.	2001	Resources Policy
Estimation of Multiplicative Effect of Oil–Producing Company on Economy of a Region	Egemberdieva, S. & Azatbek, T.	2012	Actual Problems of Economics
Explaining the Real Exchange Rate in Kazakhstan, 1996–2003: Is Kazakhstan Vulnerable to the Dutch Disease?	Kutan, A. M. & Wyzan, M. L.	2005	Economic Systems
Globalization, Regionalization and Society in the Caspian Sea Basin: Overcoming Geography Restrictions and Calamities of Oil Dependent Economies	Alieva, L.	2012	Journal of Southeast European and Black Sea
Governance and Accumulation Around the Caspian: A New Analytic Approach to Petroleum–Fueled Postsocialist Development	Liu, M. Y.	2018	Ab Imperio–Studies of New Imperial History and Nationalism in the Post–Soviet Space
Green Supply Chain as an Antecedent of Sustainable Performance in the Crude Oil Industry of Kazakhstan: Does Green Accounting Matter in the Relationship Between Green Investment Recovery and Sustainable Performance?	Toopgajank, S. et al.	2019	International Journal of Innovation, Creativity and Change
How Oil Autocracies Learn to Stop Worrying: Central Eurasia in 2008 Global Financial Crisis	Ahmadov, A. K.	2019	Post–Soviet Affairs

Impact of Oil Prices on Sovereign Funds (The Assets and Investments)	Pauhofova, I. & Svocakova, S.	2016	Ekonomicky Casopis
Importance of the Caspian Countries for the European Union Energy Security	Ibrayeva, A. et al.	2018	International Journal of Energy Economics and Policy
Improving the Competitiveness of the Oil Companies on the Basis of Innovative Development in Kazakhstan	Danabayeva, R. & Shedenov, U.	2014	World Applied Sciences Journal
Improving the Mechanism for Systematic Management of the Oil and Gas Industry at the Macro Level	Akhmetova, G. et al.	2020	Ad Alta–Journal of Interdisciplinary Research
Influence of Social Partnership on the Development of Enterprise: On the Example of Oil Industry	Sansyzbayev, A.	2019	Entrepreneurship and Sustainability Issues
Instability and Oil: How Political Time Horizons Affect Oil Revenue Management	Kendall–Taylor, A.	2001	Studies in Comparative International Development
Investment Cooperation Between Kazakhstan and Middle Eastern Countries: Problems and Prospects	Tanatarova, Z. et al.	2020	Central Asia and the Caucasus
Issues of the Cultivation of Corporate Social Responsibility for Oil and Gas Enterprises in the Republic of Kazakhstan	Buldybayeva, G.	2013	Middle East Journal of Scientific Research
Joint Venture Negotiation and Managerial Practices in the New Countries of the Former Soviet Union	Munns, A. K., Aloquili, O. & Ramsay, B.	2000	International Journal of Project Management
Kazakhstan and Azerbaijan as Post–Soviet Rentier States: Resource Incomes and Autocracy as a Double 'Curse' in Post–Soviet Regimes	Franke, A., Gawrich, A. & Alakbarov, G.	2009	Europe – Asia Studies
Kazakhstan Petroleum Industry 2008–2010: Trends of Resource Nationalism Policy?	Sarsenbayev, K.	2011	The Journal of World Energy Law & Business
Kazakhstan Pipeline Policy in the Caspian Region	Parkhomchik, L. A.	2015	Book chapter in: Oil and Gas Pipelines in the Black–Caspian Seas Region
Kazakhstan, Nazarbayev, Foreign–Investment and Oil	Elliot, G.	1993	Louisiana Law Review
Kazakhstan: Long–Term Economic Growth and the Role of the Oil Sector	Kalyuzhnova, Y. & Patterson, K.	2016	Comparative Economic Studies

Title	Author	Year	Publication
Kazakhstan: Oil Endowment and Oil Empowerment	Palazuelos, E. & Fernández, R.	2012	Communist and Post-Communist Studies
Kazakhstan: Oil, Politics and the New 'Great Game'	Jafar, M.	2004	Book chapter in: The Caspian: Politics, Energy and Security
Kazakhstan: Recent Developments and United States Interests	Nichol, J.	2012	Central Asia: Regional Affairs and U.S. Interests and Policies
Kazakhstan's Changing Geopolitics: The Resource Economy and Popular Attitudes about China's Growing Regional Influence	Koch, N.	2013	Eurasian Geography and Economics
Kazakhstan's Diversification Strategy Are Policies Building Linkages and Promoting Competition?	Howie, P.	2017	Book chapter in: Economic Diversification Policies in Natural Resource Rich Economies
Kazakhstan's Economic Challenges: How to Manage the Oil Boom?	Brauer, B.	2007	Transition Studies Review
Kazakhstan's Economy since Independence: Does the Oil Boom Offer a Second Chance for Sustainable Development?	Pomfret, R.	2005	Europe – Asia Studies
Kazakhstan's Oil	Levine, I.	2016	Book chapter in: US Policies in Central Asia: Democracy, Energy, and the War on Terror
Kazakhstan's Oil and Gas Development: Views from Russia and Kazakhstan	Olcott, M. B.	2011	Book chapter in: Russian Energy Security and Foreign Policy
Kazakhstan's Oil Boom, Diversification Strategies, and the Service Sector	Atakhanova, Z.	2021	Mineral Economics
Key Factors in Attracting Foreign Direct Investments in the Oil and Gas Industry of Kazakhstan	Darmen S. & Orazgaliyev, S.	2015	Економіка та Управління Національним Господарством
Learning Problems Efficiency of Enterprises in the Petroleum Sector	Egemberdieva, S. M., Esmagulova, N. D. & Kadyrbergenova, A. K.	2016	Bulletin of the National Academy of Sciences of the republic of Kazakhstan
Market Reforms and "Economic Miracle" in Kazakhstan	Simon, G.	2009	Economic Annals

Title	Author	Year	Journal
Measuring the Knowledge–Based Performance Efficiency in the Oil–Exported Countries	Mutanov, G., Zhuparova, A. & Zhaisanova, D.	2020	Montenegrin Journal of Economics
Mineral Wealth and the Economic Transition: Kazakstan	Auty, R. M.	1998	Resources Policy
Modeling the Caspian Sea Negotiations	Sheikhmohammady, M., Kilgour, D. M. & Hipel, K. W.	2010	Group Decision and Negotiation
Modern Aspects of Adapting Sustainable Strategic Business Planning. Studies Case from Oil Industry and the Tourism Industry	Linnik, A. et al.	2020	Journal of Environmental Management and Tourism
Motivation of Employees' Labor Activity in Oil and Gas Companies in Kazakhstan	Kurmanov, N. et al.	2013	World Applied Sciences Journal
National and International Labour Relations in Oil and Gas Trans National Corporations in Kazakhstan	Croucher, R.	2015	International Business Review
Natural Resource Policies and Standard of Living in Kazakhstan	Burak Sakal, H.	2015	Central Asian Survey
New Prospects in the Political Economy of Inner–Caspian Hydrocarbons and Western Energy Corridor through Turkey	Bilgin, M.	2007	Energy Policy
Oil and Growth Challenge in Kazakhstan	Nurmakhanova, M.	2020	International Journal of Economics and Business Research
Oil Factor in Economic Development	Humbatova, S. I. & Qadim–Oglu Hajiyev, N.	2019	Energies
Oil Prices and Kazakhstan's Real Exchange Rate: An ARDL Bound Test Approach	Agazade, S.	2020	Bilig
Oil Shock in the Caspian Basin: Diversification Policy and Subsidized Economies	Bayramov, V. & Abbas, G.	2017	Resources Policy
Perspectives on the Caspian Sea Dilemma: Russian Policies Since the Soviet Demise	Saivetz, C. R.	2003	Eurasian Geography and Economics

Title	Author	Year	Source
Pipeline Architecture of the Black Sea–Caspian Sea Region: Geographical and Political Issues	Zonn, I. S.	2016	Handbook of Environmental Chemistry
Political Insecurity and Oil: The Effect of Time Horizons on Oil Revenue Management in Azerbaijan and Kazakhstan	Kendall–Taylor, A. H.	2011	Problems of Post–Communism
Politics and Oil in Kazakhstan	Ostrowski, W.	2010	Politics and Oil in Kazakhstan
Preconditions for Competitiveness Increase of Oil & Gas Complex	Amaniyazova, G.	2013	Actual Problems of Economics
Profiles of the Petroleum Sectors in Caspian Region Countries and the Potential for a New Caspian to Middle East Gulf Export Line through Iran	Shammas, P. & Nagata, K.	2000	Energy Exploration & Exploitation
Prospects for Energy Cooperation in the Caspian Sea	Bahgat, G.	2007	Communist and Post–Communist Studies
Prospects of Export Routes for Kashagan Oil	Babali, T.	2009	Energy Policy
Purchasing Power: Oil, Elections and Regime Durability in Azerbaijan and Kazakhstan	Kendall–Taylor, A.	2012	Europe – Asia Studies
Reconstructing MNE–host Country Bargaining Model in the International Oil Industry	Orazgaliyev, S.	2018	Transnational Corporations Review
Redistribution of Oil Revenue in Kazakhstan	Najman, B. et al.	2007	Book chapter in: Economics and Politics of Oil in the Caspian Basin: The Redistribution of Oil Revenues in Azerbaijan and Central Asia
Regional Report the Caspian Sea: Potentials and Prospects	Bahgat, G.	2004	Governance
Resource Concentration, Institutional Quality and the Natural Resource Curse	Oskenbayev, Y., Yilmaz, M. & Abdulla, K.	2013	Economic Systems
Resource Nationalism	Koch, N. & Perreault, T.	2019	Progress in Human Geography
Resource Nationalism and Credit Growth in FSU Countries	Kalyuzhnova, Y. & Nygaard, C.	2009	Energy Policy

Russian Efforts to Control Kazakhstan's Oil: The Kumkol Case	Marten, K.	2007	Post–Soviet Affairs
Russian Energy Policy in the Caspian Basin	Kubicek, P.	2004	World Affairs
Resource–Rich Countries, Clean Energy and Volatility of Oil Prices	Kalyuzhnova, Y.	2017	Book chapter in: Sustainable Energy in Kazakhstan: Moving to Cleaner Energy in a Resource–Rich Country
Sharing a Multi–National Resource through Bankruptcy Procedures	Sheikhmohammady, M. & Madani, K.	2008	Conference Proceedings
Shocks to Supply and Demand in the Oil Market, the Equilibrium Oil Price, and Country Responses in Economic Indicators	Teplova, T. V., Lysenko, V.V. & Sokolova, T. V.	2019	Energy Systems–Optimization Modeling Simulation and Economic Aspects
State Governance Evolution in Resource–Rich Transition Economies: An Application to Russia and Kazakhstan	Kalyuzhnova, Y. & Nygaard, C.	2008	Energy Policy
Taxation of Subsoil Use in Kazakhstan	Sikhimbaeva, D. R., Esimseitova, K. A. & Esimseitov, M. S.	2014	Actual Problems of Economics
The CIA Made me Do It: Understanding the Political Economy of Corruption in Kazakhstan	Yeager, M. G.	2012	Crime, Law and Social Change
The Commonwealth of Independent States' Troubled Energy Sectors	Mathieu, P. & Shiells, C. R.	2002	Finance and Development
The Dependence of the Kazakhstan Economy on the Oil Sector and the Importance of Export Diversification	Azretbergenova, G. & Syzdykova, A.	2020	International Journal of Energy Economics and Policy
The Determination of Panel Causality Analysis on the Relationship between Economic Growth and Primary Energy Resources Consumption of Turkey and Central Asian Turkish Republics	Sentürk, C. & Sataf, C.	2015	Procedia – Social and Behavioral Sciences
The Digital Transformation of the Oil and Gas Sector in Kazakhstan: Priorities and Problems	Kushzhanov, N. V. & Dashqin, M.	2019	News of the National Academy of Sciences of the Republic of

Title	Author(s)	Year	Source
			Kazakhstan, Series of Geology and Technical Sciences
The Dynamics of Labor Militancy in the Extractive Sector: Kazakhstan's Oilfields and South Africa's Platinum Mines in Comparative Perspective	Evans, A. D. & Sil, R.	2020	Comparative Political Studies
The Fight for Community Justice against Big Oil in the Caspian Region: The Case of Berezovka, Kazakhstan	Watters, K.	2009	Book chapter in: Environmental Justice and Environmental Sustainability in the Former Soviet Union
The Geopolitics of Caspian oil: Rivalries of the US, Russia, and Turkey in the South Caucasus	Younkyoo, K. & Gu Ho, E.	2008	Global Economic Review
The Impact of Corruption and Local Content Policy in on Firm Performance: Evidence from Kazakhstan	Kalyuzhnova, Y. & Belitski, M.	2019	Resources Policy
The Impact of the Oil & Gas Sector on Socioeconomic Development of the Republic of Kazakhstan	Yegemberdiyeva, S., Issayeva, B. & Sadykova, P.	2014	Actual Problems of Economics
The Impact of the Oil and Oil Products Market on Economic Development: A National Aspect	Suleimenova, A. et al.	2020	International Journal of Energy Economics and Policy
The Impact of Oil Price Shocks on Oil–Dependent Countries' Currencies: The Case of Azerbaijan and Kazakhstan	Czech, K. & Niftiyev, I.	2021	Journal of Risk and Financial Management
The Kazakh Oil Industry: A Potential Critical Role in Central Asia	Dorian, J. P., Zhanseitov, S. F. & Hartono Indriyanto, S.	1994	Energy Policy
The Methodology for Economic Evaluation of Oil and Gas Investment Projects in Kazakhstan	Bogatkina, Y. G. & Eremin, N.A.	2020	Neftyanoe Khozyaystvo – Oil Industry
The Oil and Gas Resource Base of the Caspian region	Effimoff, I.	2000	Journal of Petroleum Science and Engineering
The Oil Industry in the Southern–Tier Former Soviet Republics	Sagers, M. J.	1994	Post-Soviet Geography

The Relationship Between the Oil Price Shocks and the Stock Markets: The Example of Commonwealth of Independent States Countries	Syzdykova, A.	2018	International Journal of Energy Economics and Policy
The Role of Fuel and Energy Sector in the Eurasian Economic Community Integration Process	Guliyev, I. A. & Mekhdiev, E. T.	2017	International Journal of Energy Economics and Policy
The Role of Oil and Gas in Kazakhstan's Foreign Policy: Looking East or West?	Pinar, I.	2007	Europe – Asia Studies
The Role of Oil Prices in Exchange Rate Movements: The CIS Oil Exporters	Hasanov, F. et al.	2017	Economies
The Significance of Establishing Common EAEU Gas, Oil and Petroleum Product Markets for the Republic of Kazakhstan	Tyulebekova, D., Onuchko, M. & Marmontova, T.	2019	Central Asia and the Caucasus
The Tengiz Oil Enclave: Labor, Business, and the State	Yessenova, S.	2012	Political and Legal Anthropology Review
The Trans–Caspian Energy Route: Cronyism, Competition and Cooperation in Kazakh Oil Export	Guliyev, F. & Akhrarkhodjaeva, N.	2009	Energy Policy
The US Grand Strategy and the Eurasian Heartland in the Twenty–First Century	Işeri, E.	2009	Geopolitics
Trade and Economic Cooperation Between China and Kazakhstan: Problems and Prospects	Xie, T. et al.	2021	Central Asia and the Caucasus
Transformations of the Oil and Gas Industry in the CIS	Bensaid, B.	1999	Oil & Gas Science and Technology–Revenue D IFP Energies Nouvelles
Transnational Environmental Activism in Central Asia: The Coupling of Domestic Law and International Conventions	Weinthal E. & Watters, K.	2010	Environmental Politics
Understanding China's Global Energy Strategy	Smith Stegen, K.	2015	International Journal of Emerging Markets
Using the Supply–Chain Management for Developing Oil Industries in the Republic of Kazakhstan	Mugauina, R., Madiyarova, D. & Shishmanov, K.	2020	International Journal of Supply Chain Management

Value Co–Creation Between Foreign Firms and Indigenous Small– and Medium–sized Enterprises (SMEs) in Kazakhstan's Oil and Gas Industry: The Role of Information Technology Spillovers	Heim, I. et al.	2019	Thunderbird International Business Review
Volatility, Diversification and Oil Shock in Resource–Rich Turkic Countries: Avenues for Recovery	Bayramov, V. & Orujova, L.	2017	Bilig
Ways of Clusters Formation Within Oil & Gas and Petrochemical Industries	Dzholdasbayeva, G.	2013	Actual Problems of Economics
What Price Access to the Open Seas? The Geopolitics of Oil and Gas Transmission from the Trans–Caspian Republics	Kandiyoti, R.	2008	Central Asian Survey

List of Studies excluded with Reason

Analysis of the Investment Process of the Republic of Kazakhstan at the National Economy	Yeleukulova, A. D., Baytenova, L. M. & Uandykova, M. K.	2012	Vith Ryskulov Readings: Socio–Economic Modernization of Kazakhstan Under Conditions of Global Financial Instability	Irretrievable
Assessment of the Effectiveness of the Use of the Assets of the National Fund of Kazakhstan and Ways to Improve It	Nurseiit, N. et al.	2017	Economic and Social Development	Irretrievable
Best Practices in Testing and Analyzing Multi-layer Reservoirs	–	2011	Journal of Petroleum Technology	Incidental, different focus
Business Training for a New Republic: A Seminar Series for Kazakh Oil Executives	Sergenian, G. K. & Blodgett, M.	1998	Journal of Teaching in International Business	Incidental, different focus
Caspian Petroleum	Konoplyanik, A. & Lobzhanidze, A.	1999	Pacific and Asian Journal of Energy	Irretrievable
China's Small Leap Forward in its Energy "Go–Out" Strategy	Jiang, W. & Yu, S.	2009	Geopolitics of Energy	Irretrievable
Civil Society and Politics in Central Asia	Ziegler, C. E.	2015	Civil Society and Politics in Central Asia	Incidental, different focus

Conclusions	Zonn, I. S.	2016	Book chapter in: Handbook of Environmental Chemistry	Incidental, different focus
Corporate Governance and Firm value of Kazakhstani Companies in the Conditions of Sanctions Against the Russian Federation	Zhussupova, Z., Onyusheva, I. & Baizyldayeva, U.	2016	Proceedings of the 4th International Conference on Management, Leadership and Governance, ICMLG 2016	Irretrievable
Critical Analysis of Market and Institutional Changes in Kazakhstan's Economy	Shevyakova, A. et al.	2018	Innovation Management and Education Excellence Through Vision 2020	Incidental, different focus
Crude Oil from South Kazakhstan	Urazgaliev, B. U., Dzhetpisov, B. T. & Koshebekov, D.	1988	Chemistry and Technology of Fuels and Oils	Incidental, different focus
Crude Oils from New Fields in Western Kazakhstan	Koryabina, N. M. & Kotova, A. V.	1978	Chemistry and Technology of Fuels and Oils	Incidental, different focus
Determination of the Yield of Commercial Product in Processing Kazakhstan Gas Condensates	Khairudinov, I. et al.	2011	Chemistry and Technology of Fuels and Oils	Incidental, different focus
Development of Export and Transit Potential of Oil Transportation Infrastructure of the Republic of Kazakhstan	Kabyldin, K.	2014	World Petroleum Congress Proceedings	Irretrievable
Development of Industrial Legislative Acts on Ecological Follow–up of Prospecting, Exploration and Development of Oil and Gas Fields	Koshcheev, V. P.	2003	Neftyanoe khozyaystvo – Oil Industry	Irretrievable
Development of Integration Processes in the Petroleum Industry of Kazakhstan	Zholdybaev, N. T.	2003	Neftyanoe khozyaystvo – Oil Industry	Irretrievable
Development of Oil and Gas Pipelines in North East Asia	Kandiyoti, R.	2004	Proceedings of the World Engineers' Convention 2004, Vol F–A, Resources and Energy	Irretrievable
Drilling Rigs of OMZ– Onshore & Offshore for Development of Oil & Gas Fields of Kazakhstan	Epshtein, V. E.	2003	Neftyanoe khozyaystvo – Oil Industry	Irretrievable

Title	Author	Year	Source	Reason
Drivers of Exchange Rate Dynamics in Selected CIS Countries: Evidence from a Factor–Augmented Vector Autoregressive (FAVAR) Analysis	Dreger, C. & Fidrmuc, J.	2011	Emerging Markets Finance and Trade	Incidental, different focus
Economic and Operational Assessment of the Arman Field in Kazakhstan	Kaiser, M. J. & Kubekpayeva. A.	2006	Natural Resources Research	Incidental, different focus
Economic Security in Entrepreneurship Activity Economic Security in Entrepreneurship Activity	Asainov, A. Z., Mustafayev, K. S. & Zhaulubaev, E. N.	2018	Bulletin of the National Academy of Sciences of the republic of Kazakhstan	Incidental, different focus
Energy Reforms and Foreign Direct Investments in Energy Projects in the Commonwealth of Independent States (CIS)	Brendow, K.	1995	International Journal of Global Energy Issues	Incidental, different focus
Energy Security and Its Impact on the Domestic and Foreign Policies of the Central Asian Countries	Yesdauletova, A.	2013	Book chapter in: Afghanistan and Central Asia: NATO's Role in Regional Security Since 9/11	Irretrievable
Environmental and Safety Legislation for the Offshore Oil and Gas Sector in Kazakhstan: A Critical Review	Palerm, J. et al.	2005	Journal of Environmental Assessment Policy and Management	Incidental, different focus
Estimation of the Influence on the Health of the Population of a Large Oil and Gas Complex in the Republic of Kazakhstan	Kaidakova, N. N., Skolsky, V. A. & Skolskay, E. A.	2010	International Journal of Circumpolar Health	Incidental, different focus
Europe's Energy Dependence	–	2008	Strategic Comments	Incidental, different focus
Impact of Local Content Restrictions and Barriers Against Foreign Direct Investment in Services: The Case of Kazakhstan's Accession to the World Trade Organization	Jensen, J. & Tarr, D.	2008	Eastern European Economics	Incidental, different focus
Industrial Profitability and Trade among the Former Soviet Republics	Senik-Leygonie, C. et al.	2006	Economic Policy	Irretrievable

Influence of Sino – Burmese Oil and Gas Pipeline Construction on Energy Structure in Southwest China	Guiyao, Z. & Ersi, L.	2017	Procedings of the 2nd International Symposium on Business Corporation and Development in South–East and South Asia Under B&R Initiative	Incidental, different focus
Innovation Management in the Oil and Gas Industry of the Republic of Kazakhstan	Yeleukulova, A. D. et al.	2017	Journal of Applied Economic Sciences	Irretrievable
Kazakhstan – Oil–Reserves Could Exceed Oil Reserves of Former USSR – Review of Current Projects	–	1995	Energy Exploration & Exploitation	Irretrievable
Legislative and Tax Regulation of the Kazakhstan Oil and Gas Sector	Kontorovich, A. E. & Filimonova, I. V.	2006	Neftyanoe khozyaystvo – Oil Industry	Irretrievable
Long–term Oil Outlook of Eight CIS Members	Birol, F. & Guerer, N.	1996	Revue de l'Energie	Irretrievable
Long–Term Plans for Oil and Gas Sector in Kazakhstan	Sagers, M. J.	1993	Post–Soviet Geography	Irretrievable
Modern Ways of Expanding the Functions of Personnel Services at the Enterprises of Oil and Gas Complex of the Republic of Kazakhstan	Turekulova, D. & Kurmanov, N.	2012	Vith Ryskulov Readings: Socio–Economic Modernization of Kazakhstan Under Conditions of Global Financial Instability	Irretrievable
Monotowns' Economy Diversification in East Kazakhstan Region	Zakirov, R. T.	2016	Розвиток Продуктивных Сил i Регіональна Економііка	Submitted to a Journal excluding Kazakhstan
Mutual Influence of Macroeconomic Indicators of Kazakhstan and its Trading Partners	Mukhamediyev, B. & Khitakhunov, A.	2017	Sustainable Economic Growth, Education Excellence, and Innovation Management Through Vision 2020	Incidental, different focus
New Kazakhstan Crude Oils	Bukeikhanov, N. N. & Urazgaliyev, B. U.	1992	Petroleum Chemistry	Irretrievable

New Oils of Kazakhstan	Bukeikhanov, N. N. & Urazgaliev, B. U.	1992	Neftekhimiya	Irretrievable
New Perspectives of Karamandybas Field	Kulsariev, K. U. et al.	2003	Neftyanoe khozyaystvo – Oil Industry	Irretrievable
Oil and Gas Law in Kazakhstan: National and International Perspectives	Bantekas, I., Paterson, J. & Sulemanov, M.	2006	Oil and gas law in Kazakhstan: National and international perspectives	Irretrievable
Oil Funds in Transition Economies: Azerbaijan and Kazakhstan	Wakeman–Linn, J., Mathieu, P. & van Selm, B.	2003	Book chapter in: Fiscal Policy Formulation and Implementation in Oil–Producing Countries	Irretrievable
Oil Rents and Economic Growth: Recent Evidence from Kazakhstan	Jumambayev, S.	2016	2016 International Conference on Business and Economics	Irretrievable
Offshore Kazakhstan – Ultimate Challenge for the Oil industry	Davies, G.	2003	Marine Pollution Bulletin	Incidental, different focus
Perspective Development and Improvement of Technological Processes	Pirogov, A.G. et al.	2003	Neftyanoe khozyaystvo – Oil Industry	Irretrievable
Perspective Development of Trunk Lines for Developing the Caspian Sea Shelf	Nysangaliev, A. N. & Amangali, D.	2003	Neftyanoe khozyaystvo – Oil Industry	Irretrievable
Regarding Maximal Income to the Budget in Product–Sharing Agreements	Akkaisieva, A. U.	2003	Neftyanoe khozyaystvo – Oil Industry	Irretrievable
Russia's Emerging Place in the Eurasian Hydrocarbon Energy Complex	Cutler, R. M.	2010	Book chapter in: Globalization of Energy: China and the European Union	Irretrievable
Russian Political, Economic, and Security Issues and U.S. Interests	Goldman, S. D.	2011	Book chapter in: U.S. – Russian Economic and Political Relationship	Irretrievable
Rethinking the Eastward Extension of the EU Civil Order and the Nature of Europe's new East–West Divide	Bideleux, R.	2009	Perspectives on European Politics and Society	Incidental, different focus

Sharing a Multi–National Resource through Bankruptcy Procedures	Sheikhmohammady, M. & Madani, K.	2008	Conference Proceedings	Irretrievable
Study of the Structure of Porphyrins of New Oils from Kazakhstan	Bakirova, C. F. & Yag'yaeva, S. M.	1991	Neftekhimiya	Irretrievable
Stumbling Giant–Kazakhstan's Kashagan Field	Lee, J.	2013	Geopolitics of Energy	Irretrievable
Tanking Up the Commercial and Strategic Significance of China's Growing Tanker Fleet	Collins, G. B. & Erickson, A. S.	2007	Geopolitics of Energy	Incidental, different focus
The Caspian Sea: Potentials and Prospects	Bahgat, G.	2003	Governance	Incidental, different focus
The Challenge for Industrial Development in the Central Asian Republics of the Former Soviet Union	Henley, J. S. & Assaf, G. B.	1996	Мост–Мост: Economic Policy in Transitional Economies	Incidental, different focus
The Customs Union in the CIS	Borodin, K. & Strokov, A.	2015	Journal of Economic Integration	Incidental, different focus
The Effects of Oil Prices on Turkey's Foreign Trade Relations to Azerbaijan and Kazakhstan: 1996–2016	Dikkaya, M., Doyar, B. V. & Kanbir, O.	2017	4th RSEP International Conferences on Social Issues and Economic Studies	Incidental, different focus
The Efficiency and Effectiveness of the Revenue Out Part of the Republican Budget	Shuptybaeva, D. K., Rakhimbekova, A. E. & Makhatova, A. B.	2016	Bulletin of the National Academy of Sciences of the republic of Kazakhstan	Incidental, different focus
The Energy Price Changes Impact on the Financial Market of Kazakhstan–In International Oil Prices as an Example	Cuiping, L.	2015	4th International Conference on Energy and Envronmental Protection	Irretrievable
The Eurasia Canal as a Factor of Economic Prosperity for the Caspian Region	Bekturganov, N. S. & Bolaev, A. V.	2017	Geography, Environment, Sustainability	Incidental, different focus
The Global Economy and Oil Market in Post–Recession	Alipour–Jeddi, M.	2010	OPEC Bulletin	Incidental, different focus

The Impact of Macroeconomic Indicators on Stock Exchange Performance in Kazakhstan	Oskenbayev, Y., Yilmaz, M. & Chagirov, D.	2011	African Journal of Business Management	Incidental, different focus
The New Silk Road Diplomacy: China's Central Asian Foreign Policy since the Cold War	Karrar, H. H.	2010	The New Silk Road diplomacy: China's Central Asian foreign policy since the Cold War	Irretrievable
The Potential of Energy as a Geopolitical Binding Factor in Asia	Jaffa, A. M.	2018	Post–Soviet Geography and Economics	Incidental, different focus
The Russian Trade–off: Environment and Development in the Caspian Sea	Blum, D.	1998	Journal of Environment and Development	Incidental, different focus
The Sino–Saudi Connection	Luft, G. & Korin, A.	2004	Commentary	Incidental, different focus
The Tengiz Oil–Fiedl in the Pre-Caspian Baun of Kazakhstan (Former USSR) – Supergiant of the 1980s	Lisovsky, N. N. & Gogonenkov, G. N.	1992	Book chapter in: Giant Oil and Gas Fields of the Decade 1978–1988	Irretrievable
Understanding Attitudes toward Energy Security: Results of a Cross–National Survey	Knox–Hayes, J. et al.	2013	Global Environmental Change	Incidental, different focus
Using Energy Resources to Diversify the Economy: Agricultural Price Distortions in Kazakhstan	Pomfret, R.	2009	Comparative Economic Studies	Incidental, different focus

Table 20   Studies included in the systematic review of 'corruption' and 'Kazakhstan'

Title	Author(s)	Year	Source	Approach	Method(s)	Sector
Anti–Corruption and Improving the Prospects of Criminal Responsibility in the Economic Sphere of the Republic of Kazakhstan	Yernishev, K., Saginbekov, K. & Gazayev, A.	2014	World Applied Sciences Journal	Qualitative	Descriptive statistics and document analysis	Theoretical
Are Academics in Kazakhstan Capable of Self–regulation? A Study of Faculty's Normative Structure in the Midst of Higher Education Decentralization Reforms	Rumyantseva, N. L. & Caboni, T. C.	2012	Tertiary Education and Management	Quantitative	Descriptive statistics and questionnaires	Education sector
Baker Hughes: Greasing the Wheels in Kazakhstan (FCPA Violations and Implementation of a Corporate Ethics and Anti–Corruption Compliance Program)	Holtzblatt, M. & Tschakert, N.	2014	Journal of Accounting Education	Quantitative	Document analysis	Oil sector
Blurring the Line Between Licit and Illicit: Transnational Corruption Networks in Central Asia and Beyond	Cooley, A. & Sharman, J. C.	2015	Central Asian Survey	Qualitative	Document analysis and experiment	Oil sector and telecommunication
Civil Liability for Corruption Offenses in the Kazakhstan Republic	Karibayeva, A.K.	2021	Journal of Legal, Ethical and Regulatory Issues	Quantitative	Document analysis and statistical analysis	Theoretical

Combatting Corruption in Kazakhstan: A role for Ethics Commissioners?	Janenova, S. & Knox, C.	2019	Public Administration and Development	Qualitative	Descriptive statistics, focus groups and interviews	Civil service/public administration sector
Contemporary scales of the shadow economy in Kazakhstan	Kydyrova, Z. et al.	2020	Journal of Advanced Research in Law and Economics	Qualitative	Document analysis and ethnography	Theoretical
Corruption Crimes in Public Procurement in the Republic of Kazakhstan	Kuatova, A. S.	2013	Middle East Journal of Scientific Research	Qualitative	Descriptive statistics and document analysis	Public procurement
Corruption Impact on the Formation of the Investment Climate in the Republic of Kazakhstan	Utegenova, A. M. & Serikbaeva, B. M.	2016	Actual Problems of Economics	Quantitative	Statistical analysis (multivariate regression)	Multiple sectors
Corruption in Higher Education and Government Measures for its Prevention	Feoktistova, Y.	2013	International Conference on Education & Educational Psychology 2013	Qualitative	Descriptive statistics and document analysis	Education sector
Corruption in Kazakhstan and the Quality of Governance	Satpayev, D.	2014	IDE Discussion Paper No. 475	Qualitative	Descriptive statistics and document analysis	Multiple sectors
Corruption in Post-Soviet Kazakhstan	Rigi, J.	2004	Book chapter in: Between Morality and the Law: Corruption, Anthropology and Comparative Society	Qualitative	Ethnography (participant observation and interviews)	Multiple sectors

Title	Author	Year	Journal	Method Type	Method	Sector
Criminal Policy Innovations and Legal System Improvement Problems in the Republic of Kazakhstan	Ajupova, Z. K. & Kusainov, D. U.	2014	Criminology Journal of Baikal National University of Economics and Law	Qualitative	Document analysis	Theoretical
Criminological measures to counteract corruption offences in the field of illegal gambling	Berdaliyeva, A. S. et al.	2021	Journal of Financial Crime	Qualitative	Document analysis	Illegal gambling sector
Development of Electronic Government in Kazakhstan as a Tool to Combat Corruption	Sheryazdanova, G. R. et al.	2016	Indian Journal of Science and Technology	Quantitative	Descriptive statistics, document analysis and questionnaires	E-governance
Does Good Governance Matter? Kazakhstan's Economic Growth and Worldwide Governance Indicators	Absadykov, A	2020	Otoritas–Jurnal Ilmu Pemeritahan	Quantitative	Statistical analysis	Multiple sectors
E-Government as an Anti-Corruption Strategy in Kazakhstan	Sheryazdanova, G. & Butterfield, J.	2017	Journal of Information Technology and Politics	Qualitative	Descriptive statistics and document analysis	E-governance
Effectiveness of Ecological Crimes Counteraction in Kazakhstan	Mataeva, M. H. & Mukasheva, N. K.	2014	Criminology Journal of Baikal National University of Economics and Law	Quantitative	Descriptive statistics	Theoretical
Elite Preferences and Transparency Promotion in Kazakhstan	Öge, K.	2017	Communist and Post–Communist Studies	Qualitative	Document analysis and interviews	Extractive industries
Everyday Corruption in Kazakhstan: An Ethngraphic	Oka, N.	2013	Report for: *Exploring Informal Networks in*	Qualitative	Ethnography (participant observation and interviews)	Multiple sectors

Analysis of Informal Practices			*Kazakhstan: A Multi-dimensional Approach*			
Exploitation of Natural Resources in Kazakhstan: Judicial Practice for Foreign Investment	Yessengeldin, B. et al.	2019	Journal of East Asia and International Law	Qualitative	Descriptive statistics and document analysis	Extractive industries
Foreign Experience of Formation of Anti–Corruption Strategies	Almaganbetov, P. et al.	2016	International Journal of Environmental and Science Education	Qualitative	Document analysis	Theoretical
Foreign versus Domestic Bribery: Explaining Repression in Kleptocratic Regimes	LaPorte, J.	2017	Comparative Politics	Qualitative	Document analysis	Oil sector
Formation of Negative Perception of Corruption ad Indicator of Growth of Legal Culture of Modern Kazakhstan Society	Sartayev, S. A. & Kalshabayeva, M. Z.	2015	Bullettin of the National Academy of Sciences of the Republic of Kazakhstan	Qualitative	Document analysis	Theoretical
Forming an anti–corruption culture of law enforcement agencies: National and international experience	Sitnikov, P. V. et al.	2020	Journal of Advanced Research in Law and Economics	Qualitative	Document analysis	Law enforcement sector
Gifts, Bribes, and Development in Post–Soviet Kazakstan	Werner, C.	2000	Human Organization	Qualitative	Ethnography (participant observation and interviews)	Theoretical
Grades and Degrees for Sale: Understanding Informal Exchanges in Kazakhstan's Education Sector	Oka, N.	2019	Problems of Post–Communism	Qualitative	Interviews	Education sector

Title	Author	Year	Journal			
Halfway Home and a Long Way to Go: Russian and Kazakh Roads to Sectoral and Political Corruption	Henderson, K. E.	2000	Demokratizatsiya	Qualitative	Document analysis	Theoretical
Hidden State and Municipal Services as a Corruption Factor	Filippova, N. A.	2019	Current Issues of Scientific Support for the State Anti-Corruption Policy in the Russian Federation	Qualitative	Document analysis	Theoretical
Insider's corruption versus outsider's ethicality? Individual responses to conflicting institutional logics	Muratbekova-Touron, M., Lee Park, C. & Fracarolli Nunes, M.	2021	International Journal of Human Resource Management	Quantitative	Experiment	Theoretical
Interaction of Non-Profit Organizations with Government Bodies in the Fight against Corruption as a Basis for Citizens' Economic Rights Protection	Aitimov, B. Z., Seriev, B. A. & Kopbasarova, G. K.	2015	Actual Problems of Economics	Qualitative	Document analysis	Theoretical
Investigative prevention of corruption crimes	Kassimova, M. et al.	2022	Journal of Financial Crime	Qualitative	Document analysis	Law enforcement sector
Kazakhstan Model of Anti-Corruption Drive	Seriev, B. A. et al.	2013	Middle East Journal of Scientific Research	Qualitative	Document analysis	Theoretical
Labor unions and institutional corruption: The case of Kazakhstan	Akhmetzharov, S. & Orazgaliyev, S	2021	Journal of Eurasian Studies	Quantitative	Document analysis and survey	Multiple sectors

Latent Economic and Corruption Crime as an Indicator of the Shadow Economy	Abdramanova, N. K., Abdukarimova, Z. T. & Alaukhanov, Y.O.	2020	2nd International Scientific and Practical Conference on Modern Management Trends and the Digital Economy – from Regional Development to Global Economic Growth (MTDE)	Qualitative	Document analysis	Theoretical
Manufacturing exports and institutional qualities in Central Asian countries	Taguchi, H. & Amirjon, A.	2021	Asia–Pacific Journal of Accounting and Economics	Quantitative	Statistical analysis	Theoretical
Measures of Counteracting Crimes of Corruption in the Quasipublic and Private Sectors of the Republic of Kazakhstan	Karazhanov, M. D., Karazhanova, Z. K. & Zhampeissov, D. A.	2017	Russian Journal of Criminology	Qualitative	Document analysis	Theoretical
Obesity of politicians and corruption in post–Soviet countries	Blavatskyy, P.	2021	Economics of Transition and Institutional Change	Quantitative	Statistical analysis	Theoretical
Objective or perception–based? A debate on the ideal measure of corruption	Pelizzo, R., Baris, O., Janenova, S.	2017	Cornell International Law Journal	Quantitative	Statistical analysis	Theoretical
Opportunities and Barriers of Using Blockchain in Public Administration: The Case of Real Estate Registration in Kazakhstan	Akhmetbek, Y. & Špaček, D.	2021	NISPAcee Journal of Public Administration and Policy	Qualitative	Document analysis	Public administration

Title	Author	Year	Source	Type	Method	Sector
Organized crime in Kazakhstan	Siegel, D and Turlubekova, Z	2020	Book chapter in *Organized Crime and Corruption across Borders: Exploring the Belt and Road Initiative*	Qualitative	Document analysis	Organised crime
On Certain Aspects of Acts of Corruption Countermeasures	Mamitova, Z. A. et al.	2016	International Journal of Environmental and Science Education	Qualitative	Document analysis	Theoretical
Police Corruption in Kazakhstan: The Preliminary Results of the Study	Nurgaliyev, B., Ualiyev, K. & Simonovich, B.	2015	Review of European Studies	Qualitative	Document analysis, questionnaires and interviews	Law enforcement sector
Political Corruption in Eurasia: Understanding Collusion between States, Organized Crime and Business	Kupatadze, A.	2015	Theoretical Criminology	Qualitative	Document analysis	Theoretical
Preventing Corruption Risk in Legislation: Evidence from Russia, Moldova, and Kazakhstan	Kotchegura, A.	2018	International Journal of Public Administration	Qualitative	Descriptive statistics and document analysis	Theoretical
Problems and Perspectives of Transition to the Knowledge–Based Economy in Kazakhstan	Toimbek, D.	2021	Journal of the Knowledge Economy	Quantitative	Statistical analysis	Multiple sectors
Public Procurement: Evidence from Kazakhstan	Dairabayeva, N. K.et al.	2021	Journal of Legal, Ethical and Regulatory Issues	Qualitative	Document analysis	Multiple sectors

Regime Type versus Patronal Politics: A Comparison of "Ardent Democrats" in Kazakhstan and Kyrgyzstan	Junisbai, B. & Junisbai, A.	2019	Post-Soviet Affairs	Quantitative	Descriptive statistics and survey	Theoretical
Regulating Supply Side Corruption: American Investors in the Republic of Kazakhstan	Jain, S. C. & Lehrer, B. R.	2003	Journal of East–West Business	Qualitative	Document analysis	Theoretical
Risky Business: The Political Economy of Chinese Investment in Kazakhstan	O'Neill, D. C.	2014	Journal of Eurasian Studies	Qualitative	Descriptive statistics, document analysis and interviews	Oil sector
SMEs Development and Corruption: Case of Kazakhstan	Suleimenova, G. et al.	2018	Business: Theory and Practice	Quantitative	Descriptive statistics and interviews	Multiple sectors
'Sobriety, human dignity and public morality': ethical standards in Kazakhstan	Pelizzo, R. & Knox, C.	2021	Public Money and Management	Qualitative	Document analysis	Theoretical
Social-Legal Essence of Bribery of the Office Holders in the Territory of Kazakhstan in the End of the XIX Century	Kaliyeva, G. K.	2013	World Applied Sciences Journal	Qualitative	Document analysis	Theoretical
Some Aspects of Criminal Punishment by a Fine Calculated as a Multiple of the Bribe in the Criminal Legislation of the Republic of Kazakhstan	Mercuryiev, V. V., Makhanov, T. G. & Minskaya, V. S.	2017	Russian Journal of Criminology	Qualitative	Document analysis	Theoretical

Title	Author	Year	Journal	Method type	Method	Sector
State Responses to Reputational Concerns: The Case of the Extractive Industries Transparency Initiative in Kazakhstan	Furstenberg, S.	2018	Central Asian Survey	Qualitative	Document analysis and interviews	Extractive industries
Theory and practice of criminal law combating corruption in the Republic of Kazakhstan	Siubayeva, N. Z.	2021	Journal of Financial Crime	Qualitative	Document analysis	Theoretical
The CIA Made Me Do It: Understanding the Political Economy of Corruption in Kazakhstan	Yeager, M. G.	2012	Crime, Law and Social Change	Qualitative	Document analysis	Oil sector
The E–Government Paradox in Post–Soviet Countries	Knox, C. & Janenova, S.	2019	International Journal of Public Sector Management	Qualitative	Focus groups, interviews and participant observation	E–governance
The Fit between Changes to the International Corruption Regime and Indigenous Perceptions of Corruption in Kazakhstan	Nichols, P. M.	2001	University of Pennsylvania Journal of International Economic Law	Quantitative	Document analysis and survey	Multiple sectors
The Impact of Corruption and Local Content Policy in on Firm Performance: Evidence from Kazakhstan	Kalyuzhnova, Y., Belitski, M.	2019	Resources Policy	Quantitative	Statistical analysis (multivariate regression)	Multiple sectors
The International–Domestic Nexus in Anti–Corruption Policy Making: The Case of Caspian Oil and Gas States	Pleines, H. & Wöstheinrich, R.	2016	Europe – Asia Studies	Qualitative	Document analysis	Extractive industries

The Issue Attention Cycle Model and Corruption Issues in Canada and Kazakhstan	Dyussenov, M.	2016	Public Policy and Administration	Quantitative	Descriptive statistics and document analysis	Theoretical
The other road to serfdom: The rise of the rentier class in post–Soviet economies	Sanghera, B. & Satybaldieva, E.	2020	Social Science Information	Qualitative	Document analysis	Extractive industries
The Protests in Zhanaozen and the Kazakh Oil Sector: Conflicting interests in a rentier state	Satpayev, D. & Umbetaliyeva, T.	2015	Journal of Eurasian Studies	Qualitative	Document analysis	Oil sector
The Republic of Kazakhstan Budget System Development and the Increase of its Transparency	Issatayeva, K. B. & Adambekova, A. A.	2016	American Journal of Applied Sciences	Qualitative	Descriptive statistics and document analysis	Theoretical
The Semantic Structure of Gratitude	Smirnov, A. V., Obolenskaya, A. G. & Valiev, R. A.	2016	Psychology in Russia: State of the Art	Quantitative	Descriptive statistics and survey	Theoretical
The Tengiz Oil Enclave: Labor, Business, and the State	Yessenova, S.	2012	Political and Legal Anthropology Review	Qualitative	Ethnography (participant observation and interviews)	Oil sector
Three Universities in Georgia, Kazakhstan and Kyrgyzstan: The Struggle against Corruption and for Social Cohesion	Heyneman, S.P.	2007	Prospects	Qualitative	Interviews	Education sector

| Transparent autocracies: The Extractive Industries Transparency Initiative (EITI) and civil society in authoritarian states | Öge, K. | 2017 | Extractive Industries and Society | Mixed | Statistical analysis, document analysis and interviws | Extractive industries |

List of studies excluded with reason

Title	Author	Year	Journal	Reason
Corruption as One of the Threats to Customs Bodies' Information Security in the Republic of Kazakhstan	Azhimetov, Y. et al.	2017	Journal of Advanced Research in Law and Economics	Irretrievable
Electronic Government: Motivation in Kazakhstan	Silibaevich, M. S.	2012	Vith Ryskulov Readings: Socio–Economic Modernization of Kazakhstan Under Conditions of Global Financial Instability	Irretrievable
FCPA Crackdown Tests Antibribery Compliance	Halpern, J. N. & Herrina, L. B.	2010	Oil & Gas Journal	Irretrievable
Fundamental Principles and Activities in Tackling Corruption in the Republic of Kazakhstan	Nurmaganbet, E. T. et al.	2016	Journal of Advanced Research in Law and Economics	Irretrievable
Human Resource Management Patterns of (Anti)Corruption Mechanisms within Informal Networks	Muratbekova–Touron, M. & Umbetalijeva, T.	2019	Business and Professional Ethics Journal	Irretrievable
International Legal Cooperation of Kazakhstan with the States to Combat Corruption	Akhmetbek, S.	2019	Education Excellence and Innovation Management Through Vision 2020	Irretrievable
Multiple Modernities: Features of Bureaucratic Hierarchy and Corruption in Clannish Societies	Pain, E. et al.	2017	Social Sciences (Russian Federation)	Irretrievable
Neither Boon nor Bane: Management of the Oil Boom in the Post–Soviet Space	Heinrich, A. & Pleines, H.	2013	Osteuropa	In German

On the Implementation of Article 20 of the United Nations Convention against Corruption into the Criminal Legislation of the Republic of Kazakhstan	Mamitova, Z. A.	2014	Life Science Journal	Irretrievable
Organized Crime and Corruption Across Borders: Exploring the Belt and Road Initiative	Lo, T. W., Siegel, D. & Kwok, S. I.	2019	Organized Crime and Corruption Across Borders: Exploring the Belt and Road Initiative	Irretrievable
Organized Crime in Kazakhstan	Siegel, D. & Turlubekova, Z.	2019	Book chapter in: Organized Crime and Corruption Across Borders: Exploring the Belt and Road Initiative	Irretrievable
Problems in the Implementation of the Transparency Principle in the Activities of the Public Authority Bodies of Kazakhstan	Ibrayeva, A., Seifullina, A. & Yessetova, S.	2016	Proceedings of the 4th International Conference on Management, Leadership and Governance, ICMLG 2016	Irretrievable
Problems of Implementation of the United Nations Convention against Corruption in Kazakhstan Legislation	Khassenova, A. at al.	2018	Journal of Advanced Research in Law and Economics	Irretrievable
Problems of Modernization of Kazakhstan's Economy and the Role of the State	Nailya, N. K.	2012	Vith Ryskulov Readings: Socio–Economic Modernization of Kazakhstan Under Conditions of Global Financial Instability	Irretrievable
Problems of the Legal Regulation and Practice of Enforcing Additional Punishment for Corruption–Related Offenses in Kazakhstan	Kassenova, A. M.	2019	Journal of Advanced Research in Law and Economics	Irretrievable
Resource Management and Transition in Central Asia, Azerbaijan and Mongolia	Pomfret, R.	2012	Journal of Asian Economics	Incidental, different focus
The Impact of Corruption on the Institutions of Political Power in the Republic of	Salkebayev, T. S.	2017	Journal of Advanced Research in Law and Economics	Irretrievable

Kazakhstan: The Cratological Context and Law Enforcement Activities				
To the Question of Improvement of the Anti–Corruption Legislation in the Republic of Kazakhstan	Ayupova, Z. K. & Kussainov, D. U.	2017	Bullettin of the National Academy of Sciences of the Republic of Kazakhstan	Absent from Issue 2 of 2017
To the Question of Need of Improvement of a Conceptual Framework of Counteraction of Corruption by the Legislation of the Republic of Kazakhstan	Imanov, I. A.	2016	Legal Science and Practice – Bullettin of izhniy Novgorod Academy of the Ministry of the Interior of Russia	Irretrievable
Trading in Influence: Criminal Law and Criminal Procedure Aspects	Mamitova, Z. A. at al.	2016	Journal of Advanced Research in Law and Economics	Irretrievable

Table 21   Studies included in the systematic review of 'informality' / 'informal' and 'Kazakhstan'

Title	Author(s)	Year	Source	Flavour of informality
'informality' and 'Kazakhstan'				
Between Border and Bazaar: Central Asia's Informal Economy	Karrar, H. H.	2019	Journal of Contemporary Asia	Informal economy
How to Retire Like a Soviet Person: Informality, Household Finances, and Kinship in Financialized Kazakhstan	Cieślewska, A.	2018	Journal of the Royal Anthropological Institute	Informal economy
Informal Employment in Kazakhstan: A Blessing in Disguise?	Mussurov, A., Sholk, D. & Arabsheibani, G. R.	2019	Eurasian Economic Review	Informal economy
Informal Self–Employment in Kazakhstan	Mussurov, A. & Arabsheibani, G. R.	2015	IZA Journal of Labor and Development	Informal economy
Merchants, Markets, and the State	Karrar, H. H.	2013	Critical Asian Studies	Informal economy
Negotiating State and Society: The Normative Informal Economies of Central Asia and the Caucasus	Fehlings, S. & Karrar, H. H.	2020	Central Asian Survey	Informal economy
The Bazaar in Ruins: Rent and Fire in Barakholka, Almaty	Karrar, H.H.	2020	Central Asian Survey	Informal economy
What is informality? (mapping) "the art of bypassing the state" in Eurasian spaces–and beyond	Polese, A.	2021	Eurasian Geography and Economy	Theoretical
'informal' and 'Kazakhstan'				
Adapting Agricultural Water Use to Climate Change in a Post–Soviet Context: Challenges and Opportunities in Southeast Kazakhstan	Barrett, T. et al.	2017	Human ecology: An interdisciplinary journal	Infrapolitics

Title	Author	Year	Source	Category
Agashka (Kazakhstan)	Natsuko, O.	2018	The Encyclopaedia of Informality Volume 1	Informal governance / informal payments and corruption
Baraholka (Kazakhstan)	Sholk, D.	2018	The Encyclopaedia of Informality Volume 2	Informal economy
Between Border and Bazaar: Central Asia's Informal Economy	Karrar, H. H.	2019	Journal of Contemporary Asia	Informal economy
Between Convictions and Reconciliations: Processing Criminal Cases in Kazakhstani Courts	Trochev, A.	2017	Cornell International Law Journal	Infrapolitics
Blurring the Line between Licit and Illicit: Transnational Corruption Networks in Central Asia and Beyond	Cooley. A. & Sharman, J.	2015	Central Asian Survey	Informal payments and corruption / informal governance
Borrowed Places: Eviction wars and Property Rights Formalization in Kazakhstan	Yessenova, S.	2010	Research in Economic Anthropology	Infrapolitics
Circling the barrels: Kazakhstan's regime stability in the wake of the 2014 oil bust	Skalamera Groce, M.	2020	Central Asian Survey	Informal payments and corruption
Consumer Out-of-Pocket Spending for Pharmaceuticals in Kazakhstan: Implications for Sectoral Reform	Sari, N. & Langenbrunner, J. C.	2001	Health Policy and Planning	Informal payments and corruption
Deliberate By-Catch of the Caspian Seal and the Development of Illegal Wildlife Trade (IWT) in Dagestan, Russia: A Socio-Economic Approach	Ermolin, I.	2019	Journal of Economic Sociology–Ekonomicheskaya Sotsiologiya	Informal economy
Effects of Out-of-Pocket Payments on Access to Maternal Health Services in	Danilovich, N. & Yessaliyeva, E.	2014	Europe – Asia Studies	Informal payments and corruption

Almaty, Kazakhstan: A Qualitative Study				
Experiencing Liminality: Housing, Renting and Informal Tenants in Astana	Osmonova, K.	2016	Central Asian Survey	Informal economy / infrapolitics
Foreign Versus Domestic Bribery: Explaining Repression in Kleptocratic Regimes	LaPorte, J.	2017	Comparative Politics	Informal governance / informal payments and corruption
Grades and Degrees for Sale: Understanding Informal Exchanges in Kazakhstan's Education Sector	Oka, N.	2019	Problems of Post–Communism	Informal payments and corruption
Higher Wages Vs. Social and Legal Insecurity: Migrant Domestic Workers in Russia and Kazakhstan	Karachurina, L., Florinskaya, Y. & Prokhorova, A.	2019	Journal of International Migration and Integration	Informal economy
Homeless in the Homeland: Housing Protests in Kazakhstan	Alexander, C.	2018	Critique of Anthropology	Informal economy / infrapolitics
How to Retire like a Soviet Person: Informality, Household Finances, and Kinship in Financialized Kazakhstan	Begim, A.	2018	Journal of the Royal Anthropological Institute	Informal economy
Informal Employment in Kazakhstan: A Blessing in Disguise?	Mussurov, A., Sholk, D. & Arabsheibani, G. R.	2019	Eurasian Economic Review	Informal economy
Informal Payments and Connections in Post–Soviet Kazakhstan	Oka, N.	2015	Central Asian Survey	Informal payments and corruption
Informal Politics and the Uncertain Context of Transition: Revisiting early Stage Non–Democratic Development in Kazakhstan	Isaacs, R.	2010	Democratization	Informal governance / informal payments and corruption
Informal Self–Employment in Kazakhstan	Mussurov, A. & Rezaar Absheibani, G.	2015	IZA Journal of Labor and Development	Informal economy

Informal Social Protection Networks of Migrants: Typical Patterns in Different Transnational Social Spaces	Bilecen, B. & Sienkiewicz, J. J.	2015	Population, Space and Place	Infrapolitics
Insider's corruption versus outsider's ethicality? Individual responses to conflicting institutional logics	Muratbekova–Touron, M., Lee Park, C. & Fracarolli Nunes, M.	2021	International Journal of Human Resource Management	Informal payments and corruption
Justice, Power and Informal Settlements: Understanding the Juridical View of Property Rights in Central Asia	Sanghera, B.	2020	International Sociology	Infrapolitics
Kazakhstan's Presidential Transition and the Evolution of Elite Networks	Mesquita, M.	2016	Demokratizatsiya	Informal governance
Legalized Rent–Seeking: Eminent Domain in Kazakhstan	Hanson, M.	2017	Cornell International Law Journal	Infrapolitics
Merchants, Markets, and the State	Karrar, H. H.	2013	Critical Asian Studies	Informal economy
Microfinance and Small Business Development in a Transitional Economy: Insights from Borrowers' Relations with Microfinance Organisations in Kazakhstan	Bika, Z., Subalova, M. & Locke, C.	2022	Journal of Development Studies	Informal economy
Migrant Labour in Kazakhstan: A Cause for Concern?	Anderson, B. & Hancilova, B.	2011	Journal of Ethnic and Migration Studies	Informal economy
Negotiating State and Society: The Normative Informal Economies of Central Asia and the Caucasus	Fehlings, S. & Karrar, H. H.	2020	Central Asian Survey	Informal economy
Nur Otan, Informal Networks and the Countering of Elite Instability in Kazakhstan: Bringing the 'Formal' Back In	Isaacs, R.	2013	Europe – Asia Studies	Informal governance

Party System Formation in Kazakhstan: Between Formal and Informal Politics	Isaacs, R.	2011	Party System Formation in Kazakhstan: Between Formal and Informal Politics	Informal governance
Problems of Population Informal Employment in Monotowns of Kazakhstan in the Context of Globalization	Alzhanova, N. S. & Nurzhaubayeva, R. D.	2015	Actual Problems of Economics	Informal economy
Role and Place of the Parliament of Kazakhstan in the System of Checks and Balances	Kanapyanov, T.	2018	Communist and Post–Communist Studies	Informal governance
"Run after time": the roads of suitcase traders	Lacaze, G.	2010	Asian Ethnicity	Informal economy
Rushyldyq (Kazakhstan)	Minbaeva, D. & Muratbekova-Touron, M.	2018	The Encyclopaedia of Informality Volume 1	Informal governance
Sadaqa (Kazakhstan and Kyrgyzstan)	Botoeva, A.	2020	The Global Informality Project	Informal payments and corruption
Social Precarization in Post–Soviet Countries: Common Features and Differences	Mramornova, O. V. et al.	2019	Book chapter in: Future of the Global Financial System: Downfall or Harmony	Informal economy
State Retrenchment and Informal Institutions in Kazakhstan: People's Perceptions of Informal Reciprocity in the Healthcare Sector	Sharipova, D.	2015	Central Asian Survey	Informal payments and corruption
The Conditions of Post–Soviet Dispossessed Youth and Work in Almaty, Kazakhstan	Rigi, J.	2003	Critique of Anthropology	Informal economy
The Paradox of Authoritarian Power: Bureaucratic Games and Information Asymmetry. The Case of Nazarbayev's Kazakhstan	Tutumlu, A. & Rustemov, I.	2019	Problems of Post–Communism	Informal governance / informal payments and corruption

Title	Author	Year	Journal	Category
The Precariousness Employment in the Eurasian Economic Space: Measurement Problems, Factors and Main Forms of Development	Kaliyeva, S. A. et al.	2018	Journal of Asian Finance, Economics and Business	Informal economy
The Traders of Central Bazaar, Astana: Motivation and Networks	Baitas, M.	2020	Central Asian Survey	Informal economy
Trajectory of Civil Service Development in Kazakhstan: Nexus of Politics and Administration	Emrich–Bakenova, S.	2009	Governance	Infrapolitics
Women's Progression through the Leadership Pipeline in the Universities of Kazakhstan and Kyrgyzstan	Kuzhabekova, A. & Almukhambetova, A.	2019	Compare: A Journal of Comparative and International Education	Infrapolitics
List of studies excluded with reason				
Elite Change and Political Dynamics in Kazakhstan	Schmitz, A.	2003	Orient	Irretrievable
Gender Peculiarities of the Entrepreneurship Development in Kazakhstan: Women's Participation in the "Shuttle" Business	Nurbekova, Z. A., Abenova, K.A. & Tazhieva, Z. D.	2017	Man in India	Irretrievable
Human Resource Management Patterns of (Anti)Corruption Mechanisms within Informal Networks	Muratbekova–Touron, M. & Umbetalijeva, T.	2019	Business and Professional Ethics Journal	Irretrievable
Impact of Gender Equality on Socio–Economic Development of Kazakhstan	Mukhamadiyeva, A. A. et al.	2019	Space and Culture, India	Incidental, different focus
Market Economies and Pro–Social Behavior: Experimental Evidence from Central Asia	Rosenbaum, S. M. et al.	2012	Journal of Socio–Economics	Incidental, different focus

Returning from Study abroad and Transitioning as a Scholar: Stories of Foreign PhD Holders from Kazakhstan	Kuzhabekova, A., Sparks, J. & Temerbayeva, A.	2019	Research in Comparative and International Education	Incidental, different focus
The Precarization of Employment: A Case of Kazakhstan	Jumambayev, S.	2016	Journal of Asian Finance Economics and Business	Incidental, different focus
Use of Patent Based Tax System as Tool for Reducing Informal Employment: World Experience and Prospects for Its Introduction in Russia	Shpilina, T. M.	2017	Vision 2020: Sustainable Economic Development, Innovation Management, and Global Growth	Not on Kazakhstan

Table 22   Studies included in the systematic review of 'oil', 'Venezuela', and 'Gomez'

Title	Author(s)	Year	Source
Search "oil" and "Venezuela"			
Anarchy, State, and Dystopia: Venezuelan Economic Institutions before the Advent of Oil	Rodríguez, F. & Gomolin, A. J.	2009	Bulletin of Latin American Research
Asserting State Authority through Environmental Monitoring: Venezuela in the Post–Gómez Era, 1935–1945	Kozloff, N.	2006	Bulletin of Latin American Research
British Oil Policy 1919–1939	McBeth, B.S.	1986	Book
Fueling concern: The role of oil in Venezuela	Tinker–Salas, M.	2005	Harvard International Review
Oil's Colonial Residues: Geopolitics, Identity, and Resistance in Venezuela	Kingsbury, D.V.	2019	Bulletin of Latin American Research
Oil illusion and delusion Mexico and Venezuela over the twentieth century	Rubio–Varas, M.	2015	Book chapter in Natural Resources and Economic Growth: Learning from History
Political Survival, Energy Policies, and Multinational Corporations: A Historical Study for Standard Oil of New Jersey in Colombia, Mexico, and Venezuela in the Twentieth Century	Bucheli, M. & Aguilera, R.V.	2010	Management International Review
The Enduring Legacy: Oil, Culture, and Society in Venezuela	Tinker–Salas, M.	2009	Book
Search "oil" and "Gomez"			
Cattle, Corruption, and Venezuelan State Formation During the Regime of Juan Vicente Gómez, 1908–1935	Yarrington, D.	2003	Latin American Research Review
Dictatorship and politics: Intrigue, betrayal, and survival in Venezuela, 1908–1935	McBeth, B.S.	2008	Book
Juan Vicente Gómez and the Oil Companies in Venezuela, 1908–1935	McBeth, B.S.	1983	Book

Patriotism and petroleum: Anti–Americanism in Venezuela from Gómez to Chávez	Rivas, D.	2008	Book chapter in Anti–Americanism in Latin America and the Caribbean
The intelligentsia's two visions of urban modernity: Gómez's Caracas, 1908–35	Almandoz, A.	2001	Urban History
Venezuela's Nascent Oil Industry and the 1932 US Tariff on Crude Oil Imports, 1927–1935	McBeth, B.S.	2009	Revista de Historia Economica – Journal of Iberian and Latin American Economic History

Table 23   Studies included in the systematic review of 'oil' and 'Chad'

Title	Author(s)	Year	Source
An Empirical Assessment of the Dutch Disease Channel of the Resource Curse: The Case of Chad	Kablan, S.A. & Laening, J.L.	2012	Economics Bulletin
An Obsolescing Bargain in Chad: Shifts in Leverage Between the Government and the World Bank	Gould, J.A. & Winters, M.S.	2007	Business and Politics
Betting on Oil: The World Bank's Attempt to Promote Accountability in Chad	Winters, M.S. & Gould, J.A.	2011	Global Governance
Briefing: Chronicle of a Death Foretold: The Collapse of the Chad–Cameroon Pipeline Project	Pegg, S.	2009	African Affairs
Briefing: The Chad–Cameroon Petroleum and Pipeline Development Project	Guyer, J.I.	2002	African Affairs
Can Policy Intervention Beat the Resource Curse? Evidence from the Chad–Cameroon Pipeline Project	Pegg, S.	2006	African Affairs
Chad–Cameroon Oil Pipeline: World Bank and ExxonMobil in 'last chance saloon'	Keenan, J.H.	2005	Review of African Political Economy
Chinese Outward Investment in Oil and its Economic and Political Impact in Developing Countries	Lee, C.Y.	2015	Issues and Studies
Corporate Social Responsibility and Petroleum Development in sub-Saharan Africa: The Case of Chad	Cash, A.C.	2012	Resources Policy
Dallas to Doba: Oil and Chad, External Controls and Internal Politics	Massey, S. & May, R.	2005	Journal of Contemporary African Studies
Extractive Industries and the Social Dimension of Sustainable Development: Reflection on the Chad–Cameroon Pipeline	Germond–Duret, C.	2014	Sustainable Development
Fighting for Oil When there is No Oil Yet: The Darfur–Chad Border	Behrends, A.	2011	Book chapter in *Crude Domination: An Anthropology of Oil*
Innovations of the Chad/Cameroon Pipeline Project: Thinking Outside the Box	Norland, D.R.	2003	Mediterranean Quarterly

Life in the Time of Oil: A Pipeline and Poverty in Chad	Leonard, L.	2016	Book
Lifting the Resource Curse? The World Bank and Oil Revenue Distribution in Chad	Mattner, M.	2011	Book chapter in *Social Justice, Global Dynamics: Theoretical and Empirical Perspectives*
Oil and Regional Development in Chad: Assessment of the Impact of the Doba Oil Project on Poverty in the Host Region	Aristide, M. & Moundigbaye, M.	2017	African Development Review
Oil in Chad and Equatorial Guinea: Widening the Focus of the Resource Curse	Colom–Jaén, A. & Campos–Serrano, A.	2013	European Journal of Development Research
Oil Rent and Income Disparity in Chad	Gadom, D.G., Fondo, S. & Totouom, A.	2018	Mondes en Developpement
Poverty, Petroleum and Policy Intervention: Lessons from the Chad–Cameroon Pipeline	Kojucharov, N.	2007	Review of African Political Economy
Public Investment to Reverse Dutch Disease: The Case of Chad	Levy, S.	2007	Journal of African Economies
Revisiting the Chad–Cameroon Pipeline Compensation Modality, Local Communities' Discontent, and Accountability Mechanisms	Lo, M.S.	2010	Canadian Journal of Development Studies
The Bush Administration and African oil: The Security Implications of US Energy Policy	Volman, D.	2003	Review of African Political Economy
The Chad–Cameroon Oil Pipeline – Hope for Poverty Reduction?	Ndumbe, J.A.	2002	Mediterranean Quarterly
The Chad–Cameroon Pipeline Project: Some Thoughts about the Legal Challenges and Lessons Learned from a World Bank–financed Large Infrastructure Project	Bekhechi, M.A.	2012	Book chapter in *Energy Networks and the Law: Innovative Solutions in Changing Markets*
The Effect of Public Spending on Growth in Oil-Rich, Conflict–Prone Countries: The Case of Chad	Nourou, M.	2020	Economics Bulletin
The Impact of Oil Revenues on Wellbeing in Chad	Gadom, G.D., Kountchou, A.M. & Araar, A.	2018	Environment and Development Economics

The Paradox of Petrodollar Development: Chad's Military Diplomacy in Regional and Global Security	Pemunta, N.V. & Tabenyang, T.C.J.	2016	South African Journal of International Affairs
The War on Terror, the Chad–Cameroon Pipeline, and the New Identity of the Lake Chad Basin	Fah, G.L.T.	2007	Journal of Contemporary African Studies
West African oil, U.S. Energy Policy, and Africa's Development Strategies	Ndumbe, J.A.	2004	Mediterranean Quarterly

Excluded with reason

Title	Author(s)	Year	Source	Reason for exclusion
Does Rationality Travel? Translating a World Bank Model for Fair Oil Revenue Distribution in Chad	Hoinathy, R. & Behrends, A.	2014	Africa–Europe Group for Interdisciplinary Studies	Irretrievable
Gouvernance Pétrolière au Tchad : La Loi de Gestion des Revenus Pétroliers [Petroleum Governance in Chad: The Petroleum Revenue Management Law]	Massuyeau, B. & Dorbeau–Falchier, D.	2005	Afrique Contemporaine	Irretrievable
Local Issues of Chinese Direct Investment in Africa: The Case of China National Petroleum Corporation International Chad (2006–2013)	Yorbana, S.–G.	2016	Progress in International Business Research	Irretrievable
Military Expenses: A Brake on Economic Growth in Chad?	Arsène Aurélien, N. & Jean–Claude, K.	2018	International Journal of Development and Conflict	Different focus
Nunc Dimittis or Chief Cornerstone?: Evaluating Africa's International Norm–Development Experiment in the Chad–Cameroon Pipeline Project	Duruigbo, E.	2015	Northwestern Journal of International	Different focus

Title	Author	Year	Source	
Of other Spaces? Hybrid Forms of Chinese Engagement in sub-Saharan Africa	Dittgen, R.	2015	Journal of Current Chinese Affairs	Different focus
Oil Windfall, Public Spending and Price Stability: Modelling Inflation in Chad	Kinda, T.	2013	Applied Economics	Different focus
Où va le Tchad?	Lemarchand, R.	2005	Afrique Contemporaine	Irretrievable
Petroleum Reserves in West Africa: An Overview	Copinschi, P. & Favennec, J.P.	1999	Revue de l'Energie	Irretrievable
Political Conflict and State Failure	Bates, R.H.	2007	Book chapter in *The Political Economy of Economic Growth in Africa, 1960–2000*	Chad is one of many cases
Real Exchange Rate Misalignment in the CFA zone	Devarajan, S.	1997	Journal of African Economies	Chad is one of many cases
Regulating Multinationals in Developing Countries: A Conceptual and Legal Framework for Corporate Social Responsibility	Mujih, E.C.	2016	Book	Irretrievable
Simulating Globalization: Oil in Chad	Hobbs, H.H. & Moreno, D.V.	2004	International Studies Perspectives	Different focus

SOVIET AND POST-SOVIET POLITICS AND SOCIETY

Edited by Dr. Andreas Umland | ISSN 1614-3515

1   *Андреас Умланд (ред.)* | Воплощение Европейской конвенции по правам человека в России. Философские, юридические и эмпирические исследования | ISBN 3-89821-387-0

2   *Christian Wipperfürth* | Russland – ein vertrauenswürdiger Partner? Grundlagen, Hintergründe und Praxis gegenwärtiger russischer Außenpolitik | Mit einem Vorwort von Heinz Timmermann | ISBN 3-89821-401-X

3   *Manja Hussner* | Die Übernahme internationalen Rechts in die russische und deutsche Rechtsordnung. Eine vergleichende Analyse zur Völkerrechtsfreundlichkeit der Verfassungen der Russländischen Föderation und der Bundesrepublik Deutschland | Mit einem Vorwort von Rainer Arnold | ISBN 3-89821-438-9

4   *Matthew Tejada* | Bulgaria's Democratic Consolidation and the Kozloduy Nuclear Power Plant (KNPP). The Unattainability of Closure | With a foreword by Richard J. Crampton | ISBN 3-89821-439-7

5   *Марк Григорьевич Меерович* | Квадратные метры, определяющие сознание. Государственная жилищная политика в СССР. 1921 – 1941 гг | ISBN 3-89821-474-5

6   *Andrei P. Tsygankov, Pavel A. Tsygankov (Eds.)* | New Directions in Russian International Studies | ISBN 3-89821-422-2

7   *Марк Григорьевич Меерович* | Как власть народ к труду приучала. Жилище в СССР – средство управления людьми. 1917 – 1941 гг. | С предисловием Елены Осокиной | ISBN 3-89821-495-8

8   *David J. Galbreath* | Nation-Building and Minority Politics in Post-Socialist States. Interests, Influence and Identities in Estonia and Latvia | With a foreword by David J. Smith | ISBN 3-89821-467-2

9   *Алексей Юрьевич Безугольный* | Народы Кавказа в Вооруженных силах СССР в годы Великой Отечественной войны 1941-1945 гг. | С предисловием Николая Бугая | ISBN 3-89821-475-3

10   *Вячеслав Лихачев и Владимир Прибыловский (ред.)* | Русское Национальное Единство, 1990-2000. В 2-х томах | ISBN 3-89821-523-7

11   *Николай Бугай (ред.)* | Народы стран Балтии в условиях сталинизма (1940-е – 1950-е годы). Документированная история | ISBN 3-89821-525-3

12   *Ingmar Bredies (Hrsg.)* | Zur Anatomie der Orange Revolution in der Ukraine. Wechsel des Elitenregimes oder Triumph des Parlamentarismus? | ISBN 3-89821-524-5

13   *Anastasia V. Mitrofanova* | The Politicization of Russian Orthodoxy. Actors and Ideas | With a foreword by William C. Gay | ISBN 3-89821-481-8

14   *Nathan D. Larson* | Alexander Solzhenitsyn and the Russo-Jewish Question | ISBN 3-89821-483-4

15   *Guido Houben* | Kulturpolitik und Ethnizität. Staatliche Kunstförderung im Russland der neunziger Jahre | Mit einem Vorwort von Gert Weisskirchen | ISBN 3-89821-542-3

16   *Leonid Luks* | Der russische „Sonderweg"? Aufsätze zur neuesten Geschichte Russlands im europäischen Kontext | ISBN 3-89821-496-6

17   *Евгений Мороз* | История «Мёртвой воды» – от страшной сказки к большой политике. Политическое неоязычество в постсоветской России | ISBN 3-89821-551-2

18   *Александр Верховский и Галина Кожевникова (ред.)* | Этническая и религиозная интолерантность в российских СМИ. Результаты мониторинга 2001-2004 гг. | ISBN 3-89821-569-5

19   *Christian Ganzer* | Sowjetisches Erbe und ukrainische Nation. Das Museum der Geschichte des Zaporoger Kosakentums auf der Insel Chortycja | Mit einem Vorwort von Frank Golczewski | ISBN 3-89821-504-0

20   *Эльза-Баир Гучинова* | Помнить нельзя забыть. Антропология депортационной травмы калмыков | С предисловием Кэролайн Хамфри | ISBN 3-89821-506-7

21   *Юлия Лидерман* | Мотивы «проверки» и «испытания» в постсоветской культуре. Советское прошлое в российском кинематографе 1990-х годов | С предисловием Евгения Марголита | ISBN 3-89821-511-3

22   *Tanya Lokshina, Ray Thomas, Mary Mayer (Eds.)* | The Imposition of a Fake Political Settlement in the Northern Caucasus. The 2003 Chechen Presidential Election | ISBN 3-89821-436-2

23   *Timothy McCajor Hall, Rosie Read (Eds.)* | Changes in the Heart of Europe. Recent Ethnographies of Czechs, Slovaks, Roma, and Sorbs | With an afterword by Zdeněk Salzmann | ISBN 3-89821-606-3

24 *Christian Autengruber* | Die politischen Parteien in Bulgarien und Rumänien. Eine vergleichende Analyse seit Beginn der 90er Jahre | Mit einem Vorwort von Dorothée de Nève | ISBN 3-89821-476-1

25 *Annette Freyberg-Inan with Radu Cristescu* | The Ghosts in Our Classrooms, or: John Dewey Meets Ceauşescu. The Promise and the Failures of Civic Education in Romania | ISBN 3-89821-416-8

26 *John B. Dunlop* | The 2002 Dubrovka and 2004 Beslan Hostage Crises. A Critique of Russian Counter-Terrorism | With a foreword by Donald N. Jensen | ISBN 3-89821-608-X

27 *Peter Koller* | Das touristische Potenzial von Kam''janec'–Podil's'kyj. Eine fremdenverkehrsgeographische Untersuchung der Zukunftsperspektiven und Maßnahmenplanung zur Destinationsentwicklung des „ukrainischen Rothenburg" | Mit einem Vorwort von Kristiane Klemm | ISBN 3-89821-640-3

28 *Françoise Daucé, Elisabeth Sieca-Kozlowski (Eds.)* | Dedovshchina in the Post-Soviet Military. Hazing of Russian Army Conscripts in a Comparative Perspective | With a foreword by Dale Herspring | ISBN 3-89821-616-0

29 *Florian Strasser* | Zivilgesellschaftliche Einflüsse auf die Orange Revolution. Die gewaltlose Massenbewegung und die ukrainische Wahlkrise 2004 | Mit einem Vorwort von Egbert Jahn | ISBN 3-89821-648-9

30 *Rebecca S. Katz* | The Georgian Regime Crisis of 2003-2004. A Case Study in Post-Soviet Media Representation of Politics, Crime and Corruption | ISBN 3-89821-413-3

31 *Vladimir Kantor* | Willkür oder Freiheit. Beiträge zur russischen Geschichtsphilosophie | Ediert von Dagmar Herrmann sowie mit einem Vorwort versehen von Leonid Luks | ISBN 3-89821-589-X

32 *Laura A. Victoir* | The Russian Land Estate Today. A Case Study of Cultural Politics in Post-Soviet Russia | With a foreword by Priscilla Roosevelt | ISBN 3-89821-426-5

33 *Ivan Katchanovski* | Cleft Countries. Regional Political Divisions and Cultures in Post-Soviet Ukraine and Moldova| With a foreword by Francis Fukuyama | ISBN 3-89821-558-X

34 *Florian Mühlfried* | Postsowjetische Feiern. Das Georgische Bankett im Wandel | Mit einem Vorwort von Kevin Tuite | ISBN 3-89821-601-2

35 *Roger Griffin, Werner Loh, Andreas Umland (Eds.)* | Fascism Past and Present, West and East. An International Debate on Concepts and Cases in the Comparative Study of the Extreme Right | With an afterword by Walter Laqueur | ISBN 3-89821-674-8

36 *Sebastian Schlegel* | Der „Weiße Archipel". Sowjetische Atomstädte 1945-1991 | Mit einem Geleitwort von Thomas Bohn | ISBN 3-89821-679-9

37 *Vyacheslav Likhachev* | Political Anti-Semitism in Post-Soviet Russia. Actors and Ideas in 1991-2003 | Edited and translated from Russian by Eugene Veklerov | ISBN 3-89821-529-6

38 *Josette Baer (Ed.)* | Preparing Liberty in Central Europe. Political Texts from the Spring of Nations 1848 to the Spring of Prague 1968 | With a foreword by Zdeněk V. David | ISBN 3-89821-546-6

39 *Михаил Лукьянов* | Российский консерватизм и реформа, 1907-1914 | С предисловием Марка Д. Стейнберга | ISBN 3-89821-503-2

40 *Nicola Melloni* | Market Without Economy. The 1998 Russian Financial Crisis | With a foreword by Eiji Furukawa | ISBN 3-89821-407-9

41 *Dmitrij Chmelnizki* | Die Architektur Stalins | Bd. 1: Studien zu Ideologie und Stil | Bd. 2: Bilddokumentation | Mit einem Vorwort von Bruno Flierl | ISBN 3-89821-515-6

42 *Katja Yafimava* | Post-Soviet Russian-Belarussian Relationships. The Role of Gas Transit Pipelines | With a foreword by Jonathan P. Stern | ISBN 3-89821-655-1

43 *Boris Chavkin* | Verflechtungen der deutschen und russischen Zeitgeschichte. Aufsätze und Archivfunde zu den Beziehungen Deutschlands und der Sowjetunion von 1917 bis 1991 | Ediert von Markus Edlinger sowie mit einem Vorwort versehen von Leonid Luks | ISBN 3-89821-756-6

44 *Anastasija Grynenko in Zusammenarbeit mit Claudia Dathe* | Die Terminologie des Gerichtswesens der Ukraine und Deutschlands im Vergleich. Eine übersetzungswissenschaftliche Analyse juristischer Fachbegriffe im Deutschen, Ukrainischen und Russischen | Mit einem Vorwort von Ulrich Hartmann | ISBN 3-89821-691-8

45 *Anton Burkov* | The Impact of the European Convention on Human Rights on Russian Law. Legislation and Application in 1996-2006 | With a foreword by Françoise Hampson | ISBN 978-3-89821-639-5

46 *Stina Torjesen, Indra Overland (Eds.)* | International Election Observers in Post-Soviet Azerbaijan. Geopolitical Pawns or Agents of Change? | ISBN 978-3-89821-743-9

47 *Taras Kuzio* | Ukraine – Crimea – Russia. Triangle of Conflict | ISBN 978-3-89821-761-3

48 *Claudia Šabić* | „Ich erinnere mich nicht, aber L'viv!" Zur Funktion kultureller Faktoren für die Institutionalisierung und Entwicklung einer ukrainischen Region | Mit einem Vorwort von Melanie Tatur | ISBN 978-3-89821-752-1

49 *Marlies Bilz* | Tatarstan in der Transformation. Nationaler Diskurs und Politische Praxis 1988-1994 | Mit einem Vorwort von Frank Golczewski | ISBN 978-3-89821-722-4

50 *Марлен Ларюэль (ред.)* | Современные интерпретации русского национализма | ISBN 978-3-89821-795-8

51 *Sonja Schüler* | Die ethnische Dimension der Armut. Roma im postsozialistischen Rumänien | Mit einem Vorwort von Anton Sterbling | ISBN 978-3-89821-776-7

52 *Галина Кожевникова* | Радикальный национализм в России и противодействие ему. Сборник докладов Центра «Сова» за 2004-2007 гг. | С предисловием Александра Верховского | ISBN 978-3-89821-721-7

53 *Галина Кожевникова и Владимир Прибыловский* | Российская власть в биографиях I. Высшие должностные лица РФ в 2004 г. | ISBN 978-3-89821-796-5

54 *Галина Кожевникова и Владимир Прибыловский* | Российская власть в биографиях II. Члены Правительства РФ в 2004 г. | ISBN 978-3-89821-797-2

55 *Галина Кожевникова и Владимир Прибыловский* | Российская власть в биографиях III. Руководители федеральных служб и агентств РФ в 2004 г.| ISBN 978-3-89821-798-9

56 *Ileana Petroniu* | Privatisierung in Transformationsökonomien. Determinanten der Restrukturierungs-Bereitschaft am Beispiel Polens, Rumäniens und der Ukraine | Mit einem Vorwort von Rainer W. Schäfer | ISBN 978-3-89821-790-3

57 *Christian Wipperfürth* | Russland und seine GUS-Nachbarn. Hintergründe, aktuelle Entwicklungen und Konflikte in einer ressourcenreichen Region| ISBN 978-3-89821-801-6

58 *Togzhan Kassenova* | From Antagonism to Partnership. The Uneasy Path of the U.S.-Russian Cooperative Threat Reduction | With a foreword by Christoph Bluth | ISBN 978-3-89821-707-1

59 *Alexander Höllwerth* | Das sakrale eurasische Imperium des Aleksandr Dugin. Eine Diskursanalyse zum postsowjetischen russischen Rechtsextremismus | Mit einem Vorwort von Dirk Uffelmann | ISBN 978-3-89821-813-9

60 *Олег Рябов* | «Россия-Матушка». Национализм, гендер и война в России XX века | С предисловием Елены Гощило | ISBN 978-3-89821-487-2

61 *Ivan Maistrenko* | Borot'bism. A Chapter in the History of the Ukrainian Revolution | With a new Introduction by Chris Ford | Translated by George S. N. Luckyj with the assistance of Ivan L. Rudnytsky | Second, Revised and Expanded Edition ISBN 978-3-8382-1107-7

62 *Maryna Romanets* | Anamorphosic Texts and Reconfigured Visions. Improvised Traditions in Contemporary Ukrainian and Irish Literature | ISBN 978-3-89821-576-3

63 *Paul D'Anieri and Taras Kuzio (Eds.)* | Aspects of the Orange Revolution I. Democratization and Elections in Post-Communist Ukraine | ISBN 978-3-89821-698-2

64 *Bohdan Harasymiw in collaboration with Oleh S. Ilnytzkyj (Eds.)* | Aspects of the Orange Revolution II. Information and Manipulation Strategies in the 2004 Ukrainian Presidential Elections | ISBN 978-3-89821-699-9

65 *Ingmar Bredies, Andreas Umland and Valentin Yakushik (Eds.)* | Aspects of the Orange Revolution III. The Context and Dynamics of the 2004 Ukrainian Presidential Elections | ISBN 978-3-89821-803-0

66 *Ingmar Bredies, Andreas Umland and Valentin Yakushik (Eds.)* | Aspects of the Orange Revolution IV. Foreign Assistance and Civic Action in the 2004 Ukrainian Presidential Elections | ISBN 978-3-89821-808-5

67 *Ingmar Bredies, Andreas Umland and Valentin Yakushik (Eds.)* | Aspects of the Orange Revolution V. Institutional Observation Reports on the 2004 Ukrainian Presidential Elections | ISBN 978-3-89821-809-2

68 *Taras Kuzio (Ed.)* | Aspects of the Orange Revolution VI. Post-Communist Democratic Revolutions in Comparative Perspective | ISBN 978-3-89821-820-7

69 *Tim Bohse* | Autoritarismus statt Selbstverwaltung. Die Transformation der kommunalen Politik in der Stadt Kaliningrad 1990-2005 | Mit einem Geleitwort von Stefan Troebst | ISBN 978-3-89821-782-8

70 *David Rupp* | Die Rußländische Föderation und die russischsprachige Minderheit in Lettland. Eine Fallstudie zur Anwaltspolitik Moskaus gegenüber den russophonen Minderheiten im „Nahen Ausland" von 1991 bis 2002 | Mit einem Vorwort von Helmut Wagner | ISBN 978-3-89821-778-1

71 *Taras Kuzio* | Theoretical and Comparative Perspectives on Nationalism. New Directions in Cross-Cultural and Post-Communist Studies | With a foreword by Paul Robert Magocsi | ISBN 978-3-89821-815-3

72 *Christine Teichmann* | Die Hochschultransformation im heutigen Osteuropa. Kontinuität und Wandel bei der Entwicklung des postkommunistischen Universitätswesens | Mit einem Vorwort von Oskar Anweiler | ISBN 978-3-89821-842-9

73 *Julia Kusznir* | Der politische Einfluss von Wirtschaftseliten in russischen Regionen. Eine Analyse am Beispiel der Erdöl- und Erdgasindustrie, 1992-2005 | Mit einem Vorwort von Wolfgang Eichwede | ISBN 978-3-89821-821-4

74 *Alena Vysotskaya* | Russland, Belarus und die EU-Osterweiterung. Zur Minderheitenfrage und zum Problem der Freizügigkeit des Personenverkehrs | Mit einem Vorwort von Katlijn Malfliet | ISBN 978-3-89821-822-1

75 *Heiko Pleines (Hrsg.)* | Corporate Governance in post-sozialistischen Volkswirtschaften | ISBN 978-3-89821-766-8

76 *Stefan Ihrig* | Wer sind die Moldawier? Rumänismus versus Moldowanismus in Historiographie und Schulbüchern der Republik Moldova, 1991-2006 | Mit einem Vorwort von Holm Sundhaussen | ISBN 978-3-89821-466-7

77 *Galina Kozhevnikova in collaboration with Alexander Verkhovsky and Eugene Veklerov* | Ultra-Nationalism and Hate Crimes in Contemporary Russia. The 2004-2006 Annual Reports of Moscow's SOVA Center | With a foreword by Stephen D. Shenfield | ISBN 978-3-89821-868-9

78 *Florian Küchler* | The Role of the European Union in Moldova's Transnistria Conflict | With a foreword by Christopher Hill | ISBN 978-3-89821-850-4

79 *Bernd Rechel* | The Long Way Back to Europe. Minority Protection in Bulgaria | With a foreword by Richard Crampton | ISBN 978-3-89821-863-4

80 *Peter W. Rodgers* | Nation, Region and History in Post-Communist Transitions. Identity Politics in Ukraine, 1991-2006 | With a foreword by Vera Tolz | ISBN 978-3-89821-903-7

81 *Stephanie Solywoda* | The Life and Work of Semen L. Frank. A Study of Russian Religious Philosophy | With a foreword by Philip Walters | ISBN 978-3-89821-457-5

82 *Vera Sokolova* | Cultural Politics of Ethnicity. Discourses on Roma in Communist Czechoslovakia | ISBN 978-3-89821-864-1

83 *Natalya Shevchik Ketenci* | Kazakhstani Enterprises in Transition. The Role of Historical Regional Development in Kazakhstan's Post-Soviet Economic Transformation | ISBN 978-3-89821-831-3

84 *Martin Malek, Anna Schor-Tschudnowskaja (Hgg.)* | Europa im Tschetschenienkrieg. Zwischen politischer Ohnmacht und Gleichgültigkeit | Mit einem Vorwort von Lipchan Basajewa | ISBN 978-3-89821-676-0

85 *Stefan Meister* | Das postsowjetische Universitätswesen zwischen nationalem und internationalem Wandel. Die Entwicklung der regionalen Hochschule in Russland als Gradmesser der Systemtransformation | Mit einem Vorwort von Joan DeBardeleben | ISBN 978-3-89821-891-7

86 *Konstantin Sheiko in collaboration with Stephen Brown* | Nationalist Imaginings of the Russian Past. Anatolii Fomenko and the Rise of Alternative History in Post-Communist Russia | With a foreword by Donald Ostrowski | ISBN 978-3-89821-915-0

87 *Sabine Jenni* | Wie stark ist das „Einige Russland"? Zur Parteibindung der Eliten und zum Wahlerfolg der Machtpartei im Dezember 2007 | Mit einem Vorwort von Klaus Armingeon | ISBN 978-3-89821-961-7

88 *Thomas Borén* | Meeting-Places of Transformation. Urban Identity, Spatial Representations and Local Politics in Post-Soviet St Petersburg | ISBN 978-3-89821-739-2

89 *Aygul Ashirova* | Stalinismus und Stalin-Kult in Zentralasien. Turkmenistan 1924-1953 | Mit einem Vorwort von Leonid Luks | ISBN 978-3-89821-987-7

90 *Leonid Luks* | Freiheit oder imperiale Größe? Essays zu einem russischen Dilemma | ISBN 978-3-8382-0011-8

91 *Christopher Gilley* | The 'Change of Signposts' in the Ukrainian Emigration. A Contribution to the History of Sovietophilism in the 1920s | With a foreword by Frank Golczewski | ISBN 978-3-89821-965-5

92 *Philipp Casula, Jeronim Perovic (Eds.)* | Identities and Politics During the Putin Presidency. The Discursive Foundations of Russia's Stability | With a foreword by Heiko Haumann | ISBN 978-3-8382-0015-6

93 *Marcel Viëtor* | Europa und die Frage nach seinen Grenzen im Osten. Zur Konstruktion ‚europäischer' Identität' in Geschichte und Gegenwart | Mit einem Vorwort von Albrecht Lehmann | ISBN 978-3-8382-0045-3

94 *Ben Hellman, Andrei Rogachevskii* | Filming the Unfilmable. Casper Wrede's 'One Day in the Life of Ivan Denisovich' | Second, Revised and Expanded Edition | ISBN 978-3-8382-0044-6

95 *Eva Fuchslocher* | Vaterland, Sprache, Glaube. Orthodoxie und Nationenbildung am Beispiel Georgiens | Mit einem Vorwort von Christina von Braun | ISBN 978-3-89821-884-9

96 *Vladimir Kantor* | Das Westlertum und der Weg Russlands. Zur Entwicklung der russischen Literatur und Philosophie | Ediert von Dagmar Herrmann | Mit einem Beitrag von Nikolaus Lobkowicz | ISBN 978-3-8382-0102-3

97 *Kamran Musayev* | Die postsowjetische Transformation im Baltikum und Südkaukasus. Eine vergleichende Untersuchung der politischen Entwicklung Lettlands und Aserbaidschans 1985-2009 | Mit einem Vorwort von Leonid Luks | Ediert von Sandro Henschel | ISBN 978-3-8382-0103-0

98 *Tatiana Zhurzhenko* | Borderlands into Bordered Lands. Geopolitics of Identity in Post-Soviet Ukraine | With a foreword by Dieter Segert | ISBN 978-3-8382-0042-2

99 *Кирилл Галушко, Лидия Смола (ред.)* | Пределы падения – варианты украинского буду-
щего. Аналитико-прогностические исследования | ISBN 978-3-8382-0148-1

100 *Michael Minkenberg (Ed.)* | Historical Legacies and the Radical Right in Post-Cold War Central
and Eastern Europe | With an afterword by Sabrina P. Ramet | ISBN 978-3-8382-0124-5

101 *David-Emil Wickström* | Rocking St. Petersburg. Transcultural Flows and Identity Politics in the St. Petersburg
Popular Music Scene | With a foreword by Yngvar B. Steinholt | Second, Revised and Expanded Edition |
ISBN 978-3-8382-0100-9

102 *Eva Zabka* | Eine neue „Zeit der Wirren"? Der spät- und postsowjetische Systemwandel 1985-2000 im Spiegel
russischer gesellschaftspolitischer Diskurse | Mit einem Vorwort von Margareta Mommsen | ISBN 978-3-8382-0161-0

103 *Ulrike Ziemer* | Ethnic Belonging, Gender and Cultural Practices. Youth Identitites in Contemporary Russia |
With a foreword by Anoop Nayak | ISBN 978-3-8382-0152-8

104 *Ksenia Chepikova* | ‚Einiges Russland' - eine zweite KPdSU? Aspekte der Identitätskonstruktion einer post-
sowjetischen „Partei der Macht" | Mit einem Vorwort von Torsten Oppelland | ISBN 978-3-8382-0311-9

105 *Леонид Люкс* | Западничество или евразийство? Демократия или идеократия? Сборник статей
об исторических дилеммах России | С предисловием Владимира Кантора | ISBN 978-3-8382-0211-2

106 *Anna Dost* | Das russische Verfassungsrecht auf dem Weg zum Föderalismus und zurück. Zum
Konflikt von Rechtsnormen und -wirklichkeit in der Russländischen Föderation von 1991 bis 2009 | Mit einem Vorwort von Ale-
xander Blankenagel | ISBN 978-3-8382-0292-1

107 *Philipp Herzog* | Sozialistische Völkerfreundschaft, nationaler Widerstand oder harmloser Zeit-
vertreib? Zur politischen Funktion der Volkskunst im sowjetischen Estland | Mit einem Vorwort von Andreas Kappeler | ISBN
978-3-8382-0216-7

108 *Marlène Laruelle (Ed.)* | Russian Nationalism, Foreign Policy, and Identity Debates in Putin's
Russia. New Ideological Patterns after the Orange Revolution | ISBN 978-3-8382-0325-6

109 *Michail Logvinov* | Russlands Kampf gegen den internationalen Terrorismus. Eine kritische Bestands-
aufnahme des Bekämpfungsansatzes | Mit einem Geleitwort von Hans-Henning Schröder und einem Vorwort von Eckhard Jesse
| ISBN 978-3-8382-0329-4

110 *John B. Dunlop* | The Moscow Bombings of September 1999. Examinations of Russian Terrorist Attacks at
the Onset of Vladimir Putin's Rule | Second, Revised and Expanded Edition | ISBN 978-3-8382-0388-1

111 *Андрей А. Ковалёв* | Свидетельство из-за кулис российской политики I. Можно ли делать добро
из зла? (Воспоминания и размышления о последних советских и первых послесоветских годах) | With a foreword by Peter
Reddaway | ISBN 978-3-8382-0302-7

112 *Андрей А. Ковалёв* | Свидетельство из-за кулис российской политики II. Угроза для себя и окру-
жающих (Наблюдения и предостережения относительно происходящего после 2000 г.) | ISBN 978-3-8382-0303-4

113 *Bernd Kappenberg* | Zeichen setzen für Europa. Der Gebrauch europäischer lateinischer Sonderzeichen in der
deutschen Öffentlichkeit | Mit einem Vorwort von Peter Schlobinski | ISBN 978-3-89821-749-1

114 *Ivo Mijnssen* | The Quest for an Ideal Youth in Putin's Russia I. Back to Our Future! History, Modernity, and
Patriotism according to Nashi, 2005-2013 | With a foreword by Jeronim Perović | Second, Revised and Expanded Edition |
ISBN 978-3-8382-0368-3

115 *Jussi Lassila* | The Quest for an Ideal Youth in Putin's Russia II. The Search for Distinctive Conformism in
the Political Communication of Nashi, 2005-2009 | With a foreword by Kirill Postoutenko | Second, Revised and Expanded Edi-
tion | ISBN 978-3-8382-0415-4

116 *Valerio Trabandt* | Neue Nachbarn, gute Nachbarschaft? Die EU als internationaler Akteur am Beispiel ihrer
Demokratieförderung in Belarus und der Ukraine 2004-2009 | Mit einem Vorwort von Jutta Joachim | ISBN 978-3-8382-0437-6

117 *Fabian Pfeiffer* | Estlands Außen- und Sicherheitspolitik I. Der estnische Atlantizismus nach der wiedererlang-
ten Unabhängigkeit 1991-2004 | Mit einem Vorwort von Helmut Hubel | ISBN 978-3-8382-0127-6

118 *Jana Podßuweit* | Estlands Außen- und Sicherheitspolitik II. Handlungsoptionen eines Kleinstaates im Rah-
men seiner EU-Mitgliedschaft (2004-2008) | Mit einem Vorwort von Helmut Hubel | ISBN 978-3-8382-0440-6

119 *Karin Pointner* | Estlands Außen- und Sicherheitspolitik III. Eine gedächtnispolitische Analyse estnischer Ent-
wicklungskooperation 2006-2010 | Mit einem Vorwort von Karin Liebhart | ISBN 978-3-8382-0435-2

120 *Ruslana Vovk* | Die Offenheit der ukrainischen Verfassung für das Völkerrecht und die europäi-
sche Integration | Mit einem Vorwort von Alexander Blankenagel | ISBN 978-3-8382-0481-9

121 *Mykhaylo Banakh* | Die Relevanz der Zivilgesellschaft bei den postkommunistischen Transformationsprozessen in mittel- und osteuropäischen Ländern. Das Beispiel der spät- und postsowjetischen Ukraine 1986-2009 | Mit einem Vorwort von Gerhard Simon | ISBN 978-3-8382-0499-4

122 *Michael Moser* | Language Policy and the Discourse on Languages in Ukraine under President Viktor Yanukovych (25 February 2010–28 October 2012) | ISBN 978-3-8382-0497-0 (Paperback edition) | ISBN 978-3-8382-0507-6 (Hardcover edition)

123 *Nicole Krome* | Russischer Netzwerkkapitalismus Restrukturierungsprozesse in der Russischen Föderation am Beispiel des Luftfahrtunternehmens „Aviastar" | Mit einem Vorwort von Petra Stykow | ISBN 978-3-8382-0534-2

124 *David R. Marples* | 'Our Glorious Past'. Lukashenka's Belarus and the Great Patriotic War | ISBN 978-3-8382-0574-8 (Paperback edition) | ISBN 978-3-8382-0675-2 (Hardcover edition)

125 *Ulf Walther* | Russlands „neuer Adel". Die Macht des Geheimdienstes von Gorbatschow bis Putin | Mit einem Vorwort von Hans-Georg Wieck | ISBN 978-3-8382-0584-7

126 *Simon Geissbühler (Hrsg.)* | Kiew – Revolution 3.0. Der Euromaidan 2013/14 und die Zukunftsperspektiven der Ukraine | ISBN 978-3-8382-0581-6 (Paperback edition) | ISBN 978-3-8382-0681-3 (Hardcover edition)

127 *Andrey Makarychev* | Russia and the EU in a Multipolar World. Discourses, Identities, Norms | With a foreword by Klaus Segbers | ISBN 978-3-8382-0629-5

128 *Roland Scharff* | Kasachstan als postsowjetischer Wohlfahrtsstaat. Die Transformation des sozialen Schutzsystems | Mit einem Vorwort von Joachim Ahrens | ISBN 978-3-8382-0622-6

129 *Katja Grupp* | Bild Lücke Deutschland. Kaliningrader Studierende sprechen über Deutschland | Mit einem Vorwort von Martin Schulz | ISBN 978-3-8382-0552-6

130 *Konstantin Sheiko, Stephen Brown* | History as Therapy. Alternative History and Nationalist Imaginings in Russia, 1991-2014 | ISBN 978-3-8382-0665-3

131 *Elisa Kriza* | Alexander Solzhenitsyn: Cold War Icon, Gulag Author, Russian Nationalist? A Study of the Western Reception of his Literary Writings, Historical Interpretations, and Political Ideas | With a foreword by Andrei Rogatchevski | ISBN 978-3-8382-0589-2 (Paperback edition) | ISBN 978-3-8382-0690-5 (Hardcover edition)

132 *Serghei Golunov* | The Elephant in the Room. Corruption and Cheating in Russian Universities | ISBN 978-3-8382-0570-0

133 *Manja Hussner, Rainer Arnold (Hgg.)* | Verfassungsgerichtsbarkeit in Zentralasien I. Sammlung von Verfassungstexten | ISBN 978-3-8382-0595-3

134 *Nikolay Mitrokhin* | Die „Russische Partei". Die Bewegung der russischen Nationalisten in der UdSSR 1953-1985 | Aus dem Russischen übertragen von einem Übersetzerteam unter der Leitung von Larisa Schippel | ISBN 978-3-8382-0024-8

135 *Manja Hussner, Rainer Arnold (Hgg.)* | Verfassungsgerichtsbarkeit in Zentralasien II. Sammlung von Verfassungstexten | ISBN 978-3-8382-0597-7

136 *Manfred Zeller* | Das sowjetische Fieber. Fußballfans im poststalinistischen Vielvölkerreich | Mit einem Vorwort von Nikolaus Katzer | ISBN 978-3-8382-0757-5

137 *Kristin Schreiter* | Stellung und Entwicklungspotential zivilgesellschaftlicher Gruppen in Russland. Menschenrechtsorganisationen im Vergleich | ISBN 978-3-8382-0673-8

138 *David R. Marples, Frederick V. Mills (Eds.)* | Ukraine's Euromaidan. Analyses of a Civil Revolution | ISBN 978-3-8382-0660-8

139 *Bernd Kappenberg* | Setting Signs for Europe. Why Diacritics Matter for European Integration | With a foreword by Peter Schlobinski | ISBN 978-3-8382-0663-9

140 *René Lenz* | Internationalisierung, Kooperation und Transfer. Externe bildungspolitische Akteure in der Russischen Föderation | Mit einem Vorwort von Frank Ettrich | ISBN 978-3-8382-0751-3

141 *Juri Plusnin, Yana Zausaeva, Natalia Zhidkevich, Artemy Pozanenko* | Wandering Workers. Mores, Behavior, Way of Life, and Political Status of Domestic Russian Labor Migrants | Translated by Julia Kazantseva | ISBN 978-3-8382-0653-0

142 *David J. Smith (Eds.)* | Latvia – A Work in Progress? 100 Years of State- and Nation-Building | ISBN 978-3-8382-0648-6

143 *Инна Чувычкина (ред.)* | Экспортные нефте- и газопроводы на постсоветском пространстве. Анализ трубопроводной политики в свете теории международных отношений | ISBN 978-3-8382-0822-0

144 *Johann Zajaczkowski* | Russland – eine pragmatische Großmacht? Eine rollentheoretische Untersuchung russischer Außenpolitik am Beispiel der Zusammenarbeit mit den USA nach 9/11 und des Georgienkrieges von 2008 | Mit einem Vorwort von Siegfried Schieder | ISBN 978-3-8382-0837-4

145 *Boris Popivanov* | Changing Images of the Left in Bulgaria. The Challenge of Post-Communism in the Early 21st Century | ISBN 978-3-8382-0667-7

146 *Lenka Krátká* | A History of the Czechoslovak Ocean Shipping Company 1948-1989. How a Small, Landlocked Country Ran Maritime Business During the Cold War | ISBN 978-3-8382-0666-0

147 *Alexander Sergunin* | Explaining Russian Foreign Policy Behavior. Theory and Practice | ISBN 978-3-8382-0752-0

148 *Darya Malyutina* | Migrant Friendships in a Super-Diverse City. Russian-Speakers and their Social Relationships in London in the 21st Century | With a foreword by Claire Dwyer | ISBN 978-3-8382-0652-3

149 *Alexander Sergunin, Valery Konyshev* | Russia in the Arctic. Hard or Soft Power? | ISBN 978-3-8382-0753-7

150 *John J. Maresca* | Helsinki Revisited. A Key U.S. Negotiator's Memoirs on the Development of the CSCE into the OSCE | With a foreword by Hafiz Pashayev | ISBN 978-3-8382-0852-7

151 *Jardar Østbø* | The New Third Rome. Readings of a Russian Nationalist Myth | With a foreword by Pål Kolstø | ISBN 978-3-8382-0870-1

152 *Simon Kordonsky* | Socio-Economic Foundations of the Russian Post-Soviet Regime. The Resource-Based Economy and Estate-Based Social Structure of Contemporary Russia | With a foreword by Svetlana Barsukova | ISBN 978-3-8382-0775-9

153 *Duncan Leitch* | Assisting Reform in Post-Communist Ukraine 2000–2012. The Illusions of Donors and the Disillusion of Beneficiaries | With a foreword by Kataryna Wolczuk | ISBN 978-3-8382-0844-2

154 *Abel Polese* | Limits of a Post-Soviet State. How Informality Replaces, Renegotiates, and Reshapes Governance in Contemporary Ukraine | With a foreword by Colin Williams | ISBN 978-3-8382-0845-9

155 *Mikhail Suslov (Ed.)* | Digital Orthodoxy in the Post-Soviet World. The Russian Orthodox Church and Web 2.0 | With a foreword by Father Cyril Hovorun | ISBN 978-3-8382-0871-8

156 *Leonid Luks* | Zwei „Sonderwege"? Russisch-deutsche Parallelen und Kontraste (1917-2014). Vergleichende Essays | ISBN 978-3-8382-0823-7

157 *Vladimir V. Karacharovskiy, Ovsey I. Shkaratan, Gordey A. Yastrebov* | Towards a New Russian Work Culture. Can Western Companies and Expatriates Change Russian Society? | With a foreword by Elena N. Danilova | Translated by Julia Kazantseva | ISBN 978-3-8382-0902-9

158 *Edmund Griffiths* | Aleksandr Prokhanov and Post-Soviet Esotericism | ISBN 978-3-8382-0963-0

159 *Timm Beichelt, Susann Worschech (Eds.)* | Transnational Ukraine? Networks and Ties that Influence(d) Contemporary Ukraine | ISBN 978-3-8382-0944-9

160 *Mieste Hotopp-Riecke* | Die Tataren der Krim zwischen Assimilation und Selbstbehauptung. Der Aufbau des krimtatarischen Bildungswesens nach Deportation und Heimkehr (1990-2005) | Mit einem Vorwort von Svetlana Czerwonnaja | ISBN 978-3-89821-940-2

161 *Olga Bertelsen (Ed.)* | Revolution and War in Contemporary Ukraine. The Challenge of Change | ISBN 978-3-8382-1016-2

162 *Natalya Ryabinska* | Ukraine's Post-Communist Mass Media. Between Capture and Commercialization | With a foreword by Marta Dyczok | ISBN 978-3-8382-1011-7

163 *Alexandra Cotofana, James M. Nyce (Eds.)* | Religion and Magic in Socialist and Post-Socialist Contexts. Historic and Ethnographic Case Studies of Orthodoxy, Heterodoxy, and Alternative Spirituality | With a foreword by Patrick L. Michelson | ISBN 978-3-8382-0989-0

164 *Nozima Akhrarkhodjaeva* | The Instrumentalisation of Mass Media in Electoral Authoritarian Regimes. Evidence from Russia's Presidential Election Campaigns of 2000 and 2008 | ISBN 978-3-8382-1013-1

165 *Yulia Krasheninnikova* | Informal Healthcare in Contemporary Russia. Sociographic Essays on the Post-Soviet Infrastructure for Alternative Healing Practices | ISBN 978-3-8382-0970-8

166 *Peter Kaiser* | Das Schachbrett der Macht. Die Handlungsspielräume eines sowjetischen Funktionärs unter Stalin am Beispiel des Generalsekretärs des Komsomol Aleksandr Kosarev (1929-1938) | Mit einem Vorwort von Dietmar Neutatz | ISBN 978-3-8382-1052-0

167 *Oksana Kim* | The Effects and Implications of Kazakhstan's Adoption of International Financial Reporting Standards. A Resource Dependence Perspective | With a foreword by Svetlana Vlady | ISBN 978-3-8382-0987-6

168 *Anna Sanina* | Patriotic Education in Contemporary Russia. Sociological Studies in the Making of the Post-Soviet Citizen | With a foreword by Anna Oldfield | ISBN 978-3-8382-0993-7

169 *Rudolf Wolters* | Spezialist in Sibirien Faksimile der 1933 erschienenen ersten Ausgabe | Mit einem Vorwort von Dmitrij Chmelnizki | ISBN 978-3-8382-0515-1

170 *Michal Vít, Magdalena M. Baran (Eds.)* | Transregional versus National Perspectives on Contemporary Central European History. Studies on the Building of Nation-States and Their Cooperation in the 20th and 21st Century | With a foreword by Petr Vágner | ISBN 978-3-8382-1015-5

171 *Philip Gamaghelyan* | Conflict Resolution Beyond the International Relations Paradigm. Evolving Designs as a Transformative Practice in Nagorno-Karabakh and Syria | With a foreword by Susan Allen | ISBN 978-3-8382-1057-5

172 *Maria Shagina* | Joining a Prestigious Club. Cooperation with Europarties and Its Impact on Party Development in Georgia, Moldova, and Ukraine 2004–2015 | With a foreword by Kataryna Wolczuk | ISBN 978-3-8382-1084-1

173 *Alexandra Cotofana, James M. Nyce (Eds.)* | Religion and Magic in Socialist and Post-Socialist Contexts II. Baltic, Eastern European, and Post-USSR Case Studies | With a foreword by Anita Stasulane | ISBN 978-3-8382-0990-6

174 *Barbara Kunz* | Kind Words, Cruise Missiles, and Everything in Between. The Use of Power Resources in U.S. Policies towards Poland, Ukraine, and Belarus 1989–2008 | With a foreword by William Hill | ISBN 978-3-8382-1065-0

175 *Eduard Klein* | Bildungskorruption in Russland und der Ukraine. Eine komparative Analyse der Performanz staatlicher Antikorruptionsmaßnahmen im Hochschulsektor am Beispiel universitärer Aufnahmeprüfungen | Mit einem Vorwort von Heiko Pleines | ISBN 978-3-8382-0995-1

176 *Markus Soldner* | Politischer Kapitalismus im postsowjetischen Russland. Die politische, wirtschaftliche und mediale Transformation in den 1990er Jahren | Mit einem Vorwort von Wolfgang Ismayr | ISBN 978-3-8382-1222-7

177 *Anton Oleinik* | Building Ukraine from Within. A Sociological, Institutional, and Economic Analysis of a Nation-State in the Making | ISBN 978-3-8382-1150-3

178 *Peter Rollberg, Marlene Laruelle (Eds.)* | Mass Media in the Post-Soviet World. Market Forces, State Actors, and Political Manipulation in the Informational Environment after Communism | ISBN 978-3-8382-1116-9

179 *Mikhail Minakov* | Development and Dystopia. Studies in Post-Soviet Ukraine and Eastern Europe | With a foreword by Alexander Etkind | ISBN 978-3-8382-1112-1

180 *Aijan Sharshenova* | The European Union's Democracy Promotion in Central Asia. A Study of Political Interests, Influence, and Development in Kazakhstan and Kyrgyzstan in 2007–2013 | With a foreword by Gordon Crawford | ISBN 978-3-8382-1151-0

181 *Andrey Makarychev, Alexandra Yatsyk (Eds.)* | Boris Nemtsov and Russian Politics. Power and Resistance | With a foreword by Zhanna Nemtsova | ISBN 978-3-8382-1122-0

182 *Sophie Falsini* | The Euromaidan's Effect on Civil Society. Why and How Ukrainian Social Capital Increased after the Revolution of Dignity | With a foreword by Susann Worschech | ISBN 978-3-8382-1131-2

183 *Valentyna Romanova, Andreas Umland (Eds.)* | Ukraine's Decentralization. Challenges and Implications of the Local Governance Reform after the Euromaidan Revolution | ISBN 978-3-8382-1162-6

184 *Leonid Luks* | A Fateful Triangle. Essays on Contemporary Russian, German and Polish History | ISBN 978-3-8382-1143-5

185 *John B. Dunlop* | The February 2015 Assassination of Boris Nemtsov and the Flawed Trial of his Alleged Killers. An Exploration of Russia's "Crime of the 21st Century" | ISBN 978-3-8382-1188-6

186 *Vasile Rotaru* | Russia, the EU, and the Eastern Partnership. Building Bridges or Digging Trenches? | ISBN 978-3-8382-1134-3

187 *Marina Lebedeva* | Russian Studies of International Relations. From the Soviet Past to the Post-Cold-War Present | With a foreword by Andrei P. Tsygankov | ISBN 978-3-8382-0851-0

188 *Tomasz Stępniewski, George Soroka (Eds.)* | Ukraine after Maidan. Revisiting Domestic and Regional Security | ISBN 978-3-8382-1075-9

189 *Petar Cholakov* | Ethnic Entrepreneurs Unmasked. Political Institutions and Ethnic Conflicts in Contemporary Bulgaria | ISBN 978-3-8382-1189-3

190 *A. Salem, G. Hazeldine, D. Morgan (Eds.)* | Higher Education in Post-Communist States. Comparative and Sociological Perspectives | ISBN 978-3-8382-1183-1

191 *Igor Torbakov* | After Empire. Nationalist Imagination and Symbolic Politics in Russia and Eurasia in the Twentieth and Twenty-First Century | With a foreword by Serhii Plokhy | ISBN 978-3-8382-1217-3

192 *Aleksandr Burakovskiy* | Jewish-Ukrainian Relations in Late and Post-Soviet Ukraine. Articles, Lectures and Essays from 1986 to 2016 | ISBN 978-3-8382-1210-4

193 *Natalia Shapovalova, Olga Burlyuk (Eds.)* | Civil Society in Post-Euromaidan Ukraine. From Revolution to Consolidation | With a foreword by Richard Youngs | ISBN 978-3-8382-1216-6

194 *Franz Preissler* | Positionsverteidigung, Imperialismus oder Irredentismus? Russland und die „Russischsprachigen", 1991–2015 | ISBN 978-3-8382-1262-3

195 *Marian Madeła* | Der Reformprozess in der Ukraine 2014-2017. Eine Fallstudie zur Reform der öffentlichen Verwaltung | Mit einem Vorwort von Martin Malek | ISBN 978-3-8382-1266-1

196 *Anke Giesen* | „Wie kann denn der Sieger ein Verbrecher sein?" Eine diskursanalytische Untersuchung der russlandweiten Debatte über Konzept und Verstaatlichungsprozess der Lagergedenkstätte „Perm'-36" im Ural | ISBN 978-3-8382-1284-5

197 *Victoria Leukavets* | The Integration Policies of Belarus and Ukraine vis-à-vis the EU and Russia. A Comparative Analysis Through the Prism of a Two-Level Game Approach | ISBN 978-3-8382-1247-0

198 *Oksana Kim* | The Development and Challenges of Russian Corporate Governance I. The Roles and Functions of Boards of Directors | With a foreword by Sheila M. Puffer | ISBN 978-3-8382-1287-6

199 *Thomas D. Grant* | International Law and the Post-Soviet Space I. Essays on Chechnya and the Baltic States | With a foreword by Stephen M. Schwebel | ISBN 978-3-8382-1279-1

200 *Thomas D. Grant* | International Law and the Post-Soviet Space II. Essays on Ukraine, Intervention, and Non-Proliferation | ISBN 978-3-8382-1280-7

201 *Slavomír Michálek, Michal Štefansky* | The Age of Fear. The Cold War and Its Influence on Czechoslovakia 1945–1968 | ISBN 978-3-8382-1285-2

202 *Iulia-Sabina Joja* | Romania's Strategic Culture 1990–2014. Continuity and Change in a Post-Communist Country's Evolution of National Interests and Security Policies | With a foreword by Heiko Biehl | ISBN 978-3-8382-1286-9

203 *Andrei Rogatchevski, Yngvar B. Steinholt, Arve Hansen, David-Emil Wickström* | War of Songs. Popular Music and Recent Russia-Ukraine Relations | With a foreword by Artemy Troitsky | ISBN 978-3-8382-1173-2

204 *Maria Lipman (Ed.)* | Russian Voices on Post-Crimea Russia. An Almanac of Counterpoint Essays from 2015–2018 | ISBN 978-3-8382-1251-7

205 *Ksenia Maksimovtsova* | Language Conflicts in Contemporary Estonia, Latvia, and Ukraine. A Comparative Exploration of Discourses in Post-Soviet Russian-Language Digital Media | With a foreword by Ammon Cheskin | ISBN 978-3-8382-1282-1

206 *Michal Vít* | The EU's Impact on Identity Formation in East-Central Europe between 2004 and 2013. Perceptions of the Nation and Europe in Political Parties of the Czech Republic, Poland, and Slovakia | With a foreword by Andrea Petö | ISBN 978-3-8382-1275-3

207 *Per A. Rudling* | Tarnished Heroes. The Organization of Ukrainian Nationalists in the Memory Politics of Post-Soviet Ukraine | ISBN 978-3-8382-0999-9

208 *Kaja Gadowska, Peter Solomon (Eds.)* | Legal Change in Post-Communist States. Progress, Reversions, Explanations | ISBN 978-3-8382-1312-5

209 *Pawel Kowal, Georges Mink, Iwona Reichardt (Eds.)* | Three Revolutions: Mobilization and Change in Contemporary Ukraine I. Theoretical Aspects and Analyses on Religion, Memory, and Identity | ISBN 978-3-8382-1321-7

210 *Pawel Kowal, Georges Mink, Adam Reichardt, Iwona Reichardt (Eds.)* | Three Revolutions: Mobilization and Change in Contemporary Ukraine II. An Oral History of the Revolution on Granite, Orange Revolution, and Revolution of Dignity | ISBN 978-3-8382-1323-1

211 *Li Bennich-Björkman, Sergiy Kurbatov (Eds.)* | When the Future Came. The Collapse of the USSR and the Emergence of National Memory in Post-Soviet History Textbooks | ISBN 978-3-8382-1335-4

212 *Olga R. Gulina* | Migration as a (Geo-)Political Challenge in the Post-Soviet Space. Border Regimes, Policy Choices, Visa Agendas | With a foreword by Nils Muižnieks | ISBN 978-3-8382-1338-5

213 *Sanna Turoma, Kaarina Aitamurto, Slobodanka Vladiv-Glover (Eds.)* | Religion, Expression, and Patriotism in Russia. Essays on Post-Soviet Society and the State. ISBN 978-3-8382-1346-0

214 *Vasif Huseynov* | Geopolitical Rivalries in the "Common Neighborhood". Russia's Conflict with the West, Soft Power, and Neoclassical Realism | With a foreword by Nicholas Ross Smith | ISBN 978-3-8382-1277-7

215 *Mikhail Suslov* | Geopolitical Imagination. Ideology and Utopia in Post-Soviet Russia | With a foreword by Mark Bassin | ISBN 978-3-8382-1361-3

216 *Alexander Etkind, Mikhail Minakov (Eds.)* | Ideology after Union. Political Doctrines, Discourses, and Debates in Post-Soviet Societies | ISBN 978-3-8382-1388-0

217 *Jakob Mischke, Oleksandr Zabirko (Hgg.)* | Protestbewegungen im langen Schatten des Kreml. Aufbruch und Resignation in Russland und der Ukraine | ISBN 978-3-8382-0926-5

218 *Oksana Huss* | How Corruption and Anti-Corruption Policies Sustain Hybrid Regimes. Strategies of Political Domination under Ukraine's Presidents in 1994-2014 | With a foreword by Tobias Debiel and Andrea Gawrich | ISBN 978-3-8382-1430-6

219 *Dmitry Travin, Vladimir Gel'man, Otar Marganiya* | The Russian Path. Ideas, Interests, Institutions, Illusions | With a foreword by Vladimir Ryzhkov | ISBN 978-3-8382-1421-4

220 *Gergana Dimova* | Political Uncertainty. A Comparative Exploration | With a foreword by Todor Yalamov and Rumena Filipova | ISBN 978-3-8382-1385-9

221 *Torben Waschke* | Russland in Transition. Geopolitik zwischen Raum, Identität und Machtinteressen | Mit einem Vorwort von Andreas Dittmann | ISBN 978-3-8382-1480-1

222 *Steven Jobbitt, Zsolt Bottlik, Marton Berki (Eds.)* | Power and Identity in the Post-Soviet Realm. Geographies of Ethnicity and Nationality after 1991 | ISBN 978-3-8382-1399-6

223 *Daria Buteiko* | Erinnerungsort. Ort des Gedenkens, der Erholung oder der Einkehr? Kommunismus-Erinnerung am Beispiel der Gedenkstätte Berliner Mauer sowie des Soloveckij-Klosters und -Museumsparks | ISBN 978-3-8382-1367-5

224 *Olga Bertelsen (Ed.)* | Russian Active Measures. Yesterday, Today, Tomorrow | With a foreword by Jan Goldman | ISBN 978-3-8382-1529-7

225 *David Mandel* | "Optimizing" Higher Education in Russia. University Teachers and their Union "Universitetskaya solidarnost'" | ISBN 978-3-8382-1519-8

226 *Mikhail Minakov, Gwendolyn Sasse, Daria Isachenko (Eds.)* | Post-Soviet Secessionism. Nation-Building and State-Failure after Communism | ISBN 978-3-8382-1538-9

227 *Jakob Hauter (Ed.)* | Civil War? Interstate War? Hybrid War? Dimensions and Interpretations of the Donbas Conflict in 2014–2020 | With a foreword by Andrew Wilson | ISBN 978-3-8382-1383-5

228 *Tima T. Moldogaziev, Gene A. Brewer, J. Edward Kellough (Eds.)* | Public Policy and Politics in Georgia. Lessons from Post-Soviet Transition | With a foreword by Dan Durning | ISBN 978-3-8382-1535-8

229 *Oxana Schmies (Ed.)* | NATO's Enlargement and Russia. A Strategic Challenge in the Past and Future | With a foreword by Vladimir Kara-Murza | ISBN 978-3-8382-1478-8

230 *Christopher Ford* | Ukapisme – Une Gauche perdue. Le marxisme anti-colonial dans la révolution ukrainienne 1917-1925 | Avec une préface de Vincent Présumey | ISBN 978-3-8382-0899-2

231 *Anna Kutkina* | Between Lenin and Bandera. Decommunization and Multivocality in Post-Euromaidan Ukraine | With a foreword by Juri Mykkänen | ISBN 978-3-8382-1506-8

232 *Lincoln E. Flake* | Defending the Faith. The Russian Orthodox Church and the Demise of Religious Pluralism | With a foreword by Peter Martland | ISBN 978-3-8382-1378-1

233 *Nikoloz Samkharadze* | Russia's Recognition of the Independence of Abkhazia and South Ossetia. Analysis of a Deviant Case in Moscow's Foreign Policy | With a foreword by Neil MacFarlane | ISBN 978-3-8382-1414-6

234 *Arve Hansen* | Urban Protest. A Spatial Perspective on Kyiv, Minsk, and Moscow | With a foreword by Julie Wilhelmsen | ISBN 978-3-8382-1495-5

235 *Eleonora Narvselius, Julie Fedor (Eds.)* | Diversity in the East-Central European Borderlands. Memories, Cityscapes, People | ISBN 978-3-8382-1523-5

236 *Regina Elsner* | The Russian Orthodox Church and Modernity. A Historical and Theological Investigation into Eastern Christianity between Unity and Plurality | With a foreword by Mikhail Suslov | ISBN 978-3-8382-1568-6

237 *Bo Petersson* | The Putin Predicament. Problems of Legitimacy and Succession in Russia | With a foreword by J. Paul Goode | ISBN 978-3-8382-1050-6

238 *Jonathan Otto Pohl* | The Years of Great Silence. The Deportation, Special Settlement, and Mobilization into the Labor Army of Ethnic Germans in the USSR, 1941–1955 | ISBN 978-3-8382-1630-0

239 *Mikhail Minakov (Ed.)* | Inventing Majorities. Ideological Creativity in Post-Soviet Societies | ISBN 978-3-8382-1641-6

240 *Robert M. Cutler* | Soviet and Post-Soviet Foreign Policies I. East-South Relations and the Political Economy of the Communist Bloc, 1971–1991 | With a foreword by Roger E. Kanet | ISBN 978-3-8382-1654-6

241 *Izabella Agardi* | On the Verge of History. Life Stories of Rural Women from Serbia, Romania, and Hungary, 1920–2020 | With a foreword by Andrea Pető | ISBN 978-3-8382-1602-7

242 *Sebastian Schäffer (Ed.)* | Ukraine in Central and Eastern Europe. Kyiv's Foreign Affairs and the International Relations of the Post-Communist Region | With a foreword by Pavlo Klimkin and Andreas Umland| ISBN 978-3-8382-1615-7

243 *Volodymyr Dubrovskyi, Kalman Mizsei, Mychailo Wynnyckyj (Eds.)* | Eight Years after the Revolution of Dignity. What Has Changed in Ukraine during 2013–2021? | With a foreword by Yaroslav Hrytsak | ISBN 978-3-8382-1560-0

244 *Rumena Filipova* | Constructing the Limits of Europe Identity and Foreign Policy in Poland, Bulgaria, and Russia since 1989 | With forewords by Harald Wydra and Gergana Yankova-Dimova | ISBN 978-3-8382-1649-2

245 *Oleksandra Keudel* | How Patronal Networks Shape Opportunities for Local Citizen Participation in a Hybrid Regime A Comparative Analysis of Five Cities in Ukraine | With a foreword by Sabine Kropp | ISBN 978-3-8382-1671-3

246 *Jan Claas Behrends, Thomas Lindenberger, Pavel Kolar (Eds.)* | Violence after Stalin Institutions, Practices, and Everyday Life in the Soviet Bloc 1953–1989 | ISBN 978-3-8382-1637-9

247 *Leonid Luks* | Macht und Ohnmacht der Utopien Essays zur Geschichte Russlands im 20. und 21. Jahrhundert | ISBN 978-3-8382-1677-5

248 *Iuliia Barshadska* | Brüssel zwischen Kyjiw und Moskau Das auswärtige Handeln der Europäischen Union im ukrainisch-russischen Konflikt 2014-2019 | Mit einem Vorwort von Olaf Leiße | ISBN 978-3-8382-1667-6

249 *Valentyna Romanova* | Decentralisation and Multilevel Elections in Ukraine Reform Dynamics and Party Politics in 2010–2021 | With a foreword by Kimitaka Matsuzato | ISBN 978-3-8382-1700-0

250 *Alexander Motyl* | National Questions. Theoretical Reflections on Nations and Nationalism in Eastern Europe | ISBN 978-3-8382-1675-1

251 *Marc Dietrich* | A Cosmopolitan Model for Peacebuilding. The Ukrainian Cases of Crimea and the Donbas | With a foreword by Rémi Baudouï | ISBN 978-3-8382-1687-4

252 *Eduard Baidaus* | An Unsettled Nation. Moldova in the Geopolitics of Russia, Romania, and Ukraine | With forewords by John-Paul Himka and David R. Marples | ISBN 978-3-8382-1582-2

253 *Igor Okunev, Petr Oskolkov (Eds.)* | Transforming the Administrative Matryoshka. The Reform of Autonomous Okrugs in the Russian Federation, 2003–2008 | With a foreword by Vladimir Zorin | ISBN 978-3-8382-1721-5

254 *Winfried Schneider-Deters* | Ukraine's Fateful Years 2013–2019. Vol. I: The Popular Uprising in Winter 2013/2014 | ISBN 978-3-8382-1725-3

255 *Winfried Schneider-Deters* | Ukraine's Fateful Years 2013–2019. Vol. II: The Annexation of Crimea and the War in Donbas | ISBN 978-3-8382-1726-0

256 *Robert M. Cutler* | Soviet and Post-Soviet Russian Foreign Policies II. East-West Relations in Europe and the Political Economy of the Communist Bloc, 1971–1991 | With a foreword by Roger E. Kanet | ISBN 978-3-8382-1727-7

257 *Robert M. Cutler* | Soviet and Post-Soviet Russian Foreign Policies III. East-West Relations in Europe and Eurasia in the Post-Cold War Transition, 1991–2001 | With a foreword by Roger E. Kanet | ISBN 978-3-8382-1728-4

258 *Paweł Kowal, Iwona Reichardt, Kateryna Pryshchepa (Eds.)* | Three Revolutions: Mobilization and Change in Contemporary Ukraine III. Archival Records and Historical Sources on the 1990 Revolution on Granite | ISBN 978-3-8382-1376-7

259 *Mikhail Minakov (Ed.)* | Philosophy Unchained. Developments in Post-Soviet Philosophical Thought. | With a foreword by Christopher Donohue | ISBN 978-3-8382-1768-0

260 *David Dalton* | The Ukrainian Oligarchy After the Euromaidan. How Ukraine's Political Economy Regime Survived the Crisis | With a foreword by Andrew Wilson | ISBN 978-3-8382-1740-6

261 *Andreas Heinemann-Grüder (Ed.)* | Who Are the Fighters? Irregular Armed Groups in the Russian-Ukrainian War since 2014 | ISBN 978-3-8382-1777-2

262 *Taras Kuzio (Ed.)* | Russian Disinformation and Western Scholarship. Bias and Prejudice in Journalistic, Expert, and Academic Analyses of East European, Russian and Eurasian Affairs | ISBN 978-3-8382-1685-0

263 *Darius Furmonavicius* | LithuaniaTransforms the West. Lithuania's Liberation from Soviet Occupation and the Enlargement of NATO (1988–2022) | With a foreword by Vytautas Landsbergis | ISBN 978-3-8382-1779-6

264 *Dirk Dalberg* | Politisches Denken im tschechoslowakischen Dissens. Egon Bondy, Miroslav Kusý, Milan Šimečka und Petr Uhl (1968-1989) | ISBN 978-3-8382-1318-7

265 *Леонид Люкс* | К столетию «философского парохода». Мыслители «первой» русской эмиграции о русской революции и о тоталитарных соблазнах XX века | ISBN 978-3-8382-1775-8

266 *Daviti Mtchedlishvili* | The EU and the South Caucasus. European Neighborhood Policies between Eclecticism and Pragmatism, 1991-2021 | With a foreword by Nicholas Ross Smith | ISBN 978-3-8382-1735-2

267 *Bohdan Harasymiw* | Post-Euromaidan Ukraine. Domestic Power Struggles and War of National Survival in 2014–2022 | ISBN 978-3-8382-1798-7

268 *Nadiia Koval, Denys Tereshchenko (Eds.)* | Russian Cultural Diplomacy under Putin. Rossotrudnichestvo, the "Russkiy Mir" Foundation, and the Gorchakov Fund in 2007–2022 | ISBN 978-3-8382-1801-4

269 *Izabela Kazejak* | Jews in Post-War Wrocław and L'viv. Official Policies and Local Responses in Comparative Perspective, 1945-1970s | ISBN 978-3-8382-1802-1

270 *Jakob Hauter* | Russia's Overlooked Invasion. The Causes of the 2014 Outbreak of War in Ukraine's Donbas | With a foreword by Hiroaki Kuromiya | ISBN 978-3-8382-1803-8

271 *Anton Shekhovtsov* | Russian Political Warfare. Essays on Kremlin Propaganda in Europe and the Neighbourhood, 2020-2023 | With a foreword by Nathalie Loiseau | ISBN 978-3-8382-1821-2

272 *Андреа Пето* | Насилие и Молчание. Красная армия в Венгрии во Второй Мировой войне | ISBN 978-3-8382-1636-2

273 *Winfried Schneider-Deters* | Russia's War in Ukraine. Debates on Peace, Fascism, and War Crimes, 2022–2023 | With a foreword by Klaus Gestwa | ISBN 978-3-8382-1876-2

274 *Rasmus Nilsson* | Uncanny Allies. Russia and Belarus on the Edge, 2012-2024 | ISBN 978-3-8382-1288-3

275 *Anton Grushetskyi, Volodymyr Paniotto* | War and the Transformation of Ukrainian Society (2022–23). Empirical Evidence | ISBN 978-3-8382-1944-8

276 *Christian Kaunert, Alex MacKenzie, Adrien Nonjon (Eds.)* | In the Eye of the Storm. Origins, Ideology, and Controversies of the Azov Brigade, 2014–23 | ISBN 978-3-8382-1750-5

277 *Gian Marco Moisé* | The House Always Wins. The Corrupt Strategies that Shaped Kazakh Oil Politics and Business in the Nazarbayev Era | With a foreword by Alena Ledeneva | ISBN 978-3-8382-1917-2

278 *Mikhail Minakov* | The Post-Soviet Human | Philosophical Reflections on Social History after the End of Communism | ISBN 978-3-8382-1943-1

279 *Natalia Kudriavtseva, Debra A. Friedman (Eds.)* | Language and Power in Ukraine and Kazakhstan. Essays on Education, Ideology, Literature, Practice, and the Media | With a foreword by Laada Bilaniuk | ISBN 978-3-8382-1949-3

280 *Paweł Kowal, Georges Mink, Iwona Reichardt (Eds.)* | The End of the Soviet World? Essays on Post-Communist Political and Social Change | With a foreword by Richardt Butterwick-Pawlikowski | ISBN 978-3-8382-1961-5

281 *Kateryna Zarembo, Michèle Knodt, Maksym Yakovlyev (Eds.)* | Teaching IR in Wartime. Experiences of University Lecturers during Russia's Full-Scale Invasion of Ukraine | ISBN 978-3-8382-1954-7

282 *Oleksiy V. Kresin* | The United Nations General Assembly Resolutions. Their Nature and Significance in the Context of the Russian War Against Ukraine | Edited by William E. Butler | ISBN 978-3-8382-1967-7

283 *Jakob Hauter* | Russlands unbemerkte Invasion. Die Ursachen des Kriegsausbruchs im ukrainischen Donbas im Jahr 2014 | Mit einem Vorwort von Hiroaki Kuromiya | ISBN 978-3-8382-2003-1

ibidem.eu